The Essential Guide to

PRACTICAL ASTROLOGY

April Elliott Kent

International Standard Book Number: 978-0692683576
Library of Congress Catalog Card Number: 2010917071

First Edition and Printing, 2011 by Alpha Books/Penguin
Second Printing, 2016 by Two Moon Publishing

Note: This publication contains the opinions and ideas of its author. It is intended to provide helpful and informative material on the subject matter covered. It is sold with the understanding that the author and publisher are not engaged in rendering professional services in the book. If the reader requires personal assistance or advice, a competent professional should be consulted. The author and publisher specifically disclaim any responsibility for any liability, loss, or risk, personal or otherwise, which is incurred as a consequence, directly or indirectly, of the use and application of any of the contents of this book.

Library of Congress Cataloging-in-Publications Data

Name: Kent, April Elliott, 1961–
Title: The essential guide to practical astrology / April Elliott Kent
Description: Two Moon Publishing paperback edition. | San Diego : Two Moon Publishing, 2016.
Identifiers: LCCN: 2010917071 | ISBN: 978-0692683576 (softcover)
Subjects: Astrology
Classification: LCC BF1701 .K46 2011 | DDC 133.5
LC record available at https://lccn.loc.gov/2010917071

Published by

TWO MOON PUBLISHING
PO Box 16328
San Diego, California 92176, USA

Trademarks

All terms mentioned in this book that are known to be or are suspected of being trademark or service marks have been appropriately capitalized. Two Moon Publishing cannot attest to the accuracy of this information. Use of a term in this book should not be regarded as affecting the validity of any trademark or service mark.

Dedication

To my grandfather, George—a man of many interests, from bees to astrology.

(Capricorns can surprise you.)

Introduction

Let's begin by acknowledging the elephant in the room: there are lots of books you can read to learn the essentials of astrology. Why, you might fairly ask, should you read this one?

1. It's funny, and a bit irreverent. That's how I roll. Astrology and I have kept company for several decades now, and our relationship resembles the kind of loving but contentious rapport found between old married couples. I kid astrology, because I love it.

2. You're among friends here. I'm a fan of every sign, every planet, every asteroid (okay, I'm not nuts about Chiron, but I'm learning to respect him). You're not going to read a bunch of insulting stuff about your Sun sign or about how people with your Moon sign are more likely than others to kick their dogs. There's just no need for that kind of talk.

3. This is a guide to *practical* astrology. That means it's written in plain English, illustrated with real-world examples of astrology in action. Stuff you can use, today, to better understand yourself, other people, and your world.

Practical Astronomy

Once upon a time, astrology and astronomy were one. Astronomers plotted various objects in the sky, and astrologers figured out what they meant to life on earth. Astrology was, in fact, known as "practical astronomy." The thinking was presumably something like, "It's all good and well to know where Saturn is, but what does that mean for me?" After all, life was hard, back when a simple slice of buttered toast represented an impressive amount of work—cultivating and milling wheat, chopping firewood to light the oven, baking bread, spending hours bent over a churn to produce one sad little lump of butter. No one would encourage a son or daughter to spend a lifetime studying the movements of the stars and planets unless it was going to benefit the tribe in some practical way.

So astrologers noted that when Saturn was moving through a particular constellation, harvests were meager or money was tight or livestock were sluggish about reproducing. They noticed that crops grew better when they were planted during particular lunar phases or while the Moon was in a particular sign. They warned the village to stockpile pitchforks and lighted torches when Mars rose in the morning sky, and to keep an eye out for war-making overtures from neighboring tribes.

Impractical Astrology

There are still plenty of practical uses for astrology. Astrologers still use the symbolism of the skies to predict wars, to anticipate tense moments in animal husbandry, and to monitor the ebb and flow of money and other resources. True, most of us no longer churn our own butter or have to protect our families with a pitchfork. But it can be handy to know the best times to push for a raise or take a vacation.

But are there *impractical* uses for astrology? It's tempting to say yes. There doesn't seem to be anything practical about key chains with the signs of the zodiac on them or the horoscopes in your daily paper. Even the loftier goals of modern astrology, such as self-understanding, seem more of a luxury than a necessity.

But what's more practical than a system that helps you choose a job or partner that suits you? Or to appreciate your innate strengths and weaknesses, so that you can capitalize on one and compensate for the other? That just sounds like good sense, to me.

Most astrological journeys begin with a single book—one that you find at the right moment of your life, and that speaks to you in your own language. I hope that this will be that book for you, and that our meeting between these pages will mark the beginning of your lifelong love affair with astrology. Enjoy it all!

How to Use This Book

This book covers a lot of territory. If you're like most people, you want to understand yourself and a few people close to you, and that's it. And you want it now. I respect that. The book is written and organized in such a way that you can either read it from start to finish or dip into the parts that pertain specifically to fascinating *you,* and then be on your way.

As you forage through this book, reading about the various features of your birth chart, you'll run across contradictions. That doesn't mean astrology doesn't work; it means you're complicated, and astrology is complex enough to reflect that. Sometimes, and in some situations, you behave one way; in other situations, you behave differently. You want different things from different areas of your life. You contain multitudes.

This book is divided into six parts:

Part 1, Astrology as a Second Language, introduces you to the *idea* of astrology. What is it? What's it based on? Why is your horoscope always wrong? How can you get a copy of your birth chart? And what *is* your birth chart? The chapters in Part 1 set the stage for understanding everything else that follows. If you get lost along the way, backtrack to these chapters to find your answer.

Part 2, Signs of the Zodiac, gives a rundown of those familiar favorites, the signs of the zodiac. Here's where it gets very tempting for you to dip in and just read about "your sign." Resist this impulse, because here's a secret: they're *all* your sign. Yep, each and every sign—even the one you hate because it's your old boyfriend's sign, and he was really mean to you—is represented in some part of your birth chart.

Part 3, **A Place for Everything**: Houses, introduces you to the houses of the horoscope, which symbolize where stuff happens in your life. If you're a Sun sign Cancer but you want to understand why your friends all think of you as a Leo, to paraphrase Apple, "there's a house for that"—the House of Friendship. The good news is that the 12 houses of the horoscope cover some of the same territory as the signs of the zodiac, so there's less new ground to cover.

Part 4, **Gods and Monsters:** Planets, leads you into the valley of the planets, including the Sun and Moon. This is where things really start to get interesting. Each planet of our solar system (and yes, that includes Pluto) symbolizes some motivation or need in your life—love, attention, survival, gossip. Find out which sign and house they're in, and how they relate to each other, and watch astrology really come to life!

Part 5, Cycles Made Simple, gives you some tools for understanding the cycles of astrology and how they reflect cycles in your own life. There's a daily planner to help you follow the Moon through the signs of the zodiac and anticipate the day's "mood." The monthly planner follows the Sun, Mercury, Venus, and the phases of the Moon; it can help you figure out how to get noticed, listened to, and loved this month, as well as when to start things and when to finish what you've already started. The yearly planner enlists the help of Mars, Jupiter, and Saturn to help you formulate the kinds of substantial goals that you'll be proud to include in your holiday newsletter. And the long-range planner shows you how using the cycles of Uranus, Neptune, and Pluto can help you anticipate major turning points in your life.

Part 6, Bringing It All Together, gives you an easy lesson in astrological grammar, shows you how to put all the different symbols together, and includes an example of how to analyze a birth chart. Then you learn some of the cool stuff astrologers use to make predictions. This may be a little over your head right now, but keep this book around; if you decide to move forward from the strict basics of astrology, this material represents the next logical step in your journey.

You'll also find three helpful appendixes: a glossary of astrological terms; tables of upcoming planetary activity, including New Moons and eclipses; and a directory of resources for further astrological learning.

Essential Extras

Throughout the book, you'll see additional pieces of information in sidebars. Here's what to look for:

 These boxes present interesting tips for thinking about or using the information in a chapter.

 These boxes alert you to common misconceptions or negative stereotypes about the information in a chapter.

 In these boxes you'll find simple definitions for selected key words and concepts.

You'll also see other sidebars with unique titles that present anecdotes, interesting facts, case histories, or other extended background information you should know.

Acknowledgments

I keep finding myself in the curious position of writing books I never dreamed of writing—entirely thanks to people who have more faith in my abilities than I do. This naturally includes the crack team at Alpha/Penguin, especially my brilliant and funny editors, Lynn Northrup and Randy Ladenheim-Gil, who curbed my excesses without breaking my spirit. Thanks also to my agent, Marilyn Allen of Allen O'Shea; and to Sharon Leah, whose encouragement over the years has helped nudge me from amusing myself in Internet obscurity to amusing myself in print, in front of all of you nice people.

Much gratitude and love to my astrological heroes, mentors, and colleagues, especially Diane Ronngren, Dana Gerhardt, Steven Forrest, Bill Herbst, Jeffrey Kishner, Lynn Hayes, Jim Shawvan, Simone Butler, and Jessica Shepherd. Each of you has inspired me to be a better astrologer, writer, and person, and you have my thanks. I'm also indebted to a couple of my favorite nonastrological writers, Joe Queenan and Sandra Tsing-Loh—so inspiringly witty, acerbic, and marvelous.

Thanks to Matrix Software and Astrodienst for the astrological charts and tables used in the book.

The overwhelming consensus among my family and friends is that astrology is a pretty strange way to earn a living, but since it seems to pay the bills and keeps me (more or less) out of trouble, they mostly shrug and offer their moral support. A doff of the cap, then, to Drew Elliott and Heather Galluzzi, Mari Stroud, Kathy McLaughlin, Chuck Emery, Tim Tormey, Natori Moore, John A. Rippo, Lori Rodefer, Doug Adair, and Frank Gualco—for coffee, donuts, glasses of wine, chocolate, good-natured insults, and rousing cheers.

Most of all, thanks to Jonny Kent—patient and funny, a great cook, cute as anything, and lots of fun to live with. Marrying you was the best day's work I've ever done.

Praise for
The Essential Guide to
Practical Astrology

"There's no fluff, esoteric mumbo jumbo, fringe techniques, or confusing psychobabble. The author's writing style is **clear, friendly, and intriguing** in the sense that the more you read, the more you want to learn. So beware - if you pick up this book, you will most likely be irrevocably drawn into the world of astrology."

— Dell Horoscope

"A **funny, easy-to-understand, and surprisingly thorough** beginning astrology text.... Anyone who wants to take a big, enjoyable step toward understanding (and using) astrology will learn a lot from this book."

— The Mountain Astrologer magazine

"**Highly recommended**. While this is not the only book a beginning student will ever need, it's one of the best introductions I've seen in a long, long time, and it should serve the beginner well for their first year of study and possibly beyond. It's clear, easy to use, and fun to read. Teachers take note!"

— NCGR Memberletter

"A highly readable tour through the astrological fundamentals for beginning and intermediate astrology students."

— Donna Cunningham, *author of Healing Pluto Problems*"

Contents

Astrology as a Second Language

In *Poor Richard's Almanac,* Ben Franklin wrote of astrology, "Oh the wonderful knowledge to be found in the stars. Even the smallest things are written there ... if you had but skill to read." Astrology is the language of the stars, with its own alphabet and grammar. Before you can read its wisdom about matters great and small, you first have to learn to speak the sky's language.

In this part, you'll be introduced to the ABCs of astrology and to its mysterious vocabulary. You'll discover what astrology is and what it isn't, why your horoscope can get it wrong, and why you may be nothing like your Sun sign. You'll find out how to get a copy of your birth chart, and how to make heads or tails of its upside-down world. And you'll find out what astrology is good for, other than annoying your sister (the scientist) and offending your brother-in-law (the minister).

CHAPTER 1

The Language of the Stars

What astrology is—and what it is not

How the sky "speaks" to us

How astrology works

Why your horoscope and sun sign are usually inaccurate

The most popular uses for astrology

A language you can learn!

I'm an astrologer; that's my day job, and it's the kind of profession that makes your accountant look at you funny the first time she prepares your tax return. But when I clock out at the end of the day and take off my astrologer cap, I do the same kinds of stuff that you do. That includes taking part in a variety of social rituals in which strangers break the ice by asking, "And what do you do for a living?"

That question presents an awkward moment for an astrologer. Some people really don't like astrology, and even those who do like astrology often don't understand much about it. So if I'm truthful about my job title at a cocktail party, I'm risking an evening of either trying to redeem myself in the eyes of someone who thinks I'm a complete flake, or fielding questions from someone who wants to know why Scorpios keep breaking their heart.

Which is why I usually fudge and answer truthfully, if incompletely, that I'm a writer—and then I change the subject.

Astrology is a rich, complex, fascinating study, and so thoroughly misunderstood by both its detractors and its fans that there's just no way to do the subject justice over white wine spritzers and tiny cocktail franks. So let's pretend that you and I met at this party and decided to grab a cup of coffee afterward. Comfortably ensconced in the cushy leather banquette of a dimly lit diner, sipping the worst coffee known to man, we've got nothing but time. So let's talk astrology.

What Is Astrology?

Astrology is the study of the connection between celestial activity phenomena and earthly events. Those who practice astrology are called *astrologers*. (The term "astrologist" is sometimes used, but never by astrologers; to be honest, it makes us cringe, though we're not exactly sure why.)

DEFINITION The word **astrology** comes from the Greek *astrologia*, meaning "telling of the stars." Astrology is essentially a language—the fine art of speaking in stars. An **astrologer** is someone who practices astrology.

The main tool in the astrological toolbox is the astrology chart, sometimes called a horoscope (from the Latin *horoscopus,* or "hour watcher"). Based on the date, time, and location of an event (any event, not just a person's birth but also things like marriage, natural disasters, or the founding of a country), an astrology chart is a map of the sky that's divided into 12 sections and includes the following:

- **Planets.** These include the Sun and Moon (for convenience, usually referred to as planets) and the eight known planets, including Pluto. (Yes, although its official status has been downgraded to planetoid, astrologers have observed Pluto long enough to respect and fear it as much as we do any full-fledged planet.) In their interpretations, some astrologers also include Chiron, a planetoid that orbits between Saturn and Uranus, and Ceres (a dwarf planet), Pallas, Vesta, and Juno (asteroids), which are located in the asteroid belt between Mars and Jupiter. The Sun, Moon, planets, major asteroids, and fixed stars each have specific astrological meanings that reflect fundamental human needs, such as relationship, boundaries, and intellect. If life were a play (which, in many ways, it is), then planets would be the characters.

- **Signs of the zodiac.** The zodiac is a band of fixed stars that flanks the ecliptic, which is the path the planets travel across the sky. Usually just called "signs," each of the 12 zodiac signs is associated with particular characteristics and qualities that describe personal style and defining attributes. In a play, signs would be the characters' personalities and costumes.

- **Houses.** Houses are the 12 sections of the horoscope, symbolizing the positions of the Sun, Moon, and planets in relation to the horizon and the meridian. Each house symbolizes a specific area of life experience, such as work, finances, and relationships. In a play, houses would be the settings where scenes take place.

- **Aspects.** The angular relationships between the Sun, Moon, and planets are called aspects. Aspects describe the ease or struggle of integrating various parts of your life or psyche. In a play, aspects would be the dialogue between characters.

Now that you know a little bit more about what astrology is, let's look at some of the things astrology is *not:*

- **Astrology is not astronomy.** Once upon a time, the two studies were one. Astronomy worked out the physical properties of the heavens, while astrology figured out what they meant. There was a falling out between the two disciplines around the time (1632) that Galileo confirmed the reality of a heliocentric universe (in which the earth and other planets revolve around the Sun), casting a pall over the geocentric (in which the earth is the center of the universe and everything else revolves around it) system of astrology. Today, astrology still relies on astronomical measurements as the basis for its art, while astronomy generally tries to ignore astrology's existence altogether. So whatever you do, don't call an astronomer an astrologer—or, heaven forbid, ask him "his sign." Things could get ugly!

- **Astrology is not science,** despite its reliance on scientific tools (measurements of planetary motion and complex mathematics). Astrology has not been proven, by use of the scientific method, to be a reliable predictive tool. There are astrologers who feel that, given time and funding, astrology could be proven scientifically. But for now, astrology can't claim to be a science.

- **Astrology is not clairvoyance.** Most astrologers admit to using some intuition in their interpretations, but astrology is an art of reading symbolism, not people's minds.

- **Astrology is not palm reading.** Palm readers divine human character and fate based on—well, palms. Hundreds of years ago palmistry was aligned with astrology, with each finger and mound of the hand associated with a planet. However, hands are not the heavens, and so your study of astrology will not include learning to tell the head line from the heart line.

- **Astrology does not use tarot cards.** Both are symbolic systems that can be used for divination or for self-analysis, and many (but not all) astrologers and tarot card readers know and use both systems. However, astrology and tarot are two different symbol systems, and the study of astrology will not teach you how to read tarot cards.

- **Astrology is not numerology,** which uses numbers to explore earthly affairs. Again, some astrologers know and use numerology, but numerology—since it doesn't refer to a connection between the earth and sky—is not the same thing as astrology.

No Turban Required!

The sorts of people who are drawn to astrology are often interested in a variety of other metaphysical practices as well. One day you may find yourself face-to-face with a crystal ball–peering, tarot card–reading, I-Ching–throwing, clairvoyant astrologer wearing a turban. But of all this person's many facets, it's only the part about reading charts of the sky that makes her an astrologer. For the modern practitioner of astrology, turbans are strictly optional.

A Symbolic Language

Astrology is a language; it's the sky's way of speaking to us about every facet of life, from love to investments. Astrology uses an alphabet of planets, signs, houses, and aspects and connects them into meaningful patterns with specific grammatical rules. ("Venus in Scorpio in the third house, square Mars in Leo in the twelfth house" is, believe it or not, a phrase that will mean something to you by the end of this book.)

Like any language, astrology *symbolizes* things, and interpreting language's symbols can be a complicated business. Do an online search for the word "anchor" and you'll find pictures of everything from a device for mooring ships to television news announcer Walter Cronkite. Likewise, each of astrology's individual symbols has a variety of meanings; how the symbols are interpreted depends on both context and the astrologer's skill with the language.

How Does Astrology Work?

Astrology is based on the belief that there is a relationship between what happens in the sky and what happens on earth. A favorite maxim of astrologers, "As above, so below," implies that a set of universal laws governs both earth and sky. But to be completely honest, no one seems to be sure exactly why or how this works.

Cause vs. Cosmic Coincidence

Modern astrologers mostly dismiss the concept of causation—that is, the idea that the planets physically affect life on earth. We don't imagine that planets billions of miles from earth are emanating compelling rays that move us around like pieces on a chessboard. At least, no one's proven it.

Rather, the modern view of astrology is that there is a pattern of meaningful coincidence between celestial and earthly events. Some propose that earth and heaven have a sort of fractal relationship (a fractal can be split into parts, each of which is a pint-sized replica of the larger whole). Many also point to Carl Jung's theory of synchronicity, which explores the phenomenon of two or more events occurring together in a meaningful manner, without one having appeared to cause the other to happen. For example, let's say you're sitting outside a café with a friend, recounting a dream you had last night about adopting a Jack Russell terrier. Just as you finish describing the dream, someone walks by your table with a Jack Russell terrier, which takes one look at you, leaps into your lap, and starts licking you.

Mere coincidence? Or the universe's oblique way of leading you into dog ownership?

 ASTRO ALERT Using astrology to predict specific behavior or events is unreliable, for one very good reason: human beings are unpredictable. It's that pesky free will that makes it hard to predict exactly what people will do. The less control someone has over his own life, and the less self-aware he is, the easier it is to predict what will happen to him— with or without astrology.

Astrology and Fate

Certain traditions of astrology are inclined to view astrology through the lens of fate— that is, that certain things are destined to happen to you based on the condition of the sky at the time of your birth. Generally speaking, it seems the fewer options for personal choice within a given society, the more fatalistic the tone of its astrology.

In the West, where individuality and self-determination are cherished values, we're taught from birth that we can be and do anything we want (unless we are 5'2" and wish to become a supermodel). Our astrology tends to reflect this thinking, and it's more common to find astrology used as a tool for self-understanding rather than as a window into one's fate. The prevailing thought is that astrology *reflects* life's circumstances—it doesn't create them, any more than your nationality, gender, or genetics create them. As Shakespeare rather elegantly put it, "The fault, dear Brutus, is not in our stars, but in ourselves."

But as the impossibility of being a 5'2" supermodel suggests, we are limited by certain conditions of our birth. Seen that way, it's possible that astrology describes another set of conditions imposed at birth that limit what is possible for us. In her book *The Astrology of Fate* (see Appendix C), the great astrologer and writer Liz Greene, however, uses the term "fate" unabashedly in exploring its relevance to astrology:

> As with many people, the presence of extreme suffering invokes in
> me the question of meaning. But for me, the roads of human per-
> versity and catastrophe do not ultimately lead to the comforting
> paternal arms of a benign Judaeo-Christian God whom we must not
> question nor do they lead to the indictment of society as the source
> of all ills. Rather, they lead to fate.

Regardless of whether you view astrology as a reflection of your fate or simply as a kind of cosmic blueprint for your life, all astrologers agree that even the smallest of life's details are reflected in the conditions of the heavens. The question is how rigidly we're bound to play those conditions out in a particular way.

Astrology and Prediction

"You have amazing planetary activity for marriage this year," the astrology student announces to the practice client sitting across the table from her. "You could meet some-one and be married within 10 months!"

Across the table, the practice client—his neighbor's 10-year-old daughter—blinks in confusion.

Astrologers can predict things based on knowledge of symbols and cycles. But these predictions are based on an *interpretation* of symbols. Astrology is a rich system, but it's not as though there's an astrological symbol that looks like a wedding couple on a cake, which wanders across the chart one fine Saturday and gets you married. Remember, symbols can always be interpreted in a variety of ways, and context plays an important role in all astrological interpretations.

But aside from that, I've always found the concept of prediction a bit worrisome, as it implies a static future that's sitting there waiting for you to catch up with it. How can that be, when in any given situation you usually have a number of options for how you can choose to act or react? And that doesn't even take into account the number of other people whose own decisions and choices limit and define the options available to you. Again, the matter of prediction returns us to the question of fate and its place in astrology.

Regardless of your thoughts about fate and the prediction of specific events, there's no question that astrology excels at telling you "what time it is"—which ideas and impulses are currently calling you to grapple with them. In astrology, as in life, you may not be able to choose what happens to you (perhaps that is a question of fate)—but you can certainly choose how to respond to what happens to you.

"That's Not Me!"

Scenario #1: You crack open the morning paper and sneak a peek at the horoscope column, specifically the few cryptic lines associated with "your sign." You snicker at the vague and unlikely pronouncements and shake your head. How could anyone believe such nonsense?

Scenario #2: As a gift for your early January birthday, an office friend presents you with a coffee mug emblazoned with an illustration of a goat, the word "Capricorn," and a handful of adjectives such as "serious," "mature," and "ambitious." In response to your baffled expression, your friend explains that Capricorn is your sign and so you can be described using these adjectives. Yet you're hardly the picture of maturity and ambition—you're 35 years old, you work in the mailroom, and your mother is constantly hollering at you to grow up, already. What gives?

Popularized astrology based on the signs of the zodiac, such as newspaper and magazine horoscopes and sun sign personality lore, provide a valuable service: they introduce people to astrology in a way that's practical and easy to use. The problem is that most people stop there, and base their opinions about people, situations, and astrology based on fairly shallow information. Let's take a closer look at these popular forms of astrology which, while useful in their way, can offer only limited insight.

Your Sign

When your well-meaning co-worker referred to "your sign," she was referring to the zodiac through which the Sun appeared to be moving the time of your birth. The Sun spends approximately 30 days in each sign. Of course, we're moving around the Sun, not the other way around; so when astrologers say "your Sun is in Capricorn," they really mean that the Sun *appeared* to be in Capricorn at the time of your birth.

The Sun is the single most important body in our sky; without it, we would literally perish. Its importance to life on earth is unquestioned, and therefore it holds a lot of weight and significance as an astrological symbol. In astrology, the sign symbolizes your entire reason for being, the central focus of your life. For that reason, you actually can usually tell quite a lot about a person by examining his or her Sun sign.

But not everything—because the Sun is not the *only* important object in the sky. The Moon, moving through the entire zodiac in a mere 28 days, is vitally important as well. So are the visible planets—Mercury, Venus, Mars, Jupiter, and Saturn. And Uranus, Neptune, and Pluto, though invisible to the unaided eye, are significant members of our celestial family. At any given moment, each of these is moving through a particular part of the sky, in relation to the zodiac, the horizon, and each other. Each of them offers insight into unique and fascinating you.

 ASTRO TIP To get more out of a horoscope column, read the forecast for your rising sign (see Chapter 9 for details) as well as for your Sun sign.

Horoscope Columns

There's an assumption among many that any trained monkey can sit down and write the horoscopes that appear in newspapers and magazines. I don't doubt that there are people out there with no knowledge of astrology who are simply making up horoscopes. For that matter, monkeys really are pretty smart, so maybe there's one out there that can crank out a bogus forecast. However, I've read many, many horoscope columns in my life and in each and every one I could detect the astrological rationale for the interpretations given.

The problem with horoscope columns is that they're based on what's currently happening in the sky *relative to your Sun sign*—only your Sun sign, and not the other planets and the houses of the horoscope and all that other neat stuff that makes you uniquely you. So the poor writer, struggling to make a living as either an astrologer, a writer, or (heaven forbid) an astrology writer, concocts something that's both as specific and as general as possible for each twelfth of the population born with the Sun in a particular sign.

Don't assume astrology is hopeless just because your horoscope in the newspaper misses the mark. A horoscope column is a sort of astrological caricature based on one tiny part of your full astrological profile. The answer is not fewer horoscope columns, or even better monkeys—just a broader view of why horoscopes give a limited view of things.

Practical Uses for Astrology

As far as most of us know, astrology has three important uses:

- To learn more about our favorite topic: ourselves
- To learn more about the people we're romantically interested in
- To predict the future

This is all good stuff, no doubt about it; but it presents a portrait of astrology that's painted in rather broad strokes. Actually, you might be surprised at the myriad practical uses for astrology. Most rely on the basic components of planets, signs, houses, and aspects. Let's look at some of the most popular.

Natal Astrology

Natal (related to birth) astrology assesses your characteristics and tendencies based on the day, year, exact time, and location of your birth. Newspaper horoscopes and coffee mugs with descriptions of your Sun sign, as well as in-depth readings by a trained astrologer, are all examples of natal astrology.

Relationship Astrology

Relationship astrology can help you sort out the compatibility and challenges between you and interesting others based on the day, year, exact time, and location of your respective births. Synastry compares the position of the planets in one person's birth chart with the planetary position in another person's birth chart. Composite charts are derived from a combination of the planetary placements in two birth charts—they're two charts in one!

An ethical astrologer will not give you an in-depth reading of another person's birth chart without his or her permission. If you consult an astrologer for relationship advice, you can expect an analysis of general information that helps you understand the relationship—but not an assessment of what the other person will do, or is thinking or feeling.

Electional Astrology

Electional astrology is the process of choosing ("electing") the best time to do something, such as getting married or starting a business. Save this stuff for important actions with far-reaching consequences; plotting the best time to shop for produce or get your shoes resoled is probably a bit obsessive.

Horary Astrology

Horary (from the Latin for "hour") astrology answers a question based on the moment the astrologer receives and understands it. If you need a simple answer to a burning question, such as "Does Selwyn fancy me?," you pose the question to a horary astrology specialist, who will glance at her watch, cast a chart for the moment, and deliver a simple "yes or no" answer. Horary is best suited to simple, clear-cut questions that can be answered with "yes" or "no," questions about the outcome of a particular situation, or even how to locate lost objects.

Mundane Astrology

Mundane astrology studies world affairs and events—outcomes of political elections, monarchy ascending to the throne, corporations being formed, countries picking fights with one another. This was the early astrologer's bread and butter—predicting wars, famine, plagues, and the like. There are still mundane astrologers around; in a troubled world, theirs is a nerve-wracking profession. You'll recognize them by their fretful expressions and anguished muttering.

Financial Astrology

Financial astrology relies on planetary cycles to predict gain and loss in the financial markets and the commercial marketplace. After the natal astrologer tells you you're entering a dicey time financially, a financial astrologer can talk you down with detailed advice about buying low, selling high, and diversifying your portfolio and whatnot.

Medical Astrology

Medical astrology studies the correlation between planetary symbolism and cycles and the health and illness of individuals. The signs and planets are associated with the parts of the body, and by analyzing the strengths and weaknesses of these in your birth chart, a medical astrologer can help you navigate the heartbreak of psoriasis and postnasal drip.

You Can Learn Astrology!

Like any language, astrology has a learning curve. Some people pick up a language pretty easily; others struggle. Some can learn most of what they need on their own, from books and Internet resources; others do better within the structured environment of classes and workshops.

The good news is that you already know about 90 percent of what the very best astrologers know: you understand life, the world, and human nature. You have knowledge, skill, empathy, and life experience. In other words, just because you're new to astrology doesn't mean you're a beginner at life. You're 90 percent of the way to knowing how to use astrology to better understand yourself and your world. This book is designed to teach you the other 10 percent: astrology's symbols, and how to interpret them.

Essential Takeaways

- Astrology studies the connection between the heavens and earthly affairs.
- Astrology refers to charts of the sky, not crystal balls, clairvoyance, palms, tarot cards, or numerology.
- Astrology and astronomy were once a single field of study, but are no longer connected.
- Modern astrologers do not believe the planets cause things to happen on earth, but rather that they reflect a pattern of meaningful coincidence between celestial activity and earthly affairs.
- Among the uses for astrology are understanding individuals, evaluating compatibility between people, answering pressing questions, choosing good times to act, understanding financial cycles and world affairs, and assessing physical illness.

CHAPTER 2

Reading Your Chart

Astrology's earth-centered model of the universe

Understanding the parts of a chart

Reading the symbols in the chart

How to get a copy of your birth chart

Calculating your birth chart by hand

To get the most out of this book, you'll really want to have a copy of your birth chart (also called your natal chart). Think of it as your celestial baby picture. Like the tiny hand- and footprints on your hospital birth certificate, a photo taken moments after your earthly debut, or a newspaper clipping from the day of your birth, the astrological birth chart is a representation of what the universe was like at the moment you joined us here.

This chapter will tell you how to get a copy of your birth chart—and how to understand it.

Earth: The Blue Marble

As you may recall from Chapter 1, astrology and astronomy, once peas in a celestial pod, had a nasty falling out in the seventeenth century when Galileo demonstrated that the earth orbits the Sun, and not the other way around. Up to that time, the world subscribed to a geocentric (earth-centered) model of the universe; astrology reflected this, and (mostly) still does.

A heliocentric view of the world is exemplified by the iconic photo-graph of the earth called "The Blue Marble," taken by the crew of the Apollo 17 space mission from space. The charts astrologers use to interpret the sky are like a photograph you'd take from your front yard if you had a 360-degree lens and the earth were transparent.

Why do it this way? Beyond the powerful lure of tradition, astrologers argue that our jour-nalistic beat is the connection between phenomena in the sky and earthly affairs— with an emphasis on the earthly affairs part. Astrologers were probably as excited about the 1969 Moon landing as anyone, but what really gets us going is what is happening on earth. Those of us who live on earth can hardly help having a geocentric view of things, and astrology's geocentric charts speak to our earthly interests and orientation.

The Upside-Down, AstroBizarro World

You probably have a pretty good handle on how to use the world for practical purposes. If you want to see the noonday sun, you walk outside and look up; if you want to see the midnight sun, you go to Alaska in July. If you're consulting a map of the United States, using Wichita as your reference point, you know that if you look to the east (right side of the map) you will eventually find New England; if you look to the west (left side of the map), you'll reach California. When the old-fashioned analog clock on the wall wants to represent the forward march of time, its hands move from top to bottom, and then from bottom to top, moving from the right side of the clock to the left; we call this clockwise motion. This is how things work in your world.

So when you get a copy of your birth chart for the first time and see South notated at the top of the chart and North at the bottom, East on the left side of the chart and West on the right, and the sections of the wheel are labeled from one through twelve *counterclock-wise*—well, you know you're not in Kansas anymore.

All of this fancy graphical footwork is to compensate for one inconvenient truth: the earth is tilted on its axis. In the northern hemisphere, we're actually looking down (south) to see the sun; when it reaches its daily peak, the sun is due south. So charts are drawn with south on top, representing the highest point in the sky. (In the southern hemisphere, charts are drawn the same way but the math that gets you there is somewhat different.)

How Time Works

The concept of day and night and time in general are based on our experience of dark-ness and light, not an hour on a clock. If you doubt that, spend a summer in Antarctica— it's light outside whether the clock says noon or midnight.

In the age of electricity, people organize our time with clocks, designed to approximate the movement of the Sun throughout the day and night. However, because the earth is rotating on its axis and gradually showing different areas of its surface to the Sun, people on opposite sides of the earth don't experience day and night simultaneously. This presents certain practical and logistical problems about how to keep track of the time in various parts of the world (in order to organize international conference calls and coordinate television coverage of the Academy Awards broadcast).

Look at a globe, and you'll find lines called *meridians* running from the top to the bottom at regular intervals. The line that runs through the United Kingdom (and specifically, Greenwich, England) is called the Prime Meridian. It's the reference point against which time is measured in all other parts of the world. All the other meridians basically describe how far a given place is from Greenwich, and how much sooner or later the Sun will be overhead there than in Greenwich.

DEFINITION

Meridians are imaginary lines running from the North to the South Pole at regular intervals, marking degrees of longitude from the Prime Meridian at Greenwich, England.

Time Zones

The earth's 24 main time zones roughly approximate these meridians. One time zone/meridian represents approximately 15 degrees of longitude, or about one hour of travel time for the Sun. Since the Sun rises in the east, anyplace west of Greenwich will have the Sun overhead later, and anyplace east has it earlier. So the time of day is later as you move east from Greenwich, and earlier as you move west, up to the International Date Line (longitude 180°).

Which is why when the queen is greeting the day in London, sipping a cup of Earl Grey and sneaking bites of crumpet to her corgis under the table, New Yorkers are just dragging themselves home from a late night at the clubs. New York is five meridians/time zones west of Greenwich, so when it's 6 A.M. in London, it's only 1 A.M. in New York—a full five hours before you down your coffee and bagel.

ASTRO ALERT

In 1895, a New Zealand entomologist named George Vernon Hudson proposed the idea of adding more daylight hours to the working day, the better to collect fascinating insects. He had unwittingly given birth to Daylight Saving Time, the practice of moving the clock forward one hour between spring and fall, shifting an extra hour of daylight from morning to afternoon. After a rocky start, Daylight Saving Time eventually caught on nearly everywhere. In the United States, the Uniform Time Act of 1966 standardized the beginning and end dates for Daylight Saving Time, but also allowed localities to opt out. Arizona and Hawaii, for instance, don't observe Daylight Saving Time (presumably because they get plenty of sun as it is).

Anatomy of an Astrology Chart

The astrology chart is cast for a particular moment and place in time. It can be cast for any event for which the time and place of its beginning are known: a birth (such as your birth chart), marriage, death, beginning of a job, debut of a film, or natural disaster. However, the kind of event for which the chart has been cast can't be determined just by looking at the chart. And if it's the chart of a person, you can't tell gender, sexual orientation, or marital status from looking at an astrology chart. What you can tell is something about the qualities of the moment in time for which the chart has been cast. And in astrology, it's believed that whatever begins in a moment of time has the qualities of that moment in time.

Like a human body (or a Starbucks), an astrology chart has various consistent structural components. These are the same, regardless of the event symbolized by the chart.

The Wheel

It begins with a wheel: a circle, representing the ecliptic—the path of the Sun's apparent journey across the sky. Picture it as a really big cigar band with pictures of animals and virgins and weighing machines stamped on the inside. Now picture yourself standing inside it, like one of those photographs of a formerly large person standing inside his erstwhile, now comically oversized, trousers.

If you took geometry in school, you'll recall that a circle has 360 degrees. Around 2400 B.C.E., the Sumerians came up with the 360-degree circle idea, to keep track of the Sun's journey which appeared to take 360 days. Later, the Egyptians came up with the 24-hour day; the Greeks made the hours equal in length; and the Babylonians divided the hour into fractions of 60 minutes in an hour and 60 seconds in a minute.

Basically, if you can tell time and use a calendar, you know all you need to know of math to understand an astrology chart such as the one shown here.

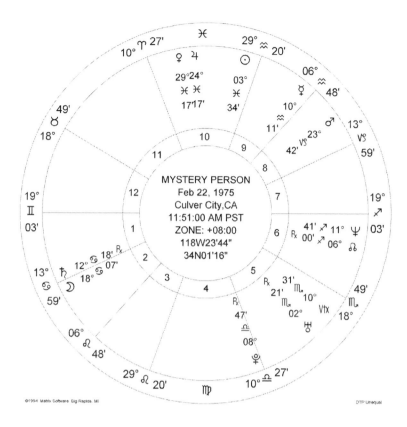

Sample astrology chart.

Your New Alphabet

So you've got this wheel. Forgetting about the Sumerians, just be aware that the circle contains 360 degrees; and that even if these degrees aren't individually represented on the chart (some-times they are, but usually they aren't), they're still there, and each one corresponds with 1 of the 360 degrees of the zodiac. Each of the 12 zodiac signs is assigned 30 degrees of the wheel.

There are also some hieroglyphics to untangle that may be a bit baffling at first:

Signs:	Planets:	Aspects:	Other:
Aries ♈	Sun ☉	Conjunction ☌	North Node ☊
Taurus ♉	Moon ☽	Sextile ⚹	Part of Fortune ⊗
Gemini ♊	Mercury ☿	Trine △	Vertex Vx
Cancer ♋	Venus ♀	Square □	Chiron ⚷
Leo ♌	Mars ♂	Opposition ☍	Ceres ⚳
Virgo ♍	Jupiter ♃	Semisextile ⊻	Juno ⚵
Libra ♎	Saturn ♄	Semisquare ∠	Pallas Athene ⚴
Scorpio ♏	Uranus ♅	Sesquisquare ⚼	Vesta ⚶
Sagittarius ♐	Neptune ♆	Quincunx ⚻	
Capricorn ♑	Pluto ♇	Parallel ∥	
Aquarius ♒		Contraparallel ⫲	
Pisces ♓			

Chapter 22 discusses the astrological alphabet and its glyphs in more detail.

Signs

The 12 signs of the zodiac take their names, symbolism, and order from the constellations along the ecliptic. Each sign is associated with a house, and is "ruled" by one or more planets.

The 12 signs of the zodiac appear in order around the perimeter of the horoscopic wheel, on the *cusp* of each house. Signs are described as being *in houses*—that is, moving through a particular area of the sky. Planets are described as being *in signs*—that is, moving through a particular constellation. (See Part 2 for more about the signs.)

Cusp is the term for the imaginary lines dividing the houses of the horoscope. Some astrologers feel that a planet that is close to a house cusp may be felt in both houses.

Houses

The chart is divided into 12 sections called houses, 6 of which represent the sky above the horizon and 6 of which represent the invisible sky below. The 12 houses have considerable correlation with the 12 signs of the zodiac. The first house corresponds to the first sign of the zodiac, Aries; the second house to the second sign, Taurus; and so on.

The houses are numbered counterclockwise beginning with the left-hand (east) point. They're divided by lines, or cusps, which point to particular degrees and signs on the ecliptic, the band of fixed stars through which the Sun makes its annual journey. We say that signs of the zodiac are in and on the cusps of particular houses; they always follow their natural order from Aries to Pisces.

There are many ways of splitting the sky into houses and considerable controversy among astrologers as to which is the best method. Suffice to say, the 12 houses are not necessarily equal in size in your chart. However, the six houses in the top hemisphere of the chart will also be the same size as their corresponding opposite houses in the southern hemisphere. So if the twelfth house is 22 degrees wide, the sixth house will also be 22 degrees wide. (Houses are discussed in detail in Part 3.)

The Natural Wheel

The *Natural Wheel* is a wheel with 12 houses of equal size, with the first degree of Aries on the cusp of the first house, followed by the first degree of each succeeding sign on subsequent house cusps.

In reality, almost nobody has a wheel like this. Yours may begin with any 1 of the 360 degrees of the zodiac on the cusp of the first house. The houses of your chart are unlikely to be exactly 30 degrees each, and some signs might appear on two house cusps in a row, with the next sign not appearing on a cusp at all.

But the Natural Wheel reflects the correlation between the signs of the zodiac and the houses of the horoscope. When we describe Gemini as the "natural" sign of the third house, we refer to the Natural Wheel and the thematic sympathy between Gemini and the third house.

DEFINITION

The **Natural Wheel** is an astrology wheel divided into 12 houses of equal size, with 0 degrees Aries on the first house cusp and 0 degrees of the succeeding signs following in order on the remaining house cusps. It's a representation of the connection between the themes of the 12 signs of the zodiac and the 12 houses of the horoscope.

Planets

The Sun and Moon are called luminaries or, for the sake of convenience, planets. Astrology charts also include Mercury, Venus, Mars, Jupiter, Saturn, Uranus, Neptune, and Pluto. Most "traditional" astrologers don't use Uranus, Neptune, or Pluto in their charts. Planets have essential meanings derived from the mythological figures for which they're named.

Planets are described as being *in signs* (that is, moving through a particular constellation) or *in houses* (moving through a particular part of the sky). Planets move through the houses of the chart in a counterclockwise motion. Planets move at different rates relative to earth, based on their distance from the Sun, with the Moon moving through the zodiac most quickly (about 28 days) and Pluto most slowly (approximately 245 years).

Each planet rules one or more signs. Planets are also classified according to their essential dignities, or strengths. In traditional astrology, the matter of essential dignities is fairly complex. It's worth knowing, however, the signs in which each planet is considered in its "house" (the sign or signs that it rules), exaltation (especially strong), detriment (the sign opposite its rulership), or fall (the sign opposite its exaltation), as shown in the following table.

Essential Dignities (Simplified)

Planet	Rulership	Exaltation	Detriment	Fall
Mars	Aries, Scorpio	Capricorn	Taurus, Libra	Cancer
Venus	Taurus, Libra	Pisces	Aries, Scorpio	Virgo
Mercury	Gemini, Virgo	Aquarius	Sagittarius, Pisces	Leo
Moon	Cancer	Taurus	Capricorn	Scorpio
Sun	Leo	Aries	Aquarius	Libra

Planets are described in more detail in Part 4.

Getting Your Hands on Your Birth Chart

Fortunately, getting a copy of your birth chart is easier than ever. Gone are the days of hauling out several large reference books; today you can calculate it online for free. Software programs that calculate charts are available at very affordable prices. Or simply turn to your favorite search engine for help and search for a phrase such as "free astrology chart."

Here's the information you'll need to calculate your birth chart:

- **Your date of birth**—This tells us the sign placements of your planets with some reliability.

- **Verified time of your birth**—You need to know this to the minute. Even a few minutes can make a big difference in your chart! I've included some tips in the next section for finding your verified time of birth.

- **Your place of birth**—City, state or province, and country. In the United States, many states have multiple cities or towns with identical names, so make sure you know the county in which you were born.

Time and place tells us the orientation of the horizon to the ecliptic, giving us your rising sign and house cusp degrees. Since the Moon moves quickly, the time and place of birth tells us its exact position at your birth.

Finding Your Birth Data

Without the time of birth, you're limited in what you can do with astrology. Prediction, in particular, gets tricky and imprecise. Because the degree on the Ascendant changes about every four minutes, and the Moon changes degree about every three hours, time is of the essence. It's worth hunting down your birth time, and it's not that difficult for most modern people. Here are some ideas to get you started:

- Check your birth certificate. If you can't find your original birth certificate in your file of important family paraphernalia, request a copy from the county where you were born. Get in touch with the Vital Records department of the county seat, or order a copy through Vitalchek (www.vitalchek.com), an online service that handles such requests for many government agencies. If you are given the option, choose a "Birth Long" or "Birth Full" record, which normally has more detailed information, such as birth time.

- If your birth certificate doesn't have a recorded time, try the hospital where you were born. If they're no help, look through baby books, family letters, or newspaper announcements.

- As a last resort, hire an astrologer who specializes in rectification to figure out your birth time based on the dates of important events in your life. This is time-consuming work that requires a high degree of skill, so expect to pay a premium for the service.

Please don't rely on your mom's memory of what time you were born. If she's like most women, she had other things on her mind at the time. Instead, get a copy of your birth certificate from the appropriate governmental office or from the hospital where you were born.

Calculating Charts with a Computer

Back in the days of manual chart calculation, errors were far too easy to make. But it's surprisingly easy to botch even computer-calculated charts. Here are a few words of caution:

- Enter your birth data correctly! I realize that sounds obvious—maybe even a bit insulting. But be sure you enter the birth date in the correct format—some programs require that you use the European format, DD/MM/YYYY, others require the U.S. format, MM/DD/YYYY. Also, some programs will automatically adjust A.M. or P.M. times to 24-hour or "military" time (e.g., 2 P.M. = 14:00), or vice versa.

- Unless it's explicitly stated otherwise, keep in mind that most calculation programs adjust automatically for Daylight Saving Time.

ASTRO TIP Here's an easy way to double-check input errors, such as using A.M. instead of P.M.: check the house placement of the Sun. The Sun should be above the horizon (houses 12, 11, 10, 9, 8, or 7) for birth times between sunrise and sunset, and beneath the horizon (houses 6, 5, 4, 3, 2, 1) for birth times between sunset and sunrise.

If you plan to calculate a lot of charts, want to maintain a personal database of birth information, or want easy access to advanced features you can grow into as you learn more about astrology, you probably will eventually want to purchase a chart calculation program. These nearly always include a built-in atlas with the longitude, latitude, and time zone of practically every city, town, berg, or mole hole in the world. They also have built-in features to adjust for Daylight Saving Time and the like. See Appendix C for a sample of user-friendly programs at a variety of price levels.

Astrology Unplugged!

Both computers and astrology are thought to be "ruled by" (associated with) the planet Uranus. It's impossible to overestimate the influence of the personal computer and the development of software designed to perform astrological calculations on the field of professional astrology. Computers have been the great equalizer, making astrology accessible to people who have a hard time with math. They make it a lot easier for astrologers to serve multiple clients in a single day. Generally, they ensure more accurate results and fewer incorrect charts and readings.

If you were born sometime after the Carter administration, you may never have run across a hand-drawn birth chart. When I was 12 years old I sent away for mine, answering an ad in the back of a paperback astrology book. It came back hand-drawn on heavy, cream-colored paper, with the astrologer's handwritten notations. It had a sort of old-world, mystical romanticism that made it seem laden with otherworldly powers and insights.

A couple of years into my professional astrology career, my mother presented me with an oddity she'd found in an old trunk: Her father's birth chart, complete with interpretations, which he'd commissioned from "a gypsy." To this day it's one of my most treasured possessions.

Are you a confirmed Luddite? Concerned with saving power? Kick it old school by arming yourself with a few tools and techniques that served astrologers well in the hundreds and hundreds of years before the advent of the personal computer.

Meet the Ephemeris

First and foremost, the *ephemeris* is your friend. Most people don't love or use it anymore, but in my lifetime—yes, even in the time I've been practicing astrology!—the ephemeris was essential for the everyday astrologer. An ephemeris is simply a table showing the planetary positions on a given day, usually calculated for midnight or noon in Greenwich, England.

DEFINITION An **ephemeris** is a table of planetary positions for a particular date. You can find one online, or buy a print copy with planetary positions for an entire century.

In my day (back when we walked 6 miles to school in the snow, barefoot), you toted around a small pocket-sized ephemeris for the current year to tell you about the daily planetary occurrences. These are still available online or in some metaphysical bookstores. You can also buy more graphically appealing annual astrology calendars (my favorite is Jim Maynard's Pocket Astrologer, available through Quicksilver Publications; www.quicksilverproductions.com) that include the ephemerides for an entire year along with helpful stuff like the Moon's void-of-course periods, daily sign, and aspects (see Chapter 18).

The serious student or professional astrologer usually owns a book of ephemerides for the entire century. Nearly the size and weight of the complete works of William Shakespeare (hardcover edition), a century's worth of ephemerides could substitute, in a pinch, for a low side table or footstool. Ephemerides are available with calculations for either midnight or noon at Greenwich.

Online Ephemeris

The digital age being what it is, you can also access an online ephemeris for free at the website of Astrodienst (www.astro.com), a Zurich-based software development company. Select "Ephemeris" from the main menu, click on the link to the year you'd like to see, scroll through to find the month and date you're looking for, and voilà—you'll see something like the following page.

Let's use the line I've highlighted in this figure as an example. It gives the planetary lowdown for Saturday, February 22, 1975, at midnight in Greenwich, England (hence the reference, at the top right-hand corner, to 00:00 UT, or zero hour and minutes, Universal Time). The top row of the table gives the symbol for each planet, and the days of the month are listed in the left-hand column. Then, from left to right, the celestial longitude is given for each planet. (Also included is the Sidereal Time (Sid.t), which for now you may safely ignore; it will become interesting and relevant if you choose to calculate charts by hand.) If there is no sign given for the planet's entry, assume it is in the most recent sign listed above it in the column.

FEBRUARY 1975 **00:00 UT**

Day	Sid.t	☉	☽	☿	♀	♂	♃	♄	♅	♆	♇	☊	☊	⚸	⚷
S 1	8 42 19	11♒29'31	12♎33	25°R13	2♓11	7♑29	19♓20	13°R27	2♏28	11♐19	9°R 8	7°R58	6♐57	29♒30	20♈24
S 2	8 46 16	12°30'24	26°37	24♒50	3°25	8°14	19°33	13♋23	2°28	11°21	9♎ 8	7♐55	6°54	29°37	20°26
M 3	8 50 13	13°31'17	10♏15	24°16	4°40	8°58	19°46	13°19	2°28	11°22	9° 7	7°D54	6°51	29°43	20°28
T 4	8 54 9	14°32'09	23°27	23°32	5°55	9°42	20° 0	13°15	2°28	11°23	9° 6	7°54	6°48	29°50	20°30
W 5	8 58 6	15°33'00	6♐18	22°39	7°10	10°26	20°13	13°11	2°28	11°24	9° 5	7°R54	6°45	29°57	20°31
T 6	9 2 2	16°33'50	18°51	21°39	8°24	11°11	20°26	13° 7	2°R28	11°26	9° 5	7°54	6°41	0♓ 4	20°33
F 7	9 5 59	17°34'39	1♑10	20°33	9°39	11°55	20°39	13° 4	2°28	11°27	9° 4	7°51	6°38	0°10	20°35
S 8	9 9 55	18°35'27	13°20	19°23	10°54	12°40	20°53	13° 0	2°28	11°28	9° 3	7°46	6°35	0°17	20°37
S 9	9 13 52	19°36'14	25°22	18°12	12° 8	13°24	21° 6	12°57	2°28	11°29	9° 2	7°38	6°32	0°24	20°39
M10	9 17 49	20°37'00	7♒20	17° 0	13°23	14° 9	21°20	12°53	2°28	11°30	9° 1	7°26	6°29	0°31	20°41
T 11	9 21 45	21°37'44	19°14	15°51	14°37	14°53	21°33	12°50	2°28	11°31	9° 0	7°13	6°26	0°37	20°44
W12	9 25 42	22°38'28	1♓ 7	14°45	15°52	15°38	21°47	12°47	2°27	11°32	8°59	6°59	6°22	0°44	20°46
T 13	9 29 38	23°39'09	12°59	13°45	17° 7	16°22	22° 0	12°43	2°27	11°33	8°58	6°44	6°19	0°51	20°48
F 14	9 33 35	24°39'50	24°51	12°50	18°21	17° 7	22°14	12°40	2°27	11°34	8°57	6°31	6°16	0°57	20°50
S 15	9 37 31	25°40'28	6♈47	12° 3	19°35	17°51	22°28	12°37	2°26	11°35	8°56	6°20	6°13	1° 4	20°53
S 16	9 41 28	26°41'06	18°47	11°23	20°50	18°36	22°42	12°35	2°26	11°36	8°55	6°12	6°10	1°11	20°55
M17	9 45 24	27°41'41	0♉57	10°51	22° 4	19°21	22°56	12°32	2°25	11°37	8°54	6° 6	6° 6	1°18	20°57
T 18	9 49 21	28°42'15	13°18	10°26	23°18	20° 6	23° 9	12°29	2°25	11°38	8°52	6° 4	6° 3	1°24	21° 0
W19	9 53 17	29°42'47	25°56	10° 9	24°33	20°50	23°23	12°27	2°24	11°38	8°51	6° 3	6° 0	1°31	21° 2
T 20	9 57 14	0♓43'17	8♊56	10° 0	25°47	21°35	23°37	12°24	2°23	11°39	8°50	6° 3	5°57	1°38	21° 5
F 21	10 1 11	1°43'46	22°21	9°D58	27° 1	22°20	23°51	12°22	2°22	11°40	8°49	6° 3	5°54	1°44	21° 7
S 22	10 5 7	2°44'12	6♋15	10° 2	28°15	23° 5	24° 5	12°20	2°21	11°41	8°48	6° 0	5°51	1°51	21°10
S 23	10 9 4	3°44'37	20°38	10°13	29°30	23°50	24°19	12°17	2°21	11°41	8°46	5°55	5°47	1°58	21°13
M24	10 13 0	4°44'59	5♌29	10°31	0♈44	24°35	24°33	12°15	2°20	11°42	8°45	5°48	5°44	2° 5	21°15
T 25	10 16 57	5°45'20	20°39	10°53	1°58	25°19	24°48	12°13	2°19	11°43	8°44	5°37	5°41	2°11	21°18
W26	10 20 53	6°45'39	6♍ 1	11°21	3°12	26° 4	25° 2	12°11	2°18	11°43	8°42	5°26	5°38	2°18	21°21
T 27	10 24 50	7°45'57	21°22	11°54	4°26	26°49	25°16	12°10	2°17	11°44	8°41	5°15	5°35	2°25	21°23
F 28	10 28 46	8♓46'12	6♎30	12♒31	5♈39	27♑34	25♓30	12♋ 8	2♏15	11♐44	8♎40	5♐ 5	5♐32	2♓32	21♈26

Delta T = 45.56 sec.

created from Swiss Ephemeris, Copyright Astrodienst AG [5.1.2003]

Sample entry from an online ephemeris.
Copyright Astrodienst AG/www.astro.com

As of midnight on this date at Greenwich:

Sun 2° ♓ 44'12

Moon 6° ♋ 15

Mercury 10° ♒ 2

Venus 28° ♓ 15

Mars 23° ♑ 5

Jupiter 24° ♓ 5

Saturn 12° ♋ 20

Uranus 2° ♏ 21

Neptune 11° ♐ 41

Pluto 8° ♎ 48

North Node (True) 6° ♐ 0

North Node (Mean) 5° ♐ 51

Black Moon Lilith 1° ♓ 51 (not covered in this book)

Chiron 21 ♈ 10

To see the planetary aspects for the day, return to the main list of years and click on the letter A to the left of the link for the year you're interested in. You'll see a list of planetary aspects in time order.

For instance, on January 1, 1960, at 7:20 A.M. Universal Time, the planet Mars ♂ made a trine aspect △ to Uranus ♅.

It's a Matter of Time

Remember, these placements are for UT (Greenwich Mean Time). So if you're in New York, subtract five hours from the time given: 2:20 A.M. If you're in Rome, one hour ahead of Greenwich, add one hour: 8:20 A.M.

ASTRO TIP Chart calculation adjusts for your distance from your local meridian, your latitude, and your time zone.

Calculating Charts by Hand

In fewer than five minutes, you can calculate a chart online. For the cost of the materials required to calculate charts by hand, you can buy a very good chart calculation program. Why, then, should you go to the trouble to learn to calculate charts by hand?

- To pass examinations for certification by an astrological organization. The major organizations awarding certification will require you to know how to calculate a variety of charts by hand.

- Your power is out, and a client will be arriving in about two hours for a reading. If you know how to calculate charts by hand and have a hard-copy ephemeris, you're in business. This will also come in handy in the event of some postapocalyptic, Mad Max future when we're all wearing tattered clothes and using an abacus for simple math.

- You want street cred among astrologers. You'd be amazed how many professional astrologers cannot calculate a chart by hand.

- To spend quality time with a chart. Okay, so this is kind of romantic. But one thing I found is that when it became a lot easier for me to calculate charts (using a computer), I spent a lot less time with each one. When you calculate charts manually, you spend time thinking about the sign and house placements of the various planets and angles, calculating aspects by hand, and drawing the thing out. Very tactile, very satisfying.

To calculate a birth chart by hand, you'll need the following:

- An atlas with time changes and time zones

- An ephemeris that covers the month you were born

- A calculator

- Appendix C of this book, which will direct you to some excellent guides to chart calculation

I realize calculating charts the old-fashioned way may seem like a completely daunting task. But although I own two software programs that calculate charts (and barely passed high school algebra), I occasionally whip out the books and the calculator and knock out a chart for old time's sake. You might be surprised to find that calculating charts manually is not only possible, but enjoyable.

Essential Takeaways

- The main component of the astrology chart is a 360-degree wheel, representing the ecliptic.
- Every chart contains the 12 signs of the zodiac; 12 houses; the Sun, Moon, and the 8 known planets (including Pluto); and planetary aspects.
- Charts can be calculated easily using online resources or specialized software.
- Learning to calculate charts manually is not difficult and may come in handy if you wish to pass a certification exam or impress your colleagues.

PART 2

Signs of the Zodiac

The zodiac. For as long as you can remember, its beasts and mythical figures (plus, inexplicably, one machine) have stared back at you from T-shirts, coffee mugs, and calendars. Almost everyone knows his or her "sign" and has read a horoscope column. For most people, the signs of the zodiac are astrology. In fact, they're not. But what does the zodiac bring to the table? Emerging from the symbolism of seasonal rhythms, constellations, and myth, the signs of the zodiac are like the personalities and costumes of characters in a play; some dress in colors of manipulation, like Lady Macbeth, others in Henry V's inspiring leadership, still others in the doomed romanticism of Juliet.

In this part, the zodiac's 12 characters are presented in four groups. Each group contains three signs of the zodiac that share certain qualities of temperament, and each has a leader, an organizer, and a Greek chorus. You'll learn which group is which and what role each sign plays within it, which will help you understand what makes each sign tick and how to anticipate their needs and behaviors in love and in work.

CHAPTER 3

The Zodiac

The 12 signs of the zodiac

Tropical versus sidereal zodiac

Using the signs to understand archetypes

Planetary rulerships of the signs

The modalities: cardinal, fixed, and mutable signs

The elements: fire, earth, air, and water signs

The 12 signs of the zodiac, usually referred to simply as "the signs," are astrology's most recognizable symbols. You probably know a little something about them; you may even have strong opinions about a few. In this chapter, you get to know the "Sky Critters"—the 12 signs of the zodiac.

The signs of the zodiac offer a vivid introduction to the 12 essential archetypes that are astrology's building blocks. They're not the be-all and end-all of astrology, but understanding their symbolism can help you understand the personal style, attitudes, and approach to life of those who wander into your orbit.

What Is the Zodiac?

The 12 signs of the zodiac take their names and symbols from the band of constellations flanking the ecliptic, which marks the Sun's apparent annual journey across the sky. Each sign represents a particular set of archetypal characteristics that are based on the time of year when the Sun moves through its part of the sky. In an astrology chart, the characteristics of the zodiac describe your attitudes, approach, and personal style.

Traditionally, the zodiac is divided into 12 signs of 30 degrees longitude each. These signs are named after 12 of the 13 constellations flanking the ecliptic. The signs serve as a kind of backdrop against which the planets, Sun, and Moon appear to move relative to earth. When we say "the Sun is in Aries," for instance, we mean that it appears the Sun is moving through the sign of Aries.

The Signs of the Zodiac

Sign	Symbol	Dates the Sun Is in Sign
Aries	Ram ♈	Mar. 21–Apr. 20
Taurus	Bull ♉	Apr. 21–May 20
Gemini	Twins ♊	May 21–June 21
Cancer	Crab ♋	June 22–July 22
Leo	Lion ♌	July 23–Aug. 22
Virgo	Virgin ♍	Aug. 23–Sept. 22
Libra	Scales ♎	Sept. 23–Oct. 22
Scorpio	Scorpion ♏	Oct. 23–Nov. 21
Sagittarius	Archer ♐	Nov. 22–Dec. 21
Capricorn	Sea Goat ♑	Dec. 22–Jan. 21
Aquarius	Water Bearer ♒	Jan. 22–Feb. 18
Pisces	Fish ♓	Feb. 19–Mar. 20

The "Wrong" Zodiac

You're sitting at dinner with friends, chatting enthusiastically about your new interest in astrology. Your friend who graduated with a degree in astronomy pipes up: "I don't know how you can believe in astrology. It's not even based on the correct positions of the stars!"

He's right. Most Western astrologers use a system known as the *tropical zodiac*, which aligns the vernal equinox with the first degree of the first sign, Aries. However, because of the precession of the equinoxes, the vernal equinox is now in early Pisces. This precession is ongoing, with the difference between tropical and sidereal positions widening about 1 degree every 72 years.

Whereas astrologers who use the *sidereal zodiac* (including the majority of astrologers in the East) refer to the current position of the stars, tropical astrology is based on the seasonal association of the signs with the season in which the sun rises in them. To tropical astrologers, who favor a symbolic or metaphorical approach to the zodiac, the fact that the vernal equinox has shifted to another constellation is beside the point. Tropical astrology is based on our relationship to the Sun, not to the stars.

DEFINITION Most modern Western astrologers use the **tropical zodiac** system. This is a metaphorical, season-based approach that aligns the vernal equinox with the beginning of Aries, the first sign. The **sidereal zodiac** uses the actual position of the Sun at the vernal equinox, which has shifted backwards into early Pisces.

So your astronomer friend is right—about tropical astrologers, anyway. In fact, the astrological community itself is divided on the topic of which zodiac is the "right" one. When you're reading horoscope columns or astrology articles in the West, however, you can safely assume that the tropical zodiac is being used, unless stated otherwise.

Signs Aren't People

As you read the chapters that follow about the signs of the zodiac, bear in mind that what we're talking about are *archetypes,* not individual people. When you read something like "Leo is magnanimous and outgoing," your mind may immediately object that your August-born aunt is, in fact, shy and retiring. This is where the astrological skeptic proclaims victory and changes the subject. But allow me to gently reintroduce the topic, with the explanation that although your aunt was born when the Sun was in Leo, she has an entire birth chart full of planets and placements and aspects that may contradict or mitigate the Leo archetype.

Think of it this way. In the world of film, there are various familiar stereotypes that allow you to grasp the essence of a character without a lot of time-consuming flashbacks or exposition. You know them as the wise-cracking best friend, the crusading cop, or the plucky career gal with the disappointing love life. But the best and most memorable films have a habit of elevating these tired stereotypes to archetypal status, representing something true and universal in the collective unconscious. The star-crossed lovers from opposite sides of the tracks are a stereotype. Positioned in an important historical context, however—such as Rose and Jack on the *Titanic,* or Scarlett and Rhett during the Civil

War—their relationship may take on archetypal importance, representing the human impact of these historic events.

Archetypes are idealized representations of some trait or quality in the collective unconscious. This is different than stereotypes, which are simplified, generalized, and often negative representations based on qualities such as gender, race, or status—or, in the case of astrology, on one or two people you once met who were born with the Sun in that sign!

Signs are not people—they're characters, archetypes. Placing different planets, like different actors, in a particular sign gives the archetype a different flavor. Signs can be thought of as a costume to be worn. Place Venus, the planet of love and also of attractive young women, in Virgo, a sign of modesty and practicality, and your film character looks a bit like a lovely and slightly shy secretary. Cast Mars, the planet of war, in analytical Virgo, and your character might be a studious young war reporter during World War II.

We're a Mix of All Signs

Nothing makes an astrologer sadder than hearing someone say, "Oh, I hate [insert sign here]." One of the favorite arguments against astrology is, "There is no way that everyone in the world can fall into 12 neat categories," and you'll get no argument from me. Gross generalizations about the signs of the zodiac are, to me, as baffling as declaring you hate vegetables just because you've eaten a couple of overcooked Brussels sprouts over the years.

The fact is, each of us contains every sign of the zodiac in our birth chart. The horoscope is a representation of the entire sky at the time of your birth. Every constellation along the ecliptic, whether it was visible or not from the place of your birth, is fully represented in the 12 houses of your birth chart. So declaring war on any sign of the zodiac is tantamount to disowning part of yourself.

You have the opportunity to experience each sign of the zodiac in your own life. If Leo falls in the sixth house of your chart, for instance, you get to "be a Leo" in sixth house areas of your life (at work, for instance). As each planet moves through a sign, it activates that archetype somewhere in your life. Some, such as the signs of the Sun, Moon, and Ascendant (cusp of the first house) at your birth, may speak through you more strongly than others. We'll learn more about how this works in practice in upcoming chapters. For now, it's enough to understand that all 12 signs are part of your birth chart, and all are relevant to your life.

ASTRO ALERT Don't disown or disparage any sign based on past experiences. If you've had a number of bad experiences with people born with the Sun in a particular sign, you may decide you "just can't get along" with people of that sign. But who knows how many people with that sign strong in their charts that you've met without knowing it, most of whom you probably got along with splendidly? Signs are not people—and all of them are a part of you.

Bright and Dark Sides

No sign is inherently good or bad. Decades of pop Sun-sign astrology have done a disservice to nearly all the signs of the zodiac, with a few signs (such as Virgo and Scorpio) suffering blows to their reputations as a result of simplistic astrology.

In astrology we regard each of these sign archetypes as symbols of essential roles in the human drama. In the hands of a "good actor," a sign's most noble traits naturally emerge. But bad motivations bring out the worst traits of signs as well as people.

A sign has a bright side and a dark side. Traditionally upbeat planets (Venus, Jupiter) or difficult ones (Saturn, Pluto) in a sign can tend to sway the balance of bright and dark one way or another for you, but ultimately, it's up to you which side shows itself most often in your life. Can you live up to each sign's best qualities, or will you give in to laziness or malevolence and portray its darker side?

Planetary Rulerships

In astrology, each sign is associated with one or more planets called the "ruler(s)" of that sign. In much the same way as a director instructs an actor how to play a part, a sign's planetary ruler gives off-screen instructions to that sign.

For example, the planetary ruler of the sign Taurus is Venus. If you were born with planets in Taurus, they will act out Taurus themes about stability, determination, and financial security. But they will also take some cues from the placement of Venus in your chart, and if Venus is in a very different kind of sign than Taurus—say, Aquarius—you will tend to experience conflict. In this case, the conflict might be between the desire for change (Venus in Aquarius) and Taurus's desire for stability.

Shared Rulerships

Two planets, Mercury and Venus, each rule two signs. Mercury is the ruler of both quick-witted Gemini and analytical Virgo, and Venus rules earthy, sensual Taurus and refined

Libra. Some astrologers suggest other rulerships for Virgo, including Vulcan (a hypothetical planet between Earth and Mercury) and the asteroid Vesta. Earth, which is usually not represented in the astrology chart, is sometimes proposed as more in keeping with the earthy, practical nature of Taurus. But this dual rulership also seems relevant to Venus's association with both money (Taurus) and relationships (Libra).

Modern vs. Traditional Rulerships

Before the discovery of Uranus, Neptune, and Pluto, the signs Aquarius, Pisces, and Scorpio were ruled by Saturn, Jupiter, and Mars, respectively. Many astrologers still refer to these "traditional" rulerships, especially in horary and electional astrology (discussed in Chapter 1).

It's also helpful to think of the modern and traditional rulerships as representing the duality of these signs. Aquarius, for instance, certainly reflects the qualities associated with its modern ruler, Uranus—rebellious, unconventional, and innovative. But Aquarius also has an extremely conventional, even conservative side that's in keeping with the symbolism of Saturn, its traditional ruler. Which makes sense, when you think about it; after all, you have to know what the rules are (Saturn) before you can break them (Uranus)!

Planetary Rulership of Signs

Sign	Modern Ruler	Traditional Ruler
Aries	Mars	Mars
Taurus	Venus	Venus
Gemini	Mercury	Mercury
Cancer	Moon	Moon
Leo	Sun	Sun
Virgo	Mercury	Mercury
Libra	Venus	Venus
Scorpio	Pluto	Mars
Sagittarius	Jupiter	Jupiter
Capricorn	Saturn	Saturn
Aquarius	Uranus	Saturn
Pisces	Neptune	Jupiter

General Approach to Life: Modalities

It takes all kinds of people to make a world. Some of us love to start new things, others prefer to nurture what already exists, and some are happiest when bringing things to completion. In the workplace, we might think of them as the executives who look ahead to the future of the organization and formulate goals; the managers who keep track of existing projects and resources; and administrators and workers who produce the work and share it with the rest of the world.

This is a useful analogy for understanding astrological *quadruplicities* (dividing the zodiac into three groups of four signs each), also known as modalities. Signs of the same modality often have a hard time getting along because they tend to compete with each other, and because each of them represents a different element (fire, earth, air, and water) and therefore a different basic temperament.

 DEFINITION

Quadruplicities, or modalities, divide the zodiac into three groups of four signs each. Signs of the same quadruplicity tend to compete with each other and have different basic temperaments. The quadruplicities are cardinal (Aries, Cancer, Libra, Capricorn), fixed (Taurus, Leo, Scorpio, Aquarius), and mutable (Gemini, Virgo, Sagittarius, Pisces).

Think of the executives as representing the cardinal signs—Aries, Cancer, Libra, and Capricorn. Managers are the fixed signs—Taurus, Leo, Scorpio, and Aquarius. And workers are the mutable signs—Gemini, Virgo, Sagittarius, and Pisces. But this analogy has a flaw. Because executives tend to be paid and otherwise valued much more than other workers, you might imagine I'm implying that cardinal sign people are more important than fixed and mutable sign people. But the truth is much more egalitarian. Each modality plays an essential role in keeping the world running. So imagine a workplace utopia in which the division of labor is distinct, but in which each contributor is equally valued and everyone collects the same salary.

Cardinal Signs

The *cardinal signs*—Aries, Cancer, Libra, Capricorn—symbolize initiative, the impulse to break new ground and keep civilization forever moving in new directions. These signs represent the cardinal points of the compass: Aries is east (where the Sun rises), Capricorn is south (where the Sun reaches its highest point in the day), Libra is west (where the Sun sets), and Cancer is north (where the Sun reaches its nadir around midnight).

DEFINITION

Cardinal signs (Aries, Cancer, Libra, Capricorn), first signs of each season, are signs of initiative and leadership.

The cardinal signs initiate the change of seasons, with the Sun entering Aries at the vernal equinox (spring), Cancer at the summer solstice, Libra at the autumnal equinox, and Capricorn at the winter solstice. Those born with cardinal signs prominent in their birth charts (planets, the Ascendant, or the Midheaven in these signs) are happiest when they're doing anything new. Whether it's exploring uncharted geography, starting a family, beginning a partnership, or founding a business, the cardinal signs love to begin a new venture.

The cardinal signs also enjoy the challenge of claiming territory. For Aries, it may be actual, physical territory. For Cancer, it may be claiming the territory of a home and family unit. For Libra, it's claiming "my marriage"; for Capricorn, the founding of "my company." Come to think of it, "my" is a popular word among cardinal sign people. And wherever you find cardinal signs in your own birth chart, you tend to be an initiator—and a bit territorial as well.

The drawback of cardinal signs is a tendency to start more things than you can possibly finish. Most of us don't have the luxury of delegating all the boring, messy details of life to others. In the real world, you have to show some follow-through on what you've started, or risk ending up with a reputation for being long on promises and short on delivery.

Fixed Signs

The Sun is in the *fixed signs*—Taurus, Leo, Scorpio, Aquarius—during the second month of each season. These signs symbolize the human need to create stability and order in the wake of change. Fixed signs are the zodiac's organizers. Taurus organizes resources, especially physical resources. Leo organizes creative ideas. Scorpio organizes shared resources. And Aquarius organizes people into groups and communities.

DEFINITION

Fixed signs (Taurus, Leo, Scorpio, Aquarius), second signs of each season, are signs of stability and organization.

Those born with fixed signs prominent in their birth charts seem to have a knack for more mundane kinds of organization as well. They love file folders and databases and those little dividers you place in a desk drawer to keep your pens and paper clips organized. They have a knack for knowing just how to approach a task to make sure it's accomplished in the most efficient manner. A cardinal sign person can cry out, "Hey kids—let's put on a show in the barn!" and be confident in the knowledge that their fixed sign brethren will set to work hiring writers, actors, and set designers and raising the money to make sure everyone gets paid.

The fixity of these signs can be a gift, but can also have drawbacks, such as a tendency toward stubbornness and intractability. Fixed signs like the challenge of managing existing routines with ever more efficiency, rather than starting new enterprises or finding new ways of doing things. They can have trouble delegating duties and can have a very hard time seeing other points of view.

Mutable Signs

The Sun is in *mutable signs*—Gemini, Virgo, Sagittarius, Pisces—in the last month of each season. These are the months when the work of each season is brought to completion and planning begins for the next. Those born with a heavy mutable sign emphasis in their birth chart are not particularly interested in spearheading new ventures or dealing with the day-to-day challenges of organization and management. Mutable signs excel at performing tasks and producing outcomes.

 Mutable signs (Gemini, Virgo, Sagittarius, Pisces), third signs of each season, are signs of flexibility and finishing things.

Mutable sign folks are happiest brainstorming with colleagues, making sales pitches to clients, tackling piles of invoices, setting up meetings, and planning parties. If there were no mutable sign people, your great idea and well-organized office space would be for naught—because nothing would ever get produced and there would be no one to share the ideas and products with the rest of the world.

On the downside, mutable signs can be undependable, lacking in initiative, and disorganized. Think of when you were finishing your last week of high school, when what we liked to call "senioritis" swept your class. When you've got one foot out the door, there's an itchy restlessness and an unwillingness to buckle down to the task at hand. Sometimes a heavy mutable sign emphasis results in a chronic inability to commit—to a job, to a relationship, or even to a set of values.

Qualities of Temperament: Elements

Each sign also belongs to a *triplicity* associated with one of the four classical elements found in nature: fire, earth, air, and water. Each triplicity contains a cardinal, fixed, and mutable sign.

In nature, some elements are naturally compatible while others are not. In astrology, signs of the same element tend to get along well with each other because they share the same temperamental quality and feed off one another's energy. Additionally, signs of the water and earth elements tend to get along, just as water nourishes the earth and the earth provides a container for water. Air and fire are also compatible, as when a strong breeze fans the flames of your beach bonfire. Astrological compatibility is a lot more complex than just comparing elements, but it's a great place to start.

 DEFINITION

Triplicities divide the zodiac into four groups of three signs each. Each triplicity represents one of the natural elements of fire, earth, air, and water. Signs of the same triplicity have similar temperaments and are compatible.

Fire Signs

The fire signs are Aries, Leo, and Sagittarius. Dynamic and passionate, with strong leadership ability, these signs generate enormous warmth and vibrancy. They're exciting to be around, because they're genuinely enthusiastic and usually friendly. But like the element for which they're named, they can either be harnessed into helpful energy or flame up and cause destruction.

Confident and opinionated, fire signs are fond of declarative statements such as "I will do this" or "It's this way." A fire sign that's out of control—usually because they're bored, or have not been acknowledged—can be bossy, demanding, and even tyrannical. But at their best, their confidence and vision inspire us to conquer new territory in the world, in society, and in ourselves.

How fire signs complement one another:

- Aries, a cardinal sign, starts the fire.

- Leo, a fixed sign, tends the fire.

- Sagittarius, a mutable sign, shares the fire.

You'll learn more about the fire signs in Chapter 4.

Earth Signs

The earth signs are Taurus, Virgo, and Capricorn. They are considered practical, reliable stewards of the earth's resources. Like earth, they can provide structure and protection, but earthquakes and landslides can extinguish fire and air and obstruct the flow of water.

Earth signs are oriented toward practical experience and think in terms of *doing* rather than thinking, feeling, or imagining. An earth sign might say, "That works/doesn't work for me." When they're out of balance, earth signs can be materialistic, unimaginative, and resistant to change. At their best, though, they provide the practical resources, analysis, and leadership to make dreams come true.

How earth signs complement one another:

- Taurus, a fixed sign, gathers and organizes resources.

- Virgo, a mutable sign, makes something from them.

- Capricorn, a cardinal sign, turns them into something else.

You'll learn more about the earth signs in Chapter 5.

 ASTRO TIP Water and earth signs are compatible because they nourish and provide structure for one another. Fire and air signs get along because they inspire and encourage one another.

Air Signs

The air signs are Gemini, Libra, and Aquarius. Sociable and communicative, these are considered the relational signs. Gemini rules casual relationships, Libra rules committed partnership among equals, and Aquarius rules friendship and group associations.

Air signs are oriented more toward thinking than feeling. Like their air element, air signs carry information and the seeds of ideas; but air can blow out fire, create violent dust storms, and evaporate water or stir up deadly waves. Air signs are fond of phrases such as "I think" or "I hear you." Out of balance, they live in their heads and can be insensitive to the feelings of others. But at their best, air signs help us form connections in all spheres of our daily lives.

How air signs complement one another:

- Gemini, a mutable sign, is skilled at making acquaintances and connecting people with one another.

- Libra, a cardinal sign, chooses from among casual acquaintances and initiates committed relationships.

- Aquarius, a fixed sign, builds on relationships to provide social organizations and networks.

You'll learn more about the air signs in Chapter 6.

Water Signs

The water signs are Cancer, Scorpio, and Pisces. Empathetic and sensitive, they are considered emotionally and psychically gifted. Water dissolves and blends almost all matter, and water signs seem able to connect empathetically with other people. They are sensitive, private, and sentimental. Water signs can say something like "I feel your pain" and be absolutely sincere.

Because they're so sensitive and vulnerable, water signs—like the creatures that symbolize them—develop strong defenses. It takes time to gain the trust of a water sign and to really get to know the person.

Out of balance, water signs are ruled by emotion, lack objectivity, and are too defensive to get close to other people. But at their best, water signs help us nourish, protect, and grow the interpersonal connections that give life meaning.

How water signs complement one another:

- Cancer, a cardinal sign, forms primary tribal units for protection.
- Scorpio, a fixed sign, protects the unit.
- Pisces, a mutable sign, brings new people into the tribe.

You'll learn more about the water signs in Chapter 7.

Essential Takeaways

- The zodiac is a band of fixed stars that mark the Sun's annual journey across the sky.
- The tropical zodiac aligns the vernal equinox with the beginning of the sign Aries and emphasizes the connection of the signs with the seasons. The sidereal zodiac uses the actual position of the stars.
- Each sign is represented somewhere in your birth chart.
- Each sign is associated with one or more planetary rulers.
- The modalities, or quadruplicities, group the signs of the zodiac into three groups that share a common approach to life: cardinal, fixed, and mutable.
- The elements, or triplicities, group the signs into four groups that are characterized by the qualities of temperament of the classic natural elements: fire, earth, air, and water.

CHAPTER 4

Fire Signs

————

Aries, Leo, and Sagittarius are the fire signs: dynamic, passionate, and inspiring

Aries is dynamic, energetic, and a born leader and pioneer

Leo is creative, inspiring, and dramatic

Sagittarius is philosophical, scholarly, and adventurous

Gaze into a roaring fire and feel yourself growing relaxed and mesmerized; this is what it feels like to bask in the glow of people who embody the spirit of the fire signs. Harnessing the energy of fire can keep you warm in winter, make your food tastier, and let you bend metal into useful tools. Understanding the needs and objectives of fire sign people can help you enjoy their warmth, zest for living, and helpful qualities—without being burned to a crisp by their incandescent personalities.

Walk into any gathering and you'll easily spot the people who have fire signs strongly represented in their birth charts. The great-looking woman surrounded by admirers, the guy who dashed in late and left in a hurry, and the one holding forth about his political views—for better or worse, fire sign people capture your attention. Enthusiastic, charismatic, spontaneous, inspiring: at their best, fire signs draw us in like a cozy fire on a cold evening. But just as uncontrolled fire quickly becomes dangerous, negative fire sign people can show a destructive side that's bossy, opinionated, pushy, and overbearing.

While the three fire signs have a lot in common with one another, each brings something unique to the table. Aries, the cardinal fire sign, symbolizes initiative, drive, and pioneer spirit. Fixed sign Leo emphasizes the cultivation of healthy ego and creativity, applying existing resources to individual self-expression. And Sagittarius, a mutable sign, symbolizes the urge to synthesize knowledge and experience into a cohesive belief system, and to formulate a vision that broadens our understanding of the world.

Aries, the Ram ♈

Though we set aside January 1 to draft New Year's resolutions, the Sun's ingress into Aries at the vernal equinox marks the real beginning of the new year. As the sign that welcomes spring's exhilarating flush of warmer weather, refreshing rains, and the first brave shoots of green after winter's fierceness, Aries symbolizes new beginnings and the return of physical potency. The sap is rising, our zest for life is renewed, and we're ready to roll up our sleeves and get to work.

For farmers and gardeners, this is an important time of year to prepare soil for new seeds. It's hard work, and the association of spring with toothy metal implements and back-breaking labor contributed to Aries's association with the planet Mars, ruler of physical work, and with metal and iron.

As the first sign of the zodiac, Aries is akin to a newborn baby: terribly small and vulnerable, without language, it must learn from the moment of its first full-throated holler how to get its needs met so it can survive. Likewise, Aries people learn to cultivate the independence and courage that allow them to thrive on insecurity, and on the thrilling terror of new experiences. Consequently, Aries natives are fiercely independent, courageous leaders, and alive with pioneer spirit. Like their symbol, the ram, they tend to jump into situations headfirst—and they never, ever back down from a challenge.

You are most likely to identify with Aries if

- You were born with the Sun, Moon, or Ascendant in Aries or in close aspect to Mars.

- You were born with a number of planets in the first house.

- You were born with Mars in the first, fourth, seventh, or tenth house.

What Makes Aries Tick

Aries is the first sign of the zodiac, and that's an easy way to remember what makes Aries run: Aries wants to be first. It's more important for you to do something first, in fact, than for you to do it best. You want to be your sweetheart's first love, the first kid in your class to get a driver's license, the first among your group of friends to be kissed; in adulthood you have to be the first in your field, the innovator, the pioneer. You have no interest in any race you can't win, and you can't stand doing the same thing day after day. Aries hits the ground running from the minute you leave the womb, and you'll never stop running, and striving, until you become the first of your friends to arrive at the pearly gates.

Aries loves a challenge. You relish overcoming obstacles and thrive on being told something is impossible, then finding a way to do it. You're ruled by the planet Mars, named for the god of war, and some Aries types do thrive on military warfare and have an affinity for weapons and a high tolerance for bloodshed. Just as many, though, find there are more than enough battles to fight in civilian life—to get ahead, blaze new trails, and develop courage and confidence.

Aries has courage and confidence to spare. The danger you face is becoming addicted to adrenalin and to doing things your own way, no matter what. You need allies who will help you temper your impulsive qualities and learn to play well with others.

Aries at its best: Brave, assertive, pioneering, quick, determined

Aries on a bad day: Aggressive, hard-headed, selfish, impulsive, impatient, brutal

How to Spot an Aries

Aries is the first to arrive and the first to leave. The one who can't sit still for long and who's not a very good listener. The impulse shopper. The impatient foot tapper. The brave pioneer who boldly goes not only where no man has gone before, but where no man ever even thought about going before. And though chivalry is as good as dead, its embers smolder in the heart of Aries—so the stranger who shimmied up a tree to retrieve your stranded tabby is the epitome of a positive Aries. Sign this person up to lead your neighborhood watch or your office safety program.

A malfunctioning Aries is easy to spot, too. He won't share his toys, can't stand buying a used car (because he wasn't the first to own it), and interrupts you when you talk. He tailgates you on the freeway, leaves abusive comments on your blog, shoves other kids off the teeter-totter, walks away distractedly in the middle of a conversation, or threatens to punch you when he gets drunk.

Above all, Aries needs to feel confident that he can get what he needs to survive. An Aries who has had to struggle too much for basic food, shelter, or attention can easily fall into a morass of anger. But an Aries who has learned that he can rely on himself when the chips are down is a calm, unflappable ninja.

The Aries archetype: Prince Lancelot, the brave and romantic rock star of King Arthur's court

The Aries stereotype: The rage-a-holic in the pickup truck who just gave you the finger after cutting you off on the freeway

ASTRO ALERT

How to handle an angry Aries? Leave him alone! Don't placate him, and don't fight back; it will just make things worse. Back off and give Aries space to cool down and collect his thoughts; he rarely stays angry for long.

Aries in Love

Ah, Aries in love. You make your lovers feel like the most special, attractive, precious, and endearing creatures who ever lived. But thanks to your sign's legendarily short attention span, the thrill doesn't necessarily last.

Aries loves a challenge, so you're fascinated by partners who are difficult to pin down. Once you've won someone's heart, that person had better keep you guessing and make you work hard to hold on to her, or else you'll soon grow bored and find some other quarry to chase. Aries tends to be uncommonly attached to conventional gender roles, so your men need to be rugged and dashing, your women dainty and ladylike.

Male or female, you tend to sweep people off their feet and, if things don't go well, to drop them just as expediently. Aries was probably the inspiration for the phrase, "Marry in haste, repent at leisure." For Aries, compromise does not come naturally. You do not instinctively take your partner into consideration before doing something (leaving your job, buying a new car, deciding to move to another country). You have to be taught to take another person into consideration; if you're with the right person, it's a lesson you'll happily learn—but the "we" of partnership will never feel quite like your native language, "I."

Most compatible signs: Fellow fire signs Leo and Sagittarius, who share your passionate nature; air signs Gemini and Aquarius, who are able to keep their cool when you lose yours

Most challenging signs: Opposite sign Libra; Cancer and Capricorn—like you, all three enjoy taking the lead, and Aries doesn't like to follow.

Aries at Work

It comes down to this, really: Aries can't abide being told what to do. Mostly, this is because you want to do things no one else has done before, and almost no boss can even imagine why you want to do them. Still, Aries doesn't particularly want to be in charge, either, though you do have natural leadership ability. Rather, you want to be left alone to do your work in exactly the way that suits you, at precisely the speed that feels right for you. And that speed, usually, will be fast—*very* fast.

Aries is best at starting things—you're a natural entrepreneur—and especially at tackling feats that daunt lesser mortals. Not all Aries fight fires, rescue people, or charge into life-threatening situations on a regular basis, but it's a safe bet that people who do this kind of work have Aries or Mars strong in their birth charts.

If Aries were to envision hell, it would involve sitting at a desk performing repetitive tasks day in, day out. You're interested in doing something exactly as long as it takes you to figure out how it should be done; then you need a new challenge. Surprisingly, though, you can be very pragmatic—and co-workers should watch their backs, because you can also be ambitious, even ruthless.

Aries-friendly careers: Traditionally, Aries was associated with careers involving sharp objects, such as surgery; weapons, such as the armed forces; and athletic skill. Aries may also be well suited to dangerous professions like fire fighting, and those that require poise under pressure, such as medical triage. Many Aries, though, can be relatively content in just about any career that offers constant challenge and independence, including soldiers, firefighters, or law enforcement; physical or speech therapists; welders or carpenters; hairdressers or other careers having to do with the head.

MISC.

Aries Fast Facts

- Symbol—The Ram
- Glyph—Ram's horns ♈
- Key phrase—I am.
- Element—Fire
- Quality—Cardinal
- Ruler—Mars
- Anatomy—Head, face, brain, upper teeth
- Natural house—First
- Opposite sign—Libra
- Key concepts—Beginnings, identity, conquering new territory, getting what you want

Leo, the Lion ♌

In the northern hemisphere, the Sun is in Leo during the hottest month of the year. Leo's season is a popular one for vacations and for recreation of all kinds—and appropriately, Leo is the sign associated with recreation and play. The most social of the big cats, lions hunt and live as part of a pride. Similarly, those born with Leo prominent in the birth chart are sociable and playful, balancing times of relaxation with periods of intense hunting and fighting. Picture Leo's totem, the lion, lying indolently beneath a shade tree in the heat of the afternoon.

The fixed nature of Leo makes it the most dependable of the fire signs. When you set your sights on a goal (usually involving recognition) you pursue it steadily, even doggedly, until you've reached it. Leo's constancy and organizational savvy regularly take the uninitiated by surprise. Beneath Leo's surface razzle-dazzle is, in fact, a steady friend in need, a loyal employee, and a devoted partner.

You are most likely to identify with the sign Leo if

- You were born with the Sun, Moon, or Ascendant in Leo, or with the Moon or Ascendant in close aspect to the Sun.

- You were born with a number of planets in the fifth house.

- You were born with the Sun in the first, fourth, seventh, or tenth house.

What Makes Leo Tick

Aries wants to be first, but Leo wants to be the best—and wants to be loved. To be second best is worse than no prize at all to Leo. Best looking, best at her job, best lover, best dressed—as long as she's acknowledged as the unrivaled master of her realm, Leo will be reasonably content.

Leo is known as the "creative" sign, which immediately brings to mind visions of paste and glitter, guitars and greasepaint. What is creativity, anyway? It's the joining of resources and individual genius. Leo people are often renaissance men and women, adept at many different artistic pursuits—indeed, pretty good at most anything they try. This is not because Leo is necessarily more gifted than anyone else, but rather because Leo is willing to bring her entire self to everything she does. Any work, any creation, any relationship is an opportunity for Leo to express her whole heart.

Leo oozes charisma, talent, and heart. The danger you face is isolating yourself through your demand to be treated as something special. Your closest friends and loved ones will give you the gift of never taking you too seriously—and will help you remember that though you are, in fact, special, so is everyone else.

Leo at its best: Regal, creative, magnetic, performer, generous, inspiring

Leo on a bad day: Vain, domineering, attention-seeking, insecure

How to Spot a Leo

Not a problem. If she looks as though she's ready to lay the side of a sword on a commoner's shoulder, or uses phrases like "We are not amused," you've got a Leo on your hands. There are loud Leos and quiet ones, but all of them are proud and, in their way, dignified. Leo may clown around with friends to get some laughs, but don't make the mistake of acting too familiar or of assuming you and Leo are equals. Her Majesty is warm, hospitable, and generous, but she is a little more special than you are, and don't you forget it.

Of course, there are benevolent monarchs and then there are ruthless dictators, which bear more than a passing resemblance to Leo when she is off her game. A Leo who is feeling insecure or overlooked can be overbearing, overtly vain, and even cruel. If you've ever seen a lion maul its prey in one of those nature documentaries, or even watched your pet tabby toy with a bird or mouse, you get the general idea.

Leo is the life of the party, the belle of the ball, the king of the castle. The one thing she is not—ever—is just another face in the crowd.

The Leo archetype: The benevolent monarch

The Leo stereotype: The shallow playboy or party girl

Leo in Love

Leo has to be the star of the show, needs to be adored, will turn to ice if neglected or betrayed. What's needed is a sort of royal consort, someone with the confidence and wry humor to hold his own in Leo's reflected glory.

Handling a Leo in a romantic relationship is dead easy, however, for someone who has the right temperament. You need a partner who is absolutely self-confident, has a negligible desire for attention, possesses the gift of smooth flattery, and is brave enough to stand up to you when you start to roar.

The good news is that with the right partner, Leo is loyal, protective, and an excellent provider. Lions mate for life, and unless you are betrayed or embarrassed by your partner, so do you!

Most compatible signs: Fellow fire signs Aries and Sagittarius, who understand your dramatic nature and aren't intimidated by you;d air signs Gemini and Libra, who are experts at flattery

Most challenging signs: Opposite sign Aquarius; Taurus and Scorpio—all three are as stubborn as you are.

ASTRO TIP

According to Debra Ronca in "How Lion Taming Works" (HowStuffWorks.com), here's how to tame a lion (works with Leos, too!):

- Introduce yourself slowly over time to earn trust.
- Distract with multiple focus of attention.
- Use positive reinforcement to shape behavior.
- Respect the animal: you never know when it may attack!

Leo at Work

President Bill Clinton, born with the Sun in Leo, was responsible for one of my favorite quotations about this sign. "Just think what it's like to be president," he mused. "They play a song every time you walk in the room. I was completely lost for three weeks after I left the White House. Nobody ever played a song any more." He was joking, of course … but no one who knows anything about Leo would be a bit surprised if he were a bit serious, too.

Most everyone wants to be recognized for the work they do. But it takes a Leo—or someone with that sign or its ruler, the Sun, very strong in the birth chart—to make being recognized a profession in and of itself. It's why Leo is a great sign for anything requiring performance—the arts, teaching and training, or leading workshops and seminars. Leo tends to be most comfortable in front of a group of people; you feel like you disappear when you're one of a crowd. But you're more than just an attention-seeking ham: Leo is also adept at inspiring others to do their best, and is surprisingly organized and reliable.

Leo-friendly careers: Leo makes an effective teacher, manager, or self-help speaker because you have a talent for motivating people. You're also well suited to a career in the arts or connected to entertainment (including parties), since you're creative, comfortable in front of an audience, and enjoy creating your own schedules and routines. Leo is also a sign of gaming and speculation, and can do well as stockbrokers, working in casinos, or developing video games.

MISC.

Leo Fast Facts

- Symbol—The Lion
- Glyph—Lion's mane ♌
- Key phrase—I will.
- Element—Fire
- Quality—Fixed
- Ruler—The Sun
- Anatomy—Heart, upper back, sides
- Natural house—Fifth
- Opposite sign—Aquarius
- Key concepts—Creativity, love, children, play

Sagittarius, the Archer ♐

The Sun rises in Sagittarius in the short, cold days leading up to the winter solstice, when the waning afternoon sunlight invites us to sit by a fire and think big thoughts. What is life all about? What happens after we die? Is there a God? Sagittarius is at home anyplace where he suspects answers to big questions can be found—in a classroom, a church, or a foreign land, or between the covers of a book.

Sagittarius is symbolized by the archer, usually represented as a *centaur* wielding a bow and arrow, or sometimes simply by the archer's arrow itself. Sagittarius is an interesting blend of cultured—even erudite—and uncivilized. The arrow that serves as his glyph represents a configuration in the constellation Sagittarius that points toward Anteres, the star known as "the heart of the Scorpion." Sagittarius seeks not just the truth (as does the previous sign in the horoscope, Scorpio), but also an *understanding* of the truth. Sagittarius naturally looks for meaning—pictures in clouds and in Rorschach tests, a philosophy of life in sacred texts and the earth's natural order.

DEFINITION

A **centaur**, from the Greek word for "hand," is a mythical creature that is half man, half beast. It is often depicted as having two natures, an untamed one and a scholarly one. Among astrologers, the centaur Chiron from Greek mythology is often thought to be associated with Sagittarius.

You are most likely to identify with the sign Sagittarius if …

- You were born with the Sun, Moon, or Ascendant in Sagittarius or in close aspect to Jupiter.

- You were born with a number of planets in the ninth house.

- You were born with Jupiter in the first, fourth, seventh, or tenth house.

What Makes Sagittarius Tick

Sagittarius is the mutable fire sign, indicating flexibility and willingness to change course when necessary. In Sagittarius, the creative vigor of the fire element is married to the ability to stretch the mind and imagine new possibilities and even new worlds. The result—as in the case of entertainment geniuses Steven Spielberg and Walt Disney, both born with the Sun in Sagittarius—can be spectacular.

Sagittarius isn't interested in details; you're too focused on the forest to take note of individual trees. While Sagittarius isn't a cardinal sign, all the fire signs are natural leaders simply by virtue of your ability to inspire others. Most people want to be involved in something that *means* something—and whether you're heading a science lab, fronting a band, or directing a film, those who are involved with you tend to be fans of yours as well.

Sagittarius knows plenty. The danger he faces is in believing he knows everything. He has a lot to share, and needs a platform for teaching and preaching—but he also needs trusted friends and loved ones who can help him keep his mind open to new ideas.

Sagittarius at its best: Philosophical, adventurous, freedom-loving, scholarly, funny, honest, athletic, traveler

Sagittarius on a bad day: Crude, blunt, know-it-all, arrogant, superior, intolerant

How to Spot a Sagittarius

On a good day, Sagittarius makes you think. He's the fellow chatting animatedly about an arcane point of philosophy, laughing loudly at his own jokes, or shrugging off a slight. At best, Sagittarius symbolizes optimism, broad-mindedness, generosity, wisdom, and humor. Woody Allen, born with the Sun in Sagittarius, is a prototypical archer whose comedic films feature protagonists obsessed with life, death, and the symbolism-rich films of Ingmar Bergman.

Unfortunately, a less inspiring form of Sagittarius also roams the earth. He's your pompous, know-it-all neighbor, the wild-eyed zealot who knocks on your door to proselytize, the relative whose blunt observations over Sunday dinner make your entire family bristle.

But these are Sagittarians who've never had someone to listen to them and tell them they're smart. At heart, every Sagittarius is a guru, a soulful clown, and a freedom-loving hobo who's just passing through.

The Sagittarius archetype: The wayfaring stranger who transforms a community with his knowledge and wisdom before moving on

The Sagittarius stereotype: The clown who trips over his gigantic shoes and throws pies in your face

Sagittarius in Love

Conventional relationships can be difficult for this freedom-loving sign. Sagittarius needs plenty of space; he's designed to explore the whole world, and he'll never be content with just a little part of it. If you want to spend your life with Sagittarius, you'd best love to laugh, be a good listener, and be content spending lots of time on your own.

Pair Sagittarius with an independent Aries or Aquarian, a fun-loving Leo, or an accommodating Libra, and he can do well. And compared with his zodiacal counterparts, Sagittarius fares well when teamed with his opposite—Gemini, a similarly cerebral and idea-loving sign.

Most compatible signs: Fellow fire signs, Aries and Leo, who share your enthusiasm and outgoing nature; air signs Libra and Aquarius, who appeal to your intellectual side and help civilize you with their social acumen

Most challenging signs: Fellow mutable signs. Opposite sign Gemini asks too many questions, Virgo is more interested in details than the big picture, and Pisces is too easily hurt by your bluntness and humor.

Sagittarius at Work

Sagittarius is a visionary, able to see a world others can't imagine. You gravitate toward any work that allows you to consider situations and ideas in a broader context and derive meaning from them. Simply put, Sagittarius likes to make sense of things. To feel happy in your work, Sagittarius must feel that daily tasks have meaning and contribute to a better understanding of the world.

Traveling, sharing ideas, and spending time in the natural world are dear to the archer's heart, and any work that includes these elements will make you happy. For instance, I know a Sagittarius who is an academic in the physical sciences and who travels extensively, giving lectures; he couldn't be happier with his career. But any workplace that values thinking and meaning and allows flexibility and freedom will provide an agreeable environment for you.

Sagittarius-friendly careers: Sagittarius has traditionally been associated with careers in academia, publishing, philosophy, writing, engineering, theology, or the clergy. Sagittarius also makes an excellent travel guide, since he loves to travel and stores up plenty of interesting stories to share with travelers. Sagittarius and its ruling planet, Jupiter, are also connected to large animals, so working with or around horses, cows, or jungle animals is a good fit.

MISC.

Sagittarius Fast Facts

- Symbol—The Archer
- Glyph—The archer's arrow ♐
- Key phrase—I understand.
- Element—Fire
- Quality—Mutable
- Ruler—Jupiter
- Natural house—Ninth
- Anatomy—Hips, thighs, upper legs
- Opposite sign—Gemini
- Key concepts—Adventure, beliefs, the higher mind

Essential Takeaways

- The three fire signs are Aries, Leo, and Sagittarius.
- Fire signs are outgoing, dynamic, and enthusiastic leaders.
- Aries is a pioneer who is impatient, likes to move fast, and is fond of starting things.
- Leo is a natural performer, sociable, magnetic, and creative.
- Sagittarius is a freedom-loving visionary who seeks to make sense of the world.

CHAPTER 5

Earth Signs

Taurus, Virgo, and Capricorn are the fire signs:
practical, resourceful, and reliable

Taurus is sensuous, steady, and patient

Virgo is analytical, discriminating, and capable

Capricorn is ambitious, pragmatic, and resourceful

Those born with the Sun or other planets in earth signs are often the most skeptical about astrology. I firmly believe it's because most of what is written about them makes them sound … a little dull. Who wants to be described as practical, resourceful, and reliable? It's true, and absolutely part of what makes earth signs what they are. But it's not the whole story.

Take a moment to contemplate earth—which, for the sake of this discussion, encompasses not just dirt, but plants, trees, gardens, caves, and mountains. Picture the majestic Himalayas, the giant redwoods of California, the Blue Grotto on the Isle of Capri. Imagine a warm, therapeutic mud bath, the feel of wet sand beneath your bare feet, acres of ripe corn under the late summer sun.

No, earth isn't dull, and neither are the earth signs or the people they symbolize. Like the earth itself, the earth signs are alive and sensuous. Those born under earth signs do, in fact, have an instinct for using the earth's resources for practical purposes. They know how to build structures that endure. They are, however, anything but dull.

Taurus, the Bull ♉

The Sun moves through Taurus in the second month of spring, when April's showers begin to subside and the days grow longer and warmer. Seeds begin to burst open into a riotous pro-fusion of vegetables and flowers. Winter and its cold and deprivation feel like ancient history now. It's a time of plenty, and of pleasure. After the mad scramble of spring planting, there's a little time for leisure—to let things be, before the hard work of the harvest. Taurus is symbolized by the bull, but this isn't a season of hard work for beasts of burden, and he stands happily in a verdant meadow, chewing grass and flirting with cows.

Taurus symbolizes the gathering and happy enjoyment of resources. It's one of the two financial signs (Scorpio is the other), but money is just a symbol for the resources one has to sell. Food, shelter, and clothing are Taurus's main concern, as well as physical health and fully functioning senses with which to enjoy it all.

This is the time of year to tend the crops and the gardens as needed, but essentially to let nature take its course. It's that steady stewardship, patience, and trust in nature that are Taurus's greatest qualities.

You are most likely to identify with the sign of Taurus if

- You were born with the Sun, Moon, or Ascendant in Taurus or in close aspect to Venus.

- You were born with a number of planets in the second house.

- You were born with Venus in the first, fourth, seventh, or tenth house.

What Makes Taurus Tick

Whenever I travel, I find myself stockpiling objects along the way—a tiny bottle of shampoo, a bag of dinner rolls, an empty box. I'm always on the lookout for anything I think might make me more comfortable on a long, deserted stretch of highway.

It's the Taurus in me, I suppose. Taurus symbolizes the desire to establish and maintain stability, comfort, and predictability. It's about blooming where you're planted, and working with what you've got—whether it's a bottle of shampoo or another person.

Nurturing and caring for living things, an unshakable, unshockable stability in the face of life's challenges, are Taurus's birthright. The Taurus souls among us help us accept the world as it is and to commit to being part of it—to celebrate experiences and knowledge that can only be gained through being embodied. Transcendence is all well and good,

Taurus might say, but you still have to get food on the table and make sure everyone has clean socks for the next day.

Taurus has a gift for making life comfortable, secure, and sane. The danger she faces is in becoming rigid, stubborn, and, in extreme cases, lazy. Taurus's most valuable companions gently move her out of her comfort zone from time to time, encouraging her to dabble with the unfamiliar and to dip a toe into the murky waters of psychological discomfort.

Taurus at its best: Patient, stable, sensible, sensuous, conservative, practical, relaxed

Taurus on a bad day: Stubborn, closed-minded, slow, possessive, bigoted, resistant to change

How to Spot a Taurus

A fixed sign, Taurus is both an immovable object and an irresistible force. You might encounter her on the day she is at peace, lounging blissfully in a hammock. Or your paths might cross on one of her bull-in-the-china-shop moods, set on a course of action and knocking over everything in her path. Taurus is essentially a slave to inertia: she has a hard time getting going, but once she does, nothing will stop her!

Taurus generally doesn't get too worked up about things. Her typical response to a question like "Didn't that make you mad?" is a shrug. She doesn't care about money per se, as long as she has as much as she needs to be comfortable, but she tends to be particular about her *stuff.* She'll have a favorite pillow, or a beloved sweatshirt that barely retains the properties of a solid. She loves plants and rocks. She loathes renting her home and will sacrifice other luxuries to buy, and if possible, to own it outright.

Taurus can sometimes be a little *too* secure, her confidence based in never moving too far from her familiar surroundings. This is a Taurus who is uncomfortable around people of different backgrounds and ethnicities, who always eats the same thing for lunch and never lets facts get in the way of her opinions. Scratch the surface and you find a Taurus who is afraid the world is moving too fast, and is worried that there aren't enough resources to go around and she might have to share her stuff with other people.

The Taurus archetype: The strong, silent type

The Taurus stereotype: The disapproving busybody

 ASTRO ALERT Do not tease, taunt, poke, or prod Taurus. Don't assume that because she is generally easygoing and slow to anger, it means she won't someday charge at you. Waving a red flat in front of a bull can get even an experienced matador hurt!

Taurus in Love

A sensuous earth sign, Taurus is especially attuned to physical and practical expressions of romantic feeling. Taurus relationships do not go unconsummated for long; for you, a relationship doesn't feel quite real unless it's physical.

Giving and receiving gifts is important to a Taurus in love; you put a lot of care into choosing something that will please your loved one, and you're deeply hurt if you receive something cheap, flimsy, or tasteless in return.

But although Taurus is thoughtful and caring, she generally dislikes sentimentality or excessive, gushing expressions of love, and generally eschews public displays of affection. In fact, you may like to give your partner a hard time in public to avoid the appearance of being "all mushy and stuff." Nevertheless, like all the fixed signs, Taurus is constant in love, supporting your partner both practically and emotionally.

Most compatible signs: Your fellow earth signs, Virgo and Capricorn, who pretty much "get" you; and water signs Cancer and Pisces, who benefit from your calm, stable nature

Most challenging signs: Your fellow fixed signs: Scorpio, your opposite sign, who likes to live on the edge; and Leo and Aquarius, who want to have their own way as much as you do

Taurus at Work

Taurus is an employer's dream: utterly reliable and competent. But like all the fixed signs, you need to be left alone to do things at your own pace—and that pace will generally be pretty deliberate. Your idea of hell is getting teamed on a project with a speedy Aries!

But Taurus brings an additional element to the workplace that is at least as valuable as meeting deadlines and doing thorough work. Taurus brings down the blood pressure of a room just by walking in, and her own no-nonsense demeanor tends to provide an element of emotional stability and keeps the overall level of workplace drama in check.

An episode of the TV show *Frontline* profiled patrons of a hair salon in New York City, all of whom had lost jobs, businesses, homes, and retirement savings in the past year. The owner of the salon is exactly the sort of sensible Taurus type who, for an hour or so every few weeks, provides these lost souls, all of whom had lost all sense of normalcy and security, with comfort, continuity, and the sense that everything will somehow work out. I could understand why her clients kept making appointments with her, even though for many it meant charging her fee on their credit card. She was providing something much more than a haircut, and much less expensive than therapy.

Taurus-friendly careers: Ruled by Venus, Taurus is suited to careers in beauty, such as hairdresser or makeup artist; in the arts (especially singing); or in financial industries careers such as banking, budgetary management, or appraisals (especially of jewelry, art, coins, carpets, and antiques). The practicality of the construction industry might appeal to you, as well as farming, gardening, or landscaping.

Taurus Fast Facts

- Symbol—The Bull
- Glyph—Bull's head and horns ♉
- Key phrase—I have.
- Element—Earth
- Quality—Fixed
- Ruler—Venus
- Anatomy—Throat, neck, vocal chords, tonsils, thyroid, tongue, mouth
- Natural house—Second
- Opposite sign—Scorpio
- Key concepts—Resources, stability, pleasure, sensuality

Virgo, the Virgin ♍

Glyph for Virgo: Variously ascribed to the Greek word for "virgin," a sheaf of barley, or an M referring to the blessed Virgin.

The Sun is in Virgo in the last month of summer and marks the season of decision. Are the crops ready for harvest, or can one wait a little longer and risk harvesting in the rain? There's an analytical quality to this time of year, of weighing and determining, that also characterizes those born under the sign of Virgo.

Virgo's powers of discrimination and knack for analysis have earned it a reputation for being critical and impossible to please. And it is difficult to satisfy Virgo, not because he wishes to be perverse but because Virgo is haunted by the specter of perfection when, as a practical earth sign, he's aware that it's an unattainable standard.

When Virgo is functioning well, it's given to statements like "It's good enough," and "It will do." When Virgo begins getting into a tizzy about imperfection, it's a sure sign that he's got too much of his ego invested in the outcome. Virgo's role is to serve the most useful outcome—and imperfect but useful is light years ahead of theoretically perfect but nonexistent.

You are most likely to identify with the sign of Virgo if

- You were born with the Sun, Moon, or Ascendant in Virgo or in close aspect to Mercury.
- You were born with a number of planets in the sixth house.
- You were born with Mercury in the first, fourth, seventh, or tenth house.

What Makes Virgo Tick

Virgo's motto is "I serve," which reminds me of a famous episode of the classic *Twilight Zone* television series, about seemingly benign aliens who have come to earth and pledged their help to mankind. One of their most revered texts is titled *To Serve Man*. Imagine the dismayed surprise of the humans who, having clasped these aliens to their bosoms, belatedly discover that the book is not a paean to intergalactic relations, as they'd imagined—but a cookbook.

It's a clever twist on not just the word, but the concept of service—which is symbolized, in astrology, by Virgo. Virgo symbolizes the very noble impulse toward usefulness. It represents the hundreds of people who impact your daily life, whether or not you ever meet each other. No matter how menial the task, others' approach to their work can have a profound influence on the quality of your day. The barista who serves up your morning coffee can set the day's tone with a smile and a little joke, or can seemingly go out of his way to annoy you. A mechanic who's having a bad day might forget an important step in servicing your car's brakes—and that could influence the rest of your life.

Virgo wants to help, wants to do good work, and wants to make the world run better. Unfortunately, the world tends toward perpetual unruliness; the dishes you just washed will need washing again tomorrow, and your car's oil will need changing again in 3,000 miles. It's this constant striving to clean up a world that can't keep its corners tucked in that makes Virgo a little cranky, and prone to fantasizing about intergalactic cookbooks.

Virgo at its best: Discriminating, thorough, scientific, clean, humane, scientific, analytical

Virgo on a bad day: Picky, critical, petty, self-centered, hypochondriac, gloomy, pedantic

How to Spot a Virgo

The women tend to be strikingly beautiful but may look a little downcast or nervous. The men favor an earthy, even sporty look, favoring baseball caps and unpretentious clothing made of natural fabrics. Virgo, like his fellow earth signs, has a soothing, calming presence. Animals gravitate to Virgo, sensing both his affection and respect, and in fact those with the sign strong in the birth chart tend to be devoted to animals and their humane treatment.

Like all earth signs, Virgo has a long fuse … which makes his eventual meltdowns all the more impressive and kind of scary. And because Virgo is ruled by Mercury, he can carve you up with an estimable blend of concise vocabulary choices and withering sarcasm, made more deadly by his careful observation of your character.

But these are the last refuge of a Virgo who feels unappreciated, or who is offended by shoddy work or mistreatment of the vulnerable. At heart, Virgo is a sweet, gentle soul who just wants to be helpful, and just wishes things could be better than they are.

The Virgo archetype: Sherlock Holmes, with his staggering powers of perception and analysis and his earthy tweed jacket

The Virgo stereotype: The quiet, slightly geeky scientist or secretary with horn-rimmed glasses and a repressed manner

Virgo in Love

The challenge Virgo faces in relationships is that while love tends to flourish in an atmosphere of unconditional acceptance, it can quickly shrivel up when exposed to Virgo's critical faculties. Virgo's powers of discernment extend to love, and it's the rare partner who can meet his exacting standards.

But there is a very sweet side to Virgo as well. Virgo shows his devotion in a thousand small, practical, helpful gestures that help your life run smoothly and efficiently. As an astrologer friend once observed, "Virgo loves in detail." Untying knots, fixing appliances, grasping the tedious syntax of a life insurance policy—these are all matters at which Virgo excels.

Don't forget, too, that Virgo is an earth sign, which means a keen appreciation for the physical expression of love. You won't rush into intimacy, but yours is a strongly sexual nature.

Most compatible signs: Your fellow earth signs, Taurus and Capricorn, who appreciate your practical expressions of love; and water signs Cancer and Scorpio, whose reserved but emotional natures are complementary to your more cerebral personality

Most challenging signs: Your fellow mutable signs, Gemini, Sagittarius, and Pisces. Pisces, your opposite sign, is somewhat too ephemeral for your tastes, while Gemini and Sagittarius tend to irritate you or make you nervous with all their chatting and moving around.

There are virgins, and then there are Virgins. Don't make too much of Virgo's symbol, the Virgin; yes, that term can refer to someone who hasn't had sex. But it can also be used to refer to someone who is whole and complete on their own, without a partner.

Virgo at Work

Virgo is often referred to as the sign of work. Of course, all signs work, but Virgo, perhaps in common with Capricorn, strongly identifies with his work. Virgo is a true craftsman—thorough, excellent at analyzing and troubleshooting problems, and exceedingly careful and detailed in his approach to any task. Virgo likes to have something to show for his work: a crisply formatted report, a bushel of corn, a new and diligently notated piece of music.

Because Virgo is so detail-oriented and ruthless at rooting out errors of logic or execution, you don't always work well with others. Few meet your standards of craftsmanship, and you refuse to have your name associated with anything that's substandard. You're best working on your own, but need to guard against becoming a workaholic.

Virgo-friendly careers: Skilled manual work such as carpentry; work requiring analysis, organization, and attention to detail, such as editing, mathematics, analysis, library science, criticism, secretarial work, and accounting. Virgo can be a wonderful healer, including work as a doctor, nurse, veterinarian, dental hygienist, or nutritionist. It's also the sign of social work, civil and domestic service, and volunteering.

Virgo Fast Facts

- Symbol—The Virgin
- Glyph—An M (maiden) crossing her legs ♍
- Key phrase—I analyze.
- Element—Earth
- Quality—Mutable

- Ruler—Mercury
- Anatomy—Intestines, upper bowel, gall bladder, liver, pancreas
- Natural house—Sixth
- Opposite sign—Pisces
- Key concepts—Service, discrimination, analysis, problem-solving

Capricorn, the Sea Goat ♑

The Sun's ingress into Capricorn marks the winter solstice, the shortest day of the year and the beginning of winter. At wintertime, the artificial construct of the calendar decrees a new year is about to begin. But our seasonal hearts experience winter differently, as the apex of an energetic cycle begun in the spring. In the cold, weak light of winter, all is revealed for what it truly is. We are either rich enough to buy holiday gifts and leave extraneous lights burning throughout the house, or we are not. We are happy because we have chosen to be so, or angry and unhappy because that was our choice. Winter solstice is a time of emotional reckoning and self-examination; like Scrooge, each of us must confront his or her own ghosts of the past, present, and future. In the long, dark days of winter, there is a lot of time to brood about what went wrong in the past and what might go wrong in the future.

When I offer Scrooge as an archetypal Capricorn figure, I don't mean to be insulting. *A Christmas Carol* hardly starts out well for the misanthropic Mr. Scrooge, but by the end of the story he's a new man. Dry, brittle, and preoccupied with material success, Scrooge is transformed by an encounter with the spirit world (Capricorn is symbolized by the sea goat, and can make his home in both the physical and spiritual realms). Confronted with spectral visions of what he is, what he has been, and what he will be if he keeps going in the same direction, Scrooge sees the light—it is, after all, a solstice tale—and opens his heart to the true wealth of friends. He recognizes, at last, that the poorest of his employees is the wealthiest of men, because he has a loving family. Seeing that the only way to find real success is to be part of a tribe, Scrooge unbends like a rose in late June and stuns his friends with a sudden warmth to rival a summer bonfire on the beach.

You are most likely to identify with the sign of Capricorn if

- You were born with the Sun, Moon, or Ascendant in Capricorn or in close aspect to Saturn.

- You were born with a number of planets in the tenth house.

- You were born with Saturn in the first, fourth, seventh, or tenth house.

What Makes Capricorn Tick

People born in the winter were welcomed by a world of brisk and biting air, holiday celebrations that disappoint as often as they delight, and a tough and scraggly landscape with bare trees. Nature's bounty was in short supply. Capricorn intuited that the world can be a harsh place, that it was up to her to make a happy and comfortable nest for herself, and that complaining was a waste of time.

Born when the midday Sun is at its lowest declination, Capricorn has a powerful urge to attain higher status. But the fame represented by Capricorn has as much to do with what other people make of us as what we make of ourselves. You might become known for doing something well, but you might just as well become known by accident—by being the son of someone famous, or being beautiful, or, like Capricorn President Richard Nixon, for resigning a powerful office in disgrace.

But achieving status is only part of what Capricorn is about. Capricorn is considered the paternal sign; her most noble path is to use its natural leadership ability and the authority she's earned to shepherd others along a constructive path. Capricorn was born to be a role model.

Capricorn at its best: Responsible, authoritative, traditional, pragmatic, hardworking, economical, serious, mature, ethical

Capricorn on a bad day: Domineering, stubborn, inhibited, unfeeling, fatalistic, judgmental, unforgiving

How to Spot a Capricorn

In her presence, you tend to stand up a little straighter. You are a little more careful with your grammar. In essence, you behave as though you've just been reunited with your particularly strict third-grade teacher.

Traditional wisdom holds that Capricorn is born old and gets younger with age. And it's true: most Capricorns seem a little out of step with their expected chronology. A teacher who is just slightly older than her students, perhaps, or someone who seems plucked from another (always earlier) era. He looks at home in tweed, likes portable typewriters, and would secretly love to carry a watch fob; she looks just right in a pillbox hat. Their clothing will be conservative and classic, of the best quality they can afford.

The Capricorn archetype: The wise elder

The Capricorn stereotype: A cranky old man or woman who keeps yelling at kids to "stay off my lawn!"

Capricorn in Love

The dark side of Capricorn's tenacity is a certain ruthless single-mindedness, and our bonds with others often suffer when we give too much to our work, sacrificing the soft, Cancerian shapes of domestic pleasure. Everyone wants love, but Capricorn in particular cries out for a partner. Specifically, he needs a mate who can help him achieve his ambitions while simultaneously keeping the home fires kindled and reminding him of his core values and important emotional connections.

Pride and Prejudice's Mr. Darcy is an archetypal Capricorn—undemonstrative, occasionally cruel, and preoccupied with social status. Yet ultimately he is able to appreciate the proud and moral Elizabeth Bennett, realizing her strong ethics and values are far more admirable than a mere accident of noble birth.

Capricorn is one of the most sexually driven of all the signs (it's sometimes represented by the satyr, a bestial and debauched centaur). You can easily slip into the unfortunate habit of being a bit mean to your lovers, so you need someone who's not impressed by your temper and who can jolly you out of your occasional black moods.

Most compatible signs: Your fellow earth signs Taurus and Virgo, who respect your ambitions; and water signs Scorpio and Pisces, who you find intriguing and soothing

Most challenging signs: Your fellow cardinal signs—Cancer, your opposite sign, who is good at stoking the home fires but can get a bit clingy about your late hours at work; and Aries and Libra, who refuse to follow your lead and do what they're told

Capricorn at Work

Capricorn, the sign that rules business and worldly achievement, is sometimes uncharitably described as cold and pragmatic. Not that all Capricorns are that way, of course; far from it. At her best, Capricorn is the kindly, sensible matriarch who guides us to achievement and to being our best selves. But each sign has its shadow side, and bottom-line pragmatism is certainly the archetypal province of Capricorn. Think of Scrooge, and of Mr. Potter from *It's a Wonderful Life*. Or the CEO who engineered an acquisition of the company where you work, and promptly discontinued the pension plan, slashed benefits, and fired 10 percent of the workforce. If a business practice doesn't improve his bottom line, such a person can't comprehend how it could possibly contribute to his success.

If you can tame your lust for power and make core values and human relationships the basis of your work, you'll be successful not only in business, but in life.

Capricorn-friendly careers: Capricorn is at home in your own business, or as the CEO or president of a corporation. Anything less will probably make you miserable. Your executive nature makes you a natural for government work or politics, and your pragmatism makes you at home in banking, economics, or engineering. Artistic Capricorns excel at sculpture or architecture; Capricorn craftsmen are drawn to carpentry, masonry, or watchmaking; and a medically inclined Capricorn would probably be a fine chiropractor or osteopath, orthopedist, or dentist. On a grim note, Capricorn is ruled by Saturn, the planet of undertakers, morticians, and those who serve the death industry. (And coincidentally, Capricorn also rules landlords—not that dissimilar from undertaking, except for the length of the lease.)

MISC.

Capricorn Fast Facts

- Symbol—The Sea Goat
- Glyph—The Sea Goat's horns and tail ♑
- Key phrase—I use.
- Element—Earth
- Quality—Cardinal
- Ruler—Saturn
- Natural house—Tenth
- Anatomy—Knees, lower legs
- Opposite sign—Cancer
- Key concepts—Resourcefulness, pragmatism, ambition, authority

Essential Takeaways

- The three earth signs are Taurus, Virgo, and Capricorn.
- Earth signs are practical, resourceful, and reliable.
- Taurus is a practical steward of resources who embraces life's pleasures and creates strong and stable foundations.
- Virgo is a born analyst who can analyze and solve problems and anticipate future needs.
- Capricorn is ambitious, goal-oriented, and a resourceful pragmatist.

CHAPTER 6

Air Signs

Gemini, Libra, and Aquarius are the air signs:
bright, communicative, and sociable

Gemini is quick, witty, and skilled with words

Libra is refined, diplomatic, and persuasive

Aquarius is friendly, unconventional, and independent

In nature, air is the most immediately necessary element. We can live without food, water, and heat much longer than we can live without air. Apart from enabling a bodily function necessary for basis survival, air helps pollinate the plants that produce our food, and bears ideas and information from one person to another.

Walk outside on a breezy afternoon, and stand under some trees in a quiet place. Listen to the wind rustling the leaves of the trees … it's the sound of the world talking to you. Sometimes it speaks a little too emphatically, in destructive tornadoes and hurricanes.

The three signs that are associated with the air element are designed to move the air around—talking, exchanging ideas, creating a breeze as they move around from one place to another. Their realms—relational, communicative—initially seem less important, somehow, than the hard earth, the nourishing water, or warming fire. But just as we can't live without air for more than a matter of seconds, our souls would asphyxiate without another soul to talk to. And having someone, or something, to talk to can be the difference between living and dying. In the film *Cast Away*, Tom Hanks plays a plane-crash survivor who, having washed ashore on a remote and deserted island, creates a companion out of a volleyball and delivers monologues to it a la Hamlet and the skull. When the volleyball is lost at sea, the Hanks character weeps as though for a human friend.

Gemini, the Twins ♊

The Sun moves into Gemini in late May, just about the time kids get out of school and start running around the neighborhood, when the first hot days signal summer's imminent arrival and birds and bees swarm lazily, drunk with pollen, around gardens in riotous bloom. Like the high voices of chattering kids at play, zooming around on their bicycles and skateboards, or birds, bees, and the wind carrying pollen from plant to plant, Gemini symbolizes a time of year when seeds—of plants, of flowers, of grass, of ideas—are carried from place to place.

The constellation Gemini is illuminated by two bright stars, named after the mythical twins Castor and Pollux, twins born of different fathers. The first of the relational air signs, Gemini symbolizes the first relationships we form outside of our parental bonds—relationships with our brothers and sisters, neighbors, classmates, and eventually co-workers. When we become infatuated with ourselves, these peers cut us down to size. They teach us the talismanic power of words, of promises and proprietary claims, of nicknames and teasing. Identical twins are famous for developing secret languages no one else can understand, but spend 10 minutes with any pair of siblings, or kids who went to grade school together, and you'll quickly encounter an impenetrable fog of in-jokes and verbal shortcuts.

Gemini rules communication—the skills of encoding and decoding messages, of understanding our world and making ourselves understood. Our earliest social interactions teach us how to argue and negotiate, how to twist the knife, how to tell a joke, and how far we can go without completely alienating someone.

You are most likely to identify with the sign of Gemini if

- You were born with the Sun, Moon, or Ascendant in Gemini or in close aspect to Mercury.

- You were born with a number of planets in the third house.

- You were born with Mercury in the first, fourth, seventh, or tenth house.

What Makes Gemini Tick

Gemini thrives on information and ideas. Like a young child learning to read, Gemini finds the whole world is endlessly fascinating. Gemini has a love of language and of vehicles that share ideas from person to person, such as books, magazines, computers, and telephones. It's the sign associated with "lower" or practical learning, such as K-12 education or trade schools in which basic skills and literacy are taught.

Like a kid on summer vacation, Gemini is easily bored. He needs variety in his routine and gets squirmy when asked to do one thing at a time. He flourishes with constant changes of scenery, and Gemini is associated with short trips and the modes of transportation that make them possible—cars, motorcycles, bikes, trains, buses, and skateboards.

Gemini at its best: Curious, inquisitive, quick witted, communicative, inventive, clever, adaptable

Gemini on a bad day: Verbally cruel, deceptive, disloyal, restless, doesn't follow through

How to Spot a Gemini

Gemini listens best when listening to two things at once, or while working with his hands. Gemini can literally watch TV while surfing the Internet and talking on the phone, and generally pays better attention to all three when doing them simultaneously. Boredom leads to distraction for Gemini. Gemini can sometimes find it hard to make eye contact while he's talking, and will look over your shoulder or into the distance while telling you something. Generally, however, he'll watch you with rapt absorption while you talk.

Gemini is always busy. In a meeting, he will be doodling or checking e-mail. At a party, he's happiest carrying food and drink from person to person, with lots of opportunities to eavesdrop on conversations.

Gossip, trivia, and word games are chicken soup for the Gemini soul. This is the sign that loves a game of Jeopardy, Scrabble, or Trivial Pursuit. A Gemini who doesn't get enough positive social interaction can become a bit of a gossip, pollinating the neighborhood with second-hand news and haunting celebrity gossip websites. Steering this sort of Gemini into journalism, research, or working with the public puts this natural curiosity to more productive use.

The Gemini archetype: The jester; clever and mischievous, your wit and agility are your best defense

The Gemini stereotype: The meddlesome neighbor, snooping and eavesdropping

ASTRO TIP A note about "two-faced" Gemini: Gemini is facile and shape shifting, as its rulership by Mercury suggests. He's easily bored and restless by nature, but he isn't necessarily a cad. You can win Gemini's loyalty easily enough: just be interesting, stimulating, and multifaceted.

Gemini in Love

In matters of the heart, Gemini has acquired something of a "love 'em and leave 'em" reputation that's not entirely fair. It's true that Gemini craves variety, but that need can be fulfilled easily by one partner who is intellectually compatible, who is a good listener, and—most importantly—can keep Gemini entertained. If you're smart and funny, quick witted, good with words, well read, and well spoken, you'll have no problem keeping Gemini satisfied.

Gemini is always interesting and amusing, or at least laughs at your jokes if you are amusing. A Gemini person likes to do things, whether it's going out to see a movie, window shopping, or visiting a farmers' market. Gemini is usually a good communicator, too. You won't have to sit around wondering what Gemini is thinking; he'll spend his life telling you!

On the other hand, there is the "easily bored" thing. Gemini is a restless sign, and if you're not smart and funny—or at least smart enough to appreciate his wit—you may not go the distance. Boredom is the kiss of death for Gemini, so he has to be free and encouraged to spend time with friends.

Most compatible signs: Fellow air signs Libra and Aquarius, who share your desire for relation-ships based on qualities of the mind; fire signs Aries and Leo, who are action-oriented and outgoing enough to keep you interested

Most challenging signs: Fellow mutable signs. Opposite sign Sagittarius is too sure of his beliefs to enjoy mental sparring, Virgo spends too much time on individual topics or activities, and Pisces can be too ethereal and sensitive.

Gemini at Work

Gemini is known for being clever with language, but what's less appreciated is his overall quickness and facility both with words and with machinery. Sometimes Gemini energy manifests itself through brilliant ideas, writing and speaking skill, and linguistic cleverness. But Gemini is also a kind of "machine whisperer," possessing a sure touch with equipment (especially communication equipment, like computers). All the air signs are pretty good at making computers work, and Gemini's skill is in his intuitive grasp of how gizmos "talk" to one another. He's the sort of fellow that can set up his own Internet connection and is an early adopter of new technology.

Of all the signs, though, Gemini is the least happy when forced to do the same thing day after day in the same way. Gemini needs a job that, for a significant portion of the day, allows him to wander around to different locations, chatting with people. The acme of a

Gemini profession would be a mail carrier, walking around the neighborhood delivering information to folks and chatting with them along the way.

Gemini-friendly careers: Gemini has a natural affinity for careers related to ideas, words, or manual dexterity. He's at home in journalism, communication, linguistics, languages, or writing. Advertising and marketing (Gemini is especially good at naming things) is a good fit for Gemini's mental agility. His manual skill makes him adept at working with computers or other machines. Gemini is a skillful networker, connecting people with resources or information. You'll also find Gemini working in professions that allow him to move around a lot, especially ground transportation, such as driving a cab or working on a train.

Gemini Fast Facts

- Symbol—The Twins
- Glyph—Roman numeral II Ⅱ
- Key phrase—I think.
- Element—Air
- Quality—Mutable
- Ruler—Mercury
- Anatomy—Collarbone, shoulders, arms, hands, lungs, nervous system
- Natural house—Third
- Opposite sign—Sagittarius
- Key concepts—Learning, intellect, skills, communication

Libra, the Scales ♎

In the northern hemisphere, the Sun enters tropical Libra at the vernal equinox, when day and night are equal. It's about balance and equality. A partner balances one's own qualities, so Libra is a sign of equal yet complementary relationships between romantic and business partners, and also between open enemies. It's also the time of year when crops are taken to market, so Libra has to do with negotiating with others.

Libra is the only sign of the zodiac that's symbolized by an inanimate object. Its symbol, the scales, was originally considered part of the constellation Scorpio, representing the scorpion's claws. In ancient Egypt, the scales were a symbol of justice used to weigh the souls of the dead against the feather of truth. Coming before the sign Scorpio, symbolizing death and rebirth, the scales of Libran justice seem especially fitting.

You are most likely to identify with the sign of Libra if

- You were born with the Sun, Moon, or Ascendant in Libra or in close aspect to Venus.

- You were born with a number of planets in the seventh house.

- You were born with Venus in the first, fourth, seventh, or tenth house.

What Makes Libra Tick

As its symbol, the Scales, suggests, Libra is committed to achieving balance. This is why Libra is not always as sweet as her reputation—it usually balances excessive niceness with confrontation. This is also behind Libra's reputation for argumentativeness. But it can also be a harmonious trait, when Libra finds a way to match her strengths with another person's weaknesses. Libra defines herself by what she's not (other people) versus what she is, so can have trouble finding a strong sense of self and standing her ground.

Libra is the sign that comes after discerning Virgo on the horoscopic wheel, and it incorporates that sign's refined tastes. Libra is generally horrified by uncouth behavior and coarse language and sets a great store by behaving like a "lady" or "gentleman." A sign of ethics, fairness, and justice, Libra believes there is a right way to behave and a wrong way—and sorting through the various shades of gray in between wrong and right is exactly what Libra is designed to do.

Libra at its best: Refined, artistic, diplomatic, sociable, peace loving, persuasive, just

Libra on a bad day: Fickle, overaccommodating, argumentative, indecisive, insincere

How to Spot a Libra

The typical Libran is pleasant, well dressed, smells good, with a dimpling smile and graceful manners. So graceful, in fact, that you hardly notice you're in an argument with Libra until you've already lost. Libra does an exceptionally good job of buttering you up first, so the sting of defeat is a lot less painful.

While they play the role of perfect lady or gentleman impeccably, Libras inhabit both gender roles with aplomb. At a party, you'll find the Libra man chatting with the ladies, and the Libra woman holding her own with the guys. Libra men generally have a strong interest in music, art, or cooking; Libra women can be exceptionally tough and ambitious businesswomen.

The contrarian of the zodiac, Libra automatically takes the opposite side of an issue and can debate either side equally well. Libra truly enjoys an argument; she loves to really examine both sides of an issue. Without a strong sense of self, Libra can easily lose track of her real convictions. Her most valuable companions are those who encourage her to take a stand and advocate on behalf of strongly held principles.

The Libra archetype: The diplomat

The Libra stereotype: The gigolo or "kept" man or woman

Libra in Love

In love, Libra seeks an equal partner—usually, one with strong opinions and decisiveness.

Libra is a natural at love and relationship. You're very alert to your partner's opinions and preferences, extremely thoughtful, and romantic without being sentimental. Saturn, the planet of commitment and maturity, is at its strongest in Libra, so this is one of the signs that is naturally made for marriage or other committed, long-term relationships.

Not all Librans find love and live in perfect harmony, ever after. Because you have a hard time making decisions, you may choose a very decisive partner and then feel railroaded into agreeing with his or her decisions. Your lack of sentimentality and raw emotion can be alienating to a water sign partner, while an earth sign partner would prefer someone who will fix her computer to someone who can write a sonnet for her.

Most compatible signs: Fellow air signs Gemini and Aquarius, who are at ease with Libra's breezy, communicative level of intimacy; fire signs Leo and Sagittarius, who enjoy Libra's flattery while encouraging you to have the courage of your convictions

Most challenging signs: Your fellow cardinal signs. Aries, your opposite sign, can be abrasive and lacks diplomacy; Cancer and Capricorn tend to see things in black and white, where you prefer shades of gray.

 ASTRO ALERT Libra has a sweet reputation that is not necessarily deserved. Her job is to balance the attitudes of others; if she is dealing with someone who is extremely accommodating, for instance, she will usually compensate by being demanding—even though it goes against her essential nature. For Libra, the desire for balance overrides even her passion for harmony.

Libra at Work

Because Libra is so attuned to what other people are doing and uses those observations to define yourself, you keep a keen eye on your competition and are always striving to get—and stay—ahead. Libra is highly competitive—a trait that often surprises those who have taken your smooth and flattering personality at face value.

It's because of that surface smoothness that Libra is especially good at pleasing customers and clients. You have a pleasing way about you that can disarm practically anyone, no matter how prickly. As a character on the TV show *Mad Men* explained in comparing a young account manager to his rival, "You're very good at solving our customers' problems. But [your rival] has the rare gift of making them feel that they *haven't* any problems." This is precisely the quality that makes Libra an unusually gifted marketer or public service representative.

Libra prefers to work independently or with a partner, not in groups, where too many points of view must be carefully weighed. It's also important to note that just because Libra is the sign of partnership and of harmonious relationships doesn't mean you're a pushover. In fact, like all the cardinal signs, Librans prefer to take the lead in their work. One Libra I knew was fond of quoting Thomas Paine: "Lead, follow, or get out of my way." Libra can work well with a trusted partner, and in fact you're at your best when you have someone to brainstorm with. But the hierarchy must be firmly established in advance—preferably with yourself at the top of the pyramid.

Libra-friendly careers: A sign of justice, Libra excels in careers related to law, justice, contracts, mediation, negotiation, and arbitration. Libra's refined taste lends itself to work in the beauty industry: cosmetics, jewelry, fashion, esthetics, interior design, and apparel. Fine art and music appeal to Libra, as well as careers that require an ability to read people, such as marketing, public relations, and human resources.

MISC.

Libra Fast Facts

- Symbol—The Scales
- Glyph—Scales ♎
- Key phrase—I balance.
- Element—Air
- Quality—Cardinal
- Ruler—Libra
- Anatomy—Lower back, kidneys, adrenal glands, appendix
- Natural house—Seventh

- Opposite sign—Aries
- Key concepts—Balance, harmony, relationship, justice

Aquarius, the Water Bearer ≈

In the northern hemisphere, the Sun is in Aquarius in the dead of winter. The cold, short days and long nights encourage people to gather together for storytelling, camaraderie, and warmth. In extreme climates and circumstances, people can in fact die without this kind of companionship. February, when the Sun is in Aquarius for most of the month, is named for Februa, the Roman feast of purification. It's one of the rainiest months of the year, and Aquarius's symbolism is connected to cleansing and renewal.

Aquarius is symbolized by the Water Bearer, a figure pouring water from a jug into a larger body of water. Aquarius wants to share his knowledge (symbolized by the water being poured from one jug) with the greatest possible number of people (the larger body of water).

The last of the relational air signs, Aquarius's realm is community—networks of people who on some level share our interests. We may have shared the same college fraternity, employment with a particular company, or interest in a sport, career, or hobby. If we've crossed paths with a person, that's basis enough for an Aquarian relationship. It's the sign of friendship—not necessarily of close, abiding soul connections, but simply of shared interests.

You are most likely to identify with the sign of Aquarius if

- You were born with the Sun, Moon, or Ascendant in Aquarius or in close aspect to Uranus.
- You were born with a number of planets in the eleventh house.
- You were born with Uranus in the first, fourth, seventh, or tenth house.

 ASTRO ALERT Because it's symbolized by a human figure pouring water from a jug, Aquarius is often mistaken for a water sign. It is actually an air sign, and the water in its symbol and the waves of its glyph are thought to suggest the flow of knowledge.

What Makes Aquarius Tick

Aquarius is a sign of acute contradictions. On one hand, Aquarius is a sociable air sign, especially attuned to working with groups and teams. On the other hand, Aquarians consider themselves unique and often find it difficult to really fit in anywhere. Aquarius seems to end up as one of the few hippies in a conservative town, or as a religious fundamentalist in a family of atheists, or some other contradictory situation where they're just not like everyone else.

These contradictions are inherent in the contradictory planets that share rulership of Aquarius. Saturn, the ruler of Aquarius before the discovery of Uranus, is the planet of rules and structure. Uranus, Aquarius's modern-day ruler, is the planet of rebellion and iconoclasm. Aquarius wants to be unique and break the rules, but of course, you have to know what the rules are before you can break them. Indeed, Aquarius may hold views that are radically different than those of the people around you; but as a fixed sign, you will defend those views to the death, and are generally impossible to sway from your opinions.

Aquarius at its best: Independent, genius, iconoclastic, rebellious, logical, scientific, progressive, intellectual, humane

Aquarius on a bad day: Eccentric, temperamental, unpredictable, cold, opinionated, radical

How to Spot Aquarius

There's a joke that goes something like this: Bob is bragging to his friend Joe that he knows everyone on the planet. "Do you know the pope?" Joe challenges him. "Sure!" Bob answers, and takes his friend to the Vatican to prove it. When the pope emerges and greets a massive throng that has gathered beneath his window, Bob is standing by his side. Down below, the man standing next to Joe elbows him and asks, "Hey—who's the guy in the funny hat with Bob?"

Aquarius knows everyone. I call a friend of mine, with Aquarius rising, "Mr. San Diego" because I literally can't mention anyone in the city without him saying, "Oh yeah, I know so-and-so." Going out with him anywhere requires numerous delays and detours as we encounter a succession of his old friends, schoolmates, and business acquaintances.

Aquarians can be a little eccentric in dress or demeanor. They're not necessarily wacky looking; sometimes it's quite the opposite, and you're charmingly anachronistic and dapper—the young man carrying a watch fob, the young woman in cat's eye glasses and a poodle skirt. But somehow, even when he's dressed in completely ordinary clothing, Aquarius manages to look like nobody else.

The Aquarius archetype: The charismatic rebel who wins over his fellow men by thumbing his nose at authority

The Aquarius stereotype: The mad scientist

Aquarius in Love

As a fixed sign, Aquarius can be very loyal and constant in love. But Aquarius is usually most successful at marriage when you've had a chance to mature, though some can also do well if you marry an older, more mature partner.

Above all, Aquarius needs a lover who is also a friend. Since Aquarians are generally independent and treasure time spent alone, you need partners who are comfortable with this. Ideally, Aquarius's partner should have lots of friends and interests to bring to the relationship—and to keep him or her out of your hair!

Your lovers may find they have to fight to get time alone with you. You usually travel with an entourage of friends, and anyone who will find that kind of arrangement threatening would probably be a difficult match for Aquarius. Your best match will be someone with a full, active social life and who is willing to share it with a quirky, interesting Aquarian like you.

Most compatible signs: Your fellow air signs, Gemini and Libra, share your love of socializing, while fire signs Aries and Sagittarius appeal to your brash, freedom-and-adventure loving side.

Most challenging signs: Your fellow fixed signs. Leo, your opposite sign, needs to feel special to you and won't like spending all your time together in groups. Taurus and Scorpio are private, a little possessive, and tend to dislike socializing except with intimate friends.

Aquarius at Work

Aquarius is a collaborative sign by nature, and you do your best work when you're around other people. You can work independently as long as there are plenty of opportunities to socialize. Aquarius is one of the few signs that really seems to enjoy office parties; you're also likely to become involved in the political structure of your workplace, such as employee-run organizations or bargaining groups.

As a fixed sign, Aquarius flourishes in a work environment with well-established routines. However, you need to feel that you're free to change the routines whenever you choose. You may enjoy contract positions that allow you to work indefinitely at a work site, while still feeling you can easily leave at any time.

Aquarius is an innovator. You have a knack for organizing ideas into forms that will really spark the imagination of large groups of people. Aquarius is a science-and-technology-oriented sign, and you thrive in innovative environments surrounded by people who are a bit quirky and thinking differently.

Aquarius-friendly careers: Aquarius's love for innovation makes you a good fit for work in electronics, engineering, aerospace, science, and computer engineering and development. Your ability to connect with large groups of people lends itself to work in media and broadcasting, human resources, politics, social work, and community relations. Astrology is also associated with Aquarius!

MISC.

Aquarius Fast Facts

- Symbol—The Water Bearer
- Glyph—Waves (of water or electricity) ≈
- Key phrase—I know.
- Element—Air
- Quality—Fixed
- Ruler—Uranus (modern) and Saturn (traditional)
- Natural house—Eleventh
- Anatomy—Ankles
- Opposite sign—Leo
- Key concepts—Knowledge, friends, associations, innovation

Essential Takeaways

- The three air signs are Gemini, Libra, and Aquarius.
- Air signs are communicative, social, and relational.
- Gemini is sociable, communicative, and craves variety.
- Libra is adept at understanding others, building relationships, and using tact and diplomacy to get things done.
- Aquarius is innovative, a little bit quirky, and a genius at building social networks.

CHAPTER 7

Water Signs

Cancer, Scorpio, and Pisces are the water signs:
sensitive, empathetic, and intuitive

Cancer is home-loving, protective, and nurturing

Scorpio is perceptive, probing, and fearless

Pisces is compassionate, intuitive, and artistic

Why are waterfront properties generally much more valuable than their land-locked counterparts? It's because we find the view soothing and inspiring. Beyond its hypnotic and restful powers, water also plays an essential role in sustaining life. We humans can live without food for a couple of weeks, but only three to five days without water. Perhaps something in us—maybe the 60 percent of our bodies that are composed of water—finds it subliminally reassuring to be close to a ready supply.

Water is an element that nurtures us both physically and spiritually. The signs of the zodiac associated with the water element are nurturing as well, and they're also known for their power to inspire through music, poetry, writing, and other forms of art. Theirs is not the self-expressive creativity of the fire signs, but rather an ability to tap into and reflect what others are feeling. A water sign really does feel your pain. And because they have the gift of sensitivity, they also bear the burden of vulnerability. If water signs sometimes seem defensive, it's because they're so easily hurt by the choppy waves of modern life.

Each of the three water signs has distinct characteristics all its own. But they all share in common the qualities of sensitivity, receptivity, empathy, artistry, and contemplative spirituality.

Cancer, the Crab ♋

The Sun's ingress into Cancer marks the summer solstice, when the Sun reaches its highest point in the sky and appears to stand still before moving across in the other direction, then turn around and move the other way. In the midst of summer vacations and trips to the beach, the Sun's journey through Cancer calls for reflection. Who we are is a construction of the family, culture, and moment in history into which we're born. But there's also a core element that makes you uniquely you. It's the job of Cancer to locate that inner compass point.

The Chaldeans, who developed a 12-constellation system that was a precursor to the zodiac, considered Cancer, the sign of the Sun's greatest elevation, to be nearest to the highest point of heaven. In his book *Star Names, Their Lore and Meaning* (Dover Publications, 1963), R. H. Allen wrote that the constellation was known as "the Gate of Men," the portal through which souls made their way to earth. Not surprisingly, Cancer is the sign associated with motherhood. The formidable matriarchs in all our lives orient us in the world by insisting on the importance of things essential and irreplaceable: history, family, lineage.

You are most likely to identify with the sign of Cancer if

- You were born with the Sun, Moon, or Ascendant in Cancer, or with the Sun or Ascendant in close aspect to the Moon.

- You were born with a number of planets in the fourth house.

- You were born with the Moon in the first, fourth, seventh, or tenth house.

What Makes Cancer Tick

I love vintage Airstream trailers—so cute, cozy, and self-contained. Shiny, portable shelter, these little land dinghies have always made me think of a crab's shell: a way of carrying home with us even as we cruise the continent. There's no more apt metaphor for the home-loving sign of Cancer. Cancer would rather be at home (or at least surrounded by loved ones) than visit the most exotic locations on earth. Familiar objects, food, and landmarks comfort you and make you feel safe. "There's no place like home," was the magical refrain of *The Wizard of Oz*'s Dorothy, one of the most Cancerian characters in film history.

Nor is it accidental that Cancer is named for the crab, a creature prized for its delicious meat and for which self-protection, therefore, is understandably a high priority. The crab's tough shell, erratic movements, and formidable claws provide some protection, and the astrological Cancer is metaphorically equipped with similar weaponry—a reticence with strangers, an indirect manner, and a tendency to get snappish when you feel threatened.

Cancer at its best: Family-oriented, nurturing, intuitive, domestic, maternal, sensitive, sympathetic, emotional, patriotic, retentive, traditional

Cancer on a bad day: Moody, touchy, oversensitive, negative, manipulative, overly cautious

How to Spot a Cancer

A Cancerian, male or female, is as comforting and nurturing as the mom in a 1950s sitcom. You find yourself wanting to confide in this kind person with the soft eyes, who offers you a cookie and agrees that the world has been pretty mean to you, all right.

Cancer evokes images of the full moon in a summer night sky, reflected in the shimmering waters of the ocean. But think for a moment about the warm days of Cancer's season, and you'll understanding the comforting warmth and charisma of these tender souls.

When Cancer is feeling threatened, though, the defenses kick in. First, disappearing into the shell—the body language stiffens, the face becomes an impassive mask. Second, the erratic movements so you can't exactly tell what he'll do next. Finally, if you ignore these signals and keep approaching, the claws make their appearance, and Cancer can be quite nasty when cornered.

The Cancer archetype: The universal mother

The Cancer stereotype: The smothering mother

Cancer in Love

In matters of the heart, Cancer is sweet, nurturing, and a bit old-fashioned. You'll do anything for the one you love; you'll cook dinner, press a shirt, take care of invalids, work two jobs. All you ask in return are loyalty and appreciation.

When Cancer is young, you often fall in love fairly quickly, usually with someone who isn't very nice. But getting your heart broken a few times usually teaches you that even when you fall fast, you should reveal your feelings very slowly. It takes you a while to feel safe with someone; your trust has to be earned.

In a 1976 interview with *Rolling Stone* magazine, singer Linda Ronstadt, born with the Sun in Cancer, talked about how she had learned to cope with having had her heart broken so often. "I try to walk that fine line between being strong and trying to avoid becoming callous. As soon as you're callous you not only shut out all the pain, but all the good stuff too. You either close the door or you open it. I keep the door open with the screen door slammed … and a strong dog at the door. That's the policy of my heart."

Only a cruel person toys with the heart of the vulnerable crab. And when you've been crossed, you buy a screen door and a big, strong dog. For Cancer, old grudges become part of the fortress that you think will protect you from further injury—but if you're not careful, it can also prevent you from forming satisfying relationships.

Most compatible signs: Your fellow water signs, Scorpio and Pisces, who understand your sensitive heart and tread lightly around your feelings; earth signs Taurus and Virgo, who soothe you with their practicality and solid support

Most challenging signs: Your fellow cardinal signs. Capricorn, your opposite sign, is as tough as you are tender; Aries is too independent to take kindly to mothering; and Libra has a breezy cerebral quality that can feel overwhelmed by your emotionalism.

Cancer at Work

Cancer is the sign of family, and if you've ever worked for a small, family-owned business, you know both the blessings and hazards of the Cancerian workplace. Cancer creates a work environment that's nurturing and protective, and flourishes in occupations that thrive on these qualities. Because of Cancer's tenacity, willingness to sacrifice, and loyalty to employees and customers, you have the capacity to build strong organizations.

All of my favorite local business people have a couple of things in common. First, they share a warm, welcoming spirit that makes me feel appreciated. And second, every one of them is wildly successful. They include a hairdresser who is booked a month in advance, a mechanic who is so busy he had to rent a new building last year, and a family-owned restaurant that always makes me feel welcome and at home when I stop by for enchiladas. They epitomize the Cancerian approach to work: creating both financial and interpersonal success by treating their customers like family.

But the Cancer energy can also turn stifling and tribal, with overt favoritism shown to intimates. Cancer can find it difficult to be assertive and direct, and this can lead to workplace misunderstandings. And Cancer's tenacity can become a liability if you refuse to let go of past conflicts, or to move on to new ways of doing things as the business environment changes.

Cancer-friendly careers: Cancer's family-loving side is taken with genealogy, history, and memorabilia; your domestic side does well in food-related careers like catering, nutrition, or restaurant management. If medically inclined you might be drawn to nursing, midwifery, obstetrics, gynecology, or pediatrics. Naturally frugal, you'd be a good financial manager, and your feel for homes gives you the edge in real estate, property management, or feng shui.

Cancer Fast Facts

- Symbol—The Crab
- Glyph—Crab's claws ♋
- Key phrase—I feel.
- Element—Water
- Quality—Cardinal
- Ruler—The Moon
- Anatomy—Stomach, breasts
- Natural house—Fourth
- Opposite sign—Capricorn
- Key concepts—Home, family, loyalty, tenacity, sensitivity

Scorpio, the Scorpion ♏

The Sun moves through Scorpio in the second month of autumn, when the leaves have already mostly fallen from the trees and cold weather creeps in. The celebrations of Halloween, Samhain (Celtic New Year, which includes harvest themes and festivals to honor the dead), and Dia de los Muertos (the Mexican "Day of the Dead") fall during the Sun's season in Scorpio, and there is a long tradition linking this sign to death, decay, and regeneration. Some things must end before new things can begin, and Scorpio symbolizes this process.

Death is an uncomfortable, even taboo subject. But Scorpio understands that life and death are two sides of the same coin, as incomplete without one another as day is incomplete without night. We see the call and response of life and death in agriculture, in the lunar phases, in the seasons; life carries a price tag of eventual death, and death is, perhaps, the portal to another kind of life. Of all the signs, Scorpio grasps that without the knowledge of death, life loses its urgency and its value.

Scorpio teaches us that life, like a temperamental lover, sometimes likes to test our commitment by showing us its ugly side. It's easy to love life when it is kind to us, when it makes sense and makes us feel good. But can we love it when it is harsh and disappointing and determined to break our hearts? Scorpio answers, "Yes." Scorpio commits to life with passion—to dancing with that temperamental lover, and to tasting every dish at life's banquet table—with spirit and with joy.

You are most likely to identify with Scorpio if

- You were born with the Sun, Moon, or Ascendant in Scorpio or in close aspect to Pluto.

- You were born with a number of planets in the eighth house.

- You were born with Pluto in the first, fourth, seventh, or tenth house.

What Makes Scorpio Tick

Of all the signs of the zodiac, Scorpio is almost certainly the most misunderstood—both by its detractors and its advocates. Its defining characteristic is its need for trust. If you're born with this sign strong in your birth chart, you constantly test people to make sure they deserve your loyalty. You have an unerring instinct for identifying others' sensitive spots, and you don't hesitate to probe them as an engineer might test a support beam with a sharp tool to gauge the extent to which termites have undermined its strength.

It's this probing quality that makes others uncomfortable around Scorpio. If you are a strong and secure Scorpio, this quality can be put to excellent use in helping others confront their own weaknesses and transcend them, often as a counselor, therapist, or hypnotist—but just as often, as a good and loyal friend or family member. But Scorpio, like all signs, has weaknesses, too. If you feel threatened, you lash out at others with a stinging, sarcastic tongue. When you're insecure you can be manipulative, secretive, and extremely jealous. This is the weakened wood in your own support beam, and must be confronted and transcended if you're to be your best self.

Scorpio at its best: Determined, probing, brave, passionate, insightful, empathetic, penetrating, investigative, powerful

Scorpio on a bad day: Jealous, suspicious, sarcastic, secretive, vengeful, manipulative

How to Spot a Scorpio

Generally, there seem to be two distinct varieties of Scorpio. There are those who proudly proclaim their sign, thinking it has menacing and powerful cache; these people tend to wear black and have a lot of body piercings. Then there are those who are reluctant to reveal anything about themselves, either out of a sense of self-protectiveness or because they simply find it more interesting to focus on others. You'll recognize them by their sunglasses and close-lipped demeanor.

The Scorpio person is deeply loyal. He doesn't give his trust easily, but if you've earned his, you have a friend for life. It's rather like having Don Corleone, the eponymous capo of *The Godfather,* on your side.

The Scorpio archetype: The magician, able to transcend the laws of nature to achieve transformation

The Scorpio stereotype: A secret agent, skilled at investigative work and most comfortable working behind the scenes

Scorpio in Love

If you're born with Scorpio prominent in your chart, you may fall in love regularly—you are a sensitive water sign, after all, and you're especially susceptible to lost souls who appear to need your help. But before you really commit to another person, you have to know you can trust them completely. That means they must prove their honesty and their loyalty. They also need to demonstrate that they can deal with the menacing side of your nature, and won't be too impressed by your temper tantrums or vows to seek revenge.

Once you've determined that someone meets these criteria, you are a passionate, if somewhat possessive lover. As long as you are sure you can trust your partner, you will be their fiercest advocate.

Most compatible signs: Fellow water signs Cancer and Pisces, who understand the sensitivity that underlies your tough exterior; earth signs Virgo and Capricorn, who have keen minds that you respect and who refuse to be intimidated by you

Most challenging signs: Your fellow fixed signs. Taurus, your opposite sign, can be too nonchalant and low energy for you; Leo and Aquarius are so gregarious and sociable that you get tired of being part of their entourage.

ASTRO TIP Over time, Scorpio has been associated with three symbols: the scorpion, the eagle, and the serpent. Modern astrologers feel that the scorpion and serpent symbolize Scorpio's lower nature, while the eagle symbolizes the proud and soaring nature of the evolved Scorpio type.

Scorpio at Work

Because you are drawn to absorbing, probing work requiring a high degree of analysis, you do your best work alone. Careers that allow you to dig deep into the core of things will always keep you interested. Because few can match your intensity or earn your trust, you're not usually a good team player, and you're quite protective of your ideas and of the work you've done.

You're drawn to the kinds of work that others may find unpleasant or frightening, from plumbing to crime scene investigation. You're talented at understanding what makes people tick, and if you're inclined, you would do very well in careers that help others understand themselves better.

Scorpio-friendly careers: You're a natural sleuth, so research and detective work might suit you. You also have a knack for getting inside people's heads, so you may be suited to hypnosis, psychology, or astrology. Scorpio is associated with shared resources, so you could also work in insurance or as a bill collector. You have a cool head in emergencies, so you could be a good surgeon, EMT, lifeguard, or security guard. Mars's rulership of your sign indicates an affinity for knives, so you could be a butcher or, if artistically inclined, a sculptor. And Pluto's rulership gives you a penchant for jobs involving what's hidden or taboo, such as plumber, locksmith, mortician, coroner, or embalmer.

Scorpio Fast Facts

- Symbol—The Scorpion
- Glyph—The Scorpion's tail and stinger ♏
- Key phrase—I desire.
- Element—Water
- Quality—Fixed
- Ruler—Pluto (modern), Mars (traditional)
- Anatomy—Genitals, reproductive organs, bladder, rectum
- Natural house—Eighth
- Opposite sign—Taurus
- Key concepts—Death, regeneration, loyalty, trust, power

Pisces, the Fish ♓

In March, the season when the Sun moves through Pisces, the days grow longer but the late winter light is weak and flat under cloudy skies. March weather is notoriously changeable and unreliable, yielding an uneasy melange of delicate late-winter flowers and tempestuous storms. In the Pisces season, nature offers a tantalizing glimpse of a vernal paradise, then delights in blowing it down and washing it away.

When we're young we lack a truly mature root structure to hold us in place. Consequently, we're a bit like March saplings that snap under a forceful gale: we can be felled with a strong breath or a harsh word. The older we get and more set in our ways, the more water and wind it generally takes to knock us down. Our sense of self grows stronger; we learn what to tune out, and how to regulate the amount of negativity we'll pay attention to. But this is a bit like tuning in to a favorite radio station: you're sure to hear something you like, but often lose some interesting possibilities in the static-y never-never land between frequencies.

As the last sign of the zodiac, Pisces symbolizes endings, illness and recuperation, imprisonment, and spiritual enlightenment. However, Jupiter, the king of the gods, was considering the ruling planet of Pisces before the discovery of Neptune, and Pisces people—like the tender saplings that take root during their season—are rarely as delicate as they seem.

You are most likely to identify with Pisces if

- You were born with the Sun, Moon, or Ascendant in Pisces or in close aspect to Neptune.

- You were born with a number of planets in the twelfth house.

- You were born with Neptune in the first, fourth, seventh, or tenth house.

 ASTRO TIP Pisces is the only one of the water signs that's symbolized by a creature without an exoskeleton—fish are protected only by scales. This symbolizes Pisces' vulnerability and occasional difficulty with maintaining personal boundaries.

What Makes Pisces Tick

Contrary to pop astrology clichés, Pisces is no more spiritual, psychic, or saintly than any other sign—but he *is* more vulnerable. The symbol for Pisces is two fish, the most tender of creatures; Cancer and Scorpio swim in the same empathetic waters, but only Pisces navigates them without a protective shell, completely exposed to both danger and ecstasy. Pisces teaches us divine vulnerability—how to lower our defenses, the better to fully empathize and blend with everyone we meet.

Like every sign, Pisces walks a razor's edge between its nobler and its baser sides, which in the case of Pisces can make itself felt in a certain lack of constancy. Pisces is compassionate and supportive; but if you lean too hard on him, he'll swim away in the blink of an eye. On one hand, this is an admirable survival skill. You can't absorb the whole world's pain and misery 24 hours a day, 365 days a year, and stay sane. You've simply got to get away from time to time, whether in a nap, a bottle, a song, or a massage. The strongest and wisest of Pisces pay close attention to their need for healthy escape. Pisces is tempted by the notion that we are one with everything, a limitless river; but without boundaries, the river overflows, often with destructive consequences.

At its best, though, the Pisces experience is one of pure enchantment. I admire Pisces as I admire water, for its quickness and its stillness, its adaptability and shape-shifting abilities. Pisces is the exotic music we hear faintly, through static, between the stronger frequencies; it is the fragile prespring flowers outside my office window, their seeds scattered here by the wind, pale and pretty in the flat, gray light of late winter—they are the youngest and most tender of flowers, yet they stand up to sudden storms with surprising strength, refusing to be blown down or washed away.

Pisces at its best: Sympathetic, compassionate, emotional, intuitive, musical, artistic

Pisces on a bad day: Impractical, timid, procrastinator

How to Spot Pisces

One of my favorite examples of Pisces is the character of Cosmo Kramer on the long-running television series *Seinfeld*. While eccentric, Kramer was also kind and helpful and had the uncanny ability to fall into sync with whoever was around him, unknowingly voicing precisely the same sentiments another character has expressed in an earlier scene. Pisces is so good at assuming the mood and posture of whatever situation he's in that he's rather like a chameleon—you have to work hard to notice him.

On the other hand, there are clues. Pisces tends to have a rather fluid sense of time, so it's possible that friend who is consistently late for every lunch date has a strong Pisces influence in his birth chart. On the plus side, that fluid sense of time allows Pisces to accomplish an enormous amount in a given day, because he's not worried about whether he has time to do everything.

Pisces is also the gentle clown who leads sing-alongs around the campfire, who drives an old VW bus plastered with bumper stickers like "Imagine whirled peas," who gives you a sentimental birthday card. He's Everyman—and yet he's not like anyone else you've ever met.

The Pisces archetype: The mystic

The Pisces stereotype: The flake

Pisces in Love

You're exceedingly sentimental and idealistic, plying the objects of your affection with flowers, goopy cards, and romantic mix tapes. Yours is a sunny, accepting, celebratory attitude toward love. But because you want to believe the best of everyone, you're not always the best judge of character, and the sensitivity and compassion that make you so dear can cause problems. You're more susceptible than most to adopting a rescuer mentality, and your early relationships are often with negative, irresponsible, even abusive partners.

What Pisces brings to a relationship is a whimsical sensibility, a joyful approach to life, surprising strength, and a warm and empathetic spirit. What you need in a partner is someone who is gentle and kind, but who can still help you cope with the knotty, practical, inconvenient details of everyday life.

Most compatible signs: Your fellow water signs, Cancer and Scorpio, who understand your sensitive nature and are naturally protective of you; earth signs Taurus and Capricorn, who provide a grounding influence and help you cope with the practical demands of daily life

Most challenging signs: Your opposite sign, Virgo, shares your compassion and adaptability but lacks your gentle imagination. Gemini and Sagittarius can injure your feelings with their witticisms and bluntness.

Pisces at Work

The trick for Pisces is to find work that plays to your strengths. You're good with people, you understand the latest trends in whatever field you're involved with, and when you set your mind to it you can squeeze an amazing amount of productivity out of a single day.

The problem is getting you to set your mind to it. It can be a challenge for you to be punctual or to hew to tight deadlines. Your best bet is to find a career in which these things just aren't as important as being sweet, inspiring, and helpful—all of which are qualities you possess in spades.

You're a natural in the helping professions, especially those with a spiritual dimension. And you usually have at least one or two social or humanitarian causes that are extremely dear to your heart that would benefit from your involvement. For instance, you have a wonderful knack for putting together social events that generate fun and excitement and could easily put those skills to work as a party planner, entertainer, or fund-raising coordinator.

Pisces-friendly careers: You'll thrive at anything that allows you to help others—counseling, guiding retreats and meditations, working for charitable or nonprofit organizations, the ministry, working in hospitals or in health care. You've got a metaphysical bent, particularly toward clairvoyance, scrying (reading crystal balls), or tarot, and you're artistic with a particular flair for painting, photography, and music. Fishermen and others who work on boats come under the purview of Pisces, as do prison workers, bartenders, and podiatrists.

Pisces Fast Facts

- Symbol—The Fish
- Glyph—Two fish joined together ♓
- Key phrase—I believe.
- Element—Water
- Quality—Mutable
- Ruler—Neptune (modern) and Jupiter (traditional)
- Natural house—Twelfth
- Anatomy—Feet
- Opposite sign—Virgo
- Key concepts—Enlightenment, kindness, imagination, compassion

Essential Takeaways

- The three water signs are Cancer, Scorpio, and Pisces.
- Water signs are sensitive, empathetic, and receptive.
- Cancer nurtures families and other groups bound together by emotion and loyalty.
- Scorpio protects loved ones and the emotional and physical resources they share in common.
- Pisces sees all people as part of one family, and attempts to love and accept everyone.

PART 3

A Place for Everything: Houses

I n life, stuff happens—and it has to happen somewhere. It happens when you're in line at the supermarket, at work, in the bedroom, or lost within your creative imagination. It happens in your home, in your marriage, on a street corner, interacting with your kids or your friends. Stuff happens everywhere.

In an astrology chart, the 12 sections of the wheel, called houses, show where the important stuff tends to happen in your life—and where your emotional baggage tends to accumulate, like last season's wardrobe in a too-small closet. In the dramatic structure of your life, the houses of your chart represent sets and props that indicate where action is taking place—a parapet, a battlefield in France, a ship. Some of these locations are more challenging territory for you than others. You tend to play out your most important scenes there; like Hamlet hanging out at his mom's house, or Richard III trapped in a deformed body, you become a particular kind of person when you enter them.

CHAPTER 8

Houses

Introducing the 12 houses of the horoscope

Dividing the horoscope into hemispheres

Ways of grouping the houses for easier understanding

Various systems used to divide the chart into houses

Understanding the basic meanings of each house

Using derivative houses to identify and describe others

Pull out your birth chart. (If you don't have your birth chart, Chapter 2 explains how you can get one.) The circle represents the sky at your birth, divided into 12 sections called houses. Each is traditionally associated with a sign of the zodiac, at least one planet, a modality, and an element. Depending on which house system you used to calculate the chart, the 12 houses are not necessarily equal in size—but as in so much of life, size isn't everything.

The houses refer to different areas of the sky, and astrologically they symbolize 12 categories of life where the action of your life takes place. The corner coffee shop, your living room, your office cubicle, a crowded train: every story has a setting, represented in one of the houses of the horoscope. As we'll see in Part 4, the planets symbolize primary motivations and lessons to be learned—but the houses tell us where you're likely to play out those motivations and learn those lessons.

Where are things happening? Understanding the houses of the chart can help you understand where you are comfortable, where you find challenge, and where the dramas of your life take place.

House Cusps

Lines, or cusps, divide the 12 houses. Starting with the first house cusp and moving counterclockwise, houses one through six begin with the cusp on the left side; houses seven through twelve begin with the cusp on the right side. The cusp of each house has a notation about the degree, minute, and sign of the zodiac associated with it, such as:

18° ♑ 37'

This notation indicates that the house cusp begins at 18 degrees and 37 minutes of the sign Capricorn. Each sign has 30 degrees of 60 minutes each, so this house cusp begins a little over halfway into the sign of Capricorn.

If this were, say, the cusp of the sixth house, we'd know that the first 18 degrees (0–17) of Capricorn lie in the fifth house. The rest falls in the sixth house. Practically speaking, if you have planets between 0 and 17 degrees of Capricorn, they are in the fifth house; between 18 and 29, they're in the sixth house.

Angles of the Chart

The cusps of the first, fourth, seventh, and tenth houses are called the angles of the chart, and are considered highly sensitive and powerful points. Signs on these house cusps, as well as planets within about 10 degrees of them, have particular significance. We'll take a closer look at the angles of the chart in Chapter 9, but here's a quick rundown:

- **The Ascendant**—The cusp of the first house. The sign on this cusp is sometimes called the "rising sign." The Ascendant marks the eastern horizon and represents your physical body and personal identity—basically, where you begin and others end. It's the "sunrise" angle of the chart, representing how you experience new beginnings.

- **The IC, or** *imum coeli* **("lowest heavens")**—The cusp of the fourth house. Sometimes referred to as the nadir, it marks the lowest or northernmost point in the chart and represents your home, family, and personal history. It's the "midnight" angle of the chart, representing privacy, rest, and the security of home.

- **The Descendant**—The cusp of the seventh house. The Descendant is the "sunset" angle of the chart, symbolizing the waning hours of the Sun's daily cycle. Since the Sun is a symbol of individuality, the angle associated with its weakest hours of the day represents the principle of relationship—giving up some measure of independence to merge with another.

- **The Midheaven or** *medium coeli* **("middle of the heavens")**—The cusp of the tenth house, often notated as MC and sometimes referred to as the zenith. The Midheaven marks the highest point in the heavens, and represents your highest worldly ambitions. It's usually called the angle of career, but that's a little misleading, since we usually think of a career as something we're paid for. We might actually think of it as symbolizing your calling—what is the work you're called to do in the world?

The Daily Circle

The circle of the chart is divided into two sets of *hemispheres*. These hemispheres can give you an understanding of the tenor of a chart just by glancing at the number of planets on one side or the other of these important lines.

DEFINITION

Hemispheres divide the horoscope using the horizon to symbolize day (above the horizon) and night (below the horizon); and the meridian to symbolize the Sun's ascent to its highest point (left of the meridian) and descent (right of the meridian) to its lowest point in the sky.

The Horizon: Day and Night

The horizon connects the cusps of the first house (symbolizing the east, or sunrise) and the seventh house (symbolizing the west, or sunset), and represents consciousness—how objective or subjective you are in how you understand the world and your place in it. Planets above the horizon are called "day" planets because they occupy the houses where the Sun travels during daylight hours. If you have lots of day planets in your chart, you tend to be outgoing, objective, and ambitious. You play to win, and you're determined to rise above your station—to improve upon the circumstances of your birth.

The Sun is reliably in these houses at roughly the same time each day (except at extreme northern or southern latitudes or near the solstice dates), so knowing which house the

Sun should be in will help you ensure that the chart you're looking at has been calculated correctly.

Day planets are those that travel through the top half of the chart at roughly two-hour intervals between sunrise and sunset:

Twelfth house	6 A.M. (sunrise)–8 A.M.
Eleventh house	8 A.M.–10 A.M.
Tenth house	10 A.M.–12 P.M. (noon)
Ninth house	12 P.M.–2 P.M.
Eighth house	2 P.M.–4 P.M.
Seventh house	4 P.M.–6 P.M. (sunset)

Planets that appear below the horizon are called "night" planets because they occupy the houses where the Sun travels at nighttime. If there are many planets in the night portion of the chart, your consciousness is somewhat more subjective, instinctual, and introverted. You're inclined to work behind the scenes and are generally less ambitious for worldly success than someone born with lots of day planets.

Night planets travel through the sixth through first houses at roughly two-hour intervals between sunset and sunrise:

Sixth house	6 P.M. (sunset)–8 P.M.
Fifth house	8 P.M. –10 P.M.
Fourth house	10 P.M.–12 A.M. (midnight)
Third house	12 A.M.–2 A.M.
Second house	2 A.M.–4 A.M.
First house	4 A.M.–6 A.M. (sunrise)

The Vertical Axis: Lust for Power

The vertical axis, or meridian, connects the cusps of the fourth and tenth houses, the points that represent the Sun's positions at midnight (fourth house) and at noon (tenth house). Planets that appear on the eastern side of the chart are called "rising" planets, because they are in the half of the chart that symbolizes the Sun's climb from its lowest to highest points. Planets that appear on the western side of the chart are called "setting" planets; they occupy the half of the chart that symbolizes the Sun's descent from its highest to lowest points.

If you were born with many planets in the rising side of the chart, your nature is assertive and your will and desire for power is strong. You tend to take action without waiting for permission from others (or, negatively, without taking others into consideration).

Rising Houses	Time of Day the Sun Is in House
Third house	12 A.M. (midnight)–2 A.M.
Second house	2 A.M.–4 A.M.
First house	4 A.M.–6 A.M. (sunrise)
Twelfth house	6 A.M.–8 A.M.
Eleventh house	8 A.M.–10 A.M.
Tenth house	10 A.M.–12 P.M. (noon)

If you were born with many setting planets, your nature is more flexible and relationship-oriented. You tend to take others into consideration before acting (or, negatively, can be indecisive).

Setting Houses	Time of Day the Sun Is in House
Ninth house	12 P.M. (noon)–2 P.M.
Eighth house	2 P.M.–4 P.M.
Seventh house	4 P.M.–6 P.M. (sunset)
Sixth house	6 P.M.–8 P.M.
Fifth house	8 P.M.–10 P.M.
Fourth house	10 P.M.–12 A.M. (midnight)

Wrangling the Houses

The houses of the chart divide each hemisphere into six houses. Each house of the chart shares certain basic themes with a sign of the zodiac, and represents an area of life experience such as partnership, career, and finances. The houses of the chart may be equal or unequal in size; it depends on which house system is used to calculate the chart.

Twelve houses are a lot to keep straight. If you refer to Chapter 2, you'll remember that each house is associated with a sign of the zodiac. The first house is associated with the first sign, Aries; the second house with the second sign, Taurus; and so on.

Still, there are a couple of ways to group the signs together that can make them a little easier to remember. Like the modalities and elements that we used to categorize signs, houses can be separated into quadrants (three groups of four signs each) and triplicities (four groups of three signs each). It's a bit easier, I think, to remember things when they're wrangled into groups rather than spilling out over one big 12-part wheel.

House Axes

Two houses opposite one another form an *axis*. The houses of these axes always share the same degree of opposite signs. If, for instance, you have 14 degrees of Cancer on the cusp of the first house, 14 degrees of Capricorn, its opposite sign, will be on the cusp of the seventh house.

Have you ever heard the maxim that what bothers us in other people are usually the very traits we deny in ourselves? Those we consider our opposites, or even our enemies, are usually more like us than we care to admit—no matter how different we may seem on the surface. Likewise, the signs on either end of the six house axes share common objectives, but they approach them from completely opposite points of view. Picture the center point on the axis as being the common ground, with the two signs inching their way toward the center from their opposite sides of the chart.

The house axes are paired as follows:

- **Houses one and seven**—Axis of boundaries: self vs. other

- **Houses two and eight**—Axis of resources: mine vs. yours

- **Houses three and nine**—Axis of knowledge: learning vs. teaching

- **Houses four and ten**—Axis of stability: home vs. career

- **Houses five and eleven**—Axis of creativity: individual vs. collective

- **Houses six and twelve**—Axis of helping: work vs. altruism

Succedent Houses by Quadrant

The *angular* houses are the first, fourth, seventh, and tenth. Associated with the cardinal signs (Aries, Cancer, Libra, and Capricorn), these are the houses of initiative and leadership. In the angular houses you define yourself (first house), create a tribe to provide security and nourishment (fourth house), join forces with equal partners (seventh house), and pursue your calling (tenth house). In these houses, you don't sit back and wait for permission to act (or even think too hard)—you operate out of instinct and don't hesitate to go after what you want. (Chapter 9 discusses angular houses in detail.)

The *succedent* houses are the second, fifth, eighth, and eleventh. Correlated with the fixed signs (Taurus, Leo, Scorpio, and Aquarius), these are houses of stabilization and consolidation of resources. In the succedent houses you gather resources (second house), use them to create things (fifth house), combine your resources with the personal resources of others close to you (eighth house), and bring together community resources for the larger work of society (eleventh house). (See Chapter 10 for more about succedent houses.)

The *cadent* houses are the third, sixth, ninth, and twelfth. Linked to the mutable signs (Gemini, Virgo, Sagittarius, and Pisces), these are houses of adaptability, synthesis, and release. In the cadent houses you exchange information (third house), analyze it and apply it to practical tasks (sixth house), synthesize it into knowledge and beliefs (ninth house), and use it to explore hidden and even mystical realms (twelfth house). (See Chapter 11 for a full discussion on cadent houses.)

Houses by Quadrant

Angular	*Succedent*	*Cadent*
First house (Aries)	Second house (Taurus)	Third house (Gemini)
Fourth house (Cancer)	Fifth house (Leo)	Sixth house (Virgo)
Seventh house (Libra)	Eighth house (Scorpio)	Ninth house (Sagittarius)
Tenth house (Capricorn)	Eleventh house (Aquarius)	Twelfth house (Pisces)

Houses by Triplicity

Houses are also categorized by the element of the sign that's naturally associated with them. There are three houses each associated with the elements of fire, earth, air, and water.

Fire houses (first, fifth, and ninth) are sometimes called "Houses of Life." If you were born with many planets in these houses, you exude energy, enthusiasm, inspiration, and dynamism. These houses represent the limits of matters suggested by the Houses of Substance: the limitations of tenth house conformity (the first house, where we celebrate our individuality); the limitations of second house acquisitiveness (the fifth house, in which we gamble our resources to create something entirely new); and the limitations of sixth house routines and logic (the ninth house, in which we seek new experiences and seek the forests rather than the trees).

Earth houses (second, sixth, and tenth) are called "Houses of Substance." If you have many planets in these houses, you're stable, practical, reliable, and materialistic. These houses represent the limits of matters described by the Houses of Relationship: the limitations of group connections (the second house, in which we learn to rely on ourselves for what we need); the limitations of casual and anecdotal information (the sixth house, in which we test theories and analyze information); and the limitations of one-on-one alliances (the tenth house, in which we seek to reach the broadest market or audience).

Air houses (third, seventh, and eleventh) are referred to as "Houses of Relationship." Having been born with a number of planets in these houses implies that you're a "people person" with a strong need for social connections. These represent the limits of matters described by the Houses of Endings: the limitations of twelfth house faith (the third house, where we ask questions and seek facts); the limitations of staying within your familiar tribe (the seventh house, in which we form our strongest connections with those outside our families); and the limitations of the resources we are able to assemble with just a few people (the eleventh house, in which we form large, strong collectives based on shared interests).

Water houses (fourth, eighth, and twelfth) are known as "Houses of Endings." With lots of planets in these houses, you are likely very sensitive, soulful, and intuitive. These houses represent the limits of matters suggested by the Houses of Life: the limitations of individual ability (the fourth house, where we connect with a tribe or family); the limitations of personal ego and creative ability (the eighth house, where we mingle our sexuality, money, and other resources with another person), and the limitations of cognitive abilities (the twelfth house, where we enter the realms of faith and psychic perception).

Houses by Triplicity

Fire Triplicity	Earth Triplicity	Air Triplicity	Water Triplicity
Houses of Life	Houses of Substance	Houses of Relationships	Houses of Endings
First house (Aries)	Second house (Taurus)	Third house (Gemini)	Fourth house (Cancer)
Fifth house (Leo)	Sixth house (Virgo)	Seventh house (Libra)	Eighth house (Scorpio)
Ninth house (Sagittarius)	Tenth house (Capricorn)	Eleventh house (Aquarius)	Twelfth house (Pisces)

Basic Meanings of the Houses

Each house of the chart symbolizes places and situations in your life, as suggested by the symbolism of its quadruplicity and triplicity and the signs and planets with which it's associated. Part 3 offers an in-depth look at the houses, but here is a summary of their key concepts:

- **First house**—An angular, fire-element house associated with the sign Aries and the planet Mars. The first house represents your physical appearance, immediate environment, and response to threatening situations.

- **Second house**—A succedent, earth-element house associated with the sign Taurus and the planet Venus. The second house indicates your attitudes about money and possessions and what things you consider valuable.

- **Third house**—A cadent, air-element house associated with the sign Gemini and the planet Mercury. The third house symbolizes your neighbors and siblings, early education, land travel, language, and communication.

- **Fourth house**—An angular, water-element house associated with the sign Cancer and the Moon. The fourth house describes your attitudes about family, your home, your history, and your country. It's believed the fourth house also represents your mother, or at least your most nurturing parent.

- **Fifth house**—A succedent, fire-element house associated with the sign Leo and the Sun. The fifth house is associated with children, creative pursuits, self-expression, recreation, gaming, and performance.

- **Sixth house**—A cadent, earth-element house associated with the sign Virgo and the planet Mercury. The sixth house relates to your job, work style, health, analytical abilities, and pets (this association probably derives from the use of animals to do work, such as on a farm, or as familiars).

- **Seventh house**—An angular, air-element house associated with the sign Libra and the planet Venus. The seventh house symbolizes your attitudes toward marriage and business partnerships, your closest friends, your open enemies or rivals, negotiation, judgment, and balance.

- **Eighth house**—A succedent, water-element house associated with the sign Scorpio and the planets Pluto and Mars. Eighth house territory includes shared resources, sexual relationships, investments, death (especially in the sense that "death" of the self is required in order to merge with another), and communal funds of limited membership (investments, taxes, insurance, or inheritance).

- **Ninth house**—A cadent, fire-element house associated with the sign Sagittarius and the planet Jupiter. The ninth house describes higher education, international travel, belief systems, philosophy, and attitudes toward those who are different from you.

- **Tenth house**—An angular, earth-element house associated with the sign Capricorn and the planet Saturn. The tenth house represents your profession or calling, reputation, status, ambition, employer, and achievements. It's also believed that the tenth house represents your father, or more specifically the parent who had the strongest influence on your career.

- **Eleventh house**—A succedent, air-element house associated with the sign Aquarius and the planets Uranus and Saturn. The eleventh house is connected to your capacity for friendship, your social ease, long-range goals, step-children, politics, professional or social organizations, and money earned from your profession.

- **Twelfth house**—A cadent, water-element house associated with the sign Pisces and the planets Neptune and Jupiter. The twelfth house indicates hidden strengths and weaknesses, covert enemies, secrets, illness and suffering, behind-the-scenes activities, and places of confinement (hospital, prison).

 ASTRO ALERT Some houses, like some signs, have rather ominous-sounding associations. Death! Hidden enemies! Illness and confinement! Let's face it: life has a nasty side, and if astrology is going to present a complete picture of life, it has to find a way to include its unhappier dimensions. However, resist thinking of any house as intrinsically "bad" or "scary." After all, you'll find death and taxes in the eighth house, but you'll also find sex and inheritance!

Signs and Houses

Each house has a natural association with a particular sign of the zodiac that shares its essential themes. However, your own chart also has a secondary sign associated with each house, based on the time and place of your birth, which colors your experience of that house.

For instance, the first house is naturally associated with Aries and with the Sun's rising each morning in the east. However, let's say you were born at the time of day when the sign of Gemini was rising on the eastern horizon. Your first house still has an Aries agenda: the search for personal identity, blazing of new trails, and self-defense. But you will use

Gemini strategies such as communication and information gathering to do the work of the first house, defining and defending yourself by your ability to learn and communicate.

The degree of the zodiac that's rising in the east at any given moment is called the Ascendant, and it changes approximately every four minutes. This is why knowing the precise time of your birth is so important in calculating your birth chart—four minutes can be the difference between being having a bouncy, optimistic Sagittarius Ascendant or a serious, subdued Capricorn Ascendant.

 ASTRO TIP The sign rising in the east at the moment of your birth is sometimes called the "rising sign." it symbolizes your personal appearance, personality, and style of dealing with new situations.

The signs of the zodiac always follow the same order from Aries to Pisces, just as the alphabet has an established order from A to Z; so the sign on the Ascendant determines the signs associated with the other houses. If you were born with Pisces on the Ascendant, then most likely Aries will appear on the cusp of the second house, Taurus on the cusp of the third, and so on.

In some house systems, however, it's not unusual for some signs not to appear on any house cusps at all, while some signs may appear on more than one (sequential) house. In these cases, all 30 degrees of the sign are "intercepted" in a house. The sign is still represented in your chart, but its influence may be more subtle and somewhat more difficult for you to express.

House Systems

Walk outside on a clear evening and take a look up at the sky. You'll see some constellations, and perhaps the Moon and some planets. What you won't see, however, are lines dividing the sky into houses. Houses are a helpful but almost completely artificial construction, derived from the viewer's perspective relative to fixed points such as the horizon and the Sun's zenith.

There is some controversy among astrologers about the best system of slicing up the horoscopic pie (called "house systems"). That's a nice way of saying that most astrologers have their favorite and if you try to convince them their system is inferior to yours, you're itching for a fight.

Let's take a closer look at some of the most popular house systems.

Whole Sign

This is one of the oldest house systems, used in the Hellenistic and early Medieval traditions and also in Indian astrology. In the whole sign system, the horoscope is divided into 12 houses that are exactly 30 degrees each. The first house begins at 0 degrees of the zodiac sign in which the Ascendant falls. The rest of the houses begin with 0 degrees of the subsequent signs, in order. In other words, each house contains a whole sign.

Equal House

In the equal house system, each house also contains 30 degrees. However, the degree of the Ascendant marks the beginning of the first house instead of 0 degrees of the sign (as in the whole sign system). For instance, if you were born with 13 degrees of Scorpio rising, the second house would begin with 13 degrees of the next sign, Sagittarius, and so on.

Placidus

Placidus (pronounced *PLA-si-dus*) is the most common house system in modern Western astrology. If you've ever had your birth chart calculated using a computerized chart service, it was probably calculated using Placidus houses.

Unlike the whole sign and equal house systems, Placidus houses may be much larger or much smaller than 30 degrees and there is the possibility of intercepted signs. Charts calculated using the Placidus house system produce very odd house sizes for locations at extreme northern or southern latitudes. The farther north or south of the equator that you were born, the more likely your chart will have a few very large houses and then a lot of very small ones.

Koch

The Koch (pronounced *COKE*) house system is a variation on the Placidus house system that uses a slightly different method of calculating the cusps of the succedent and cadent houses. Like the Placidus system, it can be a bit unpredictable at extreme latitudes. The Koch house system is especially popular in German-speaking countries (it originated in Germany), but it has gained favor around the world with astrologers who feel it may work more accurately for predictive work. This was my astrology teacher's preferred method, so I adopted it as my own—which, to be honest, is the way many astrologers settle on their favorite house system.

Derivative Houses

Astrology is a complete system; your birth chart symbolizes absolutely everything—and everyone—in your life. From your mother to your best friend in high school to the cabbie who cut you off on your way to work this morning, everyone who has crossed or will cross your path can be found in your chart. You just have to know where to look.

Each house symbolizes places, situations, and types of relationships, but there are only 12 houses. How can they cover all the characters, both major and minor, in your life's story? *Derivative houses* is a method of finding relationships through the inherent connection between the houses in your chart. If you're trying to analyze a situation, possibly involving a person for whom you don't have a birth chart, the derivative house system allows you to use your own birth chart to do it. The cusp of the house in your chart that symbolizes the essential nature of the relationship becomes the Ascendant, and a new chart derived from this new Ascendant will help you find the person or matter in question.

DEFINITION

Derivative houses is a method that allows you to read a "horoscope," derived from the houses of your chart, for any person in your life. In derivative houses, a particular house of your horoscope is treated as though it were the Ascendant, and the rest of the chart is read relative to that house.

Let's say you're trying to track down the neighbor of your brother's ex-wife (you suspect he stole your teacup pig). Which house of your horoscope can give you information about the alleged thief? Here are the steps you would take to find out:

1. Find your brother. Siblings are found in your third house.

2. Locate your sibling's ex-wife. Spouses past, present, and future are represented by the seventh house. Beginning with the *third house* (your sibling), count seven houses: the third, fourth, fifth, sixth, seventh, eighth, and ninth. Your brother's ex is represented by the *ninth house*.

3. Now, to find that elusive neighbor. Neighbors are represented by the third house; so beginning with the *ninth house*, which represents the ex-wife (it's her neighbor, not yours), count three houses: ninth, tenth, and eleventh.

4. Voilà! Your brother's ex-wife's neighbor is represented by the *eleventh house* of your chart. The condition of planets in this house or the ruler of the sign on the house cusp describes the person and his current situation.

The pig is a different matter altogether. Livestock is associated with the sixth house. Should you find a connection between the sixth house (the pig) and eleventh house (the sibling's ex-wife's neighbor)—say, Taurus is on the sixth house cusp, ruled by Venus, which is in the eleventh house—it might be time to stand outside your brother's ex-wife's neighbor's house and start hollering "Soo-eeeeeee!"

Essential Takeaways

- The 12 houses of the horoscope represent where action takes place in your life.
- The hemispheres of the chart divide the horoscope in half, representing day and night and sun's daily ascent and descent.
- Like the signs of the zodiac, the 12 houses can be grouped together by quality and by element.
- Each house is naturally associated with a particular sign and planet.
- There are different methods used to split the chart into 12 houses. Depending on which is used, houses may be different sizes or all exactly the same size.
- Don't have a birth chart for someone in your life? You can read about your connection to them by using the houses of your own chart using derivative houses.

CHAPTER 9

Celestial Navigation: Angular Houses

The angular houses: first, fourth, seventh, and tenth

Each angular house is associated with one of the cardinal signs

The first house: self, personality, and physical body

The fourth house: home, family, and roots

The seventh house: partners, close friends, and open enemies

The tenth house: career, authority, and reputation

Opinions vary about what happens to us before birth and after shucking off the mortal coil. But one way to think of it is that when you're born, your spirit gets attached to the corporeal world, like a butterfly pinned up in an etymology exhibit. The angular houses of the chart, representing observable points in space, symbolize the primary experiences that "pin" you to a particular place and set of circumstances.

Your physical body (first house), family and nation (fourth house), vital primary relationships (seventh house), and career or calling (tenth house) are the orienting points on your personal compass. When things change in these areas of your life—even when you initiate the change, as is often the case in these cardinal-energy houses—the entire compass of your life shifts. Such are the con-sequences of being human: you're no longer free to go where you wish on a whim, and walking into walls is going to get you a big lump on your head. On the plus side, you get to wiggle your toes, enjoy a good meal, and hug your loved ones.

The cusps of the first, fourth, seventh, and tenth houses are considered especially powerful and sensitive points. Also referred to as the "angles" of the chart, these cusps, unlike the cusps of the other houses, have special names. Defined in your birth chart by the time and location of your birth, they are the compass points that help you figure out where you are and to navigate the waters ahead.

First House: The House of Self

Imagine for a moment what it must feel like to be a newborn baby. You've left the soothing comfort and security of your mother's womb in a bloody, terrifying process, ultimately landing in a bright, cold, scary new place. You're tiny, you're naked, and you don't speak the language of the natives. How will you protect yourself? How will you get fed? How will you survive? The first house of the horoscope marks the alignment of the western horizon with the zodiac at the moment you drew your first breath. Had you been born someplace else, or slightly earlier or later, a different part of the zodiac may have been rising. The first house describes what makes you unique from all the other babies being born on the same day. And it symbolizes how you, a tiny, naked, terrified infant who's scrambling to get a handle on a new environment, will figure out how to get your needs met.

Babies have a standard repertoire of attention-seeking behaviors—crying, laughing, and grasping. But as a baby grows—as you grew—you developed other strategies for keeping yourself safe, getting what you needed, and figuring out what makes you different from every other baby in the nursery. We find a description of those strategies in the first house of the birth chart.

Rulerships and Key Concepts

The first house is associated with Aries, the first sign of the zodiac, and with its ruling planet, Mars. Like Aries, the first house belongs to the cardinal quality and the fire element.

Key concepts of the first house: Self, identity, physical body, personality, appearance, beginnings, thresholds, self-defense, war

The Ascendant

The angle associated with the first house is called the Ascendant, and it refers to the degree and sign that was rising in the east at the moment and location of your birth. The

Ascendant describes your physical body, which is your most instantly recognizable personal characteristic. But it also describes your sense of personal identity, your assertiveness, and how you go about getting what you want. The Ascendant symbolizes the way you handle the world. It's the welcome mat at your door, the receptionist that limits the world's outside contact with you, and your personal bodyguard. The sign on the Ascendant, as well as its ruling planet, tell us a great deal about what we'll experience when we shake your hand, knock on your door, ask you out on a date, pick a fight with you, or interview you for a job. The Ascendant may or may not reflect much about who you really are inside; it's essentially a Halloween costume you wear year-round.

Signs

The first house of the chart covers much of the same territory as the sign Aries. In your chart, the first house is also strongly influenced by the following:

- The sign on the Ascendant and signs contained in the first house

- Planets in the first house

- The planet that rules the sign on the Ascendant

Aries in the first house—Born with Aries in the first house, you're conditioned to live life on the offensive. You tend to move fast, talk fast, and take action without hesitation. You exude self-confidence and seldom second-guess yourself, traits that make you a magnetic leader. You do have a formidable temper and, when you're feeling insecure, can be pretty domineering. Because you're often in a hurry, Aries rising can tend to be accident prone, especially when angry.

Taurus in the first house—With Taurus in the first house, you think carefully before speaking or acting. You exude sex appeal and quiet confidence, and win others over with your easygoing charm and magnetism. Others instinctively feel that they can rely on you. Taurus rising can find it difficult to get moving, but once set on a course of action nothing can stop you. You have a long fuse, but when you lose your temper people take notice. The placement of Venus in your birth chart can modify all of these traits.

Gemini in the first house—Gemini in the first house is restless and sensitive to external stimuli. You may find it difficult to sit still for long and enjoy the stimulation of sitting in public, people watching and eavesdropping on conversations or chatting with your own friends. With Gemini rising, you rely on your quick wit to defend yourself; you can often get away with saying things that others can't. You're prone to irritability, especially when you've been sitting in one place for too long, but rarely show real anger. When you do, your favored weapon is fast-talking sarcasm.

Cancer in the first house—Cancer in the first house radiates warmth and humor, but is excruciatingly sensitive to perceived hurts. Because you're vulnerable, you prefer to take an indirect approach in most situations and are a bit wary and defensive with new people. When you trust enough to open up, though, you endear yourself to others with your sweetness, your sense of humor, and your desire to take care of them. You withdraw when you feel threatened, but when you're cornered you defend yourself by getting very snappish; those claws can draw blood!

Leo in the first house—When you walk in a room, people notice—you have regal bearing, dignity, and charisma. You're friendly with new people, but you're slow to trust them, and you loathe familiarity from strangers. You have a quick and ferocious temper but are generally forgiving of minor transgressions. It's when you become icy that you should really be feared! You generally go on the offensive only to protect those you care about, but you never back down when someone directly threatens you.

Virgo in the first house—Quirky but quietly attractive, you radiate intelligence, competence, and self-sufficiency. If pressed, you would admit that you find the world pretty tiring and prefer to spend time alone, preferably engaged in some constructive activity. Because you appear to be a substantive person with high standards, others want to please you. Like your fellow Mercury-ruled Gemini Ascendant, you tend toward irritability rather than anger. Unlike Gemini, though, you have a volcanic temper when angered, and your Mercurial facility with words becomes a fearsome weapon.

 ASTRO TIP — The degree on the Ascendant changes approximately every four minutes, and a new sign is rising about every two hours (depending on the sign of the zodiac and the latitude of your birthplace). That's why it's important to know the exact time of birth before calculating a birth chart. Even a few minutes can make a big difference, especially when you are working with predictive tools (see Chapter 23).

Libra in the first house—You're smooth, Libra rising. You're assertive and proactive, but you're so charming and flattering that others rarely notice what you're up to! The original steel magnolia, you learned early on that you catch more flies with honey than with vinegar. You're competitive, and good at getting what you want—often because you know whom you need to sweet-talk. Libra rising does get angry, but you're adept at using strategy to disarm your opponent. To paraphrase President Abraham Lincoln, you destroy your enemies by making them your allies.

Scorpio in the first house—Scorpio in the first house is a sign of the secret agent. You may be reasonably friendly, but you don't give away much information about yourself;

information is power, and you don't willingly give power to anyone. In a threatening situation, your unerring ability to detect an opponent's weak spots, combined with your control over your emotions, gives you a distinct advantage. You simply devastate your opponent with a withering observation about his Achilles' heel, then coldly engineer his destruction.

Sagittarius in the first house—Friendly and open, you never met a stranger and you have nothing to hide. You don't keep secrets because you value your freedom too much to risk being controlled by someone who threatens to expose them. Sagittarius rising often develops self-deprecating humor as a defense mechanism, and deals with threats by making jokes. Sagittarius, like his fellow fire signs, has a quick temper—usually triggered by someone impugning his knowledge or beliefs—but rarely stays angry for long.

Capricorn in the first house—Your preferred method of dealing with the world is by being a grown-up who handles the pragmatic challenges that daunt lesser mortals. Even when you were young, you probably had to take care of younger siblings—or even your parents. Consequently you grew up fast, and others—including people older than you are—look up to you. Capricorn rising, like his fellow earth sign Ascendants, is slow to anger but scary when he's worked up—cold, sarcastic, and harsh. And other than Scorpio, few signs hold a grudge longer.

Aquarius in the first house—Aquarius rising is cool and poised, but doesn't quite fit in anywhere—either because you're a little quirky and eccentric, or simply because you're not who others expect to be dealing with a particular situation (male when they expect female, black when they expect white, young when they expect old). Your personality is somewhat reserved, yet everyone seems to know you and most of them like you. You're threatened by attempts to control you, and your weapons are your willingness to cut offenders out of your life permanently, and to take your enemy down even if it means suffering setbacks yourself.

Pisces in the first house—You're sweet and a little dreamy, and others like you but have a tendency not to take you seriously. You're bubbly and eager to please, and generally quite popular because everyone feels you'll be nice to them. When you've been pushed too far, however, you will defend yourself; your main weapons are your ability to escape—you just seem to disappear from the person's life—and of course, the element of surprise. No one expects you to get angry, and when you do, they're astonished and a little ashamed of themselves for having offended such a nice person.

Fourth House: Bloom Where You're Planted

"Where are you from?" In certain parts of the world, that's a question even more ubiquitous than the well-worn "And what do you do?" (which is a question related to the tenth house, opposite from the fourth). And, of course, where you were born and raised, the family in which you spent your formative years, and the rich genealogical loam from which you sprang have an enormous impact on the person you become.

Unlike the first house, in which you fashion your own identity and individual mythology, the fourth house is the umbilical cord that fed you the impulses to create that myth in the first place. Who were "your people"? How did they see themselves, and how did they treat you? Maybe you learned kind lessons from them, and maybe some of the lessons weren't so benign. Certainly, though, they had a big hand in making you what you are.

Many of us never drift far from our familiar beginnings and the people we've known all our lives. Others can't wait to escape the tyranny of our personal history and start over. Can you ever really do that, though, even if you want to? If your earliest memories were of magnolias and soft, drawling accents, will you ever feel truly at home in Maine? If you were born in poverty, is it reasonable to assume you'll ever have the confidence of one born to wealth and privilege?

If the first house tells us about the persona you created to handle the world, the fourth house tells us the motivation behind that persona. Where are you from? Are you likely to leave, or is it more likely you'll dig in your heels, determined to bloom where you've been planted?

Rulerships and Key Concepts

The fourth house is associated with the sign of Cancer and its ruler, the Moon. It belongs to the cardinal modality and the water element.

Key concepts of the fourth house: Home, mother, history, birthplace, genealogy

The IC or *Imum Coeli*

The angle associated with the fourth house is called the IC, or *imum coeli* ("lowest heavens"). This angle specifically refers to the degree and sign at the northernmost point in the sky (the lowest point in the chart); it's sometimes called the nadir.

The IC is a sort of umbilical cord that connects you to your home, family, personal history, and subconscious. Think of the IC as a cosmic homing device, helping you find your way to safety whenever you've wandered too far into dangerous territory. The sign on the

IC, and its ruling planet, tell us what you need to feel safe and secure, what you're like in your private life, and a lot about your basic motivations. Planets near the IC in your birth chart suggest additional family baggage and emphasize the importance of home, family, or privacy to you.

Signs

The fourth house of the chart covers much of the same territory as the sign Cancer. In your chart, the fourth house is also strongly influenced by the following:

- The sign on the IC and signs contained in the fourth house

- Planets in the fourth house

- The planet that rules the sign on the IC

Aries in the fourth house—Your early home life left you sensitive to conflict; you may not have always felt safe. Perhaps there was a military influence in your family; an importance placed on weapons, hunting, or self-defense; or just an environment that forced you to learn to defend yourself. You're motivated to use what you learned about conflict to help yourself and others find peace and harmony.

Taurus in the fourth house—Your early home life was likely secure but a bit dull and materialistic. The early emphasis on money and possessions and discomfort with emotionally sensitive subjects motivates you to live simply and honestly, and to develop interests and relationships that you feel passionate about.

Gemini in the fourth house—Your early home life left you sensitive about your intelligence, competence, and ability to communicate effectively. Perhaps you were considered exceptional in these areas, whether highly intelligent or rather slow. Your primary motivation is to use your intelligence and learning to pursue knowledge and to find meaning in life.

Cancer in the fourth house—Your early home life left you sensitive to nurturing; you may have felt smothered, or else not closely supervised enough. Because you learned to take care of yourself at an early age, or perhaps because you long to prove you can be self-sufficient, your primary motivation is to be independent, worldly, and respected for your competence.

Leo in the fourth house—Your early home life left you sensitive to being noticed; you may have gotten too much special attention, or not enough. Feeling (or wanting to feel) special can be isolating and lonely; your primary motivation is to seek like-minded allies who appreciate your unique gifts while also making you feel as though you fit in.

Virgo in the fourth house—Your early home life left you sensitive to orderliness and health. Whether you lived in a very orderly, health-conscious household or a chaotic one where you lived on junk food, your early environment motivates you to seek a reasonable balance between order and chaos, and between practical affairs and spiritual fulfillment.

MISC.

At Home in the Fourth House

The fourth house symbolizes your physical home, and signs in the fourth house describe the kind of home that makes you feel comfortable:

- Aries—New construction, with an office, workshop, and/or fitness room
- Taurus—Comfortable and unpretentious
- Gemini—A home on wheels, or a duplex
- Cancer—Cozy, with pets and family photos
- Leo—Luxurious and impressive
- Virgo—Simple and tidy
- Libra—Harmonious and tasteful
- Scorpio—Dramatic and private
- Sagittarius—On a large lot surrounded by nature; filled with books
- Capricorn—On a hill, classic and well built
- Aquarius—Quirky and unorthodox
- Pisces—Peaceful, quiet, restful

Libra in the fourth house—Your early home life left you sensitive to fairness, good manners, and getting along. There may have been a message at home that being nice is more important than getting ahead. This early emphasis on being nice and playing by the rules motivates you to become more assertive, by using your social skills to help you go after whatever you want out of life.

Scorpio in the fourth house—Your early home life left you sensitive to secrecy and power. You learned from an early age to read between the lines and figure out what was really going on in any situation; you're able to use these skills to improve your security and financial standing. Your primary motivation is to develop relationships with people you can trust and to enjoy life instead of dwelling on its dark side.

Sagittarius in the fourth house—Your early home life left you sensitive to strong beliefs, foreignness, and higher education. Your family may have been immigrants, strongly religious or ideological, or zealous about the importance of higher education; it's likely you always felt like an outsider. Your primary motivation is to cultivate open-mindedness—to question the beliefs you grew up with, and to find a place where you feel like you fit in as part of a community.

Capricorn in the fourth house—Your early home life left you sensitive to responsibility and self-sufficiency. Perhaps you had to care for younger siblings, or maybe strict and even harsh discipline overshadowed nurturing in your family. Your primary motivation is the desire to help others learn to take care of themselves—emotionally as well as materially.

Aquarius in the fourth house—Your early home life left you sensitive to disruption and not fitting in. Your family might have moved often, or an early trauma may have caused considerable upheaval at home. Whatever the reason, your primary motivation is to maintain stability, prepare for the unexpected, and feel as though you belong somewhere.

Pisces in the fourth house—Your early home life left you sensitive to discord, suffering, and untidiness. There may have been illness or an untimely death in your family, something that undermined the peace, order, and guidance that a young child craves. Your primary motivation is to develop practical confidence and emotional stability that will give you the inner tranquility.

Seventh House—Meeting the Other

"Like attracts like." "Opposites attract." "Out of sight, out of mind." "Absence makes the heart grow fonder." Platitudes about love and relationships are confusing, and offer numerous mixed messages. Which is it, then: are we meant to be with someone who is like us, or someone who is different enough to balance our weaknesses with their strengths? Is it healthier to spend a certain amount of time away from our partner, or is that inviting estrangement and indiscretions?

There's no single answer to these questions, of course, which is why the language, music, literature, and art devoted to the topic of love and relationships are so contradictory. Sometimes, we expect a partner to fill in the gaps of our own development—assertive where we're timid, witty where we're dull. This approach can work, but it can also backfire in a string of relationships with people who are temperamentally incompatible.

The seventh house's message of balance suggests that the ideal partner is one who encourages you to fill in your own gaps, someone who teaches by example but who insists that you strive to be your best, most complete self. It's interesting that the seventh house, along with symbolizing marriage, partners, and close friends, is the house of "open enemies." A wise person once told me that "your enemies are your treasure. They show you the best and worst of what you can be." Pay attention to the best qualities of your rivals, because those are the qualities you need to develop in yourself. Then find a partner that can help you be those things.

Rulerships and Key Concepts

The seventh house is associated with the sign of Libra and its ruling planet, Venus. Like Libra, the seventh house belongs to the cardinal modality and the air element.

Key concepts for the seventh house: Partners, marriage, close friends, open enemies, customers, the public marketplace, negotiation, balance

The Descendant

The Descendant, opposite the Ascendant, is the cusp of the seventh house and represents the western horizon, where the Sun sets. This is the pivotal relationship point of the chart. Planets close to this angle in your birth chart, or crossing over it by transit and progression, symbolize relationship timing.

Signs

The seventh house of the chart covers much of the same territory as the sign Libra. In your chart, the seventh house is also strongly influenced by the following:

- The sign on the Descendant and signs contained in the seventh house

- Planets in the seventh house

- The planet that rules the sign on the Descendant

Aries in the seventh house—Your rivals are assertive and decisive, and your ideal partners help you develop these qualities in yourself. Because you tend to avoid conflict and approach others diplomatically, you're often drawn to partners who are very assertive and direct, even abrasive. As they teach you to be more assertive, you teach them how to be more diplomatic.

Taurus in the seventh house—Your rivals are calm and stable, and your ideal partners help you develop these qualities in yourself. Because you are intense and secretive, you're often drawn to partners who are easygoing and uncomplicated. As they guide you toward greater stability and emotional security, you help them confront uncomfortable emotions and find their passion.

Gemini in the seventh house—Your rivals have an open mind and the gift of gab; your ideal partners help you develop these qualities in yourself. You can have a tendency to be a bit naive and trusting, and to pretend you know more than you do, and so you're drawn to partners who are canny, skeptical, and questioning. They help you keep an open mind, and you help them figure out what believe.

Cancer in the seventh house—Your rivals are nurturing and giving, and your ideal partners help you develop these qualities in yourself. Because you're pragmatic and ambitious, you're drawn to partners who are sensitive and nurturing. They help you keep in touch with the emotional side of your decisions; you encourage them to pursue their goals and to take things less personally.

Leo in the seventh house—Your rivals are confident and know how to get noticed; your ideal partners help you develop these qualities. You have the ability to get along with just about anyone in any situation, and you're drawn to partners who demand to be acknowledged as special. They help you realize that being true to oneself is as important as fitting in; you remind them that individuals can have greater impact when they form alliances with others.

Virgo in the seventh house—Your rivals are capable and discriminating; your ideal partners help you develop these qualities. Because you empathize with everyone and aren't terribly practical, you're drawn to partners who make sure the bills get paid on time and are choosy about the company they keep. They teach you to be more practical and avoid getting taken advantage of; you teach them to enjoy life—and other people—more.

 ASTRO ALERT "There are no planets in my seventh house," you moan. "Does that mean I'll never get married?" No, an "empty" seventh house doesn't mean that at all. (Actress Elizabeth Taylor has been married eight times, despite having not a single planet in her seventh house!) Look to the planet that rules the sign on the Descendant to tell the story of whom, how, and when you'll marry.

Libra in the seventh house—Your rivals are charming and cooperative, and your ideal partners help you develop these qualities. You're a "shoot first, ask questions later" kind of person, and you're drawn to partners who are polite and have good social skills. They teach you about the power of using charm and persuasion to get what you want; you teach them to be assertive and decisive in pursuing their goals.

Scorpio in the seventh house—Your rivals are passionate and intense; your ideal partners help you develop these qualities. You're an easygoing, self-effacing type who is drawn to passionate, emotionally dramatic partners. They teach you to understand what's going on beneath the surface of your life, while you help them develop trust, patience, and humor.

Sagittarius in the seventh house—Your rivals have strong beliefs and the ability to laugh at themselves; your ideal partners help you develop these qualities. You're a restless, curious, wise-cracking jack of all trades; you're drawn to partners who are focused, intellectually confident, and knowledgeable. They encourage you to see the big picture; you help them from becoming a know-it-all.

Capricorn in the seventh house—Your rivals are ambitious and worldly; your ideal partners help you develop these qualities. You wear your heart on your sleeve and are preoccupied with home, family, and security; you're drawn to partners who keep their feelings to themselves and have worldly ambitions. They help you open your mind to a larger world beyond your little corner of it, and you help them remember that ambition isn't everything.

Aquarius in the seventh house—Your rivals are iconoclastic and independent; your ideal partners help you develop these qualities. You consider yourself special and a bit extraordinary, and you're drawn to partners who treat you like an equal. They help keep you from becoming imperious and self-important; you teach them that everyone is special—at least, to their partner.

Pisces in the seventh house—Your rivals are fun-loving and empathetic; your ideal partners help you develop these qualities. You have high standards and a low tolerance for frivolity, and you're drawn to partners who are accepting of others and who live in the moment. They help you loosen your tight hold on perfectionism and enjoy life; you help them untangle problems and take a responsible approach to the practical side of life.

Tenth House: Who's Your Daddy?

My teacher used to say that the first house and the Ascendant describe the impression someone gets when they meet you face-to-face. But the tenth house and the Midheaven symbolize the reputation that precedes you—what someone perceives to be true about you based on your public persona, including your job, your father's work, or where you went to school.

When I occasionally visit the small farming community where I was born and where my family had lived for generations, I'm recognized immediately, no matter how much older I've gotten. Most of the people I meet don't know me at all. But they knew my parents, what my father did for a living, what fraternal lodge he belonged to, and how much land we owned. Based on all that, they probably feel they have a pretty good idea of who I am.

The tenth house describes this inherited reputation. But it also symbolizes the need to create your *own* reputation, one that's deliberate and earned: to be the author of your own life. One way this is done is through your work, or more specifically what used to be called a "calling." You might be called to raise a family, to raise wheat, or develop iPhone applications. A calling doesn't necessarily pay the bills; in fact, you may have to take a job to support pursuing your calling. But whether you earn money with it or not, you'll only feel like a success if you heed the tenth house's call.

Rulerships and Key Concepts

The tenth house is associated with the sign of Capricorn and its ruling planet, Saturn. Like Capricorn, the tenth house is associated with the angular modality and the earth element.

Key concepts for the tenth house: Career, status, authority, being the boss, being a paternal and mentoring figure.

The Midheaven

The angle associated with the tenth house is called the Midheaven; it refers to the degree and sign that was directly overhead at the moment and location of your birth. The Midheaven symbolizes the way the world sees you. It's the angle of career, calling, authority, and reputation; if you were famous, it's the kind of information about you that appears in magazines, subject to distortion and misunderstanding.

The Midheaven describes the way you approach your career, and possibly something about the nature of your career. But it also symbolizes the heights you aspire to reach, some qualities of character that, if you were to realize them, would make you feel that your life is a success.

Signs

The tenth house of the chart covers much of the same territory as the sign Capricorn. In your chart, the tenth house is also strongly influenced by the following:

- The ruling planet of the sign on the Midheaven

- Planets in the tenth house

- Aspects from other planets to the Midheaven

Aries in the tenth house—The legacy: Assertive, ambitious, and somewhat contentious. The calling: A natural entrepreneur, you're called to careers that challenge you and encourage independence and pioneering spirit.

Taurus in the tenth house—The legacy: Easygoing, reliable, and not particularly energetic. The calling: Stable and well organized, you're called to careers that celebrate the senses and require wise stewardship of money, property, and other resources.

Gemini in the tenth house—The legacy: Smart and well spoken, but a dilettante. The calling: Your inquisitive spirit is called to careers that let you ask questions, explore and share ideas, and enjoy a wide variety of experiences.

Cancer in the tenth house—The legacy: A nurturing figure from a matriarchal background who takes care of others. The calling: Your caring, protective nature calls you to careers that allow you to nourish and empower others, including teaching them to care for themselves.

Leo in the tenth house—The legacy: A rock star; creative and expressive. The calling: Warm and inspirational, you're called to careers in which you help others reach their full personal and creative potential.

Virgo in the tenth house—The legacy: Practical and capable support person. The calling: Resourceful and analytical, you're called to help others untangle their problems and put their lives in order.

ASTRO TIP

The sign on your Midheaven will often describe the qualities and attributes you most admire in others. Your favorite teachers, bosses, and other authority figures almost certainly embody at least some of the best characteristics of your Midheaven sign.

Libra in the tenth house—The legacy: Pleasant and cooperative social director. The calling: You're called to careers that let you bring beauty, harmony, and balance to the world.

Scorpio in the tenth house—The legacy: Powerful but perhaps a little scary. The calling: Trustworthy and truthful, you're called to careers that allow you to listen to people's secrets and help them become stronger people.

Sagittarius in the tenth house—The legacy: Jolly and generous, a cross between Santa Claus and Ronald McDonald. The calling: Well informed and optimistic, you're called to careers that allow you to teach, advise, or explore.

Capricorn in the tenth house—The legacy: Serious and stern. The calling: A natural authority, you're called to careers that allow you to lead others.

Aquarius in the tenth house—The legacy: The rebel without a pause. The calling: A freedom-loving iconoclast, you're called to work that allows you to reach large numbers of people with innovative solutions for a more exciting future.

Pisces in the tenth house—The legacy: A tree-hugging, granola-snarfing hippie. The calling: You're called to work that capitalizes on your ability to empathize with others, to "meet them where they are" and to encourage them along a spiritual and compassionate path.

Essential Takeaways

- The angular houses are the first, fourth, seventh, and tenth houses. They're associated with the cardinal signs: Aries, Cancer, Libra, and Capricorn.
- Angular houses represent the orienting compass points of your life: self, others, home, and career.
- The Ascendant and first house symbolize your appearance, personality, identity, and assertiveness.
- The IC and fourth house symbolize your connection to home and family.
- The Descendant and seventh house symbolize partnerships.
- The MC and tenth house symbolize your public status and calling..

CHAPTER 10

Getting Grounded: Succedent Houses

The succedent houses: second, fifth, eighth, and eleventh

Each succedent house is associated with one of the fixed signs

The second house: money, possessions, and personal values

The fifth house: creativity, recreation, and children

The eighth house: intimate relationships and shared resources

The eleventh house: friends, groups, and future legacy

You've just started a new job, moved to a new house, gotten married, or lost a substantial amount of weight. The shape of your daily landscape has radically changed. What's your next step?

Getting grounded.

You establish new routines. You assess what you have and make a list of what you need. You buy new clothes, or decorate your house or workspace in a way that makes you comfortable and reflects your personality. You negotiate with your partner about the best way to merge your possessions, money, and friends. You figure out how to express your individuality in a new environment, and work to develop alliances based on shared goals.

The succedent houses are associated with the fixed signs of the zodiac, and these are the houses that represent the processes that lend stability and security to our lives, our relationships, and even our society. In them, you amass possessions (second house), learn to use them creatively (fifth house), share them with others (eighth house), and use them to contribute to society's future (eleventh house). These houses represent the cornerstones in the foundation of your life.

Second House: Collect What You Need

Close your eyes, and imagine you're in a completely safe, comfortable place. You have every-thing you need; you're not worried about where your next paycheck or meal will come from. You have good health, affectionate relationships, great hair, and a fabulous figure.

Where are you? What are you doing? Are you lying in a hammock between two palm trees, gazing out at the ocean while you sip a cool beverage? Sitting serenely at the top of a craggy mountain, enjoying a breathtaking view? Lying on your back in a meadow, watching puffy clouds in an azure sky?

Now open your eyes. Welcome back … you've just visited your second house—a place where no one goes without or feels threatened or alone.

The second house was traditionally called the "House of Money." Without taking anything away from money (in the real world, most of us find it handy, if not essential), it has no intrinsic worth. Its worth lies in what it represents: resources, and the ability to exchange them for other resources. So the second house is about your relationship with money, but it's also about what you consider valuable. If you grew up without enough food to eat, you probably value a hearty meal and a full pantry. If you were raised to think your physical appearance is your most important asset, you'll value good grooming and an attractive wardrobe. If you were born into wealth, you might value a friend who likes you for something other than your money.

What you value is connected to the resources you have available, and the second house symbolizes not just your attitude about possessions, personal comfort, and security, but also the natural resources of personality, gifts, and character that you bring to the table. The challenge of navigating the second house is to use all of your resources wisely, and to cultivate a relationship to the physical world that reflects what's truly important to you— to avoid ending up being someone who, as Oscar Wilde once said, knows "the cost of everything and the value of nothing."

Rulerships and Key Concepts

The second house is associated with the second sign of the zodiac, Taurus, and its ruling planet, Venus. Like Taurus, it's of the fixed quality and the earth element.

Key concepts of the second house: Money, resources, contentment, security, property, banks, gardens, farms, coins

Signs

The second house shares a lot of territory and concerns with the sign of Taurus. In your chart, the second house is also strongly influenced by the following:

- The sign on the second house cusp and signs contained in the second house

- Planets in the second house

- The planet that rules the sign on the second house cusp

Aries in the second house—You value action, initiative, and enterprise, and your greatest resources are courage, energy, and daring. Impulsive in your spending, you're a financial risk taker. You're willing to do whatever it takes to get money or anything else you need for your comfort and security. You have an entrepreneurial spirit and do best when your pay is directly based on your own initiative (such as through bonuses and commission).

Taurus in the second house—You value stability, practicality, and comfort, and your greatest resources are patience, tenacity, and a calm temperament. You like *things* and can be rather possessive about your stuff; you take good care of your property and finances. However, you have a weakness for easy money and can sometimes be taken in by get-rich-quick schemes.

Gemini in the second house—You value intellect, variety, and curiosity, and your greatest resources are your wit, adaptability, and open mind. You're not materialistic, but you're fascinated by money, reading spreadsheets for fun and spending a lot of time thinking and talking about financial matters. You prefer to have at least two sources of income, and you're always looking for new ways to increase your earnings.

Cancer in the second house—You value safety, family connections, and your home; your greatest resources are your caring nature, tenacity, and ability to connect with others emotionally. Money and possessions are emotional territory for you; they represent safety and security. You don't part with money easily, but can be generous with immediate family and close friends (though you're easily hurt if you don't feel appreciated). Your caution may prevent you from earning a lot of money, but you're an accomplished saver.

Leo in the second house—You value fun, creativity, and appearances, and your greatest resources are your charisma, loyalty, and dependability. You're a bit of a big spender; you love to pick up the check at restaurants, loathe cheapness, and are impatient with talk of budgets, bargains, and coupon clipping. You're generous, especially with the children in your life, and you have a touch of the gambler in you.

Virgo in the second house—You value prudence, efficiency, and quality, and your best resources are discrimination, analytical ability, and the ability to figure out how things work. You're fascinated with the efficient use of resources; nothing makes you happier than finding a great deal or developing ways to lower your electric bill. You abhor waste and prefer to spend money on things that will last, instead of expensive dinners and vacations.

Signs in the Second House Go Shopping

- Fire signs (Aries, Leo, Sagittarius) are impulse spenders. They spend because it feels good!

- Earth signs (Taurus, Virgo, Capricorn) are practical spenders. They're generally frugal and spend because that's the only way to get what they want.

- Air signs (Gemini, Libra, Aquarius) are relational spenders. They spend on the people in their lives, or because of peer pressure.

- Water signs (Cancer, Scorpio, Pisces) are emotional spenders. They spend to make themselves feel better.

Libra in the second house—You value relationships, beauty, and fairness; your finest resources are refinement, diplomacy, and good judgment. You'll spend money on beautiful things and on pampering services, but only after an exhaustive search to find exactly what you want. It's not easy for you to make financial decisions, and you rely on your partner to help you decide on purchases and investments. You're gifted at marketing and can usually develop sources of passive income, such as royalties.

Scorpio in the second house—You value loyalty, passion, and intimacy; your greatest resources are your passion, intuition, and trustworthiness. You value money only as a means of maintaining control over your own life. Scorpio is the sign of "other people's money," and you have excellent instincts about investments and are very talented at making money for other people.

Sagittarius in the second house—You value freedom, honesty, and adventure; your greatest resources are your vision, independence, and understanding. For you, money is a means of securing your freedom. You're generous, mostly because you don't care much about money. You tend to wander into financially lucrative situations, which is perhaps why you have a trusting and optimistic attitude about money.

Capricorn in the second house—You value responsibility, success, and maturity; your greatest resources are pragmatism, persistence, and self-reliance. You're haunted by fears of poverty and deprivation, and you don't trust anyone else to provide for you. Because of this fear, you can be tight-fisted with your money. However, you can often build up a substantial empire, or at least a nest egg, because you're frugal, resourceful, and determined to get ahead financially.

Aquarius in the second house—You value freedom, friendship, and equality, and your best resources are sociability, stamina, and innovation. You find the subject of money intellectually stimulating, particularly financial markets and long-range financial planning. Your income tends to fluctuate, often because you're drawn to careers like consulting or contract assignments that allow you more control over your schedule. You're generous with friends and with your favorite charitable organizations.

Pisces in the second house—You value art, social welfare, and imagination; your best resources are your kindness, popularity, and adaptability. You find financial management tedious and can be trusting and impractical when it comes to money, with an "easy come, easy go" attitude about possessions. You'll give help to anyone who needs it, and you trust that if you ever need help, it will be forthcoming.

Fifth House: Create, Express, Play

To understand the fifth house, think for a moment about midevening, when the Sun moves through the fifth house each day. This is the time of day after dinner is finished but before bedtime, a time when we give ourselves over to leisure and recreation, watching television, playing a video game, going out to hear a concert. On weekends, it's the time when things really begin to heat up, with parties hitting their stride and the headlining act taking the stage.

The fifth house symbolizes the urge to play. It's where you find leisure, playful enjoyment, and the expression of creative energy. But the leisurely tone of the fifth house is not just about recreation, any more than a child at play is simply having fun; unstructured time offers opportunities for exploring fresh ideas and approaches that inform a creative, stimulating approach to life. The fifth is a storytelling house. In the same way children play make believe to try on various roles, the fifth house symbolizes the act of crafting a compelling vision of who you are. Imagination is one of mankind's most precious resources, and it first rears its head in the fifth house.

The fifth house was traditionally called the "House of Children," and in an earlier era children were considered important practical resources, providing labor and caretaking. Children hold a different position in the modern family, and the fifth house has increasingly become associated with fun, play, and self-expression. It's the house of transforming your resources into something that didn't exist before, except in your imagination. It's a house of gambling, of using up resources on games or the stock market, or the thrill of creating something that may not pay off in practical dividends. When a kid salvages an old wooden box and some wheels and builds a box cart with them, those resources are no longer available for other, more practical uses. But the return on his investment of time and materials is the thrill of hurdling down the steepest hill in town on his very own magic carpet.

Rulerships and Key Concepts

The fifth house is associated with Leo, the fifth sign of the zodiac, and its ruler, the Sun. Like Leo, the fifth house belongs to the fixed quality and the fire element.

Key concepts of the fifth house: Children, creativity, performance, self-expression, gaming, recreation, fun, romantic relationships that are committed

Signs and the Fifth House

The fifth house shares a lot of territory with the sign of Leo. In your chart, the fifth house is also strongly influenced by the following:

- The sign on the fifth house cusp and signs contained in the fifth house

- Planets in the fifth house

- The planet that rules the sign on the fifth house cusp

Aries in the fifth house—You love a creative challenge and push hard to develop your talents and get them noticed. If you have children, you'll push them hard to reach their potential. Your idea of a good time is to exert yourself physically or creatively; you're a bit of a lone wolf, preferring leisure activities that allow you to move at your own pace. Passionately romantic, you love the thrill of the romantic chase.

Taurus in the fifth house—You love music, the arts, dinner parties with good friends, and generally living the good life. You adore children and create stable, affectionate environments for them. Sentimental in love, you favor old-fashioned expressions of affection. You enjoy games of all kinds and enjoy being outdoors, but aren't usually strenuously athletic. You can get a little stuck in the same old recreational grooves, however, and benefit from friends who can nudge you out of your comfort zone.

Gemini in the fifth house—Good conversation, reading, and writing are your favorite forms of recreation. You have little patience with the long, rambling, repetitive stories of young children, but are a favorite confidant of teens because you listen and speak to them on their level. You're astonishingly creative, generally good at writing, playing an instrument, painting, or acting, and are restless without tasks, handcrafts, or puzzles to keep your busy mind occupied.

Cancer in the fifth house—You have a gift for touching people's hearts with your creative gifts; you're a natural artist, whether painting a landscape or creating a delicious meal, but are a bit shy of the spotlight. You're wild about kids of all ages, shapes, sizes, and temperaments. You're not good at dating—you get attached too quickly and get your heart broken a lot; but once in a committed relationship you keep the romance alive. You rarely relax; taking care of your loved ones is a full time job.

Leo in the fifth house—You're a natural, joyful, unselfconscious performer—you're good at everything, and you make it all look easy. You love children and are good at joining them in their play and helping them develop their own creativity. You fall in love like other people breathe and genuinely enjoy dating, socializing, and parties. You have a zest for enjoying life, and others gravitate to you to try to catch some of your magic.

Virgo in the fifth house—You're an artisan, a craftsperson whom others look to as a standard bearer. You're your own worst critic, so many of your creative projects never see the light of day. You have a romantic heart but impossible standards; you hate dating and are uncomfortable at parties. You dislike the noise and messiness of children, though you're a gentle parent to kids of your own. You adore animals and the outdoors, and your ideal vacation would enjoy camping, hiking, or just exploring some lovely place and its wildlife.

Pets: Animals ... or Children?

In traditional astrology, household pets were associated with the sixth house, along with beasts of burden and the animals that tend to show up on your dinner plate. Some astrologers feel that modern pets, the kind who wear cunning outfits and are spoiled rotten, are more appropriately placed in the fifth house with the rest of the children in our lives. My own experience is that the sixth house of my chart describes my pets better than the fifth house; then again, I think my cats are cute enough wearing only fur.

Libra in the fifth house—You have a tremendous gift for beauty. A natural musician or painter, you also have a great gift for creating beautiful environments and helping others beautify themselves. A romantic marriage is crucially important to you; you're the type to have date nights even after you're married and have specific ideas about how your partner should observe special occasions, often picking out your own gifts. Your children are taught to be well mannered and charming, but you prefer to vacation with your partner alone.

Scorpio in the fifth house—You're passionately creative, favoring art that is a bit disturbing or confronts taboos. You're secretive about your creative projects, and people often never know how talented you are until suddenly, one day, you've written a book or invented some fantastic gadget that makes you rich. You're great with your children when they're young but can have power struggles with teenagers. You're hopeless at relaxing, but approaching some challenge with intensity and focus is great fun for you.

Sagittarius in the fifth house—A creative visionary, you're always at least one step ahead of everyone else. You think big and always reach for the widest possible audience. You're bighearted with your children and encourage their education and life experiences, but often feel that children tie you down from doing what you'd like to be doing. Travel and spending time outdoors are your favorite pastimes.

Capricorn in the fifth house—You don't create anything without harboring the ambition of being the very best—and usually you reach that goal, becoming respected for your creative efforts. You're inclined to be a hands-off parent, as long as your children perform well in school and don't create discipline problems. "Fun" is a bit of an alien concept to you; to you, work is more fun than anything else.

Aquarius in the fifth house—You have the popular touch in whatever you create and are able to connect with a large audience without sacrificing your uniqueness. You tend to relate to children as a friend, and are an excellent step- or foster parent. You enjoy having a houseful of people, and parties or group activities with friends are your favorite form of fun.

Pisces in the fifth house—You have a lyrical, poetic, creative sensibility and are a natural musician, dancer, or poet; art is an escape for you, and you need a lot of quiet time alone to devote yourself to creativity. You love children and enjoy leading them in play and in art projects; you're a soft touch, and as a parent you need a partner who is willing to be the disciplinarian. You have a good time all the time, but especially enjoy spending time near the water.

Eighth House: Urge to Merge

Before I got married, my therapist asked me how well I thought I knew my husband-to-be. "Pretty well," I answered. "We were close friends for a full year before we ever got involved romantically." She thought about that for a moment. "April," she said, "you never truly know another person until you share a bank account with them."

She was right, of course. In the seventh house you meet and fall in love with someone who fits your particular psychological schema, and make serious, public promises about sticking it out together until you die. But the eighth house, traditionally called the "House of Other People's Money," symbolizes the next step in relationship, when things get really interesting. The process of pooling resources—including money, possessions, secrets, and bodily fluids—makes you utterly vulnerable. Without this complete openness to another person, you can't really be intimate.

If your seventh house powers of judgment have served you well, and you've chosen a partner with complementary abilities and values, merging your resources makes each of you stronger. The process of setting up house (or a business) together is a delicate one, exploring the limits of our trust, but the end result is greater and stronger than the sum of its parts.

Rulerships and Key Concepts

The eighth house is associated with Scorpio, the eighth sign of the zodiac, and its ruler, Pluto. Like Scorpio, the eighth house belongs to the fixed quality and the water element.

Key concepts of the eighth house: Shared resources, including joint bank accounts with a partner, investments, insurance, and taxes; death, particularly in the sense of submerging individual identity to a partnership; sexual relationships

Signs

The eighth house shares a lot of territory and symbolism with the sign of Scorpio. In your chart, the eighth house is also strongly influenced by the following:

- The sign on the eighth house cusp and signs contained in the eighth house

- Planets in the eighth house

- The sign and house placement of the planet that rules the sign on the eighth house cusp

Aries in the eighth house—The sign of individuality is an uncomfortable fit with the house of shared resources. Aries enjoys the sexual dimension of the eighth house, but doesn't generally enjoy sharing turf or mingling resources. Merging with another person is unlikely to be a smooth process for you; you don't like conferring with someone before spending money or painting the living room. You do best with someone who is independent, and it may be a good idea to keep your finances separate.

Taurus in the eighth house—You tend to get attached to your stuff, and you want things your own way. Still, you're inclined to be generous with your partner unless it's obvious they're not going to carry their own weight. Fortunately, you have a gift for attracting partners who are financially secure and who are dedicated to your ease and comfort.

Gemini in the eighth house—From an early age, you're interested in sex, death, and emotional intrigue. People tell you their secrets, and though you love to gossip you're astonishingly good at honoring individual confidences. You're only comfortable becoming intimate with someone who doesn't smother you and who is interesting to talk to; if you stray in a relationship it's because you're bored mentally, not physically.

Cancer in the eighth house—You loathe talking about sex and money; these are intensely private matters to you, and you have to know and trust someone very much indeed to wade into these waters with them. You feel terribly vulnerable relying on someone else for your financial security, and are rarely promiscuous because once you've had sex with someone you become immediately emotionally attached.

Leo in the eighth house—You might as well have been born a Scorpio, because you live for the mystery and sexual intrigue symbolized by the eighth house. You're intensely loyal, financially reliable, and generous with your intimate partners—but you can also be kind of bossy, because you're convinced your way of dealing with money, sex, or anything else is the only way!

Virgo in the eighth house—You often seem to end up in intimate relationships in which you and your partner are not contributing equally. There can, in fact, be the sense that one partner has to sacrifice a considerable amount in order to support the other. There is often a powerful sexual component that sustains the relationship.

Libra in the eighth house—Fairness and equality are essential to you, and in a relationship you need to feel both parties are contributing equally and sharing the decisions about joint resources. You enjoy sexual intimacy most within a committed relationship; you may also create art that has mystical, sexual, or death-related themes.

ASTRO ALERT The eighth house seems to be less connected to your own death than to the role of mortality in your life. Fascination with death is certainly eighth house territory, as is the "death" of individual ego that's necessary to become really intimate with another person.

Scorpio in the eighth house—Sexual intimacy, loyalty, and shared resources are deadly serious to you. Someone who betrays you in any of these areas will never get a second chance.

Sagittarius in the eighth house—Intimacy, for you, requires only fairness, honesty, and freedom. You can't bear feeling tied down or hemmed in by a partner, and at the first hint of manipulation or dishonesty you're out the door.

Capricorn in the eighth house—You fear debt and hate to owe anybody money, so you're frugal and always live within your means. There's a sense of having to rely on yourself because others seem to let you down or rely on you to provide for them.

Aquarius in the eighth house—This is the original commune/hippie/1960s ethos of sharing resources communally and taking a free-love approach to sexual intimacy. It's a utopian ideal that works well on a kabutz, but may get you into tight spots with more conventional or possessive types.

Pisces in the eighth house—Generous both emotionally and financially, you can often find yourself overextended in both areas. You're fond of giving away your possessions, regularly purging your home and giving things away. You always assume that somehow there will be enough and you'll be taken care of, and usually you're right!

Eleventh House: Touch the Future

I used to love the television program *Northern Exposure*. Set in the tiny fictional town of Cicely, Alaska, it offered a warm and heartfelt (if somewhat idealized) depiction of small-town life. In a small town, everyone knows everyone else and has distinctive characteristics and eccentricities. In Cicely, a retired astronaut, a big-city doctor, a woman pilot, a May–December couple of restaurateurs, and many other disparate characters found a way to get along, mostly because their survival depended on it—not just the survival of Alaska's extreme weather and rugged topography, but the survival of isolation from other people.

With a traditional name of the "House of Friendship" (but I prefer to think of it as a house of community), the eleventh house moves you beyond the eighth house challenge of merging your resources with one other person and into the realm of contributing to large-scale efforts that provide social stability. Government is one example of eleventh house collectivism, but so are social or political movements that join groups of people in opposition to the status quo. Like the unlikely bedfellows of Cicely, Alaska, societies are formed when individuals marshal their resources to achieve common aims.

Eleventh house territory transports you beyond the present and your own smallness and allows you to touch the future—to leave the legacy of a dream realized. Whether it's a corporation, an invention, a scientific breakthrough, or the constitution for a fledgling democracy, a legacy is not something that can be created alone; it's a collaboration between you and the society in which you live. What people create together from their combined resources is what survives long after they're gone. Even a painting created by a brilliant artist is not a legacy until it's embraced by an audience.

Rulerships and Key Concepts

The eleventh house is associated with Aquarius, the eleventh house of the zodiac, and its rulers, Uranus and Saturn. Like Uranus, the eleventh house belongs to the fixed quality and the air element.

Key concepts of the eleventh house: Friendship, social organizations, groups, politics, income from career

Signs

The eleventh house shares similar territory with the sign of Aquarius. In your chart, the eleventh house is also strongly influenced by the following:

- The sign on the eleventh house cusp and signs contained in the eleventh house

- Planets in the eleventh house

- The sign and house placement of the planet that rules the sign on the eleventh house cusp

Aries in the eleventh house—You're not really a joiner and don't really gravitate toward existing groups or organizations—though you might start some. You're a leader among your friends and have a knack for motivating people to take action, and if you do get drawn into an organization you're likely to be made president. Pioneering is your legacy.

Taurus in the eleventh house—You're drawn to artistic people and organizations, or those celebrating "the good life"—epicureans, country clubs, wine-tasting groups. You are likely to earn considerable wealth from a career you find meaningful, making it possible you could leave a significant philanthropic legacy.

Gemini in the eleventh house—You seem to know everyone; you're a one-person social network. You're drawn to networking organizations or groups that help improve communication skills; within an organization you're a secretary or newsletter editor. Yours is a legacy of information.

Cancer in the eleventh house—You're especially drawn to organizations that are devoted to the causes of women, children, the hungry, and the homeless. Your friends are carefully chosen, because you hang on to them for life. Others feel you really understand them; empathy is your legacy.

Leo in the eleventh house—First among equals, you're a rock star among your friends and are drawn to organizations that celebrate creativity, artistic expression, children, and performance. You inspire others to explore their own creative side; creative expression is your legacy.

Virgo in the eleventh house—Passionately devoted to environmental causes, animal rights, and health (especially reproductive health), you're drawn to organizations that want to improve the health of the planet and all those who live on it. You'll offer any practical assistance you can to a cause you believe in; service is your legacy.

ASTRO TIP The eleventh house was traditionally called the "House of Friendship." However, your very closest friends are the purview of the seventh house. Eleventh house friends tend to run in packs—groups of people bound by common interests and circumstance, like your local astrology group or the gang of work friends who get together for Friday happy hour.

Libra in the eleventh house—You're adept at getting along with others and making friends, but you strongly feel that friendship is a two-way street and won't waste time with people who don't make an effort. You're more interested in one-on-one relationships than groups, but you are committed to social justice, human rights, and arts-related organizations. Yours is a legacy of harmony.

Scorpio in the eleventh house—You don't shy away from troubled people or difficult issues, and you're a loyal friend. You're drawn to organizations that help victims of sexual abuse or torture, and those that are connected to weapons, including guns and nuclear weaponry. Your willingness to confront taboos and expose horrors makes yours a legacy of truth telling.

Sagittarius in the eleventh house—Your friends reflect a wide range of backgrounds, beliefs, and cultures. You don't much care for groups, but you're vocal about education, religion, and cultural issues. You don't insist that your friends believe exactly as you do, so long as they believe strongly in something and their beliefs are based on a sound philosophy. Your legacy is one of understanding and tolerance.

Capricorn in the eleventh house—Your friends are often older or younger than you are, and intergenerational concerns figure prominently in your sense of community involvement. You're the elder of your tribe, the mother or father figure, and the keeper of the ethical flame. Your friends are those you work with and who share your cause, and your tireless work for your community is a legacy of achievement.

Aquarius in the eleventh house—Friends and organizations are vital to your sense of well-being. You like your autonomy, but you are happiest when you exercise your independence within a larger communal framework of family, friends, workplace, church, or career. You have strong opinions and are often part of the radical, polarizing edges of any group. Yours is a legacy of community.

Pisces in the eleventh house—Your enormous number of friends are drawn from your varied interests in music, dance, social causes, and spirituality. Your charm and ability to take others as they are makes you a beloved friend and a welcome addition to any group or organization. You are interested in peace and human rights, and your support of groups that advocate in these areas is your legacy of love.

Essential Takeaways

- The succedent houses are the second, fifth, eighth, and eleventh houses. They're associated with the fixed signs: Taurus, Leo, Scorpio, and Aquarius.
- The succedent houses represent areas of life in which resources are gathered and shared, and where you seek stability.
- The second house symbolizes where and how we gather personal resources.
- The fifth house symbolizes how we use those resources to create, including creating a new generation.
- The eighth house symbolizes how we merge our resources with a partner.
- The eleventh house symbolizes how we contribute our resources to the community and in service of future generations.

CHAPTER 11

Where You Dance: Cadent Houses

The cadent houses: third, sixth, ninth, and twelfth

Each cadent house is associated with one of the mutable signs

The third house: communication, siblings, neighbors, and short trips

The sixth house: work, health, habits, and service

The ninth house: higher education, knowledge, long journeys, and religion

The twelfth house: faith, the unconscious, confinement, and illness

To modern ears, "cadent" is an odd, archaic-sounding word. It's related to "cadence," or rhythm in dance or music; in music, a cadence is a progression of chords moving toward a resolution. These are houses of resolution, then, but even more interesting is the part about rhythm.

In the cadent houses, you learn to dance with life by attuning yourself to its rhythms. In the third house you master the rhythms of language; in the sixth, the rhythms of work and daily rituals; in the ninth, the rhythms of the workings of the universe; and in the twelfth, the rhythms of rest and release. In the cadent houses, you learn to handle the discord and tension that come just before release. You learn to adapt to new realities and to expand your effectiveness and consciousness. You learn to loosen your grip on structure and routine, in preparation for making changes. In the cadent houses, you learn to let yourself go—and ultimately, just to let go.

Third House: Dances with Words

The third house was traditionally called the "House of Communication." We often equate communication with speaking, and certainly the third house symbolizes the learning and mastery of written and spoken language. But communication is a two-way street, requiring a listener as well as a speaker. The third house is also about perception, the ability to listen, observe, and notice things.

The third house also symbolizes your siblings, neighbors, and early education. Your brothers and sisters taught you the talismanic power of words, of promises and proprietary claims, of nicknames and teasing. Identical twins are famous for developing secret languages no one else can understand, but if you spend 10 minutes with any pair of siblings who are reasonably close, you will quickly encounter an impenetrable fog of in-jokes and verbal shortcuts. Siblings teach us the skill of encoding and decoding messages, of understanding our world and making ourselves understood. Our interactions with siblings teach us how to argue and negotiate, how to twist the knife, how to tell a joke, and how far we can go without completely alienating someone.

By negotiating a role for ourselves among our siblings, we define ourselves. To a lesser extent this is also true of our neighbors, to whom we're also yoked by common turf, mutual interests, and subtle competition. Few of us would admit that we feel pressure to "keep up with the Joneses," but it's difficult not to compare your old jalopy and crabgrass-infested lawn to your neighbor's bright new sedan and expensive landscaping. We naturally compare ourselves to those whose circumstances closely resemble our own—just as we might compare ourselves with a brother or sister.

Rulerships and Key Concepts

The third house is associated with the Gemini, the third sign of the zodiac, and its ruling planet, Mercury. Like Gemini, the third house belongs to the mutable quality and the air element.

Key concepts of the third house: Communication, learning, memory, practical skills, siblings, neighbors, early education, short trips, land transportation

Signs

The third house shares a lot of territory with the sign of Gemini. It symbolizes your style of communication, relationship with neighbors and siblings, and ability to collect and share information. In your chart, the third house is also strongly influenced by the following:

- The sign on the cusp or signs contained within the third house

- Planets in the third house

- The sign and house placement of the planet that rules the sign on the third house cusp

Aries in the third house—You are a straight shooter, speaking directly, plainly, and sometimes impulsively. You think fast on your feet and are an able and incisive debater. Relationships with your siblings may be strained, with a lot of competition and arguments, and you may also find yourself at odds with your neighbors. You are probably well suited to a career in transportation or communication (such as journalism).

Taurus in the third house—You consider your words carefully before speaking, which can sometimes give the mistaken impression that you think slowly as well. You're a person of few words, with a calm manner and a mesmerizing speaking voice. Your relationships with your siblings are generally good, although there may be more than the usual squabbles about sharing, and your relationships with neighbors are slow to develop but generally cordial.

Gemini in the third house—You are one of the smartest people around, with a balanced intellect, the ability to listen as well as you speak, and the ability to figure out how to do almost anything. You're probably extremely close to at least one of your siblings, even if you don't necessarily agree on everything. You like to be on a first-name basis with your neighbors but generally avoid getting too close to them.

Cancer in the third house—You're extremely perceptive, very funny, and rather secretive, even with people you know well. You tend to be closely attached to your siblings, whether for good or for ill. You are either the social hub of your neighborhood, the lynchpin that draws everyone together, or else you jealously guard your privacy and rarely so much as make eye contact with your neighbors. You're extremely sensitive to noise and discord.

Leo in the third house—You're a dazzling communicator, artistically gifted, adept at writing and speaking but better at expressing than perception. Hopefully you and your siblings enjoy one another, but you probably compete strenuously for attention. You're warm and friendly with neighbors and are usually well known in your community.

Virgo in the third house—You're formidably intelligent and an excellent analyst; nothing escapes your notice. You're a little self-conscious about speaking in public, and your tendency to edit yourself while you're creating can make creative writing a challenge, but you're an excellent teacher or editor. You're protective of younger siblings but your relationships with older ones can be harshly critical. You like to be of help to your neighbors, but can grow irritable if they take advantage of your kindness.

Short Journeys Over Land

The opposite house from the ninth ("House of Long Journeys Over Water"), the third house represents short trips, particularly by land. It's the house of cars, trains, bicycles, motorcycles, skateboards, and buses. In contrast to the ninth house's academic bent, the third is the house of folklore and storytelling.

Libra in the third house—You have a naturally artistic temperament and a refined way of expressing yourself. You're a natural at negotiation, and your keen sense of public relations could be put to good use in your profession. You tend to have intense rivalries with your siblings, but to build strong friendships among your neighbors. You are likely to marry the boy or girl next door, or at least someone who shares a background very much like your own.

Scorpio in the third house—You fear others having the power to divine your thoughts, so you're secretive, sarcastic, and blunt. Your friends value your willingness to be completely—even brutally—honest; everyone else fears your sharp tongue. Relationships with your siblings are fiercely loyal or almost completely estranged, with no in-between. You often gravitate to "difficult" neighborhoods with many who are down on their luck; you like living in environments that are a little raw.

Sagittarius in the third house—Unlike Scorpio in the third, you have no secrets and are open and effusive. You're a lively speaker and teacher and are a natural at communicating through visual media such as film; you are more interested in conveying your knowledge and beliefs than gathering new information. You may hardly know your siblings, or feel you have little in common with them.

Capricorn in the third house—Like all the earth signs, you think before you speak. You prefer communication to serve a practical purpose, and may well make a career in communication. You can have a hard time being friendly in casual situations, and may find it hard to get close to your neighbors or, in your youth, to your classmates. You do best in situations where you're clearly a teacher/mentor or a student/protégé, and not a peer. You're often a surrogate parent to your siblings, or otherwise feel responsible for them.

Aquarius in the third house—No one knows what will come out of your mouth or your computer keyboard—you're an original thinker, and you like to shake people up and make them think when you speak or write. Your siblings are your best friends, and your best friends feel like siblings. You generally like your neighbors, and you like to settle in and stay in one place for a long time, so you generally get to know everybody.

Pisces in the third house—Imaginative and sensitive, you may seem otherworldly but you absorb everything around you and miss nothing. You are easily overwhelmed by talk and noise, probably a bit psychic, and need to retreat periodically to rest your nerves. Usually you get along fine with your siblings, even if you feel you don't have much in common; you probably maintain a bit of distance with your neighbors because you don't have the energy to get sucked into their dramas.

Sixth House: Meaningful Habits

The sixth house was traditionally called the "House of Servants." For those of us who don't have servants, it's associated with the routines that comprise most of our days—working, running errands, preparing meals—as well as the habits we form while repeating these routines. For the most part, we regard the boring minutia of daily life as necessary but dull, and entirely separate from the really important work of our careers and relationships. The domestic tasks associated with the sixth house are denigrated, and when possible, delegated.

But something is lost, I think, in our determination to avoid these humble occupations; the sixth house is also the house of ritual, the performance of activities for symbolic purposes. Both habit and ritual involve doing particular things at regular intervals in a particular way. What distinguishes them from one another? Intention, and consciousness. You can sweep the kitchen floor each evening and hardly notice doing it, beyond a vague desire to have it over with as quickly as possible. But imagine you instead treat the chore as a ritual, giving your full attention to sweeping the floor carefully and thoroughly, visualizing the debris and disorder of your mind being swept away with the breadcrumbs. Feel the difference?

Why make such a big deal out of sweeping a floor? Because life is a finite resource, and it's maddening to waste five minutes every day—more than 30 hours each year!—on an activity that is meaningless. And yet the floor needs to be swept—a consequence of inhabiting a body that walks on things, eats things, and spills crumbs. If you don't occasionally sweep up the debris, pretty soon it offends the senses and can even breed disease. So why not enjoy sweeping the floor, clearing it of life's thriving, lively messiness? Why not use those five minutes as a sort of practical prayer, to celebrate being alive?

Rulerships and Key Concepts

The sixth house is associated with Virgo, the sixth sign of the zodiac, and its ruler, Mercury. Like Virgo, the sixth house belongs to the mutable quality and the earth element.

Key concepts of the sixth house: Work, service, routines, health, adaptation, analysis, fixing problems

Signs

The sixth house shares a lot of territory with the sign of Virgo. In your chart, the sixth house is also strongly influenced by the following:

- The sign on the sixth house cusp and signs contained in the sixth house

- Planets in the sixth house

- The sign and house placement of the planet that rules the sign on the sixth house cusp

Aries in the sixth house—A natural leader in the workplace, you also thrive in work environments involving danger or risk (firefighter, EMT). Strenuous, competitive, solitary exercise is your key to good health; health problems are related to anger, frustration, or accidents, with the head and teeth being especially vulnerable.

Taurus in the sixth house—A steady and reliable worker, you're most comfortable with a leisurely pace and a regular work routine. You're drawn to the arts and to work involving personal finance. You hate strenuous workouts and sweat; your best health regimen involves a moderate diet combined with stretching and comfortable walks. You're generally healthy, but overindulgence and inactivity can lead to problems with your throat, thyroid, and neck.

Gemini in the sixth house—You need a work routine with variety and flexibility; solitude or too much sameness will drive you nuts. You're suited to work in communications, telecom, or transportation. Avoid overwork and especially stress, which can lead to health problems related to the nervous system, your lungs, and your shoulders and hands.

Cancer in the sixth house—You have a gift for creating a family atmosphere in the workplace, and are suited to work related to public advocacy, children, women's issues, or domestic issues (food, hunger, or shelter). Health problems commonly emerge in the stomach and breast areas and are due to internalizing emotional stress; swimming is an excellent workout for your mental and physical health.

Leo in the sixth house—You need to stand out at work, to be considered the best at what you do, and to have the respect of your colleagues. You're a steady and reliable worker, but you get temperamental if you're ignored or treated as an underling. You're well suited to careers with a performance aspect to them, such as teaching or training. Your heart and back are your vulnerable spots; yoga would be an excellent workout to relieve your stress and promote flexibility.

Virgo in the sixth house—You're a superb technician and craftsman, flexible and versatile and good at almost everything. You're at home in health care, science, teaching, or analytical jobs; above all, you need to feel that you're making a useful contribution and are encouraged to do quality work. You're vulnerable to digestive problems and need exercise that relieves stress, a careful diet, and plenty of rest and quiet.

ASTRO TIP

The sixth house is associated with jobs, the daily tasks that fill your days and hopefully earn your living, whereas careers are found in the tenth house. Ideally, you'll find a way to bring your sixth house job into alignment with your tenth house calling—but sometimes, of course, a sixth house job is necessary to pay the bills while you pursue your tenth house dream career.

Libra in the sixth house—Above all, you need a social work environment and the feeling of contributing to beauty, justice, and fairness. You're at home in the arts, human resources, public relations, marketing, or law, but you're happiest when you're in charge or working in an equal partnership. A balanced diet and emotional equilibrium are essential for your health; your vulnerable areas are your kidneys, lower back, and adrenal system.

Scorpio in the sixth house—You need a job that allows you to be in control of your own work and takes advantage of your ability to handle life-or-death situations, such as surgery, EMT, firefighter, or lifeguard. You're not terribly diplomatic in the workplace; health problems are aggravated by resentment, anger, and power struggles. A solitary form of exercise such as swimming can help you avoid problems with the reproductive organs, genitals, bladder, and rectum.

Sagittarius in the sixth house—You need to feel that your work has meaning; you're unhappy in a job that doesn't have a connection to what you consider your calling. Academia, science, publishing, and travel are also congenial work environments for you. Get exercise that increases flexibility, stretches muscles, and is done outdoors, such as horseback riding or hiking. Your vulnerable spots are your hips, thighs, and upper legs.

Capricorn in the sixth house—A resourceful and tireless worker, you're effective in any kind of business as long as you have the authority to make important decisions in your work. You're particularly well suited to banking, building, or government work. Your vulnerable areas are the joints and skin, so exercise should focus on encouraging flexibility, strengthening the muscles around your joints, and relieving stress (good for the skin).

Aquarius in the sixth house—A dependable and innovative worker, you need a regular routine and a convivial workplace. Your talents and temperament are suited to technology, nonprofit organizations, government work, and science (especially social science). Your ankles are vulnerable to injury, so get gentle, low-impact exercise such as bicycling that improves flexibility and coordination and strengthens muscles around joints.

Pisces in the sixth house—You're imaginative and have a talent for tapping into what the public wants, but you need an unstructured daily routine and work that feels meaningful. You might be drawn to social work, commercial art or advertising, or metaphysical practice (especially tarot). Your feet are your vulnerable area, so get low-impact exercise such as swimming and yoga.

Ninth House: What Do You Know?

The ninth house was traditionally known as the "House of Long Journeys Over Water." It represents long-distance travel, but the "water" of its traditional name is metaphorical as well. You also experience the ninth house in situations and interactions that are very different from the ones you grew up knowing, and any scenario—travel, education, religion—that stretches you to grow in a fuller understanding of the world. Whether you're boarding an international flight, eating Ethiopian food for the first time, or struggling to stay awake in a university lecture hall, you've entered ninth house territory.

I was born with many planets in this house of the chart; it's little wonder that I grew up to be the first in my family to graduate from college and that I married someone from another country. And from an early age, I had strong beliefs about the way the world worked. When I was small, my parents sent us to the tiny country church down the road from our house. I didn't enjoy it; in particular, I disliked the preacher who yelled at the congregation about hellfire and damnation until his face turned red. "Why, he doesn't even know me!" I remember thinking. "How does he know whether I'm going to hell?" One Sunday morning, in the middle of one of his tirades, I simply stood up and walked out. When I got home I announced in no uncertain terms that I would not be going back. I had my own ideas about salvation, and they didn't include getting yelled at.

The more emphasis on the ninth house of your chart, the more you care about *knowing*. Religion offers one way of knowing, science another; academia teaches us how to convert information into real knowledge. You may take any one of these paths, or all of them, or none. The ninth house of your chart describes your relationship to knowledge and believing. Is yours a pragmatic philosophy or an idealistic one? How driven are you to explore the farthest reaches of the world and of the ideas you grew up with?

Rulerships and Key Concepts

The ninth house is associated with Sagittarius, the ninth sign of the zodiac, and its ruler, Jupiter. Like Sagittarius, the ninth house belongs to the mutable quality and the fire element.

Key concepts of the ninth house: Higher education, overseas travel, teaching, religious occupations, foreigners, foreign languages

Signs

The ninth house shares a lot of territory with the sign of Sagittarius. It symbolizes your beliefs, education, knowledge, desire to travel, and experience of being an outsider. In your chart, the ninth house is also strongly influenced by the following:

- The sign on the ninth house cusp and signs contained in the ninth house

- Planets in the ninth house

- The sign and house placement of the planet that rules the sign on the ninth house cusp

Aries in the ninth house—You're a pioneer at heart and love foreign travel and people from different backgrounds. You believe in the need for survival and self-preservation, and that one of the best qualities a person can have is a fighting spirit.

Taurus in the ninth house—You're probably not completely wild about long-distance travel; it's too uncomfortable, and you're constantly having to change your routine and cope with unfamiliar things. Your philosophy of life tends to be gentle, nonconfrontational, and based in practical, everyday lessons.

Gemini in the ninth house—Language is the most daunting part of international travel for you. If you take long trips, you'll tend to enjoy short stays in many places rather than long stays in a couple of places. You probably find all religions pretty interesting but have a hard time completely embracing any one. You'll tend to favor either higher education related to information and communication, or done by correspondence or in a trade school.

Cancer in the ninth house—You believe in the importance of family and belonging, and that each of us has a responsibility to take care of others. You may make your home in a land far from the country of your birth.

Leo in the ninth house—You believe in the primacy of the individual, that each of us is unique and has something to say that's worth listening to. You're creatively inspired by other cultures, by travel, and by education and pride yourself on your ability to connect to people from other backgrounds.

 In the third house you gather information, in the sixth house you analyze the information, and in the ninth house you seek to understand the facts as you know them. But the ninth is a cadent house, so don't get too attached to what you know; in the twelfth house you let go of rational understanding and enter the realm of faith.

Virgo in the ninth house—You believe in the importance of service. Any religion you're drawn to will emphasize service and helping, and the betterment of oneself.

Libra in the ninth house—You believe in fairness, that each of us must pull our weight and put as much into life as take from it. You may find yourself connected to foreign lands or new religious traditions through marriage or other partnerships.

Scorpio in the ninth house—You believe in honesty, loyalty, and the importance of seeing things as they truly are. Experiences of death or trauma directly influence your beliefs and are an important component of them. You keep your beliefs close to your vest and can converse about religion or politics without revealing your own thoughts.

Sagittarius in the ninth house—You're convinced that you've got the world figured out and that your beliefs are the right ones. You have strong feelings about religion—either devout or agnostic. You believe in taking a scholarly approach to beliefs. You tend to be very vocal, even occasionally preachy, about your beliefs.

Capricorn in the ninth house—You believe in individual responsibility, and for you "the buck stops here." If you are religious, you will probably rise to a position of leadership and authority in your church. Your career is likely related to ninth house matters such as publishing, travel, academia, or religion.

Aquarius in the ninth house—You believe in personal liberty and individual freedom, yet are likely to be associated with food co-ops, unions, or other collectives. You're given to radical beliefs and a strong rebellion against the beliefs you grew up with or that are imposed upon you.

Pisces in the ninth house—You believe in kindness and helping others. You're unlikely to be strongly attached to a particular religion, likely considering yourself more spiritual than religious. You are likely to spend time abroad and are likely interested in working for human rights or other groups in helping the underdeveloped world.

Twelfth House: Letting Go

The twelfth house was traditionally known as the "House of Troubles." The astrology books of an earlier era generally had hard words for the twelfth house. It was the house of confinement, imprisonment, illness, even insanity—the house of hidden enemies and self-undoing.

There's no doubt that prisoners, invalids, and monks are still among us and are certainly a feature of the twelfth house landscape. But relatively few of us will spend significant time behind bars, laid up in a sick bed, or devoted to prayerful solitude. What's the twelfth house mean for us?

You know, being a little bit sick can be a good thing. When you're a bit too ill to go to school or work, but not too ill to enjoy a movie on cable or a good book, illness can be a way of getting time out from your usual routines. Like a vacation, but without the expense or the onus of having to visit every notable attraction within a 50-mile radius, having a bad head cold may be one of our few opportunities to take a time out.

The twelfth is a house of rest, reflection, and letting go. Modern times are hectic, and it's hard to carve out time to devote to these tasks. It's no wonder many of us struggle to get a good night's sleep, to understand what's in our heads and hearts, and to let go of the hurts, slights, and torments that undermine our happiness. Signs or planets (see Part 4) associated with the twelfth house indicate where and how you find refuge, and the work you need to accomplish through rest and retreat.

Rulerships and Key Concepts

The twelfth house is associated with Pisces, the twelfth sign of the zodiac, and its rulers, Neptune (modern) and Jupiter (traditional). Like Pisces, the twelfth house belongs to the mutable quality and the water element.

Key concepts of the twelfth house: Faith, the unconscious, rest, reflection, illness, confinement

Signs

The twelfth house shares similar territory with the sign of Pisces. In your chart, the twelfth house is also strongly influenced by the following:

- The sign on the twelfth house cusp and signs contained in the twelfth house

- Planets in the twelfth house

- The sign and house placement of the planet that rules the sign on the twelfth house cusp

Aries in the twelfth house—It's not easy for you to relax. If you have Taurus on the first house cusp, others rarely suspect just how much anger and competition lies beneath your placid exterior. Getting strenuous exercise is a good way for you to relax and let go of your anger and your need to be first.

Taurus in the twelfth house—You're pretty good at relaxing, enjoying spalike indulgence, great food and drink, and pampering. You're willing to spend significant money on luxury items and getaways, but especially if you have Gemini in the first house, few would suspect that you have a materialistic, even hedonistic side. It's hard for you to admit to your craving for *things.* Focusing on the enjoyments of the natural world is a good way for you to relax.

Gemini in the twelfth house—Resting is not easy for you because you have a hard time turning off your brain. You relax through writing, reading, and learning, but if caring Cancer is in your first house, others will little suspect your cerebral and restless side. It's hard for you to let go of your need to maintain free agent status and to explore an endless variety of interests.

Cancer in the twelfth house—You keep your private thoughts to yourself and consider time spent with your family to be sacred. If you have outgoing Leo in the first house, others would be amazed to find out just how vulnerable and easily hurt you are. It's hard for you to let go of your need for safety and nurturing.

Leo in the twelfth house—Time spent alone is vital to your physical and creative vitality. If you have modest Virgo rising, few realize your need for recognition and how hurt you can be if you're overlooked.

Virgo in the twelfth house—You never relax, probably don't sleep well, and are quite susceptible to stress-related illness. Gentle exercise such as walking or yoga, and meditation or prayer, are extremely beneficial for you. If you have upbeat Libra in the first house, few suspect just how hard you work to make everything look so easy, and how critical you can be of yourself as well as others.

ASTRO ALERT The twelfth house symbolizes the ability to surrender, to admit when you are exhausted or discouraged and need help. Trying to be strong all the time can lead to illness, disruptions in sleep, and even phobias. No one likes to admit they're feeling overwhelmed by troubles, but it's better than ending up in the hospital, jail, or an asylum (all associated with the twelfth house!).

Libra in the twelfth house—You relax by spending time with your partner or through music and art. If you have intense, protective Scorpio rising, few realize just how much you want to be liked. It's very hard for you to give up the "disease to please," and to let go of the desire to avoid unpleasantness and conflict at almost any cost.

Scorpio in the twelfth house—You relax by retreating into your fertile imagination and spending time alone. If you have a happy-go-lucky Sagittarius Ascendant, people would be shocked to know how dark your view of the world can be, and how tenaciously you hold on to a grudge. It's extremely hard for you to let bygones be bygones, and to let go of your need to constantly be in control.

Sagittarius in the twelfth house—You relax best when you're outdoors, especially in a beautiful and preferably unfamiliar place. If you have conservative Capricorn in the first house, few suspect that you can be funny and that you always feel a little bit like an outsider. It's very hard for you to admit you're wrong about anything, or to change your point of view even in the face of indisputable evidence.

Capricorn in the twelfth house—Like Virgo in the twelfth, you never relax, but you're made of iron and rarely let infirmity slow you down. If you have friendly Aquarius rising, few suspect that you're tough as nails and extremely ambitious; it's hard for you to let go of a plan, even if it's clearly not working out.

Aquarius in the twelfth house—You relax by connecting with like-minded souls—your fellow "inmates." You're the stereotypical geek living in your mother's basement and chatting in Internet forums. If you have loving, accepting Pisces rising, others would be amazed by how opinionated you can be and how easily you can detach from others.

Pisces in the twelfth house—You escape through sleep, and sometimes drugs, alcohol, food, or other addictions. If you have feisty Aries rising, others would be stunned to learn just how sensitive you are. You find your concern for others so overwhelming that you look for any way to escape from it. It's hard for you to develop appropriate boundaries while still remaining emotionally open to your loved ones.

Essential Takeaways

- The cadent houses are the third, sixth, ninth, and twelfth houses. They're associated with the mutable signs: Gemini, Virgo, Sagittarius, and Pisces.
- The cadent houses represent areas of life in which information and skills are gathered and synthesized into knowledge and beliefs.
- The third house is where you master language and remedial skills.
- The sixth house is where you turn these skills into gainful employment.
- The ninth house is where you develop a broader understanding of the world.
- The twelfth house is where you rest, reflect, and cultivate faith.

PART 4

Gods and Monsters: Planets

───────

Named for figures from mythology, the planets of our solar system dazzled our ancestors as they strutted across the sky's stage. Planets move through the signs of the zodiac at varying speeds, changing costumes (signs) and sets (the houses of your chart) along the way, improvising dialogue (aspects) as their proximity to one another changes. Watching the planets moving across the sky was the closest thing our ancestors had to television. Ancient sky watchers invented stories based on what they observed when particular planets were prominent in the sky. Sometimes the planets behaved well, like gods; other times they were mischievous, angry, or immoral, like monsters. Sometimes their dialogue was tender, sometimes rough. After all this time, human nature hasn't changed, and neither has the sky; and the stories our ancestors told about the planets are timeless.

These gods of love, war, money, and learning represent your personal mythology as well. If life were a play, the planets would be its players. In this part, you'll meet the planetary players of your chart, and learn what their sign and house placement say about you. Are they gods or monsters? That's up to you.

CHAPTER 12

Your Intimate Circle: Personal Planets

The Sun, symbol of the sense of self that holds your inner "universe" together

The Moon, symbol of nurturing and protective influences

Mercury, symbol of how you think and express yourself

Venus, symbol of what gives you pleasure

The Sun, Moon, Mercury, and Venus are often called the "personal planets." Because they move through the zodiac relatively quickly, their placements differ more from day to day than those of their more ponderous planetary brethren.

They're planets of subjectivity, symbolizing your essential character—your identity, security and instincts, thought processes, and pleasures.

Your Inner Superstar: The Sun ☉

"I'm not myself today," you might tell a friend when you've just behaved in an uncharacteristic way. Snappish when you're normally calm, hasty when you're ordinarily careful; whether you're under stress or just didn't get a good night's sleep, feeling like you're "not yourself" can be disorienting.

But what does it mean to be "yourself"? In astrology, the Sun symbolizes identity—what makes you *you*. The symbol for the Sun—a tiny speck surrounded by a circle—is a bit like the bull's-eye of a target, with the astrological Sun describing both the goals that you're aiming for and how you must develop yourself as an individual in order to reach that target.

The Sun also symbolizes confidence, and those situations and pursuits that, when you're "not yourself," help restore your feeling that the world makes sense again. Each of us begins life as a tiny, nearly invisible speck; surrounds ourself with empty, insulating space; and then builds a solid circle around it all, a boundary to safely contain our fearsome smallness.

The Sun rules the sign of Leo, and is said to be exalted, or especially strong, in the sign of Aries. Its themes of identity and self-expression are a more challenging fit for the signs of Aquarius (detriment), which feels most itself in a group; and Libra (fall), which is most at home in a partnership.

Essential dignities are a system of evaluating the essential strengths of a planet based on its sign or degree. A planet is considered most strong in the signs of its rulership or exaltation, which are the signs whose symbolism is essentially compatible with the planet's objectives. A planet is considered least strong in the signs of its detriment (the sign opposite its rulership) and fall (the sign opposite its exaltation); these are signs whose symbolism is essentially at odds with the planet's purpose.

Sun Fast Facts

- Key concepts—Self, life goals, ego, charisma
- Cycle—Takes one year to complete a cycle of the zodiac
- Rules—Leo
- Exalted—Aries
- Detriment—Aquarius
- Fall—Libra
- Glyph—Circle of infinity
- Anatomy—Heart, upper back, spleen, circulatory system, sperm, right eye (male), left eye (female)

The God: Our Hero

In school, at work, or in your social circle, there are one or two people who stand out. They may not be the best-looking people you know, or the best at what they do. Yet they have an indefinable something—charisma, a magnetism as strong as Earth's gravitational attraction to the Sun. They know who they are and who they aren't, and don't feel they have much to prove to anyone else. Others follow them around like a rock star's groupies, basking in reflected glory and hoping for a morsel of personal attention from their hero.

In drama, such people are the heroes of the story, the magnetic protagonists who drive the narrative. And in the story of your life, you are the hero. The Sun in your birth chart indicates the personal style and settings that define your charisma and magnetism. Whenever someone looks up to you, copies what you do or say or how you dress, or lobbies hard for your attention, they're responding to the Sun in you. And when you walk through the world with your head held high, feeling pretty good about yourself, and perhaps with a little strut in your step, you're responding to your sunny side, too.

The Monster: The Zero

Some are born with a natural ability to celebrate the Sun's energy in their lives. Their dispositions are "sunny," open, and welcoming. But many of us are raised to think that calling attention to ourselves is selfish and unattractive. Where my husband comes from, they call this the "Tall Poppy Syndrome." Sometimes when people feel frustrated in their own lives, they try to "chop down" anyone else who succeeds in standing out from the crowd (the "tall poppy"). If you spent your life among smaller poppies, it might have been difficult for you to develop and embrace "solar" energy in your life—the universal human need for recognition and self-expression.

Nearly every day, I'll bet you encounter someone whose ego is undernourished, frantically lobbying for validation. It may be a tedious party guest who dominates the conversation with talk of himself, who seems, at first glance, to be pretty self-infatuated. But, of course, anyone who has to work that hard to convince you that he's impressive is probably not too sure of himself. And anyone who is jealous of another's success, or has a hard time giving others their due, is probably fairly insecure.

When you find yourself trying too hard to be noticed, showing off and putting on airs, you're a quart low on Sun energy. Understanding the Sun in your chart can help you understand what you can do to feel truly good about yourself—and to cultivate magnetism and an infectious joy for living.

The Sun in Signs and Houses

The Sun's sign in your chart describes the outward style of your inner hero. Does he or she look more like Superman, Gandhi, or Joan of Arc? The Sun's house placement pinpoints the areas of life in which you naturally shine (fighting crime, championing human rights, leading others in battle). This section blends the meanings of the Sun's sign and house placements into 12 parts instead of 24, since the themes of certain signs and houses are similar.

 Be sure to read both paragraphs that pertain to the Sun's sign and house placement in your birth chart. And remember that aspects between your Sun and other planets in your chart can also affect the way you experience your inner hero.

Sun in Aries/first house—*The hero:* You feel most "yourself," and are most charismatic, when you're doing something new and going after what you want. *The zero:* When you find yourself taking foolish risks and picking fights, it may be a sign that you are avoiding going after something that's truly important to you.

Sun in Taurus/second house—*The hero:* The Sun shines brightest in you when you're enjoying the pleasures of the material world and creating an atmosphere of stability and security. *The zero:* Boasting that your possessions are "the best" and that your way of doing things is the only "right" way are signs that you feel insecure or disrespected.

Sun in Gemini/third house—*The hero:* You're at your most magnetic when you're telling stories and sharing ideas and information. *The zero:* If you find yourself talking too much, listening too little, or engaging in destructive gossip, it's a sign you're not feeding your mind with enough variety and stimulation.

Sun in Cancer/fourth house—*The hero:* You feel most creative and confident when you're creating a nest of comfort and nurturing for yourself and others. *The zero:* When you find yourself clinging to what's familiar or feeling that others are taking advantage of you, it's probably time for you to step back and move your own priorities to the top of the list for a while.

Sun in Leo/fifth house—*The hero:* You're a charismatic powerhouse when you're expressing yourself through art or by lighting up a party with your joyful sense of play. *The zero:* When you feel ignored or ordinary, you can become a classic show-off, determined to grab the spotlight at any cost. That's a sign that you need rest and relaxation to fuel your true creativity.

Sun in Virgo/sixth house—*The hero:* You're irresistible when you're making the world more manageable; it's fun to watch you at work, doing something you love. *The zero:* When you feel unappreciated or woefully imperfect, you can become cranky and caustic; that's when it's time to work on something out of love, rather than just to be helpful.

If you don't identify with your Sun sign, it could be that there are other factors in your birth chart that contradict its symbolism. But it could also be that you haven't yet "grown in" to your Sun sign. After all, the Sun symbolizes something we reach for, and we're not necessarily born knowing how to make the most of its gifts!

Sun in Libra/seventh house—*The hero:* When the Sun's energy is strong in you, you're charming, pleasant, and have a gift for making others feel you're just delighted to see them walk through the door. *The zero:* When you lose sight of what makes you unique and wonderful, you can let yourself get pushed around; that's when it's time to stand up for yourself, in your own charming way.

Sun in Scorpio/eighth house—*The hero:* Your charisma is based in your emotional strength; others feel they can trust you with their deepest secrets. *The zero:* If you find yourself feeling overburdened or betrayed, you can be caustic and manipulative; let go of what isn't serving you rather than scattering your energies in revenge or bitterness.

Sun in Sagittarius/ninth house—*The hero:* You're most "yourself" when you're sharing your knowledge and embarking on adventures, and others are drawn to your vision and optimism. *The zero:* If you find yourself giving unsolicited advice, feeling hemmed in, or lacking inspiration, it's time to dream new dreams, get out of your comfort zone, and think bigger for yourself.

Sun in Capricorn/tenth house—*The hero:* Your no-nonsense pragmatism and insistence on excellence are the keys to your charisma; others want to please you and to live up to your example. *The zero:* If you find that you're neglecting your loved ones in pursuit of worldly goals, it's time to remember the emotional ties that motivate all worthwhile goals.

Sun in Aquarius/eleventh house—*The hero:* You have a gift for making other people feel that they belong; you're the social glue that holds your community together. *The zero:* When you begin to feel overcommitted or that you have no time for yourself, you can become rebellious and erratic. That's when it's time to take a hard look at your social commitments and pare them down to just the ones that really mean something to you.

Sun in Pisces/twelfth house—*The hero:* You're at your most charismatic when you're living in the moment and helping others have fun or feel better, through art, music, comedy, or spiritual pursuits. *The zero:* If you let yourself become overwhelmed by other people, you can become unreliable and physically ill; it's essential that you develop strong boundaries and to recognize when you need down time to recharge your batteries.

Your Inner Mom: The Moon ☽

Every mother knows that no matter how good a job she does of protecting her young, the day will eventually come when the offspring leaves the nest and her care. That's why mothers spend the first part of our lives keeping us safe—and most importantly, teaching us how to keep ourselves safe.

The Moon in your chart represents Mom: her story, her personality, her history, and your relationship with her. But it also symbolizes your inner Mom, the one that was installed in your psyche during your formative years. It symbolizes the ways you protect yourself, comfort yourself, and how you take care of others based on how you were cared for. It symbolizes the way you like to live, your nesting instinct, and how connected you feel to your family and the place where you grew up. In the story of your life, the Moon is the matriarch, holding together home and hearth and tending emotional needs, while the patriarch hunts wildebeests and farms the land.

The Moon is symbolically connected to the sign of Cancer, and informs that sign's domesticity and protective instincts. It's also associated with the fourth house of the chart, and shares that house's symbolism of history, family, and sense of place. The Moon is exalted, or especially strong, in the sign of Taurus, which lends stability to the Moon's fluctuations and moods. It's in its detriment in Capricorn, a sign whose worldliness is at odds with the Moon's domestic nature. And the Moon is in its fall in Scorpio, where it can symbolize suspicion and mistrust.

MISC.

Moon Fast Facts

- Key concepts—Comfort, nurturing security, home, family
- Cycle—Takes 28 days to complete a cycle of the zodiac
- Rules—Cancer
- Exalted—Taurus
- Detriment—Capricorn
- Fall—Scorpio
- Glyph—First quarter Moon
- Anatomy—Stomach, breasts, digestion, fluids and glandular secretions, left eye (male), right eye (female)

The Goddess: Good Mom

The 1950s were the golden age of television mothers, epitomized by *Leave It to Beaver*'s June Cleaver, the quintessential "good mom". Nurturing, supportive, protective, and kind, June maintained an impeccable home, greeted her sons after school with a plate of warm cookies, and prepared sumptuous meals for Beaver, Wally, and their dad, Ward—all while wearing fetching housedresses, pearls, and pumps.

June Cleaver is an unreasonable role model for any mortal woman. But the archetype of a woman who is completely loving and devoted to you alone is a compelling one. After all, there was a time, living in your mother's womb, that you were completely safe and the object of her entire care; it's a state to which part of you longs to return, no matter how old you are. The Moon in your chart describes your inner caretaker—the things you do to comfort, nurture, and protect yourself, just as any good mother would do.

The Monster: Bad Mom

Like the old saying goes, "No one can push your buttons quite like your mother can. After all, she installed them." A mom who doesn't know when to back off, to take off the training wheels and let you ride your bike alone, can feel smothering. And a woman who resents the constraints of motherhood can pass that resentment on to her children.

When your lunar processes run off course, you can become clingy with those you love, over-protective, and a slave to your fears and to your unconscious. Or you may find yourself growing resentful and short-tempered with those who look to you for nurturing and comfort. Taken to extremes, lunar energy run amok becomes Joan Crawford in *Mommie Dearest,* the ultimate "bad mom." These are signs that you need to be a good mom to yourself and help give yourself the healthy emotional support we all need. The sign and house of the Moon in your chart describe the things you should do to make yourself feel better; astrological chicken soup for the soul, if you will.

ASTRO TIP

A Mom Never Forgets
Ever wonder why your mom never, ever forgets the rotten things you did when you were a kid? It's simple: the Moon is the astrological symbol that's associated with both mothers and memory.

The Moon in Signs and Houses

The Moon's sign in your chart describes the outward style of your inner mom. Does she resemble June Cleaver, Roseanne, or Joan Crawford? The Moon's house placement symbolizes the areas of life in which you seek and offer nurturing and emotional connection.

This section blends the meanings of the Moon's sign and house placements into 12 parts instead of 24, since the themes of certain signs and houses are similar.

 ASTRO TIP Be sure to read both paragraphs that pertain to the Moon's sign and house placement in your birth chart. And remember that aspects between the Moon and other planets can also influence the qualities of your inner mom.

Moon in Aries/first house—*Good mom:* A feisty pioneer woman who crossed the continent in a covered wagon and kept a rifle under the buckboard. *Bad mom:* Emotionally volatile and impulsive. *Nurturing yourself:* Strenuous physical activity, tackling challenges, and developing assertiveness.

Moon in Taurus/second house—*Good mom:* A practical, calming Depression Era mom, able to provide necessities and make any situation work, no matter how grim. *Bad mom:* Rigid and narrow-minded. *Nurturing yourself:* Emotionally stable, you rarely give in to blue moods. But working outdoors, indulging in creature comforts, and building collections are sources of comfort.

Moon in Gemini/third house—*Good mom:* A multitasker, talking on the phone while updating her Facebook page and catching up on her favorite TV shows. *Bad mom:* Nervous, distracted, caustic. *Nurturing yourself:* Your moods pass quickly; you can shake them off by writing, reading, or having a chat with someone.

Moon in Cancer/fourth house—*Good mom:* A domestic goddess, hanging laundry with a baby on her hip. *Bad mom:* Manipulative, clingy, passive-aggressive. *Nurturing yourself:* Gather for a meal with loved ones. Put your house in order.

Moon in Leo/fifth house—*Good mom:* Playful, creative, and glamorous. *Bad mom:* Self-absorbed, melodramatic, domineering. *Nurturing yourself:* Do something creative, watch a movie or play, or dress to the nines and hit the town.

Moon in Virgo/sixth house—*Good mom:* A tranquil, frugal, working mom who makes self-sufficiency and problem solving look easy. *Bad mom:* Critical, nagging, nervous. *Nurturing yourself:* Do one small, useful thing: balance your checkbook, clean a drawer, or change the oil in your car.

Moon in Libra/seventh house—*Good mom:* Pleasant, polite, and fair. *Bad mom:* Vain, false, indecisive. *Nurturing yourself:* Spend time with your partner; create or enjoy art or music; offer grooming services.

Moon in Scorpio/eighth house—*Good mom:* Magical, honest, and impossible to fool. *Bad mom:* Jealous, suspicious, vengeful. *Nurturing yourself:* Renovate or transform something; throw out unneeded stuff; get therapy or counseling.

Moon in Sagittarius/ninth house—*Good mom:* Good-humored and adventurous. *Bad mom:* Inflexible; thinking your way is the only way. *Nurturing yourself:* Laugh. Get some exercise outdoors. Read, teach, travel, or just try something new.

Moon in Capricorn/tenth house—*Good mom:* High standards and emotional maturity and restraint. *Bad mom:* Very tough on yourself when you fall short of your own standards. *Nurturing yourself:* Make lists of goals; busy yourself with a practical, constructive task with tangible results.

Moon in Aquarius/eleventh house—*Good mom:* Friendly, sociable, spontaneous. *Bad mom:* Unpredictable, distant, eccentric. *Nurturing yourself:* Gather some friends together for a group activity; tinker with gadgetry; watch TV, or create a short film on your computer.

Moon in Pisces/twelfth house—*Good mom:* Intuitive, empathetic, and lives in the moment. *Bad mom:* Poor boundaries; emotionally overwhelmed; in denial. *Nurturing yourself:* Go swimming, sit on the beach, meditate, take a nap, lose yourself in a book or movie.

Your Inner Sidekick: Mercury ☿

Excited about her latest crush, a fifth-grader urges her friend Becky to do reconnaissance. "Go and find out if he likes me! Tell him I like him!" Becky scurries away, delivers the message, and soon returns with news of requited affection. After a couple more rounds, a summit has been arranged in which the young lovers will meet to plight their troth. Satisfied with a morning's work well done, Becky flits away to report on every detail of her activities to a cluster of interested classmates.

She probably has no idea, but Becky is working for Mercury. The god of communication was in charge of moving information around amongst the other gods; according to some legends, he even transported the dead to the front door of the afterlife. Mercury symbolizes your desire and aptitude for gathering information, getting the message out, and bringing people together. Since Mercury never orbits farther than about 28 degrees from the Sun, I like to think of him as the press agent for your inner superstar, able to broadcast news of your latest adventures, organize interviews with the press, and schedule meetings with influential people.

Mercury is most comfortable in the signs of Gemini, Virgo (rulership), and Aquarius (exaltation). He has a more difficult job expressing himself in Sagittarius and Pisces (detriment), which prefer to focus on the big picture rather than the details and trivia that delight Mercury, and Leo (fall), in which Mercury's perceptions tend to be overly subjective (it won't do for the press agent to believe his own hype).

Mercury Fast Facts

- Key concepts—Perception, communication, skill
- Cycle—Takes 88 days to complete a cycle of the zodiac
- Rules—Gemini, Virgo
- Exalted—Aquarius
- Detriment—Sagittarius, Pisces
- Fall—Leo
- Glyph—The god Mercury's winged cap
- Anatomy—Hands and arms, respiratory system, hormones, nervous system, brain, eyes, mouth, tongue

The God: The Sidekick

If only life were like the movies (an idea I heartily endorse), each of us would be assigned our own sidekick. A sidekick is a secondary character—usually the lead character's slightly less attractive but witty best friend—who provides comic relief, helps move the story along with a well-timed word in the lead's ear, and is the only one who can tell the protagonist that he or she is about to make a big mistake. In some stories, the sidekick is a wacky scene stealer; in others, the straight man for the brilliant protagonist, a sort of Dr. Watson to the Sun's Sherlock Holmes.

The Sun in your chart symbolizes your inner superstar, but Mercury describes your inner sidekick. When a situation calls for you to toot your own horn, do you sound like a wise-cracking secretary, a self-effacing best friend, or a patient sounding board?

The Monster: The Mouthpiece

A traitor who reveals state secrets, the neighborhood gossip, or a friend who spreads rumors behind your back are all examples of "Monster" Mercury at work. When Mercury's cleverness and resourcefulness are used for ill, the result can be dishonesty, unreliability, and indiscretion.

What's the motivation for lying, deceit, and double-crossing? Remember that Mercury always serves the Sun; so when Mercury is up to no good, it's because the ego—the

Sun—has malfunctioned. Trading in sensitive information can make you feel important and bolster a wounded ego, but it can damage your credibility in the long run. When your inner hero has turned into a villain, Mercury ceases to function as comic relief and becomes a hapless henchman.

 ASTRO ALERT Planets or signs in the third house of your chart can strongly influence your style of thinking and communicating. Mercury in Libra combined with Aries or Mars in the third house, for instance, can mask Aries/Mars's iron fist in Libra's velvet glove.

Mercury in Signs and Houses

Mercury's sign in your chart describes the outward style of your inner sidekick—is your Mercury the zany best friend, the partner in crime, or the court jester? Mercury's house placement symbolizes the areas of life that you find especially interesting, and where you find it easy to gather and share information.

This section blends the meanings of Mercury's sign and house placements into 12 parts instead of 24, since the themes of certain signs and houses are similar.

 ASTRO TIP Be sure to read both paragraphs that pertain to Mercury's sign and house placement in your birth chart. And remember that aspects between Mercury and other planets can also influence the qualities of your inner sidekick.

Mercury in Aries/first house—*The sidekick:* You're the hot-headed sidekick with the itchy trigger finger, ready to defend the hero with impulsive words and a vocabulary that would make a sailor blush. *The mouthpiece:* You think fast, but not always wisely, and words are some of your sharpest weapons. Remember the old adage: measure twice, cut once!

Mercury in Taurus/second house—*The sidekick:* You're the laconic, patient sidekick who is just plain comfortable to be around. You don't say much, but what you do say is worth listening to (and often said in a beautiful voice); you don't believe in talking when your actions—or gifts—can speak more eloquently. *The mouthpiece:* You're not much of a talker, so you're not much good at promoting the hero—or yourself. It takes you so long to get to the point that you often forget what you were trying to say.

Mercury in Gemini/third house—*The sidekick:* Witty and wisecracking, you're the classic fast-talking, fast-moving sidekick. You have the gift of gab, hatch ingenious schemes, and can think and talk circles around almost anyone. *The mouthpiece:* The wit that some people find delightful is profoundly annoying to others. Slow down and take a breath once in a while!

Mercury in Cancer/fourth house—*The sidekick:* Tender-hearted, sensitive, and fiercely loyal, you're the Melanie Wilkes (*Gone With the Wind*) of sidekicks. Shy, retiring, and primly old-fashioned, you smile timidly, blush easily, and seem altogether harmless—until your inner superhero is threatened, and then your tongue grows claws. *The mouthpiece:* Sometimes you overthink your emotions; other times you get so emotional that you can't think or talk clearly.

Mercury in Leo/fifth house—*The sidekick:* You're the crowd-pleasing sidekick who steals the show—you're just so colorful and charismatic! Every time you open your mouth it's like that old E.F. Hutton commercial: everyone around you stops to listen, because you're a dazzling storyteller. *The mouthpiece:* Do you ever stop talking about yourself? Self-promotion is all good and well, but give others a chance to discover your charms for themselves!

Mercury in Virgo/sixth house—*The sidekick:* You're M*A*S*H's Radar O'Reilly, so attuned to the needs of others that you know what they need before they do. This is one of Mercury's strongest signs, and you're smarter and more capable than most—including your inner superhero, who knows it (and hopefully values you for it). *The mouthpiece:* You overanalyze, nit-pick, and offer criticism when it wasn't asked for. Now and then, go ahead and throw some money down on the table without calculating the tip to the last penny.

Mercury in Libra/seventh house—*The sidekick:* You're the smooth, sweet-talking sidekick who distracts the bad guys while the superhero is doing something sneaky in the background. Like Mercury in Taurus, you have a way of talking that others find enchanting, so much so that they hardly notice what you're saying. *The mouthpiece:* You make it impossible for people to know where you stand on a matter, can be maddeningly indecisive, and often give too much ground in an argument.

Mercury in Scorpio/eighth house—*The sidekick:* You are the quietly strong, intensely loyal sidekick who speaks softly but carries a mighty big stick (with nails in it). *The mouthpiece:* No one messes with you; you're incredibly perceptive about people's sensitive spots and, when crossed, you don't hesitate to call attention to them. You're not always nice, but you are an effective mouthpiece.

Mercury in Sagittarius/ninth house—*The sidekick:* You're the fun-loving, clownish cowboy sidekick, taking comical pratfalls and generally yucking it up. Which makes it all the more surprising when you pipe up with some philosophical word of wisdom. Mercury's not at his best here, but you do have a way of endearing others to you with the naïve wisdom of your words. *The mouthpiece:* You're notoriously gaffe-prone, sticking your foot in your mouth, telling secrets out of school, and being so cheerfully blunt that people want to murder you.

Mercury in Capricorn/tenth house—*The sidekick:* You're the stoic, glowering henchman in the pinstripe suit who pays off prospective suitors of poor rank. Highly strategic and a pragmatist, you're an asset to any superhero. *The mouthpiece:* It can be disturbingly easy for you to excise all human emotion from your decisions, and to lock up enemies below deck while your inner superhero takes over the ship.

Mercury in Aquarius/eleventh house—*The sidekick:* You're the crazy inventor/professor, not unlike Doc Brown in the *Back to the Future* movies. You're an innovative thinker, so much so that people often think you're a little bit bonkers. *The mouthpiece:* You're *extremely* opinionated, and you are probably a little bit bonkers. It's not a great combination.

Mercury in Pisces/twelfth house—*The sidekick:* You're either a ghostly sidekick or the sweet, harmless girl or boy next door. Exceptionally empathetic, you have a genius for speaking to others on their level, using their language; you get on their wavelength and voice their thoughts. You don't always think or speak in a straight line, but nevertheless your insights often save the day. *The mouthpiece:* You speak in endless circles about your mantra, your guru, and your poetry. Sometimes, you burst into song. This is no way to get your inner superhero taken seriously.

Your Inner Consort: Venus ♀

What makes you feel good? What kinds of people do you find attractive? Why do you collect the things you do—ticket stubs, marbles, glass figurines, stocks and bonds? What's your relationship with money?

Venus, the traditional planet of money and relationships, is best thought of as the planet of pleasure. Venus in your chart describes what you truly enjoy, what you find attractive, what you are willing to spend money on, and how you adorn, treat, and pamper yourself.

Venus is also considered the relationship planet, though that's a bit simplistic. Really, every planet is a relationship planet; but Venus symbolizes the pleasure and affection of relationships, the factor and attraction that draws us in. Even someone who married for money is marrying for Venus, since Venus is also the goddess of money.

Venus is happiest in the signs of her rulership, Taurus and Libra, where she feels prosperous and pretty, and loving Pisces, the sign of her exaltation. She has a harder time expressing beauty and harmony in the tough-edged signs of Scorpio and Aries (detriment) and in analytical Virgo (fall).

Venus Fast Facts

- Key concepts—Desires, values, finances, partners
- Cycle—Takes 224 1/2 days to complete a cycle of the zodiac
- Rules—Taurus, Libra
- Exalted—Pisces
- Detriment—Aries, Scorpio
- Fall—Virgo
- Glyph—Venus's mirror
- Anatomy—Throat, cheeks, sense of taste, kidneys, ovaries, internal reproductive organs, venous blood circulation, skin's sensory organs

The Goddess: Beauty

Venus-filled people have a gift of making others feel good. It may be physical beauty and grace, artistic talent, or simply an honestly affectionate and happy nature that makes them so popular. But usually, it's the fact that they demonstrate an honest interest in you. They ask questions about you, and actually listen to your reply without jumping in with stories of their own. They laugh at your jokes, and the laughter is sincere. They say nice things about other people behind their backs. They're gracious in the face of compliments or praise of their own virtues. And yet they also give the impression—by their own aura of healthy self-esteem—of being people whose esteem is worth having.

You have the capacity to be such a person, by understanding and honoring your own Venus gifts and beauty and by learning to find beauty in others.

The Monster: The Beast

Imagine a creature that's physically beautiful but so vain, selfish, promiscuous, spoiled, and wasteful that its physical gifts are wasted. In fact, you need journey no farther than your supermarket checkout line to find stories about vapid, pampered starlets and heiresses whose only claim to fame is wealth or beauty.

But even regular folks can be pretty unpleasant, even with far less money and fame than *People*'s last cover model. No one likes a whiner, or someone who barely tolerates your presence as she preens in a mirror or as he looks over your shoulder in the hope of finding someone more interesting. The moocher, the freeloader, the gigolo, the "kept woman" are looked down upon, for they've exchanged their beauty and grace for mere money.

Venus is the planet of love and relationships. This is because relationships, at their best, unite us with partners who complement us. But it's also because relationships are expected to enrich us and make us feel good.

Venus in Signs and Houses

Venus's sign describes the outward style of your inner consort. Venus in houses pinpoints the areas of life in which you find pleasure and beauty in yourself, your environment, and in others. For the sake of space, I'm blending 24 paragraphs into 12.

ASTRO TIP Be sure to read both paragraphs that pertain to Venus's sign and house placement in your birth chart. And remember that aspects between Venus and other planets can also influence the qualities of your inner consort.

Venus in Aries/first house—*Beauty:* You find pleasure in battle, challenges, and physicality. You make others feel good about their physical appearance, assertiveness, and ability to defend themselves. *Beast:* Spends impulsively, overidealistic in love, demanding.

Venus in Taurus/second house—*Beauty:* You find pleasure in whatever appeals to your senses. You spend money on art, music, and creature comforts. You make others feel good by giving them a massage or singing for them. *Beast:* Possessive, materialistic, and self-indulgent.

Venus in Gemini/third house—*Beauty:* You find pleasure in words, thoughts, variety, and wit. You spend money on books and cars. You make others feel good by making them laugh or talking to them. *Beast:* Empty-headed, shallow, gossipy.

Venus in Cancer/fourth house—*Beauty:* You find pleasure in domestic arts, cooking, baking, and buying things for your home. You make others feel good by cooking for them or sharing your home with them, making them feel cozy and accepted. *Beast:* Smothering, financially stingy, sulky.

Venus in Leo/fifth house—*Beauty:* You find pleasure in creating works of art, in playing games and recreation, and in being noticed. Financially and emotionally generous, you make others feel good by appreciating their creative efforts or including them in your fun. *Beast:* Vain, bossy, financially imprudent.

Venus in Virgo/sixth house—*Beauty:* You find pleasure in doing things really well, and making something work, helping someone out. You make others feel good by doing practical things to make their lives easier. *Beast:* Cheap, critical of lovers.

Venus in Libra/seventh house—*Beauty:* You find pleasure in striking the right balance in a relationship and feeling you've anticipated and met another person's needs. You make others feel good by being elegant and appealing and creating beautiful spaces. *Beast:* Prissy, snobbish, can't commit.

Venus in Scorpio/eighth house—*Beauty:* You find pleasure in magic, makeovers, and sexual mingling. You make others feel good by loving them for their ugly, broken bits as well as their beautiful ones. *Beast:* Jealous, suspicious, destructive.

Venus in Sagittarius/ninth house—*Beauty:* You find pleasure in nature, in the open sky and wind, and in anything that feels like an adventure. You make others feel good by making them laugh and introducing them to new things. *Beast:* Blunt, restless, financially careless.

Venus in Capricorn/tenth house—*Beauty:* You find pleasure in structure, form, rules, and routines; you even find pleasure in doing without, because it makes you feel self-sufficient. You make others feel good by holding them to high standards and helping them feel that the world is in control. *Beast:* Greedy, opportunistic, lacking affection.

Venus in Aquarius/eleventh house—*Beauty:* You find pleasure in weirdness, in wires and shiny bits of metal, marble, machinery. You make others feel good by treating them as equals and making them feel included. *Beast:* Aloof, preoccupied with money, don't make partners feel special.

Venus in Pisces/twelfth house—*Beauty:* You find pleasure in imagination, beauty, poetry, music, and dance. You make others feel good by inspiring them to be better, kinder, and more loving. *Beast:* Unreliable, escapist, financially unrealistic, easily deceived.

Essential Takeaways

- The inner, or personal, planets are the Sun, Moon, Mercury, and Venus. These planets symbolize identity and subjectivity.
- The Sun symbolizes your ego and your personal magnetism.
- The Moon symbolizes your subconscious and the way you nurture yourself and others.
- Mercury describes how you think, perceive, and express your identity and thoughts.
- Venus symbolizes what gives you pleasure, and how you give pleasure to others.

CHAPTER 13

Your Social Circle: Mars, Jupiter, Saturn

Mars, planet of war, conflict, and sexuality

Jupiter, planet of expansion, exploration, and higher learning

Saturn, planet of rules, limits, authority, and consequences

Mars, Jupiter, and Saturn symbolize your individual encounters with society, through competition for resources (Mars), under-standing others (Jupiter), and living within societal boundaries (Saturn).

Your Inner Gladiator: Mars ♂

The planet Mars, traditionally known as the "lesser malefic" (translation: a bad guy, but not as awful as Saturn, the greater malefic), is a sort of symbolic shorthand for a handful of qualities and impulses that essentially boil down to "survival instinct." Mars's astrological trademarks—anger, aggression, violence, competition, bravery—are side effects of the primal, biological urge to live.

No matter how sweet, kind, and peace loving a person you think you are, Mars is somewhere in your birth chart and your psyche. If you doubt it, think about how angry you get when someone cuts you off in traffic, or how you'd struggle if you were attacked. And remember, too, how you came to exist in the first place. Out of all the spermatozoa making a play for Mom's egg, yours was the winner. Yours got there first, and you won a coveted ticket to life on earth.

You want to live. You intend to survive. If you and a mob of other starving people were thrown a loaf of bread, Mars would propel you into the mosh pit to grab for a slice. The urge to help the human race survive is also a Mars function hard-wired into your psyche; Mars is named for the god of war, and symbolizes the willingness to take up arms. And if you and a member of the opposite sex were the only two people left on earth, Mars would turn down the sheets and urge you to get busy perpetuating the species.

Mars rules the sign of Aries, and along with Pluto is the co-ruler of Scorpio. Mars is exalted, or especially strong, in the sign of Capricorn, which provides discipline, focus, and structure to Mars's raw energy. Mars's themes of individualism and open aggression are a difficult fit for the polite, partnership-oriented sign of Libra (detriment); and Cancer (fall), which values collectivism and prefers an indirect approach to settling disagreements.

MISC.

Mars Fast Facts

- Key concepts—Action, initiative, energy, aggression, competition, work, sexuality
- Cycle—Takes 22 months to complete a cycle of the zodiac
- Rules—Aries, Scorpio (traditional ruler)
- Exalted—Capricorn
- Detriment—Libra
- Fall—Cancer
- Glyph—Shield and spear (or, um, certain parts of the male anatomy)
- Anatomy—Head and face, red blood corpuscles, adrenal glands, external reproductive organs

The God: The Hunter

The great astrologer and author Steven Forrest describes Mars as offering us two choices: to be the hunter, or the prey. I'll take the liberty of expanding on that a bit to say that, at its best, Mars is also our fierce guardian and protector.

After an evening with friends at a new club, you find yourself walking down a dark street, alone, in a bad part of town. Every nerve and sinew vibrate with attention; your intuition, like antennae, restlessly scans the perimeter for potential threats. Suddenly, from the shadows, a loud noise, a blur of motion. You take off running down the street, adrenaline propelling you faster than you've run since childhood ….

In your second year working at a company that hired you for an entry-level job, an opening becomes available for a position several pay grades higher than your current one. You have most of the qualifications and a gut instinct that you'd be absolutely brilliant at the job. But could you possibly succeed? Are you being too aggressive, reaching so high, so soon in your career? There's no reason to believe you'll succeed. Yet you apply for the job, dazzle the interviewers, and get the promotion ….

Mars is the instinct that gets us out of danger, but he doesn't just play defense. He also encourages us to take risks and pursue opportunities. When someone tells you to be careful, or that you can't do something, or that no one in your position has ever been promoted so quickly, Mars responds with a sassy, "Oh, yeah? Watch me."

Meet the Malefics

In traditional astrology, Mars was known as the lesser malefic planet and Saturn as the greater malefic. Symbolizing violence, war, and conflict (Mars) as well as hardship and limitations (Saturn), these planets were thought to represent everything that was bad (malefic) about being alive. Modern astrologers take a less dire view of both planets and mostly use the terms "greater malefic" and "lesser malefic" when we wish to sound mysterious.

The Monster: Predator or Prey

Mars in his monster guise tends to take two distinct forms: predator or prey. The predator is aggressive, bullying, and domineering; the prey is too afraid to stand up for himself. Both represent a failure to live up to Mars' highest potential of leadership and courage.

Look at any playground, any workplace, and you'll find your share of both Mars "monsters." In school, the "predators" were the bullies who shoved other kids (their prey) off the teeter totter and heckled them in physical education class. When you grew up and entered the workforce, you found the players and tactics had changed, but the game remained the same. Workplace "predators" take credit for other people's work, abuse their employees, or steal another company's intellectual property, all in the name of getting ahead.

There's nothing wrong with going after what you want, and Mars will help you do it. But when Mars gets out of control, he becomes a bully; and when we will not live our lives with the courage and assertiveness that Mars demands of us, we become his victim.

Mars in Signs and Houses

Mars in houses pinpoints the areas of life in which you are assertive and courageous. Because the signs and their natural houses share similar themes, I'm blending 24 paragraphs into 12.

ASTRO TIP — Be sure to read both paragraphs that pertain to Mars's sign and house placement in your birth chart. And remember that aspects between Mars and other planets can also influence the qualities of your inner gladiator.

Mars in Aries/first house—*The hunter:* A master of self-promotion, you radiate charisma, physicality, and courage. You're a natural leader and relish competition. *The predator:* Uncontrolled temper or libido, physical aggression, domineering, recklessness. *The prey:* Cowardice; refusing to pursue what you want.

Mars in Taurus/second house—*The hunter:* Your voice and physical magnetism attract others to you, and your patience and persistence eventually get you what you want. *The predator:* Jealous, selfish, stubborn. *The prey:* Getting stuck in a rut.

Mars in Gemini/third house—*The hunter:* Quick-minded, facile, a formidable and wily verbal opponent. Also a shameless, sweet-talking flirt. *The predator:* Verbal aggression, reckless driving, vicious gossip, lying. *The prey:* Negative thought patterns; depression.

Mars in Cancer/fourth house—*The hunter:* Passionate about protecting the people you care about, competitive on behalf of your family (soccer mom) and close friends. *The predator:* Passive aggression, defensiveness, emotional manipulation, anger toward family. *The prey:* Inability to break away from family; guilt; need for security limits your success.

Mars in Leo/fifth house—*The hunter:* Motivated and assertive in pursuing creative projects, a master of self-promotion, competitive at games and recreational activities. *The predator:* Overbearing; temperamental; treating others as unimportant. *The prey:* Feeling unimportant, untalented; constantly being told you're "too full of yourself."

Mars in Virgo/sixth house—*The hunter:* Self-assured, competent, and a champion of quality work, attention to detail, and good grammar. *The predator: Sarcasm;* using language as a weapon. *The prey:* Feeling incompetent, unappreciated, and taken for granted.

Mars in Libra/seventh house—*The hunter:* Charming, socially adept, graceful, flattering. Prospective partners (in romance or business) crawl right into your net and believe the whole thing was their idea. *The predator:* Using your charm or popularity to make others feel inferior or to do things they wouldn't normally do. *The prey:* Letting others walk all over you; being unable or unwilling to make decisions.

Mars in Scorpio/eighth house—*The hunter:* Focused, stealthy, and hypnotically attractive, you can persuade anyone to do just about anything. *The predator:* Psychological warfare, manipulation, cruelty. *The prey:* Mars in Scorpio would rather die than become prey.

Mars in Sagittarius/ninth house—*The hunter:* Bold, risk-taking, optimistic, you go after anything you want without considering for a moment that you might fail. *The predator:* Overzealous, fanatical, intolerant of differences. *The prey:* Naive; afraid to pursue your dreams.

Mars in Capricorn/tenth house—*The hunter:* Boldly ambitious, a pioneer in your career, and thriving on challenges. *The predator:* Ruthlessly competitive, authoritarian, cruel, unethical. *The prey:* Self-pitying, morose.

Mars in Aquarius/eleventh house—*The hunter:* Brilliant networker, able to connect with almost anyone, innovative and friendly. Your social connections are the key to getting what you want. *The predator:* Insisting others go along with your way of doing things. Dropping social contacts when they no longer benefit you. *The prey:* Feeling like you don't fit in and that you're nothing special.

Mars in Pisces/twelfth house—*The hunter:* Flexible, imaginative, and gentle, you can "whisper" other people into cooperating with you. *The predator:* "Bewitching" others into doing things for you. Taking advantage of others' kindness. *The prey:* You're so kindly and agreeable that others take advantage of you mercilessly.

Your Inner Adventurer: Jupiter ♃

Jupiter has lots of meanings, but they can be summed up in a single word: adventure. Ad-ventures of the mind (education), adventures of the spirit (religion), and physical adventures (travel) are all the province of Jupiter. It's the planet that lifts us out of our everyday experience and tries to make a very large world make sense, and seem familiar.

Growing up on a farm in the Midwest, I spent hours lying on my back in a wheatfield, looking up at the sky. Its sheer size excited my imagination; who knew what lay outside my world of flat, yellow light and buzzing insects? The first time I traveled across country by car, I got my taste of a larger world beyond Indiana. Passing through towns with exotic names like Tucumcari and Amarillo, trying to pronounce the Spanish street names in Los Angeles, learning to eat Mexican food—all were thrilling adventures.

When I took my first airplane ride and glimpsed the other side of those clouds I'd long admired, I was awestruck. And the first time I touched down in a foreign country, I was astonished to find how ordinary it seemed … skies, land, trees. From my tiny farm, the world had seemed dauntingly huge and foreign. But by the time I stood on the ground of Sydney, Australia, at the age of 27, the world didn't seem so big after all. Being there felt like an adventure—but it also felt quite a lot like coming home.

Jupiter rules the sign of Sagittarius and co-rules Pisces. Before the discovery of Neptune, Jupiter was the ruler of Pisces and is sometimes called its "traditional ruler." Jupiter is exalted, or especially strong, in the sign of Cancer; that sign's domestic, family-oriented symbolism provides much-needed roots and emotional ballast for Jupiter. Jupiter's themes of optimism, exploration, and big-picture thinking are not an easy fit for Gemini (detriment), a sign that is too rational to be optimistic and prefers to observe and describe the present rather than envision the future; or for serious, conservative, pragmatic Capricorn (sign of its fall).

ASTRO TIP

Jupiter Fast Facts

- Key concepts—Expansion, optimism, benevolence, higher mind
- Cycle—Takes 12 years to complete a cycle of the zodiac
- Rules—Sagittarius, Pisces (traditional ruler)
- Exalted—Cancer
- Detriment—Gemini
- Fall—Capricorn
- Glyph—First letter of the Greek spelling of Zeus (the Roman Jupiter's Greek counterpart)
- Anatomy—Liver, thighs, hips, blood circulation, pancreas, right ear

The God: Thinking Big

Let's say you've got this friend, Joe, who's had a passport since he was 6 months old; he thinks nothing of hopping on a plane to vacation in a third-world country. Joe's got an advanced degree, is fluent in several languages, and can talk to just about anyone on a wide variety of topics. He was raised in a family in which education and travel were the norm, and consequently he's at ease in just about any situation, instinctively knowing how to dress, how to behave, and what to order from the menu. He knows what's going on in the world, including recent political developments in countries you've never heard of.

Joe was born and (more or less) raised in the same country you were, but he seems a little bit different. His shoes, which he bought on a trip to Europe, are not like the shoes that are sold here. He doesn't have the same rabid, knee-jerk response to social or political issues that inflame your other friends, because he doesn't have quite the same investment in them that you do. For while Joe is a citizen of the same country that you are, he's more than that. He's a citizen of the world. He's a living, breathing embodiment of everything Jupiter represents in astrology: the willingness to immerse himself in everything life and the world have to offer, the enlarged perspective of the seasoned traveler, and the trained mind of the academic.

The Monster: Thinking Small

Now let's say you've got another friend, named Bob. Bob has lived in the same small town since the day he was born there, 35 years ago. He's never left the country; in fact, he's never been on an airplane. He barely graduated from high school. He speaks only English, and without much skill or grace. You call to ask him out to lunch, but Bob sneers when you ask if there's a good sushi restaurant in town. "What, hamburger isn't good enough for you?"

Over burgers, you mention your upcoming trip to Africa; you're very excited about it. "Why would you want to go there?" he scoffs. You mention that you're volunteering for a nonprofit group to develop a water system for a small Nigerian village. No sooner does the phrase "nonprofit" leave your lips than Bob rolls his eyes and launches into a 20-minute screed about "do-gooders," and allows as how you couldn't pay him enough to go to a place like that, "not," he notes, "that you'll be getting paid."

Instead of making the large world more familiar to him, Bob's response to Jupiter's call was to make his own small part of the world even smaller. So small, in fact, that he can confidently claim to know everything about it.

ASTRO TIP

Big Planet on Campus

Jupiter comes by his astrological reputation for "bigness" honestly. In Roman mythology, Jupiter was considered the most powerful of all the gods, and the planet named for him is far and away the largest planet in our solar system, with two-and-a-half times the mass of all the other planets combined! In your chart, Jupiter exaggerates the symbolism of the sign and house in which he's placed.

Jupiter in Signs and Houses

Jupiter's sign describes the outward style of your inner adventurer. Jupiter in houses pinpoints the areas of life in which you explore beliefs, knowledge, and new experiences. For the sake of space, I'm blending 24 paragraphs into 12, since the signs and their natural houses share similar themes.

 ASTRO TIP Be sure to read both paragraphs that pertain to Jupiter's sign and house placement in your birth chart. And remember that aspects between Jupiter and other planets can also influence the qualities of your inner adventurer.

Jupiter in Aries/first house—*Thinking big:* The sky is the limit; new experiences, foreign lands, and new ways of thinking fill you with joy. *Thinking small:* Timid and unadventurous; angered or threatened by foreign or unfamiliar people, places, or concepts.

Jupiter in Taurus/second house—*Thinking big:* You believe in being wise with your resources, but you also feel that money, good health, security, and comfort are to be shared and enjoyed. *Thinking small:* Being content with too little, selling yourself short, overindulging in food, drink, or stimulants; an "easy come, easy go" attitude.

Jupiter in Gemini/third house—*Thinking big:* The ability to transform information, data, and symbols into larger meaning. *Thinking small:* Being too attached to your native language, your beliefs, and your knowledge to entertain different ones.

Jupiter in Cancer/fourth house—*Thinking big:* Being at home anywhere in the world. *Thinking small:* Staying in your comfort zone, spending too much time with people and situations that are familiar.

Jupiter in Leo/fifth house—*Thinking big:* Writing a life story that is so creative and magnificent, others are inspired to follow your example. *Thinking small:* Settling for being a big fish in a small pond.

Jupiter in Virgo/sixth house—*Thinking big:* Making a practical contribution to an important cause, one that makes a real difference in determining whether people live well or die miserably. *Thinking small:* Hypochondria, sweating the small stuff, and dwelling on the reasons why something can't be done.

Jupiter in Libra/seventh house—*Thinking big:* Forging relationships with equal partners whose joy and vision broaden your own experience of the world. *Thinking small:* Living vicariously through others.

Jupiter in Scorpio/eighth house—*Thinking big:* Walking fearlessly into other people's secrets, mysteries, and fears; seeking to understand what's really going on beneath the surface. *Thinking small:* Using your gift for insight to play head games and manipulate people.

Jupiter in Sagittarius/ninth house—*Thinking big:* Taking big chances and seeking out experiences that help you understand the whole world, not just a tiny part of it. *Thinking small:* Thinking you understand the whole world just because you understand a tiny part of it.

Jupiter in Capricorn/tenth house—*Thinking big:* Inspiring the world with your knowledge, ethics, and graceful, inclusive leadership. *Thinking small:* Being a boss who doesn't care about what your company does or whether your employees feel they're making a contribution.

Jupiter in Aquarius/eleventh house—*Thinking big:* Inspiring others to feel that they're part of something important, and that together you can create a legacy that will influence future generations. *Thinking small:* Being an outsider on the fringes of society, with no influence beyond a small niche.

Jupiter in Pisces/twelfth house—*Thinking big:* Becoming significantly involved in alleviating the suffering, pain, and unhappiness in the world. *Thinking small:* Getting stoned and watching TV.

Your Inner Teacher: Saturn ♄

Before the discovery of Uranus, Neptune, and Pluto, Saturn was the farthest known planet from the Sun, marking the outer limits of our solar system. Perhaps this is how it came to be known as the planet of limitations, restrictions, and rules.

Saturn is known as the "greater malefic"—the baddest of planetary bad guys, the Darth Vader of the solar system. Over the years, I've heard many people complain about Saturn in their charts, about the terrible misery and deprivation it has wrought. And I'm reminded, every time, of outspoken U.S. President Harry Truman who, in response to those who told him "Give 'em hell, Harry!" replied, "I never gave anybody hell. I just told the truth and they think it's hell."

All of us have limitations and failings. Our actions have consequences. And we all face tests. Saturn is the symbol that says, "Life is hard. But you can't even begin to make it better unless you first face up to reality and take responsibility."

Saturn rules the sign of Capricorn. It's exalted, or especially strong, in the sign of Libra, which offers a keen appreciation for how our decisions and ambitions affect others. Saturn's themes of patiently overcoming hardship, living by the rules, and pursuing worldly ambition are at odds with the nurturing, security-loving, domestic world of Cancer (the sign of its detriment), and with the impatience and independence of Aries (the sign of its fall).

Saturn Fast Facts

- Key concepts—Discipline, responsibility, security, wisdom, aging, ambition, limitations
- Cycle—Takes 28 to 30 years to complete a cycle of the zodiac
- Rules—Capricorn, Aquarius (traditional ruler)
- Exalted—Libra
- Detriment—Cancer
- Fall—Aries
- Glyph—Sickle of Chronos, the god of time
- Anatomy—Skin, skeletal system, teeth, ligaments, knees, gallbladder

The God: The Mentor

I once had a boss who was tough as nails, provoked me to tears on several occasions, and made me spend every Sunday dreading Monday. She was a merciless taskmaster who taught me it's never acceptable to shift the blame for failure—even when the failure wasn't my fault.

She was the best boss I ever had.

She taught me about responsibility, one of Saturn's favorite words. Somehow our modern minds confuse the word responsibility with the concept of blame; we feel that taking responsibility in a situation means accepting the blame for what has happened. But the two are not related. Blame means you caused the problem. But responsibility means, simply, that you are *able to respond* to a situation. There is something you can do to affect the circumstances or outcome.

Saturn is the planet that symbolizes taking that responsibility and running with it. Like the toughest but best mentor, Saturn's the god who refuses to let you complain about your circumstances, pass the buck, depend on others to help you out of a jam, or ever give up. It's the planet of problems, and hardship, yes; but more importantly, it's the planet of proving to yourself and the world that you can overcome those problems and hardships. That you, and you alone, are the author of your fate.

The Monster: The Oppressor

It's Christmas Eve, and George Bailey is standing at the edge of a bridge, debating whether to throw himself into the icy river below. George's nemesis, the cold and ruthless Mr. Potter, has stolen $8,000 that was meant to be deposited in George's business account. And now, after a lifetime spent helping others at the expense of pursuing his own ambitions, George is on the verge of bankruptcy and scandal.

In the movie *It's a Wonderful Life,* Mr. Potter is clearly playing the role of "monster" Saturn: "the greater malefic," a cruel, ruthless, oppressive jerk. But while it might seem that we're kicking poor George while he's down in saying so, he's also playing out "monster" Saturn: giving in to despair, depression, and failure. Giving up.

The only way to fight the Saturn monster is to keep plugging away, moving forward when you think you can't take another step, and doing it without excuses or self-pity. Although the sulking voice within complains about how everyone else has it so much easier than you do, such complaints don't become you. And they'll never lead you to the role of leadership and authority that is your birthright.

ASTRO ALERT

It's fashionable among people who know something about astrology to complain about Saturn. Saturn is picking on them, Saturn is keeping them from having what they want, and why can't they have Saturn surgically removed from their birth chart? But complaining about Saturn is like complaining about a tough teacher who demands your best work—yes, doing your best is hard, but you always feel better about yourself when you've left everything you have on the playing field.

Saturn in Signs and Houses

Saturn's sign describes the outward style of your inner taskmaster. Saturn in houses pinpoints the areas of life where you find obstacles that must be overcome. For the sake of space, I'm blending 24 paragraphs into 12, since the signs and their natural houses share similar themes.

ASTRO TIP — Be sure to read both paragraphs that pertain to Saturn's sign and house placement in your birth chart. And remember that aspects between Saturn and other planets can also influence the qualities of your inner teacher.

Saturn in Aries/first house—*The mentor:* Teaches you to defend yourself and your boundaries, to develop a strong body and a distinctive personal "brand" and to assert yourself appropriately. *The oppressor:* Tells you that you are incapable of defending yourself and that you're not worthy of being noticed.

Saturn in Taurus/second house—*The mentor:* Teaches you to take care of your body and possessions, and to grow prosperous, healthy, and secure. *The oppressor:* Encourages your insecurity, low self-esteem, fear of poverty, and poor physical condition.

Saturn in Gemini/third house—*The mentor:* Encourages you to improve your mind, develop strong communication skills, and make yourself heard. *The oppressor:* Compares you unfavorably to your siblings, calls you stupid, and tells you that you don't have anything to say that's worth listening to.

Saturn in Cancer/fourth house—*The mentor:* Encourages you to learn to nurture yourself, build a family and a comfortable home, and feel safe. *The oppressor:* Makes you feel unsafe, unwanted, and all alone in the world.

Saturn in Leo/fifth house—*The mentor:* Encourages you to let yourself have fun, be noticed, and develop creative outlets; to celebrate your uniqueness and to embrace life with joy. *The oppressor:* Makes you feel ordinary, untalented, and unlovable.

Saturn in Virgo/sixth house—*The mentor:* Encourages you to develop practical skills, find meaningful work, and organize your daily affairs; to be of practical service in solving the world's problems. *The oppressor:* Tells you that you're incompetent, not very bright, and useless.

Saturn in Libra/seventh house—*The mentor:* Encourages you to maintain a balanced lifestyle and to achieve harmonious relationships that balance both individuals' needs. *The oppressor:* Tells you that life isn't fair and that you'll always be alone.

Saturn in Scorpio/eighth house—*The mentor:* Encourages you to form intimate, sharing, and supportive relationships; to trust your own judgment; and to let others give to you. *The oppressor:* Discourages you from trusting others or accepting their help or support.

Saturn in Sagittarius/ninth house—*The mentor:* Encourages you to cultivate understanding and wisdom and to open your mind to other cultures, views, and beliefs. *The oppressor:*

Discourages you from seeking truth and from learning about people, cultures, and beliefs that are different from your own.

Saturn in Capricorn/tenth house—*The mentor:* Encourages you to pursue your ambitions and accept the risk of not reaching them; to take responsibility for your life and decisions; and to become a mentor yourself. *The oppressor:* Tells you you're doomed to be a failure and that no one likes or respects you.

Saturn in Aquarius/eleventh house—*The mentor:* Encourages you to be yourself while being part of a community; to act as a focal point for friends and like-minded people, and to lead them in collective action. *The oppressor:* Tells you that you'll never fit in, that you're hopelessly weird, and that you might actually be a little crazy.

Saturn in Pisces/twelfth house—*The mentor:* Encourages you to have faith, to accept impermanence and not knowing what the future brings, and to have compassion for yourself and others. *The oppressor:* Tells you that faith is no substitute for knowledge, that uncertainty is frightening, and that people are, inherently, no good.

Essential Takeaways

- Mars, Jupiter, and Saturn symbolize the way you interact with society.
- Mars symbolizes how you handle aggression, competition, and anger.
- Jupiter symbolizes the way you make sense of the world.
- Saturn symbolizes how you deal with limitations and rules and achieve your goals.

CHAPTER 14

Your Generational Circle: Uranus, Neptune, Pluto

Uranus, planet of revolution, rebellion, and innovation

Neptune, planet of spirituality, enlightenment, and compassion

Pluto, planet of mortality, empowerment, and transcendence

Uranus, Neptune, and Pluto are called generational planets because they move so slowly that entire generations are born with these planets in the same sign. These planets tell us about the cultural touchstones (Pearl Harbor, poodle skirts, Woodstock, savings bonds with an annual yield of more than 1 percent) that you share with most everyone born around the same time that you were.

The generational planets symbolize spiritual and psychological processes that take time to play out, and that describe the "zeitgeist" of a particular moment in history. Think of it this way: plant summer squash and you'll see fruit within a month; plant an oak tree and it could be many years before your kids get their tree house. The faster-moving "personal" planets—the Sun, Moon, Mercury, and Venus—are summer squash. The slower-moving planets, especially Uranus, Neptune, and Pluto, are trees.

You're a member of a generation—perhaps a post–World War II baby boomer with self-obsessed Pluto in Leo (1940–1957) and a dusty collection of Rolling Stones LPs, or a Generation X "slacker" with Pluto in Libra (1971–1984) and an anatomical portfolio of tattoos. But you also experienced your generation's defining issues on a personal level; that experience is symbolized by the placement of Uranus, Neptune, and Pluto in the houses of your chart.

Your Inner Revolutionary: Uranus ♅

Whenever you see news footage of people rioting in the streets, marching for causes, or engaging in civil disobedience, you're watching Uranus in action. It's the planet of revolution, tearing down structures that stifle individual expression, and generally sticking it to "The Man." Even its physical orientation (it rotates sideways) and its name (there are at least three common pronunciations, at least one of which is certain to elicit giggles) bear mute testimony to its overall weirdness.

And that's what Uranus represents: weirdness. Being different from everyone else, and rebelling against the status quo. The way your generation rebelled against the one that came before, and was viewed askance by your parents ("Those kids with their crazy haircuts/loud music/piercings and tattoos"). And the ways you, personally, feel that you don't fit in and are inclined to a certain twitchy rebelliousness.

Uranus is symbolically connected to the unconventional, even revolutionary, sign of Aquarius. Uranus is exalted, or especially strong, in the sign of Scorpio, a sign of transformation that lends a sense of larger purpose to Uranus's radical changes. It's in its detriment in Leo, a sign whose emphasis on individual creativity is at odds with Uranus, which represents the principle of egalitarianism. And Uranus is in its fall in Taurus, a sign that values stability and security and doesn't welcome the kind of disruptive change symbolized by Uranus.

MISC.

Uranus Fast Facts

- Key concepts—Awakening, invention, originality, science, the future, electricity, revolution, unexpected events, natural disasters

- Cycle—Takes 84 years to complete a cycle of the zodiac

- Rules—Aquarius

- Exalted—Scorpio

- Detriment—Leo

- Fall—Taurus

- Glyph—The glyph commonly used by astrologers looks like a stylized H, an homage to Herschel, the discoverer of Uranus. Astronomers use a glyph that looks like the planet Mars pointing upright with a dot in the middle of the circle.

- Anatomy—Ankles, nervous system, body electricity

The God: The Lightning Bolt

You've lived your whole life in a tiny, homogeneous, and fairly dull town in the middle of nowhere. It's the first day of seventh grade, and you're looking down the barrel of another long, boring school year, spending day after day with the same kids you've known since your mothers were in the hospital delivery room together.

Then, a latecomer enters the classroom. Your teacher asks the class to welcome Buzz, a new student from Malibu, California. Buzz wears the kind of clothes you've only seen on television, and he oozes as much cool confidence as a 12-year-old possibly can. As he shakes his hair out of his eyes and flashes a devastating grin, an electric current pulses through the classroom as the entire seventh grade—as one—falls a little bit in love with Buzz.

In a close-knit community, whether it's a classroom, workplace, or town, an outsider can have a tremendous impact. Buzz is occasionally baffled by your alien customs, and he asks questions that are innocent, but unsettling. Why aren't there any African Americans in your class? Why do people still smoke cigarettes and eat so much red meat in this part of the country? Friendships are tested as girls vie for Buzz's attention. Modest Midwestern boys spend hours in front of their bedroom mirrors, cultivating the "Buzz" look. Even Ms. Evans, your teacher, seems to wield her chalk with more energy.

And to you, suddenly, the world looks different. Why should you stay in one place your whole life, eating what your parents eat and following the unspoken rules of your upbringing? Finally, one night, as you watch your mom and dad light up cigarettes after their steak dinner, you blurt out, "I'm gonna be a vegetarian from now on, and I'm never, ever gonna smoke!"

Their startled expressions tell you that you've turned into Buzz.

ASTRO TIP

Astronomers pronounce Uranus "UR-uh-nus." Some folks (and all fifth-graders) pronounce it "Ur-AY-nus." And among astrologers I've also heard it pronounced "Ur-AH-nus." Any way you pronounce it, you're going to encounter some snickers from the peanut gallery. And, of course, that's just the way Uranus likes it.

The Monster: The Outcast

Usually, a "Buzz" is a perfectly normal kid who is strange only by virtue of having been raised a bit differently, or having a distinctive personal style. But occasionally, a Buzz relishes his role as exotic and rebellious outsider. He pits friend against friend, daughter against parents, and teacher against principal. He exists to stir up trouble and controversy for their own sake, and to break down the happy associations that keep a community functioning smoothly. Like lightning, Uranus can generate electricity or wreak destruction.

And then, too, a Buzz might be somewhat less attractive, less cool, his "weirdness" less alluring. Then he becomes a sad exile whose occasional contributions to classroom discussions draw snickers, who eats alone at lunchtime, and who never seems to wear the right clothes or say the right thing. Uranus can represent the part of you that feels like an outcast—all rough, pointed edges, a square peg with no business trying to fit into a round hole. In society, entire classes of people can feel like outcasts, with no status or sense of belonging within their own culture.

What happens when an outcast has been cut off from society for too long? Usually, he rebels against the culture that rejected him. Occasionally, he grows into his genius and changes the world. In extreme cases, he seeks to destroy it—through revolution, and sometimes with violence.

Uranus in Signs

Uranus describes the outward style of your inner revolutionary. Because Uranus moves through the zodiac so slowly, everyone born within the same (roughly) seven-year period shares the same Uranus sign. As a generation, you and those who share your Uranus sign are helping to awaken society to prepare it for new insights and innovations in the areas represented by Uranus's sign.

ASTRO TIP There is some overlap between the Uranus generations, while Uranus was making long retrograde journeys back into the previous sign. If you were born during a year when Uranus was changing signs, you'll need to look at your birth chart to find out exactly where it was at your birth.

Uranus in Aries (1928–1934; 2010–2018)—*The lightning bolt:* A can-do spirit, the ability to cope with upheaval and revolution, a knack for survival. *The outcast:* Survivalism; united with others only for the purpose of waging war.

Uranus in Taurus (1934–1942)—*The lightning bolt:* The equalizer, dispersing wealth and property throughout society. *The outcast:* Disruption of economic and societal stability.

Uranus in Gemini (1943–1949)—*The lightning bolt:* The ability to grasp concepts, formulate new ideas, and revolutionize technology and transportation. *The outcast:* Disruption of communities, disjointed thoughts, extreme ideas.

Uranus in Cancer (1949–1956)—*The lightning bolt:* Radical reconfiguration of home, family, and traditional motherhood. Women seeking fulfillment outside the home. Birth control. *The outcast:* Estranged families, societal insecurity.

Uranus in Leo (1956–1962)—*The lightning bolt:* Sexual freedom, self-expression, changes in parenting style. *The outcast:* Exhibitionism, neglect of children, shocking entertainment.

Uranus in Virgo (1962–1968)—*The lightning bolt:* Civil rights and equality for all. Health-care advances. Technology as part of everyday life. *The outcast:* Mechanization displacing skilled workers. The workforce shaken up by the entrance of more women and minorities.

Uranus in Libra (1968–1974)—*The lightning bolt:* Free love, unconventional relationships, women's liberation. *The outcast:* Rising divorce rates; shocking music and art.

Uranus in Scorpio (1974–1981)—*The lightning bolt:* Rapid advances in computer technology, videotapes, cable TV. Exposure of taboos and corruption. *The outcast:* Realignments in sexual attitudes and behavior. Shocking and explicit media.

Uranus in Sagittarius (1981–1988)—*The lightning bolt:* Popularity of video games, end of the Cold War, advent of personal computer, court rulings on school prayer. The *Challenger* explosion and the examination of "groupthink." *The outcast:* Radicalization of religious organizations and figures. Increased media emphasis on extreme religious views.

Uranus in Capricorn (1905–1911; 1988–1996)—*The lightning bolt:* Upheavals in politics, government, and big business. The beginning of the popular rise of the Internet. *The outcast:* Genocide, riots, terrorism.

Uranus in Aquarius (1912–1919; 1996–2003)—*The lightning bolt:* Brilliant ideas and technological advances. Networking through technology. *The outcast:* Global disruption (war, pandemics), radical political movements.

Uranus in Pisces (1919–1928; 2003–2011)—*The lightning bolt:* Challenges to institutional prejudice, cruelty, victimization; breakthroughs in genetics, health-care technology. Unifying theories. *The outcast:* Unchecked racism and fascism, radicalized religious movements.

ASTRO TIP

Saturn's Dad

Uranus was initially named Herschel, after its discoverer, Sir William Herschel. The name, incongruous among the mythical names of the other planets, never really caught on outside of Herschel's own Britain. It was astronomer Johann Elert Bode who suggested that the new planet, orbiting on the outside of Saturn, should be named after Saturn's father, just as Saturn, orbiting on the outside of Jupiter, was named after Jupiter's father. Herschel proposed the name Uranus, the Latin version of Ouranos, Greek god of the sky.

Uranus in Houses

Uranus's house placement in your chart marks the areas where your generation's rebelliousness and innovation collides with your personal experiences. It's where you, personally, are rebellious, innovative, iconoclastic, and determined to do things your own way. It's also the symbol for the triggers that can literally drive you crazy if you're prevented from exercising your freedom in a particular area of life.

Uranus in your first house—*The lightning bolt:* You do things no one ever imagined doing, blazing new trails for "your people" and going head-to-head with societal rules and mores. *The outcast:* Your appearance is distinctive and unusual, you're uncompromising, and you're kind of hard to get close to. You're unpredictable and can be destructive when your freedom is threatened.

Uranus in your second house—*The lightning bolt:* Your philanthropy or quirky attitude toward money and possessions awakens others to new ideas about what is valuable. You demand freedom from financial constraints; you don't want to be "owned" by either your money or your poverty. *The outcast:* Your financial status, whether extreme poverty or wealth, may set you apart from those around you.

Uranus in your third house—*The lightning bolt:* You awaken the world with new ways to think, educate, and communicate. You insist on the freedom to speak your mind without interference or censorship. *The outcast:* The way you think and speak sets you apart as radical.

Uranus in your fourth house—*The lightning bolt:* You offer the world new ideas about what it means to belong to a family or to a country. You seek freedom from family obligations, traditions, and allegiances of birth or nation. *The outcast:* Emotionally estranged from your family, uncomfortable in your own country, difficulty forming meaningful emotional connections.

Uranus in your fifth house—*The lightning bolt:* You refuse to be told who you are, who you can be, or how to express yourself. You demand that the world adopt new attitudes about the importance of individual freedom, expression, and happiness. *The outcast:* Your creative interests or your attitudes toward sex or childrearing mark you as different or even radical.

Uranus in your sixth house—*The lightning bolt:* You're very good at figuring out innovative solutions to mundane problems. You refuse to conform to rules about work, health, or wealth. *The outcast:* Everyday rebellion. In the movie *The Wild One*, Marlon Brando's character is asked, "What're you rebelling against, Johnny?" His reply: "Whaddya got?"

Uranus in your seventh house—*The lightning bolt:* You are able to think about relationships and social justice in fresh, innovative, fair ways. Your relationships will be very different from the ones you grew up watching. If your parents were advocates of free love who refused to get married, you're likely to walk down the aisle at an early age. *The outcast:* You can be a bit socially "tone deaf," missing social cues. By turning your back on societal rules about relationships, you also forfeit some of society's support for conventional relationships such as marriage.

Uranus in your eighth house—*The lightning bolt:* You are able to break down barriers between people, and organize others to use shared resources for good. You will do almost anything to avoid being subject to someone else's control. *The outcast:* You're not good at sharing, may seem a little scary, and don't respect people's privacy.

Uranus in your ninth house—*The lightning bolt:* You have an innovative way of thinking about the world of knowledge and beliefs. You take an unconventional educational path and generally hold religious or philosophical beliefs that are very different from those of the people around you. You feel strongly about religious freedom. *The outcast:* The best way for someone to ensure you will never, under any circumstances, subscribe to his or her belief system is to tell you it's the only one that's valid and that bad things will happen if you don't believe. Sometimes this amounts to cutting off your nose to spite your face.

Uranus in your tenth house—*The lightning bolt:* You refuse to follow the career path that's expected of you, preferring to follow your own unorthodox calling. You're a born leader, one who shakes up the status quo and promises a more egalitarian approach to government. *The outcast:* You just don't get the way the world works. You're constantly in trouble with parents, teachers, cops, bosses, anyone in authority. It can be hard for you to achieve much because it's hard for you to commit to a goal.

Uranus in your eleventh house—*The lightning bolt:* You refuse to give in to peer pressure, and yet you have a talent for bringing people together. *The outcast:* You probably like people, but you really don't have a feel for group interactions. You are good at bringing groups of people together, but you dislike the politics that inevitably emerge, so you quickly distance yourself.

Uranus in your twelfth house—*The lightning bolt:* You see the world and all its people as interconnected. You refuse to be controlled by fear, bigotry, illness, or imprisonment. *The outcast:* You're a bit too sensitive and impractical to deal with other people much on a regular basis. You may love everyone in theory, but in reality you need lots of quiet time alone.

Your Inner Angel: Neptune Ψ

None of us is a saint. But all of us have the ability, on our best days, to be a little bit better than we'd imagined we could be. We have moments of real grace, kindness, and compassion. We can turn the other cheek. We put another's feelings ahead of our own. We show faith and forbearance in the face of tragedy, and offer kindness to strangers.

No, we're not saints. But on a good day, we can behave as though we were. Neptune symbolizes how, and in what circumstances, you are most likely to show your sweetest, most compassionate side.

Neptune is symbolically connected to the compassionate, spiritually sensitive, artistic sign of Pisces. Its signs of exaltation and fall have not been determined; but its sign of detriment is Virgo, whose practical, discriminating, and analytical nature makes an uncomfortable home for Neptune's unconditional love, intuition, and faith.

Neptune Fast Facts

- Key concepts—Spirituality, compassion, unconditional love, empathy, art, psychic sensitivity
- Cycle—Takes 165 years to complete a cycle of the zodiac
- Rules—Pisces
- Exalted—Not determined
- Detriment—Virgo
- Fall—Not determined
- Glyph—Poseidon's trident
- Anatomy—Feet, pineal gland, white corpuscles of the blood, spinal column

The God: The Dream

Every now and then, usually when I've been driving too much, I get to feeling pretty exasperated with my fellow man. I start griping to my poor husband, loudly and at some length, about how perfectly nice, civilized people become animals the minute they get behind the wheel. Wringing my hands (metaphorically, for my actual hands are on the wheel, I promise), I bemoan the general breakdown of civility in modern society, always ending up on the same thought. "The heck of it is," I'll observe to my (now glassy-eyed, desperate for this familiar monologue to end) spouse, "If I were crossing the street right now and got hit by a car, probably a dozen people would stop their cars and run over to help me."

It's true: disaster and human suffering bring out the best in people. Watch video footage of the aftermath of a disaster. There is suffering, yes; also pain, deprivation, loss, even death. Chaos reigns—rubble in the streets, ashes, bits of aircraft, flooding. But there are also feet on the ground, rushing around with food, water, medicine, and tourniquets, voices clamoring to donate blood.

And even many miles away, most of us instinctively open our hearts, our wallets, our pantries, or our guestrooms, ready to help. In a moment of almost painful clarity, we see what's important and real: our connection to other humans. Make it a big enough disaster shared by enough of us, and the usual distinctions of status, gender, race, and age evaporate completely. We're one people, brothers and sisters; we love each other, and we'd do anything for one another. Neptune, the god of oneness, has washed us into each other's arms and baptized us in unconditional love.

The Monster: Not My Problem

But what if it wasn't a big enough disaster? What if the only people affected were not like us—didn't speak the same language, have the same skin color, or worship the same god? Maybe we watch the news for a little while, initially stunned at the misery unfolding before our eyes—but then we quickly find a way to absolve ourselves from caring. "They should never have built a city there." "Why did they build with stones in a place that gets massive earthquakes?" "I'm broke and they're halfway around the world; it's not like there's anything I can do for them." And we turn the channel, and convince ourselves that those people have nothing to do with us.

Neptune is described as the planet of deception, escapism, and denial. And when Neptune is in his Monster mode, the sensitivity and compassion that serve us so well in a catastrophe are brushed under the rug. We sense the truth—"I don't love him, he doesn't love me, I don't deserve that raise"—but we choose to ignore it. We watch others suffering and pretend we can't do anything about it, and in order to absolve our guilt we blame the victim. The cheater thinks, "It's not my fault he was stupid enough to trust me." The thief believes, "She was just asking to be robbed." Instead of talking to the ones we love about things that are important, we spend our evenings drinking, eating too much, smoking dope, or surfing the Internet for hours at a time.

 ASTRO ALERT Neptune is often associated with negative qualities, especially deception. But while those who practice deception almost certainly have strong Neptune placements in their chart, not all with strong Neptune choose to use it in a negative or destructive way. Beware of interpreting Neptune in your chart, or anyone else's, with the assumption that it means deception, substance abuse, insanity, or any of the other traditional Neptune scourges.

Neptune in Signs

Neptune describes the outward style of your inner saint. Because Neptune moves through the zodiac so slowly, everyone born within a 13- to 14-year period shares the same Neptune sign. As a generation, you are moving society toward a specific dream of spiritual enlightenment; and from time to time, you awaken to find the world isn't necessarily the way you thought it was.

 ASTRO TIP There is some overlap between the Neptune generations, while Neptune was making long retrograde journeys back into the previous sign. If you were born during a year when Neptune was changing signs, you'll need to look at your birth chart to find out exactly where it was at your birth.

Neptune in Aries (1861–1875; 2025–2039)—*The dream:* An individual person (or nation) can save the world. All men are created equal. *The awakening:* As the American Civil War demonstrated, fighting wars doesn't necessarily make anyone free or equal.

Neptune in Taurus (1874–1889; 2038–2052)—*The dream:* A gilded age of wealth and luxury, impressionistic art, opulence and philanthropy. *The awakening:* Bitter racial and class divisions. The poor wish to dream their own dreams.

Neptune in Gemini (1888–1902; 2051–2066)—*The dream:* Efficiency of production, better access to transportation, the ability to communicate more efficiently and effectively. *The awakening:* The products aren't necessarily any better, there's not necessarily any place worth traveling to, and there aren't necessarily any ideas worth communicating.

Neptune in Cancer (1901–1915)—*The dream:* Willingness to sacrifice for family and nation; security, caring, and patriotism as ideals. *The awakening:* Safety is an illusion, and anyone who promises it is not to be trusted.

Neptune in Leo (1915–1929)—*The dream:* Glamour, mesmerizing forms of entertainment, getting rich quick, and the party that never ends. *The awakening:* The party always ends eventually, and there's a lot of cleaning up to do when it does.

Neptune in Virgo (1929–1943)—*The dream:* The highest values are service, usefulness, and sacrifice. Anything is possible if you're willing to work hard. *The awakening:* Sometimes, hard work is not rewarded, sacrifice is not appreciated, and your real responsibility is not to a noble cause, but to the fellow fighting alongside you.

Neptune in Libra (1943–1955)—*The dream:* All you need is love! Make love, not war! Peace! Can't we all just get along, man? As long as we both shall love …. *The awakening:*

Nice guys finish last. Creating art is great, but even better if it pays the bills. The problem with being free to love anyone you want is that the people you love are free to do the same thing.

Neptune in Scorpio (1956–1970)—*The dream:* Sacred sexuality, Eastern philosophy, mysticism, creating sexually themed art and music, abandoning romanticism. *The awakening:* Sex and intimacy are not the same thing. Having all the answers doesn't mean you're asking the right questions.

Neptune in Sagittarius (1971–1984)—*The dream:* Cleaning up government, thinking up a new vision, believing in something. *The awakening:* Nothing you believed is true. None of the institutions who taught you your values can be trusted.

Neptune in Capricorn (1985–1998)—*The dream:* We are the world. Dissolving of national borders. Global activism and practical dreams. *The awakening:* Multinational corporations, decentralized government, corporatized faith.

Neptune in Aquarius (1998–2012)—*The dream:* The entire world connected by technology. Shared knowledge. *The awakening:* Mass delusion, wide-scale groupthink, the emergence of radical fringe groups.

Neptune in Pisces (2012–2025)—*The dream:* Boundaries between individuals and nations are dissolved. Empathy and compassion as universal ideals. *The awakening:* Scapegoating, environmental disintegration, denial of reality.

Neptune: Catch a Wave
Neptune is the Roman version of Poseidon, the Greek god of the sea, storms, and earthquakes. Astrologically, Uranus is more closely associated with earthquakes, but Neptune retains bragging rights over rain, flooding, and tidal waves. He also gets to carry around that cool trident (which provided the inspiration for his glyph).

Neptune in Houses

Neptune's house placement in your chart personalizes the generational themes of Neptune in the signs, and indicates where you seek enlightenment, escape, and spiritual meaning in life. When it's being expressed negatively, Neptune can describe where you get lost in a fog of deception or denial.

Neptune in your first house—*We are one:* Willingness to fight for and defend others and to champion your beliefs. *Not my problem:* Feeling that nothing is worth fighting for. Difficulty exerting your personality; projected anger.

Neptune in your second house—*We are one:* Use of money and other resources for philanthropic/charitable causes. Lack of attachment to material things. Espousing the ideal of material security and peace for all. *Not my problem:* Financial impracticality, unclear values, being easily exploited.

Neptune in your third house—*We are one:* Your ideal is to give expression and voice to humanity's greatest fears and pain. Belief in facts and communication. Able to read between the lines. Imaginative writing, enchanting way of speaking. *Not my problem:* Deceptive or easily deceived; trouble with siblings or neighbors; trouble thinking or speaking clearly.

Neptune in your fourth house—*We are one:* Belief in the importance of family and home, willingness to help your family and community, ability to heal troubled family history. Creating a foundation of love and acceptance for everyone in your life. *Not my problem:* Hiding out at home. Family history of substance abuse, illness, or parental absence. Blaming family for your problems.

Neptune in your fifth house—*We are one:* The artist, a gifted and moving performer, an inspirational figure, a compassionate champion of children. *Not my problem:* Unrealistic about creative abilities, inflated ego, shallow sexual relationships, ambivalence about children.

Neptune in your sixth house—*We are one:* You dream of a perfect world and work hard to make your ideals a reality. You devote each day of your life to making some part of the world better. *Not my problem:* Too overwhelmed, disorganized, untidy, and impractical to help anyone else.

Neptune in your seventh house—*We are one:* You believe in love, peace, and fairness. You're able to understand others, meet them on their level, and accept them. You have the ability to create a truly loving and equal partnership. *Not my problem* Escaping into your relationships; letting partnership overshadow your own identity. You can be deceived by partners or give too much in a relationship.

Neptune in your eighth house—*We are one:* You believe in magic and the ability to transform. You love what is broken. Your dream is to share your whole self, completely, with another person, and in doing so to transcend yourself. *Not my problem:* Paranoia; obsessing about your romantic relationships until you're not able to give much to anyone else.

Neptune in your ninth house—*We are one:* Knowledge and understanding are your highest ideals. You're likely to describe yourself as spiritual rather than religious. You inspire others with your beliefs, through writing, educating, travel, or religious leadership. *Not my* *problem:* Willful ignorance. Believing without questioning; imposing beliefs onto others; being deceived by religious figures, teachers, or gurus.

Neptune in your tenth house—*We are one:* A spiritual leader and loving parent or mentor; involvement in a business with a philanthropic motivation. Providing a public example of compassion, empathy, and giving. *Not my problem:* Putting all your faith in authority figures to solve society's problems. Abusing your authority. Being an absent parent.

Neptune in your eleventh house—*We are one:* Great love and compassion for your friends. Ability to move the public with your artistic and inspirational works, and to demonstrate that we are all part of the same society. The ability to connect with almost anybody. *Not my problem:* Immersing yourself in friendships that are not what they seem or friends who are addicted to drugs or alcohol and constantly in need of help.

Neptune in your twelfth house—*We are one:* Receptive to psychic or subliminal influences and the power of suggestion. Powerful dreams. Naturally artistic and musical; able to give voice to collective emotions, images, thoughts, and fears. Good at reading symbols and signs. *Not my problem:* Losing yourself in your own daydreams, musings, and fears. Using victimhood as an excuse not to move forward with your life. Phobias and obsessions.

Your Inner Phoenix: Pluto ♀

Life offers us plenty of things to fear. We fear our own deaths, and the deaths of our loved ones. We fear illness, losing our jobs, or finding out our spouses have been unfaithful.

But there's something else that we fear even more, I think, and that's the fear of feeling small and helpless. We fear the kind of freakish *Twilight Zone* scenario of waking up one day to find that nobody cares about us as individuals—a prisoner in an internment camp, a poor child starving to death in Kenya, or a poor person clinging to the roof of a house in New Orleans.

We fear powerlessness, and we fear being treated inhumanely by those who have power over us. But when we're faced with life's most terrifying and threatening situations, we can surprise ourselves by transcending the fear and emerging stronger than ever, like a phoenix rising from the ashes. In astrology, the fear and the transcendence of that fear share the same symbol: Pluto.

Pluto is symbolically connected to Scorpio, the powerful sign of transformation. The signs of Pluto's exaltation and fall have not been determined; it's in its detriment in Taurus, a sign whose need for stability and security place it fundamentally at odds with Pluto's message of transformation.

Pluto Fast Facts

- Key concepts—Power, transformation, obsession, cycle of birth and death, kidnapping, hidden things, dictatorships, generation, regeneration, and degeneration
- Cycle—Takes approximately 248 years to complete a cycle of the zodiac
- Rules—Scorpio
- Exalted—Not determined
- Detriment—Taurus
- Fall—Not determined
- Glyph—The cross of matter, the crescent moon, and the circle of infinity
- Anatomy—Elimination and reproductive systems, abnormal growths, pituitary gland

The God: Fearless

The goal of Pluto is to make you strong—to give you the kind of strength that comes with integrity, and living clean without secrets, dishonesty, or waste. Pluto is the plumber who keeps the nasty consequences of being human rushing through pipes and away from your house. He's the garbage collector who takes away your smelly, unneeded refuse. He's the chemotherapy that kills cancerous cells. He's the awesome movie character, known as a "fixer," who shows up after a murder has been committed to quietly and efficiently remove all evidence of the crime.

Pluto has only one interest: to get rid of what isn't making you strong. Our attachments in this world are what cause us pain—attachment to a body, to possessions, to other people. Pluto takes a hard, clinical glance at you and says, "What can this person do without? What is weighing this person down, undermining her?" And then he takes it away, whether or not you felt you were finished with it.

Losing other people is probably the hardest Pluto lesson we learn. We lose the ability to interact with someone we loved; we lose the person we were when we were around them. But speaking as someone who has lost half my family, I can say that they probably left when the time was right. It might not have been the right time for me, but I'm fairly certain it was the right time for them.

The Monster: Fearful

As I said, there are plenty of things to fear in life. People who know about astrology often fear times when Pluto will be active in their chart by transit (see Chapter 23) because they imagine at least a few of those awful things will happen to them. And when bad things happen in life—when things are taken away from us that we really don't want to give up—Pluto is invariably nearby, lurking in the shadows.

Someone gets chemotherapy, a treatment that many claim is worse than the disease it treats and worse than death. It might take away diseased cells and give you a chance to keep living … but it can make you feel as though you don't necessarily *want* to keep living. Monster Pluto is a cancer of nihilism, taking away zest for living.

Pluto: Planet or Planetoid?
Discovered in 1930, Pluto was considered our solar system's ninth planet until 2006, when it was demoted to "dwarf planet" status by the International Astronomical Union. This decision was not without controversy in the scientific community, with many astronomers objecting to the decision. The decision was almost entirely without controversy in the astrological community, however: astrologers still overwhelmingly include Pluto in their charts.

Pluto in Signs

Pluto describes the outward style of your inner terminator. Because Pluto moves through the zodiac so slowly, everyone born within roughly 20 years of you shares the same Pluto sign. As a generation, you are helping society achieve greater strength and integrity by removing the dead wood of dishonesty, artifice, hubris, and anything else that's unnecessary. Together, you create a myth that defines your generation. But every generation also has a shadow side, in which unacknowledged fears become potentially destructive.

There is some overlap between the Pluto generations, while Pluto was making long retrograde journeys back into the previous sign. If you were born during a year when Pluto was changing signs, you'll need to look at your birth chart to find out exactly where Pluto was at your birth.

Pluto in Aries (1822–1851)—*The myth:* The Wild West, celebrating rugged individualism and pioneer spirit. *The shadow:* Impulsive, self-serving violence. Genocide.

Pluto in Taurus (1851–1884)—*The myth:* The golden age of agriculture, a time of enormous wealth and ease for privileged landowners. *The shadow:* Getting rich off the backs of others. Slavery.

Pluto in Gemini (1882–1913)—*The myth:* Transformation of travel, communications, and paradigm-busting novelists like Hemingway and Fitzgerald. *The shadow:* The sinking of the *Titanic* and the mixed blessing of automation.

Pluto in Cancer (1912–1939)—*The myth:* Fighting to protect the safety and security of family and nation. Doing anything to make sure your family is fed. *The shadow:* Isolationism. Not allowing others to face hardships that build strength and character.

Pluto in Leo (1937–1958)—*The myth:* The sovereignty of the individual; everyone is special, and everyone can be a star. *The shadow:* Self-absorption, terror of aging, neglect of children.

Pluto in Virgo (1956–1972)—*The myth:* Bringing ideals down to earth, practical problem solving, and correcting the excesses of the previous generation. *The shadow:* "Perfection" as the enemy of the "good." Disillusionment; surrendering ideals altogether because they seem impossible to realize.

Pluto in Libra (1971–1984)—*The myth:* Facing interpersonal conflicts and negotiating solutions. Healing divisions that destroy marriages and nations. *The shadow:* Giving in too easily. Peace at any cost.

Pluto in Scorpio (1983–1995)—*The myth:* Empowerment through uncovering evil, dark, and twisted impulses in society. Demystifying taboo subjects. *The shadow:* Nihilism. Giving up in the face of so much ugliness and so many lies. Preoccupation with mortality.

Pluto in Sagittarius (1995–2008)—*The myth:* The explosion of the Internet and pervasive globalism, making the world a smaller and more intimate place. *The shadow:* The need to be right at all costs. Scapegoating those who are different. Religious zealotry.

Pluto in Capricorn (2008–2024)—*The myth:* The rise of powerful governments, and wise leaders guiding a new vision of the world. Some who seek to uncover truths about bureaucracies. *The shadow:* Dictators, tyrants, and plutocrats overseeing shadow governments and oppressive empires. Enslavement.

Pluto in Aquarius (2023–2044)—*The myth:* Innovation and exploration. Forming societies based on shared values rather than family connections. *The shadow:* A rebellious, fractured society, unable to connect with one another emotionally.

Pluto in Pisces (2043–2068)—*The myth:* Transcending individuality; revealing the untruths behind sentiment and uncovering those who use faith as a tool of manipulation. *The shadow:* Religious wars or oppression. In the previous transit of Pluto in Pisces, the French Revolution marked the end of the age of enlightenment.

ASTRO TIP

Because Pluto is so secretive, he has two different glyphs—one for popular usage and one that he uses as an alias, for undercover work. Actually, one is a styled version of the letters PL—the first two letters of Pluto, and also the initials of Percival Lowell, the discoverer of Pluto. The other looks kind of like an atomic mushroom cloud—an appropriate symbol for the planet associated with nuclear weapons.

Pluto in Houses

The house placement of Pluto in your chart personalizes the generational Pluto themes and symbolizes where you are secretive, protective, and probing; it's where you're trying to uncover the truth, get rid of what isn't necessary, and make yourself truly strong. Negatively, Pluto's house placement can describe what areas of life bring out your jealous, destructive, and controlling side.

Pluto in your first house—*Fearless:* You look at the world realistically and help others face difficulties head-on. You're good in emergencies. *Fearful:* Your drive to protect your privacy and physical safety can give an edge to your personality. When you feel threatened, you may tell harsh truths with the intention of hurting people.

Pluto in your second house—*Fearless:* You're willing to take terrifying chances to prove that you're secure and independent. You refuse to let financial fears rule your life. *Fearful:* You might not feel you deserve to have anything. You have the potential for great wealth, but your fear may lead you to make other people rich at the expense of your security.

Pluto in your third house—*Fearless:* You have uncanny perception and tend to remark on unsettling truths—you're a natural detective. You also have the ability to heal with your words. *Fearful:* Fear of saying the wrong thing. A pretty dark attitude about life and a caustic way of expressing yourself.

Pluto in your fourth house—*Fearless:* You have the ability to create a safe emotional place for people, where they can be completely themselves. *Fearful:* Fear of displeasing your family; self-sufficient to a fault and emotionally withholding.

Pluto in your fifth house—*Fearless:* Creating works of art that reflect dark and taboo themes; uplifting and inspiring others through your fearless self-expression. *Fearful:* Fear of being completely unimportant; empty sexual relationships and self-sabotage.

Pluto in your sixth house—*Fearless:* Doing meaningful work and creating a healthier, more compassionate world. *Fearful:* Fear of being imperfect. Neglect, selfishness, overwork, guilt, criticism.

Pluto in your seventh house—*Fearless:* Trusting someone. Understanding and healing the shadow. *Fearful:* Fear of being alone; cynicism about love; being secretive and controlling with partners..

Pluto in your eighth house—*Fearless:* You've seen it all, and when ugly stuff happens, you're someone people can talk to. *Fearful:* Fear of depending on someone; moodiness and emotional isolation, especially when you're hurting.

Pluto in your ninth house—*Fearless:* You have strong beliefs about the great questions of life, and when you speak, people listen. You're a natural philosopher, academic, or religious leader. *Fearful:* Fear of being wrong; refusing to speak out for fear of being punished.

Pluto in your tenth house—*Fearless:* You were born to do great things and to be a leader and an example to others. Don't wait for permission; carpe diem! *Fearful:* Fear of being a failure; becoming a petty tyrant, stuck in a puny, dead-end job.

Pluto in your eleventh house—*Fearless:* Join with passionate allies, and when they're wrong, tell them so. *Fearful:* Fear of being an outcast; keeping your mouth shut when the group is going in the wrong direction.

Pluto in your twelfth house—*Fearless:* You have the strength to love anyone, no matter how messed up and ugly and twisted they are. *Fearful:* Fear of being a bad person; cynicism about the suffering of others.

Essential Takeaways

- The generational planets are Uranus, Neptune, and Pluto. Because they move so slowly, entire generations are born with these planets in the same signs.
- The sign these planets are in describe your generation's defining qualities. The house the planets are in symbolize where you, personally, experience the qualities of the planet.
- Uranus is a planet of awakening, change, disruption, and rebellion.
- Neptune symbolizes illusion, clarity, compassion, intuition, spirituality, and faith.
- Pluto symbolizes honesty, hard truths, and getting rid of what isn't needed.

CHAPTER 15

Asteroids and Other Nonplanets

Chiron: healing and higher learning

Ceres, Vesta, Juno, and Pallas

The lunar nodes: past experience and future opportunity

The Part of Fortune and other Arabic parts

The vertex: relational turning points

When I began my formal astrology studies in the late 1980s, the use of asteroids in astrology was still pretty new. (My teacher, in fact, referred to them as "transiting gravel.") Demetra George had just published her pioneering book *Asteroid Goddesses* (see Appendix C), and some astrologers started to get pretty excited about these new symbols. Named for goddesses, the major asteroids seemed to offer feminine perspective that was sorely lacking in a modern astrology chock-full of manly symbolism.

Today, many astrologers swear by asteroids, using them (especially Chiron—ironically, the token male of the group) in a way very similar to planets in the chart. Asteroids can be interpreted in the birth chart or by transit according to their placement by sign, house, and in aspect to each other and to the planets and angles.

The asteroids commonly used in astrology are Chiron, which orbits between Saturn and Uranus, and the planetoids that orbit between Mars and Jupiter. Once classified as planets (in the early nineteenth century), they are Ceres (reclassified from asteroid to a dwarf planet in 2006), Vesta, Juno, and Pallas.

Asteroids are not included in most planetary ephemerides. However, most computer programs and online sites with calculation services (see Appendix C) include them upon request. Just ask for a chart that includes the asteroids and Chiron.

Chiron, the Wounded Healer ⚷

The myth: Chiron is by far the most popular asteroid among astrologers. Those who use Chiron *love* Chiron, interpreting it in connection to healing (especially holistic healing) and higher knowledge.

Chiron was an outcast centaur (his family considered him a freak, what with the whole half-man, half-horse thing) who pulled himself up by his hoofstraps to become exceptionally learned and gentle. Chiron was a great healer, a really smart guy, and a mentor for unruly youth. Then he was accidentally wounded by his student, Hercules, with a poison arrow to his knee. Sadly, despite his knack for healing, Chiron was unable to cure himself—a bummer, because he was both immortal and in terrible pain. Eventually Chiron figured that since he was suffering anyway, he would give himself up to switch places with Prometheus, who was undergoing some painful trials of his own. So Chiron, along with his other great qualities, was pretty noble as well.

The moral of the story: Enduring emotional and physical pain can make you more sensitive to the suffering of others, and a more insightful healer.

How to interpret Chiron in the birth chart: In astrology, Chiron symbolizes traumas or wounds that are incurable but which can, through consciousness, be transformed into great strengths. Chiron is a symbol for healing and healers, holistic health, higher knowledge, and the mind/body connection. Joyce Mason, in her ebook *Chiron and Wholeness: A Primer* (www.joycemason.com), offers Michael J. Fox and his battle with Parkinson's disease; the late Christopher Reeve, who became a quadriplegic after a horse-riding accident; and Caroline Kennedy Schlossberg, who's lost most of her family in tragic circumstances, as examples of Chiron's transformative principle at work.

MISC.

Chiron Fast Facts

- Key concepts—Healing, wounds, higher knowledge
- Symbolism—Chiron the centaur, half-horse, half-man
- Glyph—A skeleton key that opens all doors

- Orbit—49 years to complete a tour of the zodiac
- Possible rulerships—Virgo, Sagittarius

Ceres, the Great Mother ⚷

The myth: Ceres was the first asteroid discovered and is by far the largest. It's named for the Roman goddess of agriculture and the harvest. (The cereal you ate for breakfast this morning takes its name from Ceres.) It's Ceres's association with agriculture that leads astrologers to associate her with the qualities of nurturing, caretaking, parenting, and nourishing others.

Ceres also figures prominently in one of the great resurrection myths. Persephone is a maiden who is abducted and taken to live with Hades (whom we call by his Roman name, Pluto) in the underworld. This upsets her mother, Demeter (Ceres is the Roman equivalent of the Greek goddess), so much that she goes to Hades to beg for her daughter's release. Eventually, Hades gives in—but then Hermes manages to trick Persephone into eating forbidden fruit, the seeds of the pomegranate, which will bind her forever to the underworld. In a cruel intimation of the future of custody arrangements, it's decided that Persephone will spend half the year below ground and the other half above ground—hence, the division between winter/autumn and summer/spring.

The moral of the story: Whenever you love someone or something, you will eventually experience loss and grief—however fiercely you try to protect what you care about.

How to interpret Ceres in the birth chart: Where in your life are you a nurturing caretaker? What do you love enough to fight for as ferociously as a mother fights for her child? Ceres symbolizes the nurturing instinct. Its sign and house placement indicate your willingness to protect and defend people under your care, or even things, interests, or ideas that you care deeply about.

MISC.

Ceres Fast Facts

- Key concepts—Nurturance, self-worth, attachment, loss, grief, sharing, productivity, self-reliance
- Symbolism—Goddess of agriculture, the Great Mother
- Greek name: Demeter
- Glyph—The sickle, symbol of agriculture
- Orbit—1,680$\frac{1}{2}$ days (a little over 4$\frac{1}{2}$ years) to complete a tour of the zodiac
- Possible rulerships—Cancer, Virgo, Taurus, Scorpio

In her classic *Asteroid Goddesses,* Demetra George suggests the following rulerships for Ceres:

- Cancer: Nurturing, providing for others

- Taurus-Scorpio polarity: Attachment and aversion, loss and rejection, capacity for grief, sharing

- Virgo: Productivity, growth, self-reliance, work

She offers Ceres as a symbol of parenting (especially mothers), pregnancy, and childbirth, as well as physical, emotional, and spiritual nurturing. These qualities, combined with her connection to agriculture, make Ceres the consummate Earth Mother. If Ceres is negatively aspected in your birth chart, it may represent negative early parenting—the equivalent of being thrown into the waters of responsibility before you knew how to swim. You may have never known unconditional love, feel that you are unworthy of love, or believe you're not capable of independence and assertiveness.

Vesta, Keeper of the Flame ⚶

The myth: Vesta is the Roman counterpart of the Greek Hestia, born to Cronus and Rhea. After a lively beginning in which she and her siblings were devoured by their father (who feared a prophecy that they would overthrow him), Hestia—having perhaps had her fill of domestic drama—chose to remain a virgin. She refused offers to marry Apollo or Poseidon (both up-and-coming gods with good prospects). She was worshipped as the goddess of hearth and home.

Vesta, the Roman correlary to Hestia, was honored in every Roman home with a sacred fire that was never allowed to go out. Vestal virgins kept Vesta's eternal flame alive in the temple devoted to her. The job of the virgins, who took the job at age 6 and vowed 30 years of service and chastity, was to purify the shrine and keep the sacred flame burning. In exchange, they were granted the unusual privileges of owning property, freeing criminals, being buried within city limits, and safeguarding wills and contracts.

The moral of the story: Devote all your energy and focus to your sacred task and you will serve a higher purpose and achieve respect and improved status.

How to interpret Vesta in the birth chart: Where in your life are you whole, complete, centered, and focused? Vesta symbolizes the ability to be alone, without comfort and companionship. Its sign and house placement indicate your willingness to make sacrifices in order to be of service in some area of your life.

Vesta Fast Facts

- Key concepts—Work, devotion, sacrifice, commitment, fear of intimacy, groups based on common beliefs, safety, fanaticism
- Symbolism—Goddess of the hearth
- Greek name: Hestia
- Glyph—The sacred flame
- Orbit—1,325 days (a little over 3$\frac{1}{2}$ years) to complete a tour of the zodiac
- Possible rulerships—Virgo, Scorpio

Juno, the Sacred Consort ⚹

The myth: Mythological Juno is the Roman counterpart to the Greek goddess Hera. Hera was Zeus's wife and main concubine and was known as the "Queen of Gods." Hera had a temper, and not one to look the other way when Zeus messed around, she would often kill the other woman or the children she bore for Zeus.

The moral of the story: Hell hath no fury like a woman scorned.

How to interpret Juno in the birth chart: What do you need in order to feel happy in love, or that your marriage is a success? And if you don't get it, how jealous and angry are you apt to get?

Juno Fast Facts

- Key concepts—Relatedness, marriage, intimacy, manipulation, jealousy
- Symbolism—Goddess of marriage, queen of the heavens
- Greek name—Hera
- Glyph—A royal scepter
- Orbit—1,595$\frac{2}{5}$ days (a little under 4$\frac{1}{2}$ years) to complete a tour of the zodiac
- Possible rulerships—Libra, Scorpio

Pallas, the Warrior ♀

The myth: The most popular of the myths involving Pallas has her springing fully formed, clad in full battle gear, from the head of her father, Zeus (a surprise, as he'd assumed he just had a nasty headache). Zeus quickly forgot the pain of Pallas's birth and favored her among all his children. Born from the head of a male, Pallas came to represent intellectual creativity and great wisdom, symbolizing a patriarchal schism between creative intellect and femininity (since she wasn't born through typical female reproduction). She was revered by Greeks as their protectress—a warrior goddess, but a warrior of the Libran variety, emphasizing justice and diplomacy rather than bloodshed. And it's a long story, but she's frankly a feminist nightmare, siding with patriarchy and against the civil and parental rights of women.

The moral of the story: Intellectual strength is superior to both reproductive power and brute force.

How to interpret Pallas in the birth chart: Are you smart, creative, and a late bloomer sexually? If you're a woman, how do you feel about having children? And if you're a man, do you get a lot of really bad headaches? (Kidding!) Are you a daddy's girl, a staunch defender of patriarchy? Do you fear success, especially worrying that it will preclude you from romantic satisfaction? Are you dedicated to influencing society to believe that women shouldn't be in positions of influence? You could well have been born with Pallas prominent in your birth chart.

Pallas Fast Facts

- Key concepts—Intelligence, creativity, courage, fear, wisdom, the arts, politics, androgyny

- Symbolism—Goddess of wisdom and justice

- Latin name—Minerva

- Glyph—Spear

- Orbit—1,686.044 days (a little over $4\frac{1}{2}$ years) to complete a tour of the zodiac

- Possible rulerships—Libra, Leo, Aquarius

Cosmic Hula Hoops: Lunar Nodes ☊☋

Like the angles of the chart, the lunar nodes aren't physical objects, but rather points where the Moon's orbital path intersects with the ecliptic (the Sun's apparent path). To get a mental picture of this, imagine a clutch of hula hoops swinging around you at various angles and occasionally knocking into one another. The nodes are the points where they come together.

All planets have nodes, but the lunar nodes are the only ones commonly used in astrology and included in charts. The nodes are symbolized by symbols that look like horseshoes: the North Node is the horseshoe right-side up, the South Node is the horseshoe upside down. Usually, only the North Node is included on a chart, but the South Node is always at exactly the same degree as the North Node in the opposite sign.

The North Node is sometimes referred to as the dragon's head, and the South Node as the dragon's tail. The dragon's head "eats" new experiences, and the dragon's tail is where past experiences are eliminated.

The Meaning of the Nodes

The lunar nodes represent the polarity between past experience and future opportunity. The South Node represents your early environment and experiences (according to some astrologers, your past-life experiences), your unconscious mind, and your psychological safety zone. The North Node symbolizes your pathway to growth, people and situations that force you out of your comfort zone, and challenges that offer the promise of great reward.

True vs. Mean Nodes

Unlike the planets, the lunar nodes move backward (retrograde) through the zodiac and clockwise through the houses of the birth chart. Their complete lap around the zodiac takes about $18^1/_2$ years. But there's a catch: the Moon wobbles slightly, and its nodes don't move at exactly the same rate each day.

The *mean node* is calculated by taking the average rate of motion and averaging it out over $18^1/_2$ years. This was the tried-and-true method before the joyful advent of computers, which are able to calculate the *true node* position without breaking a sweat.

The two placements are only a couple of degrees apart, so in most cases it doesn't really matter which you use. But if your nodes are close to the beginning or end of a sign, or if you're using particular predictive techniques involving the nodes, you're better off using the true node.

DEFINITION

The Moon's **mean node** is calculated by averaging the node's average rate of motion over its 181/2-year journey through the zodiac. The **true node** is the actual position of the node on a particular day. The two are usually only a degree or two apart, so it doesn't matter too much which you use—though why be mean when you can be true?

Lunar Nodes by Sign and House

The sign placement of the nodes is generally shared by all people born within an approximate 18-month period, and refer to common evolutionary experiences. The house placement of the nodes refers to the areas of your life where this evolutionary struggle is experienced.

North Node in Aries/first house, South Node in Libra/seventh house—*Your gift:* The ability to relate to others. *Your challenge:* To learn how to stand up for yourself and to fight for what you want. *Your mission:* Cultivate relationships that support your independence, assertiveness, and ambitions.

North Node in Taurus/second house, South Node in Scorpio/eighth house—*Your gift:* Insights, sensitivity, and honesty. *Your challenge:* To develop trust, security, and material stability. *Your mission:* Learn to trust your insights, integrity, and judgment; they are your path to true security.

North Node in Gemini/third house, South Node in Sagittarius/ninth house—*Your gift:* Knowledge, understanding, and confidence in your beliefs. *Your challenge:* To maintain an open mind and keep trying new things. *Your mission:* Keep learning and trying new things; otherwise, your beliefs will be founded on incomplete information.

North Node in Cancer/fourth house, South Node in Capricorn/tenth house—*Your gift:* Pragmatism, shrewd judgment, and executive ability. *Your challenge:* Connecting in a nurturing way with family and community. *Your mission:* In order to feel like a true success, use your practical ability and leadership skills to mentor and nurture others.

North Node in Leo/fifth house, South Node in Aquarius/eleventh house—*Your gift:* You know what it feels like to be an outsider, and you know how to befriend practically anyone. *Your challenge:* To let yourself to stand out from the crowd, and to seek recognition of your creative gifts. *Your mission:* Only by standing out will you ever fit in.

North Node in Virgo/sixth house, South Node in Pisces/twelfth house—*Your gift:* Compassion, intuition, faith, and spiritual grace. *Your challenge:* To master the practical minutia of everyday life, such as good work and health habits. *Your mission:* To approach the routines of daily life as a personal spiritual practice.

North Node in Libra/seventh house, South Node in Aries/first house—*Your gift:* You know how to assert yourself and how to fight for yourself. *Your challenge:* To form good relationships, based on cooperation and compromise, with equal partners. *Your mission:* To use your warrior abilities and confidence to help others learn to take care of themselves.

North Node in Scorpio/eighth house, South Node in Taurus/second house—*Your gift:* You know who you are and you're happy with what you have. *Your challenge:* To share with others, and to become familiar with uncomfortable truths about life. *Your mission:* Your strong inner resources will allow you to delve deeply into life's mysteries without getting lost.

North Node in Sagittarius/ninth house, South Node in Gemini/third house—*Your gift:* Your curiosity, facility with language, and ability to connect with people. *Your challenge:* To know when you have enough facts and skill to make a contribution to the world. *Your mission:* Stop asking everyone else what they think, and start telling them what you know.

North Node in Capricorn/tenth house, South Node in Cancer/fourth house—*Your gift:* Your tender, sensitive, nurturing spirit; you're a giver. *Your challenge:* To take yourself seriously. *Your mission:* You nurture others more effectively by helping them set high standards for themselves.

North Node in Aquarius/eleventh house, South Node in Leo/fifth house—*Your gift:* Your playful, joyful, creative approach to life, and your ability to get noticed. *Your challenge:* To play well with others. *Your mission:* Working collectively with others will let you use your creative abilities for a larger purpose.

North Node in Pisces/twelfth house, South Node in Virgo/sixth house—*Your gift:* Your ability to analyze situations, see what's wrong, and make things work. *Your challenge:* To be accepting and empathetic. *Your mission:* Living ecstatically in each moment will give you a more intuitive insight into how you can really be helpful.

Arabic Parts

The *Arabic parts* (or lots) don't represent physical points in the sky. Rather, they're mathematically derived from three points in the chart, such as planets or angles. The distance between two points is added to the position of the third to come up with the degree and sign of the part.

DEFINITION

Arabic parts (or lots) originated in Arabia during the Middle Ages. Each part is derived from three points in a horoscope and represents a sensitive point in the chart that is connected to the three planets or other points from which is was derived. There are hundreds of Arabic parts, but today most astrologers use only the Part of Fortune, derived from the Sun, Moon, and Ascendant.

The Part of Fortune ⊗

There are Arabic parts for a dazzling array of things, from marriage to pomegranates, but only one will commonly show up in your chart: The Part, or Lot, of Fortune. It represents the body, fortune, and health, as an indicator of material well-being. Since it's derived from the placements of the Sun, Moon, and Ascendant, it seems a sort of macrocosm of your ego, unconscious, and personality.

The formula for deriving the Part of Fortune differs depending on whether you were born during the day (the Sun is above the horizon in the chart) or at night (the Sun is below the horizon). Most computer programs take this into account, but if you're calculating it by hand, be sure you use the right formula:

- For day charts, the formula is: Ascendant + Moon − Sun

- For night charts, the formula is: Ascendant + Sun − Moon

The Part of Fortune is the one that regularly shows up in charts, and you'll probably never need to know how to calculate it. But if you want to, the instructions follow. The first two steps are the same for calculating any of the Arabic parts.

1. Translate each sign of the zodiac into degrees of the 360-degree horoscopic wheel:

Aries	0–29
Taurus	30–59
Gemini	60–89
Cancer	90–119
Leo	120–149
Virgo	150–179
Libra	180–209
Scorpio	210–239
Sagittarius	240–269
Capricorn	270–299
Aquarius	300–329
Pisces	330–359

2. Translate each planetary placement in the formula into a degree.

Example (for a daytime birth, use Ascendant + Moon – Sun):

Sun 13° 25" Cancer   90 (first degree of Cancer)
          + <u>13.25</u> (degree of natal Sun)

          103.25 (degree on horoscopic wheel)

Moon 24° 19" Libra   180 (first degree of Libra)
          + <u>24.19</u> (degree of natal Moon)

          204.19 (degree on horoscopic wheel)

Ascendant 5° 08" Virgo 150 (first degree of Virgo)
          + <u>5.08</u> (degree of natal Ascendant)

          155.08 (degree on horoscopic wheel)

3. Add the horoscopic degrees for the Ascendant and Moon together:

       204.19
       + <u>155.08</u>

       359.27 (Ascendant/Moon total)

4. Subtract the horoscopic degree of the Sun from the Ascendant/Moon total:

       359.27
       – <u>103.25</u>

       256.02 (Ascendant/Moon – Sun total)

5. Convert the result to a horoscopic degree:

       256.02 (falls between 240–269 Sagittarius)
       – <u>240.00</u> (first degree of Sagittarius)

       16.02 (Part of Fortune: 16° 02" Sagittarius)

Interpreting the Part of Fortune

The part of fortune is interpreted as a point in your chart that describes your worldly success. Planets or angles in close aspect to the Part of Fortune, the planet(s) ruling the sign of the Part of Fortune signify your calling and talents, as well as how easy or difficult it will be for you to make something of them. The sign and house placement of the Part of Fortune describes how, and in which areas of life, you're likely to find success.

MISC.

Other Cool Arabic Parts
Since you went to the trouble of learning the math, here are a few other fun Arabic parts that you can calculate and toss into your chart:

- The Part of Love: Ascendant + Venus – Sun
- The Part of Marriage (for a woman): Ascendant + Saturn – Venus
- The Part of Marriage (for a man): Ascendant + Venus – Saturn
- The Part of Sudden Happiness: Ascendant + Uranus – Jupiter

Notice that the formula for Part of Marriage for a woman *adds* Saturn (responsibilities) and *subtracts* Venus (pleasure), while the formula for a man is the reverse. (Hmmm ...)

The Vertex ☒

The vertex, like the lunar nodes, is another reference point in space rather than a physical object. The vertex marks the spot where the ecliptic (which, as you no doubt recall, is the hula hoop that marks the Sun's apparent annual journey across the sky, highlighted by the signs of the zodiac) meets the prime vertical. The prime vertical is a hula hoop that runs at right angles to the meridian and divides the celestial sphere from front to back (like a center part in your hair). The vertex can be interpreted according to its sign, house placement, and aspects to planets in your birth chart. It can be activated by transits, progressions, and the planets in another person's birth chart.

Except in rare instances at extreme latitudes, the vertex falls in the houses on the right (western, other-oriented) side of your chart, usually the fifth, sixth, seventh, or eighth house. Because of this orientation, it's thought that the vertex has something to do with fated relationships and pivotal meetings with people who catalyze growth. You may be the one catalyzed, but sometimes you may be the catalyst.

Vertex in the fifth house: Children, creative partners, lovers, givers of enjoyment, playmates who share hobbies or other recreational interests.

Vertex in the sixth house: Co-workers, healers, servants, and those who share a bond of service.

Vertex in the seventh house: Equal partners, spouses, open enemies, adversaries in lawsuits, rivals.

Vertex in your eighth house: Intimate partners, people in a power-based relationship, those who share a joint bank account or property, insurers, inheritance, psychotherapy.

The Antivertex

The point exactly opposite the vertex is called the antivertex. It falls on the left (eastern, or self-oriented) side of your chart, usually in the twelfth, eleventh, first, or second house. You'll almost never find it marked in the chart, but it's the same degree as the vertex and in the opposite sign and house. Here, there are situations and people who reinforce the personal status quo, allowing or even encouraging each other to remain pretty much as they are. This is not always negative, and may be done with kind intentions, but the net result is a nagging feeling that you're not growing.

Antivertex in the eleventh house: Peers who encourage conformance to a group. More positively, friends and associates who are accepting of each other based on having many things in common.

Antivertex in the twelfth house: Your priest, your hidden enemies, your psychic, or your drug dealer. These people are invested in your blind side, where you can't see the whole picture and must rely on intuition or faith.

Antivertex in the first house: People who respond to your looks, personality, drive, and assertiveness. These are people who encourage you to look out for number one.

Antivertex in the second house: Those with whom you exchange money, gifts, or other forms of security. These may be customers or admirers, or you may be their customer or admirer.

Like the Ascendant and Midheaven, the vertex is an extremely time-sensitive point. If you don't have your exact birth time, don't bother with the vertex. Honestly, most people don't—not even those who know their exact birth time.

The Vertex in Your Chart

Hardly anyone uses the vertex or writes about the vertex, but it's commonly assumed to have some relevance in how you relate to other people or to events. Some astrologers assert that it's connected to turning points, ah-ha moments, and fateful encounters with others. The vertex can be activated by transits, progressions, or directions (see Part 6); by the planets in another person's chart; or if you move to a new place. The house and sign position can offer clues as to where the change or turning point may take place and in what way.

Essential Takeaways

- The asteroid Chiron is linked to healing and higher learning.
- The dwarf planet Ceres is associated with nurturing, motherhood, and loss.
- Vesta, a planetoid, represents devotion, work, and sacrifice.
- The planetoid Juno symbolizes marriage, the principle of relatedness, and jealousy.
- The planetoid Pallas is associated with intelligence, wisdom, and the arts.
- The Moon's nodes mark the points where the Moon's orbital path intersects with the Sun's apparent path. They represent the polarity between past experience and future opportunity.
- Arabic parts, or lots, are mathematically derived from three points in the chart. The one commonly included in birth charts, the Part of Fortune, represents body, fortune, health, career, and material success.
- The vertex is the point where the ecliptic meets the prime vertical. It is connected to fateful encounters with others that catalyze change.

CHAPTER 16

Planetary Aspects

How to find aspects between planets

Easy aspects: the conjunction, sextile, and trine

Difficult aspects: the square and opposition

Major and minor aspects

Interpreting aspects between planets

How signs and houses work with aspects

Planets move at different speeds, moving past each other, saluting from across the ecliptic. Their proximity to each other is always changing. When they reach particular angular relationships to each other along the zodiac, we call this proximity the "aspect," or angular relationship, between planets.

Planets in aspect are like characters in a play who have dialogue with each other. They are in some way acquainted. Perhaps they get along well, sometimes they torment one another, they might fall in love or get in a fight. One thing's for certain: they are not indifferent to one another.

Rules of Engagement

In astrological grammar, the faster-moving planet aspects the slower-moving planet. The Moon aspects everyone; Mercury aspects everyone but the Moon; the Sun aspects Venus through Pluto; Venus aspects Mars through Pluto. You get the idea.

When a faster-moving planet is within a certain number of degrees of an exact aspect to a slower-moving planet, we say it's making an approaching, or applying aspect. These are usually more powerful aspects than separating ones, because they refer to energy that is gathering momentum, and the suspense of building toward a particular moment.

After the aspect is exact and the faster planet begins moving away, the aspect is separating. There's still a connection, but it's reached its peak of intensity and its influence is waning. Think of a girl who's left her boyfriend to go away to college; the longer she's away, the more remote the connection between them and the dimmer the memories of their courtship.

Finding Planetary Aspects

For my money, planetary aspects are the richest, most fascinating, and most reliable dimension of astrology. Signs and houses are extremely valuable, but in a pinch, an astrologer can glean an awful lot from just knowing the relationships between the planets in a chart.

In teaching astrology, I've found that planetary aspects are a kind of moment of truth that marks the dividing line between serious students and those who are happy knowing a little bit more than the signs of the zodiac. That's because aspects bring us into the realm of 3-D astrology and its terrifying suburb, geometry. But relax. I mastered planetary aspects before I learned anything at all about geometry.

Easy aspects generally occur between planets in signs that are compatible: air with fire, water with earth. There are exceptions to this rule. Oppositions occur between planets of compatible element that are on opposite sides of the chart. Also, because there is a little leeway given between exact aspects, it's possible for a planet at the end of one sign to be in difficult aspect to a planet at the beginning of another sign, even if those signs are compatible. This is called a *dissociate* or *out-of-sign* aspect.

DEFINITION

Dissociate or **out-of-sign** aspects are between planets that are in aspect but whose signs are not in the same relationship. For example, a trine aspect naturally occurs between planets in signs of the same element. But a planet at the end of Aquarius (an air sign) can form a trine aspect to a planet in the first degrees of Cancer (a water sign).

An Aspect Grid

When you have your chart calculated by a computer program, it will usually spit out a convenient grid showing the aspects between planets. It'll look something like this:

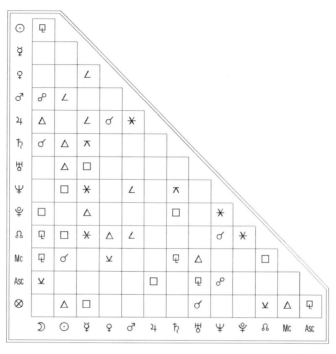

©1994 Matrix Software Big Rapids, MI   Aspect Wheel

Planetary aspect grid.

Read the grid from left to right and top to bottom. The column underneath the symbol for the Moon shows the aspects from the Moon to the slower-moving planets on the right. If you see a lot of triangles and stars in this column, your Moon plays well with the other planets; if there are a lot of squares and little things that look like barbells or side views of picnic tables, you've got a Moon that's a little cranky.

Orbs: How Close Is Close Enough?

You and an attractive stranger live in the same city, but up to now you haven't met. Then one evening you find yourselves at an art exhibition. If you were planets, you'd have just entered one another's orb.

221

For the first 20 minutes, you work the room at different speeds, never noticing one another. Then the stranger stops next to a potted palm, and as you're reaching for a glass of chardonnay, you both look up and notice each other from across the room. The orb is getting tighter.

Gradually, you each work your way across the room, greeting friends, spilling wine on the carpet, until you're close enough to introduce yourselves. The aspect is exact.

Orbs are tricky. Not all astrologers agree on the number of degrees on either side of an exact aspect that two planets need to have to be considered "in aspect." Some astrologers might say that you and the attractive stranger were not in orb until you get within wine-spilling distance; others feel you were in orb from the time you both found yourselves living in the same city. Most astrologers use different orbs for different kinds of aspects, and some might adjust orbs depending on the planet itself. The orbs provided in the rest of this chapter are merely guidelines; in time you'll form your own opinions on the subject, so you can hold your own in any group of screaming astrologers.

> **ASTRO TIP**
>
> The only thing that can animate a group of astrologers more than the great house system debate (see Chapter 8) is the subject of planetary orbs. A standard rule of thumb gives major aspects (conjunction, square, trine, opposition) an orb of 7 degrees. The sextile and quincunx (discussed later in the chapter) are given an orb of 5 degrees, and minor aspects only 1 degree. Some astrologers (the ones with a strong Jupiter) favor much more generous orbs, while others (with a strong Saturn or lots of Virgo planets) hew to tighter orbs.

A Planetary Dinner Party

Aspects can be hard to visualize. So to illustrate them, I've used a familiar setting: the family dinner party, shown in the following figure. Imagine all the planets are guests—the usual collection of siblings, cousins, mothers, children, and even pets—and that the dining table is the wheel of a birth chart. Each guest has a relationship to the others that's represented by the seating arrangement. Two guests sitting opposite each other have an "opposition" relationship; they are sitting 180 degrees apart. Two guests sharing the same bench have a conjunction relationship; they are sitting 0 degrees apart.

Will sesquiquadrate warfare break out between Pete's girlfriend Marge and his sister Janet? Will the contentious square aspect between them prompt Uncle Hank to throw a dinner roll at Ted? Use this planetary seating chart as your guide to the cast of characters

I'll return to in this chapter. The planets in your own chart may be sitting in different seats at the table, but they share many of the same relationships as this family.

Planetary seating chart.

Easy Aspects

Flowing, compatible, do not interfere with one another, enabling … having some easy aspects in your chart is like having some oil in your car's engine: it keeps the works running smoothly, without making dreadful screeching noises and ruining the metal. However, having too many easy aspects is like being a spoiled rich kid who's had everything handed to him his whole life, has never had to work for anything, and has never paid consequences for any of his actions.

Conjunction ☌

Degrees of separation: 0°

Recommended orb: 7°

Key concepts: Beginnings, fusion, melding, intensity, concentration, drive, emphasis

By far the easiest aspect to spot in a chart, planets in a conjunction are sitting right next to each other at the same degree of the same sign. They've been thrown into a room together, and they're standing toe to toe and eye to eye.

The conjunction is more of a neutral aspect than an easy one, actually. Planets in a conjunction are like members of the same family: they share a strong connection, history, and genetics, but not necessarily compatible personalities. As you know from Thanksgiving dinners past, you can have a lot in common with your family—even love them—without actually getting along that well.

For example, seat your chatty, restless younger brother Carl (Mercury) next to glowering, taciturn Uncle Hank (Saturn) at the Thanksgiving table. And I do mean *next to him*—you ran out of chairs, and the two have to share a piano bench you dragged in from the living room. Will Mercury find a way to engage Saturn in conversation? Or will Saturn win the day and silence your chattering brother with a chilly glance?

Much depends on the sign where the conjunction is taking place, and whether or not one of these planets is stronger in that sign than the other. If the sign is Gemini, where Mercury is strong, then Carl's indefatigable gift of gab will win the day and his chattering will drive Uncle Hank half mad. If the sign is Capricorn, then Saturn rules; Uncle Hank will settle the kid down with a dirty look and finally get some peace and quiet. However, if the sign is Aquarius, which is a comfortable sign for both Mercury and Saturn, your brother will hit on a topic (finance, taxidermy) that will draw Uncle Hank out, and both will be happy.

Sextile ⚹

Degrees of separation: 60° (two signs)

Recommended orb: 5°

Key concepts: Opportunity, attraction, friendship, expression, spark

Sitting two seats away from Carl and Uncle Hank, at a 60-degree angle, is ravishing, charming cousin Angela (Venus). Carl loves nothing more than to tease Angela, and she takes it with good humor. He would have preferred to sit next to her at dinner, but as it is, he can still manage to chat with her if he works at it. He has to crane his neck around Uncle Hank and Aunt Leticia (more about her later) and holler a little bit, but he still manages to throw some witticisms toward Angela, and she giggles appreciatively.

Two planets separated by 60 degrees are in sextile aspect. The sextile usually occurs between planets that are in complementary signs but not the same element—fire with air, and earth with water. My teacher once described the sextile as being like a cross between a trine and a square; it yields the gifts of a trine if you're willing to do the work of a square. Planets in sextile are usually in signs of compatible element; temperamentally, they aren't exactly alike, but they're complementary.

Carl (Mercury) and Angela (Venus) are in a sextile aspect. They still get to have fun with each other, but it takes a little work.

Planet in This Sign …	Look for Sextiles to Planets in …
Aries	Gemini, Aquarius
Taurus	Cancer, Pisces
Gemini	Leo, Aries
Cancer	Virgo, Taurus
Leo	Gemini, Libra
Virgo	Cancer, Scorpio
Libra	Leo, Sagittarius
Scorpio	Virgo, Capricorn
Sagittarius	Libra, Aquarius
Capricorn	Scorpio, Pisces
Aquarius	Aries, Sagittarius
Pisces	Taurus, Capricorn

ASTRO ALERT

"Easy" aspects aren't always "good." Easy aspects point to noninterference. For instance, the chart for the 9/11 attacks had a lot of harmonious aspects to Mercury (the planet of transportation and logistics), and those horrific events were noteworthy for the ease with which the hijackers carried out their mission.

Trine △

Degrees of separation: 120°

Recommended orb: 7°

Key concepts: Flow, ease, harmony, laziness, inspiration, noninterference

Sitting two seats to Angela's right is your other brother Pete (Neptune). Carl and Pete have a clear eye line to one another and have no problem communicating all through dinner, even though they can't easily chat with each other. Their in-jokes and body language work together to give them an almost telepathic rapport, and they regularly burst into laughter. Pete's easygoing and gentle, but Carl brings out his mischievous side. They spend the entire dinner rolling their eyes every time Angela's husband Ted opens his mouth (more about him later).

Carl (Mercury) and Pete (Neptune) have a trine aspect between them. The trine, which normally occurs between planets in signs that share the same element, indicates ease, harmony, and instinctive rapport. Carl and Pete don't have to work at their interaction at all—they totally get each other, and are seated in such a way that they can see each other clearly and communicate. Of course, when they've both had a little too much wine and start horsing around, tossing rolls at each other, everyone might wish they didn't get along quite so well.

Planet in This Sign ...	*Look for Trines to Planets in ...*
Aries	Leo, Sagittarius
Taurus	Virgo, Capricorn
Gemini	Libra, Aquarius
Cancer	Scorpio, Pisces
Leo	Aries, Sagittarius
Virgo	Taurus, Capricorn
Libra	Gemini, Aquarius
Scorpio	Cancer, Pisces
Sagittarius	Aries, Leo
Capricorn	Taurus, Virgo
Aquarius	Gemini, Libra
Pisces	Cancer, Scorpio

Difficult Aspects

Difficult or "hard" aspects symbolize an uneasy relationship between planets in signs that have little in common. They're often in signs of the same quality, but of different elements; so they want some of the same things, but they go about them in very different ways.

Difficult aspects represent challenges that must be overcome—both the challenges that the world throws at you and the challenge of your own inner conflicts. Difficulties can make you angry, frustrated, and driven, but they can also motivate you to get things done. (As my mom used to say, "If you didn't have any problems, you'd never get anything done.") So don't be wary of the difficult aspects in your chart; many can be stressful, but you need a few to motivate you and build character.

 ASTRO TIP "Hard" aspects aren't always negative, though they may feel that way. On the contrary, hard aspects build character in the same way pumping iron builds muscles.

Square □

Degrees of separation: 90° (four signs)

Recommended orb: 7°

Key concepts: Accomplishments, breakthroughs, action, tension, challenge, friction

Sitting at cousin Angela's right is her husband Ted (Jupiter). Ted doesn't enjoy conversation; he enjoys giving monologues. He's a happy, boisterous guy, but he does have a way of dominating the conversation. Both Carl (Mercury) and Uncle Hank (Saturn) find Ted intensely annoying—Uncle Hank because (as we know) he's not so much a fan of the talking, and Carl because he'd like to get the odd word in edgewise himself.

On the other hand, Ted's presence forces Carl to curb his own tendency toward exhausting blather, and refine his message and delivery to sneak between the cracks in Ted's monologue; and Ted's determined vivacity and corny jokes occasionally get Uncle Hank to *almost* break a smile, despite his best efforts to maintain maximum grumpiness.

Carl (Mercury) and Uncle Hank (Saturn) are in a square aspect to Ted (Jupiter). They don't like the cut of his jib. They find him irritating. They wish he'd shut up. But they're also benefiting from Ted's presence; he's making them into slightly better versions of themselves.

Planets in square aspect experience friction with each other. They're usually in signs of incompatible element and the same quality (cardinal, fixed, mutable). If you've got two planets opposite each other but both square another planet, you've got yourself a T-square configuration, which I think of as the "an enemy of my enemy is my friend" aspect. Both the opposing planets have a beef with the third planet, so they work together to settle their differences with him.

Planet in This Sign …	Look for Squares to Planets in …
Aries	Cancer, Capricorn
Taurus	Leo, Aquarius
Gemini	Virgo, Pisces
Cancer	Aries, Libra
Leo	Taurus, Scorpio
Virgo	Gemini, Sagittarius
Libra	Cancer, Capricorn
Scorpio	Leo, Aquarius
Sagittarius	Virgo, Pisces
Capricorn	Aries, Libra
Aquarius	Taurus, Scorpio
Pisces	Gemini, Sagittarius

Opposition ☍

Degrees of separation: 180° (six signs)

Orb Recommended: 7°

Key concepts: Judgment, conflict, balance, awareness, projection, reaching out

Across the table from cousin Angela is cousin Phoebe (the Moon). Phoebe is Angela's molecular opposite: shy, quiet, and sensitive. The two cousins have little to say to one another; they regard each other from across the table as ambassadors from different countries, in different hemispheres, possibly from different planets.

But they also rather admire one another. Angela (Venus) sometimes feels she could benefit from being a little quieter and nurturing her inner life (the Moon); Phoebe would love to have a makeover and be as glamorous and socially at ease as Angela. It's as though they're missing halves of a two-piece puzzle. The potential for two planets in opposition

228

is that, since they're in signs of complementary element, they can learn from each other how to develop the qualities they envy in one another.

Planets in opposition are coming from different places (opposite houses) and often behave in very different ways (opposite signs). But like Angela and Phoebe, they can't avoid looking at each other because they're seated directly opposite each other. They can envy each other, try to emulate each other, or declare open warfare on each other; one thing they can't do is ignore each other.

Planet in This Sign ...	Look for Oppositions to Planets in ...
Aries	Libra
Taurus	Scorpio
Gemini	Sagittarius
Cancer	Capricorn
Leo	Aquarius
Virgo	Pisces
Libra	Aries
Scorpio	Taurus
Sagittarius	Gemini
Capricorn	Cancer
Aquarius	Leo
Pisces	Virgo

 ASTRO TIP Minor aspects are fascinating, but when you're first learning astrology you can safely disregard them. Focus on major aspects to get the big picture; minor aspects add richness and dimension, like shading on a portrait, but you can still get a clear picture without them.

Minor (But Not Trivial) Aspects

While the louder, more extravagant aspects grab the spotlight, other, more subtle influences are also at work. Think of the extras in a film; they don't have dialogue that the audience hears, but you see them in the background chatting animatedly with one another. Apparently, however, it's not conversation that drives the story's central drama.

Around your Thanksgiving table (and huddled around the kids' table) are several minor dramas unfolding. You'll have to look closely to notice them, but they contribute significantly to the overall mood of the gathering.

I believe that minor aspects represent blind spots, where you really don't stop to ask yourself what's going on. Major aspects can absolutely not be ignored; they represent crucial, defining characteristics of you and your life. But minor aspects offer answers to questions you don't really think to ask, about matters that are sometimes troubling and irritating but that you accept, sort of like wallpaper.

Semisextile ⊻

Degrees of separation: 30° (one sign)

Recommended orb: 1°

Key concepts: Correction, reaction

Sitting next to Uncle Hank is Aunt Leticia (Uranus). They're the type of couple that prompt head-scratching bewilderment of the "How in the heck did those two end up together?" variety. Aunt Leticia is breezy, affable, and as offbeat in dress and personality as Uncle Hank is conservative and grumbly.

And yet, they've been married for 40 years and seem to get along swimmingly. If it weren't for Aunt Leticia, Uncle Hank probably wouldn't have a friend in the world, but she has dragged so many people home to dinner over the years that some of them have stuck and have become Hank's friends, too. If it weren't for Uncle Hank's steadying influence, Aunt Leticia would probably veer off the rails, careening from endearingly offbeat to flamboyantly eccentric.

Planets in semisextile are in the same degree of adjacent signs. Signs next to each other on the natural wheel share nothing in common—not element, not quality, nothing (except Capricorn and Aquarius, which share Saturn as a ruler). And yet surprisingly often they—like Uncle Hank and Aunt Leticia— benefit from their wildly divergent natures, each curbing and correcting the gravest excesses of the other.

Planet in This Sign ...	Look for Semisextiles to Planets in ...
Aries	Pisces, Taurus
Taurus	Aries, Gemini
Gemini	Taurus, Cancer
Cancer	Gemini, Leo
Leo	Cancer, Virgo

Planet in This Sign ...	Look for Semisextiles to Planets in ...
Virgo	Leo, Libra
Libra	Virgo, Scorpio
Scorpio	Libra, Sagittarius
Sagittarius	Scorpio, Capricorn
Capricorn	Sagittarius, Aquarius
Aquarius	Capricorn, Pisces
Pisces	Aquarius, Aries

Semisquare ∠

Degrees of separation: 45° (one-and-a-half signs)

Recommended orb: 1°

Key concepts: Irritation; annoyance; a feeling of "itchiness"

Two planets are semisquare if they're 45 degrees ($1^1/_2$ signs) apart. They're related to squares and oppositions; oppositions divide the horoscope in two, squares divide the horoscope into four, and semisquares divide the horoscope into eight.

The semisquare feels intensely itchy. It's the driving urge (square) to resolve diametrically opposed needs (opposition). In a positive way, we can think of it as an aspect that encourages (okay, *demands*) integration of the themes represented by these two planets.

At the dining table, Carl and Pete's mom, Regina (the Sun), is simmering at a low boil. She's annoyed by the constant struggles between Pete and his girlfriend Marge (each sitting 45 degrees from her), who keep throwing nasty looks and heated comments at each other. She's about to lock them in the powder room together until they sort things out and can act like grown-ups. (Don't mess with Regina.)

Quincunx ⊼

Degrees of separation: 150° (five signs)

Recommended orb: 5°

Key concepts: Adjustment, imbalance, compromise, dissatisfaction

Angela's cousin Ted has a secret: although he's deeply in love with his wife, he's always had a little bit of a crush on her cousin Phoebe. There's something mysterious about her that appeals to Ted, probably because her quiet personality is completely different from his own open, friendly nature.

Like Ted and Phoebe, the quincunx (or inconjunct) aspect separates two planets by 150 degrees (five signs). You find whether a planet is involved in a quincunx fairly easily, as minor aspects go. Just look to the sign opposite the one the planet is in, and find the signs on either side of it; that's where you'll find quincunxes.

When you're trying to spot aspects in the chart, count signs, not houses. A quincunx, for instance, usually occurs between planets that are five signs away from each other. But since an entire sign is sometimes hidden (intercepted) within a house, quincunx planets are not necessarily five houses away from each other.

The quincunx naturally forms an uneasy alliance between planets in signs with nothing in common (other than Taurus and Libra, signs which are quincunx each other but share a common planetary ruler, Venus). They are from different elements and different modalities, so they have different temperaments and ways of approaching things. And the quincunx is an aspect of inherent inequality; one party is enthralled by—and willing to be the devoted servant of—the other.

These planets/signs just don't get each other. As with Ted and Phoebe, that sense of mystery can be sexually compelling, under the right circumstances, so you often see these signs hooking up. But their very different natures can also wear on the nerves. Constant adjustments and compromises must be made, and it seems only one planet/sign can be happy at a time.

Planet in This Sign ...	Look for Quincunxes to Planets in ...
Aries	Virgo, Scorpio
Taurus	Libra, Sagittarius
Gemini	Scorpio, Capricorn
Cancer	Sagittarius, Aquarius
Leo	Capricorn, Pisces
Virgo	Aries, Aquarius
Libra	Taurus, Pisces
Scorpio	Gemini, Aries
Sagittarius	Taurus, Cancer

Planet in This Sign ...	Look for Quincunxes to Planets in ...
Capricorn	Gemini, Leo
Aquarius	Cancer, Virgo
Pisces	Leo, Libra

Sesquisquare ⊡

Degrees of separation: 135° (four-and-a-half signs)

Recommended orb: 1°

Key concepts: Tension, exasperation

Smoldering moodily to Carl's left, his sister Janet (Pluto) is debating whether to murder Pete's girlfriend Marge with a fork or by water torture. Pete had assured his sister that she and Marge would really hit it off and would be great friends; as it turns out, each finds the other extraordinarily irritating—the last straw on an afternoon when both are already having their share of relationship problems.

Janet and Marge represent the sesquisquare, also known as the sesquiquadrate, separates planets by 135 degrees. It naturally occurs between planets in signs that are trine or quincunx each other. If the sesquisquare occurs in trine signs, we've got one of these situations where it looks on paper like the planets should get along beautifully ... and yet they really want to strangle each other. If they occur in signs that are quincunx, they don't expect to get along and just give over to their mutual antipathy.

What can you expect from an aspect that's like a semisquare (45 degrees) added to a square (90 degrees)? Imagine you're pushing a massive boulder uphill, all by yourself, while a thousand flies bite at you. The irritating, abrasive quality of this aspect feels like the quivering tension of a wishbone that's ready to snap. It's insult to injury, the straw that broke the camel's back, and dealing with your sister's annoying girlfriend on a day when you and your mother are already at each other's throats. For that reason, I think of the sesquiquadrate as the "I don't need this!" aspect.

Parallel ∥ and Contraparallel ∦

Parallels are a bit different from other aspects because they measure declination, or two planets' distance from the celestial equator, rather than their celestial longitude. Not that you need to know much about that. Suffice to say that if two planets are within a degree of the same declination (their latitude, projected onto the celestial sphere), they're parallel, which has the feel of a conjunction. If they're within a degree of the same declination but one is north of the equator and the other is south, they're contraparallel, which is sort of like an opposition.

Back at the dinner table, I neglected to mention before that Regina is holding the family's 20-pound tabby, Oliver, on her shoulders. It just worked out that way. After Regina finished eating, the cat leaped into her arms, then sidled up onto Regina's shoulders where he is perched in a state of supreme satisfaction. He's awesome to behold, and he knows it. Everyone digs his cute expressions, and when the tension gets too thick, Oliver can be counted upon to do something cute and relieve the pressure.

Meanwhile, hiding under the table at Regina's feet is Rufus, the family dog. Rufus is happy with his place in the family, happy to eat the scraps that fall to the floor, content to be mostly overlooked, stepped on, and hollered at. Until he catches the occasional glimpse of Oliver, on top of the world and the beloved center of attention.

Oliver the tabby cat is parallel to Regina, occupying the same general space but a bit higher up. Rufus is contraparallel to Oliver—in line with Regina but lower down and out of sight.

Interpreting Planets in Aspect

Getting a handle on planetary aspects can be tricky. The usual rookie mistake is to break off too big a piece of the pie all at once. If you've bitten off, say, the Moon *in Leo* AND *in the sixth house* AND *trine* Jupiter *in Sagittarius* AND *in the tenth house*—well, that's a mouthful, and it's no surprise if you choke on it a bit.

So take it slow. Start with the planets; who are the characters you're dealing with? The Moon, your inner June Cleaver, and Jupiter, your inner Indiana Jones. Think about those two for a moment; how would those two get along, if Indy should happen to stop by the Cleaver house-hold, whip in hand and fedora on head? June would be polite, of course. She'd offer to take his hat and whip and to serve him a cool beverage, but she'd probably be a bit annoyed about the mud on his shoes. Indy would politely accept the drink, but would be looking over her shoulder, into Ward's study, where he spots a globe and something that looks like a big dictionary or atlas ….

Within you, there is a connection between the desire to be comfortable and to nurture yourself and others, and the desire to explore the larger world of ideas and adventure. What is the nature of the connection? A trine, an easy aspect between planets in signs of the same element. June, noticing Indy's interest, leads him into Ward's study to show him the beautiful atlas she gave her husband as a birthday gift. She asks her visitor to show her the most interesting country he's ever visited. For his part, Indy compliments her on the lemonade, which is a perfect balance of tart and sweet, and comments on the comfort and graciousness of her home. Your Moon—your nesting instinct, and the things that make you comfortable—is at ease with the world of adventure. You like exotic strangers who stop by wearing a fedora. You decorate your home with artifacts from other lands. Depending on the rest of your chart, you might even someday make your home (the Moon) in a land far from your birth (Jupiter).

Incorporating Signs and Houses with Aspects

That's a lot of information, just from the planetary aspect. What about the signs and houses? Well, the Moon is in Leo, an attention-grabbing sign; your home is a bit of a show-piece, per-haps, because you need to feel proud of where you live. And it's in the sixth house, a house of order and also of work; perhaps you feel most at home when you're at work, or you might work at home. Within you, the concepts of domestic contentment and work are synonymous.

Jupiter is in Sagittarius, the sign it rules, so your need for adventure and your interest in life's great questions are strong indeed. It's in the tenth house, the house of calling, career, and authority; this is an area of your life where you think big. Publishing, writing, traveling, religion—all are of interest to you.

We know by the trine that joins them that these two parts of your life complement one another. Perhaps you travel a lot as part of your career (Jupiter in Sagittarius in the tenth house) and bring home creative (Moon in Leo) yet practical (Moon in the sixth house) items for your home (Moon in Leo), or ideas for your home business (Moon in the sixth house). There are a lot of possible interpretations, of course, but hopefully this example will get your own interpretive juices flowing.

Essential Takeaways

- Aspects are angular relationships between planets or other important points in the chart.
- The "easy" aspects are the conjunction, sextile, and trine. They symbolize harmony and compatibility.
- The "hard" aspects are the square and opposition. They represent conflict, challenge, and incompatibility.
- Major aspects represent defining characteristics and major life issues; minor aspects symbolize more subtle dynamics requiring compromise or changes in perspective.
- Interpreting planetary aspects is easier if you take it slowly. It can be helpful to imagine the planets as characters having a dialogue.
- Interpretations of the aspects between planets includes the sign and house placements of the planets.

PART 5

Cycles Made Simple

The cycles of the planets define the landscape of your life. Some planets move very slowly. Their cycles are like towering granite monuments, marking major milestones: graduations, marriages, births, deaths, career achievements. They're few, but they can be seen for miles around. Other planets move a little more quickly. Their cycles are like tall, well-lit, eye-catching billboards commemorating the year's top events—a job promotion, a new house, an overseas vacation. This is the stuff of holiday newsletters and conversation around the Thanksgiving table. Other planets whip through a sign of the zodiac in a single month. Their cycles are like colorful flyers slapped on telephone posts, advertising your company's monthly sale, a lost or found pet, a class that you're teaching.

Handwritten and cheery, propped up on a curb outside your favorite restaurant, a chalk-board lists the day's specials. What sounds good, fun, appealing, and tasty today? Of the many projects on your to-do list, which is the one that will get your attention today? Look to the Moon, which covers the entire zodiac in a month.

CHAPTER 17

The Circle of Seasons

Equinoxes and solstices

Planetary cycles

Critical life cycles

Retrograde planets

How to work with planetary cycles

Remember the movie *Groundhog Day?* Bill Murray plays a misanthropic TV weatherman who finds himself reliving the same day again and again. He moves through the stages of denial, anger, and depression, and abuses his immortality by engaging in bizarre pranks, and every morning he wakes up to do it all again. Eventually it dawns on him that he can use the time a little more wisely, and embarks on a project to improve himself, learn new things, and use every bit of skill and ingenuity to live that same day better and better.

Life is cyclical. We don't live exactly the same day again and again, but sometimes it feels as though we are. It's lunchtime again, and our birthday again, and Christmas time again, and it feels like we've done it all before.

Astrology's greatest gift, to me, is that it provides a framework for understanding the cycles of your days, your seasons, and your lifetime—to recognize more quickly where you are on the circle of your life, identify when it's time to tackle a particular lesson, and make conscious decisions that increase your enjoyment of, and contribution to, your world.

The Circle of the Month

Each month, the Moon makes a full circle around the zodiac. Its cycle is a lovely microcosm of the annual rhythm of the seasons; its phases are, in fact, like miniseasons. Each New Moon offers the springtime energy of new beginnings and fresh starts. The First Quarter Moon is like summer, a time to actively tend your crops and enjoy watching them grow. Full Moon is like autumn, the month's harvest time, when you get a full picture of how things are progressing. And Last Quarter Moon is like wintertime, time to review your results, discuss them with others, and make resolutions for the next cycle.

In Chapter 18, you'll learn more about the Moon's journey through the zodiac, and in Chapter 19 you'll learn how to use its monthly phases to make better use of your time and energy.

Seasonal Turning Points

As we've seen in previous chapters, the four cardinal signs (Aries, Cancer, Libra, Capricorn) and the four angular houses of the horoscope (first, fourth, seventh, tenth) symbolize the turning wheel of your life and signal major change and events. Four times each year, the Sun enters one of the cardinal signs, marking the transition to a new season. Because the Sun's tour of the zodiac is not exactly the same length as a calendar year, the date of these seasonal changes can vary from year to year by one day, but they're roughly as follows:

March 20/21	Sun enters Aries	Spring	Vernal equinox
June 20/21	Sun enters Cancer	Summer	Summer solstice
September 22/23	Sun enters Libra	Autumn	Autumnal equinox
December 21/22	Sun enters Capricorn	Winter	Winter solstice

Note that this information refers to the seasons of the Northern Hemisphere. In the Southern Hemisphere, the dates and months of the equinoxes and solstices are the same, but the seasons are reversed. So down under, the vernal equinox takes place in September and the autumnal equinox in March; the summer solstice is in December, and the winter solstice is in June.

These seasonal turning points are of particular interest to mundane astrologers, the intrepid souls who use astrology to study world affairs. Mundane astrologers cast charts for the moment the Sun enters one of these cardinal signs in various world capitals, and then they use the charts to anticipate the mood and major events of the coming three-month period. These charts are called *ingress charts*, because they're cast for the moment of the Sun's ingress, or entry, into a sign of the zodiac.

All Things Being Equal: Equinoxes

The word *equinox* comes from the Latin *aequus* (equal) and *nox* (night); it refers to the phenomenon of day and night being at about equal length on the day of the equinox. Equinoxes occur twice each year and mark the beginning of spring (March 20 or 21) and autumn (September 22 or 23). Between the spring and autumn equinoxes, the Sun spends more time above the horizon than below it in a 24-hour period, reaching the maximum hours of daylight at the summer solstice; between autumn and spring equinoxes, the reverse is true, reaching minimum hours of daylight at the winter solstice.

The vernal or *spring equinox* corresponds to the Sun's ingress into the sign of Aries and the beginning of a new seasonal year. The *autumnal equinox* marks the Sun's ingress into the sign of Libra. The balance of night and day echoes the archetypal symbolism of the Aries/Libra polarity: the need to balance individual (Aries) concerns with the needs and concerns of others (Libra). The dance of relationship requires honoring both sides of the equation; obviously you can't have a good relationship without taking the needs of both partners into consideration, but you also can't have a good relationship unless you have a good understanding of who you are and what you need from life.

When Time Stands Still: Solstices

The word *solstice* comes from the Latin *sol* (sun) and *–stitium* (stoppage). Over the course of the year, the Sun's elevation (relative to the horizon) at noon rises, reaching its peak at the summer solstice; then seems to stop and change direction, with the Sun reaching a lower elevation at noon each day until at the winter solstice it reaches its lowest point.

The *summer solstice* refers to the longest day of the year, when the Sun reaches its maximum elevation at noon. The *winter solstice* refers to the shortest day, when the Sun reaches its minimum elevation at noon.

The summer solstice marks the Sun's ingress into the sign of Cancer; at the winter solstice, the Sun moves into Capricorn. The Sun's highest and lowest points at the solstices reflect the symbolism of the Cancer/Capricorn polarity, which contrasts inner/emotional and familiar connections (Cancer) with worldly ambitions and reputation. The chilly characteristics of Capricorn are embodied in archetypal Christmas/winter solstice figures such as Dickens's Mr. Scrooge and Mr. Potter of *It's a Wonderful Life*. The warm, nurturing, family-oriented Cancer imagery finds its way into summer's backyard barbecues and beach holidays.

DEFINITION

The **spring** and **autumn equinoxes** mark the equal length of day and night. Between spring and fall, the Sun spends more hours above the horizon; between fall and spring, it is below the horizon for more time each day. The **summer** and **winter** solstices mark the longest (summer) and shortest (winter) days of the year. Between the winter and summer solstices, the Sun gradually rises in elevation at noon, and between summer and winter it gradually lowers.

Planetary Cycles and the Seasons of Your Life

The Sun, Moon, and planets move through the sky at different speeds relative to our earthly perspective. Some move quickly, changing signs every month, or even every couple of days; others glide along at a somewhat more sedate pace, taking a couple of months or a couple of years to finish their celestial journey; still others lumber at a glacial rate, taking an entire generation to get through a single sign of the zodiac.

The planetary positions at the moment of your birth are static—for you. But the planets didn't stop in their orbits when you were born; they continued moving, and have been running their relay races ever since. Understanding the full picture of astrology means understanding the rudiments of these cycles, and interpreting what it means when the relationships between the planets gradually change.

Cycles of Inner Planets

The inner planets, sometimes called the "personal planets," are Mercury and Venus. Like a sprinter running in the innermost track, inner planets move through the zodiac quickly, in one year or less. Astrologers refer to the Sun and Moon as planets for the sake of convenience, and because the Sun moves through the zodiac in about a year and the Moon covers the same ground in only 28 days, they are included in this group. For more information about planning your daily and monthly affairs with the cycles of the inner planets, including descriptions of their trip through particular signs of the zodiac and houses of your chart, see Chapters 18 and 19.

Sun—The Sun takes one year to make a full trip around the zodiac (from our perspective; in reality, of course, we're the ones taking the trip, around the Sun) and will pass through every house of your birth chart in one year as well. The Sun takes about one month to move through a sign of the zodiac. Its entry into the cardinal signs marks the beginning point of each season (in the Northern Hemisphere, Aries for spring, Cancer for summer, Libra for autumn, Capricorn for winter). The Sun's cycle is descriptive of vitality, procreation, liveliness, creativity, and warmth. See Chapter 19 for more about the Sun's annual journey through the signs of the zodiac and the houses of your chart.

Moon—The earth's Moon takes about 28 days to make a full cycle through the zodiac, changing signs about every $2\frac{1}{2}$ days. The Moon's cycle is descriptive of emotional fluctuations, sensitivity, the public and its moods, and domestic and agricultural activities. Its eight major phases, symbolizing its relationship to the Sun, delineate an important monthly cycle of beginnings, adjustments, reevaluations, and endings. See Chapter 18 for more about the Moon's monthly journey through the signs of the zodiac, and Chapter 19 for more about the Moon's monthly phases.

Mercury—Mercury takes 88 days to make a full circle around the zodiac. It never orbits farther than 29 degrees from the Sun, and it turns *retrograde* several times each year for about three weeks at a time. Mercury cycles indicate optimal times for learning, communicating, and documenting information.

Venus—Venus takes 245 days to make a full circle around the zodiac. It never orbits farther than 45 degrees from the Sun, and it turns retrograde every year and a half for full cycle. Cycles of Venus represent the ebb and flow of personal relationships and financial matters.

 Retrograde is the term used for when a planet appears to move backward in its orbit.

Cycles of Societal Planets

The societal planets—Mars, Jupiter, and Saturn— orbit between the earth and Saturn. The societal planets aren't as speedy, or their focus as subjective, as the inner planets; they symbolize the process of socialization, of learning to work within societal structures. Their trips around the zodiac ranges from $2\frac{1}{2}$ years to 29 years, and symbolize important milestones of a 1- to 2-year period. For more information about using the cycles of these planets to help plan your year ahead, see Chapter 20.

Mars—Mars takes about $2\frac{1}{2}$ years to take a full turn around the Sun. It turns retrograde once every two years, for anywhere from 58 to 81 days. Mars cycles represent assertiveness, beginnings, individual pursuits, and sexuality.

Jupiter—Jupiter takes about 12 years to orbit the Sun, changing signs once every 12 months. It's retrograde for about half of every year. Jupiter's cycles represent higher knowledge and education, long-distance travel, adventure, and the development of your belief system.

Saturn—The full cycle of Saturn is $29\frac{1}{2}$ years. It spends about $2\frac{1}{2}$ years in each sign of the zodiac, and is retrograde for about half of every year. Saturn's cycles are related to career, ambition, parenthood, leadership, and worldly pursuits.

Cycles of Generational Planets

The generational planets—Uranus, Neptune, and Pluto—are the planetary runners in the outermost tracks, and they take so long to orbit the Sun that they affect entire generations of people in similar ways. Their journeys through the zodiac range from 84 to 245 years, and symbolize important cycles of often life-changing importance. For more information about anticipating major milestones using the cycles of the generational planets, see Chapter 21.

Uranus—Uranus makes a full cycle of the zodiac in 84 years. It's retrograde for about half of each year, and it changes signs once every seven years. Cycles of Uranus are related to individuality, rebellion, change, chaos, and revolution.

Neptune—Neptune takes 165 years to make a full circle around the zodiac. It's retrograde for half of each year; it changes signs only once every 12 years or so. Cycles of Neptune are associated with spirituality, enlightenment, clarity, and togetherness.

Pluto—Pluto takes 245 years to make a full circle around the zodiac and is retrograde for half of each year. Because of its erratic orbit, it spends much more time in certain signs than others; in recent history, it's spent as few as 12 years and as many as 33 years in a single sign. Cycles of Pluto are associated with power, control, strength, and destruction.

ASTRO TIP Certain important planetary cycles converge in everybody's charts when we reach particular ages. There's some comfort in knowing that little Johnny's terrible twos, your teenager's rebellious phase, or your husband's midlife crisis are all part of a predictable planetary schedule!

Planetary Traffic Jams

Ever have one of those years? One that's like a country song, when your lover leaves, your dog runs away, and someone spills beer on your new boots? Sure, we all have years like that. And there are certain ages when we all have one of those years. They're the terrible twos, the first years of high school, turning 21, looking down the barrel of 30, hitting the midlife crisis, and preparing for retirement. That's because the slower-moving planets have cycles that converge, pretty reliably, at particular times of life.

The Terrible Twos

What happens when a kid hits the terrible twos? Astrologically speaking, two things: Junior gets his first Mars return at about age $2^1/_2$, when Mars returns to the same degree of the same sign it was in at his birth. This is when a kid will typically discover his inner No, which is usually charmingly accompanied by the classic kicking, screaming temper tantrum. You gotta love a human being of any age who is completely in the thrall of hot-tempered, self-centered, me-centric Mars! Or not.

Secondly, Jupiter makes a square aspect to its position in Junior's birth chart. He's ready to be a big boy. He's thinkin' big. He's outgrowin' all his clothes. He wants a trike. Together with the willfulness of Mars, this makes for a handful cocktail. He settles down a bit between 3 and 5, but then he hits school and Saturn makes its first difficult aspect to Saturn in his birth chart and he gets his first taste of society's rules.

High School Horror

Around the age of 14, Junior hits high school. He has a Jupiter square to natal Jupiter, and Saturn reaches the opposition point to his natal Saturn. Suddenly, his parents and counselors are urging him to figure out what to do in the present to make his dreams come true in the future. It's a lot of pressure. Back in my day, *every* kid got his or her driver's permit at age 15 and applied for a license on his or her sixteenth birthday; that's just how one spent one's sweet 16. It was all about authority, and Saturn kicking us to step to the plate and claim a taste of adulthood. Meanwhile, we were sassing our parents and teachers and refusing to do what anyone told us; such is the nature of a Saturn opposition.

Legal Adulthood

In the United States you're legally an adult—meaning you can enter into legal agreements and vote—at the age of 18, but you can't legally drink until the age of 21. This happens to coincide with one of the most volatile periods a young person has yet faced: squares from Jupiter, Saturn, and Uranus to their positions in the birth chart, all within a 3- to 4-year period. If your parents don't kick you out of the house, you're eager to kick yourself out by this time. You have places to go and things to do, you want to really prove you're a grown-up, and you absolutely can no longer abide being told what to do by your parents. So you go away to college or get a job and move into your own place.

First Chance for Failure: 28–29

Between the ages of 28 and 29, you'll have a Saturn return: Saturn will return to the position it was in at your birth. There are some other Jupiter aspects during this period that intensify the experience, but essentially this is all about Saturn, the planet of worldly ambition and success, and whether or not you've achieved any or are at least on track to do so. If you're not remotely living up to your potential, you will, for the first time, get a real taste of what it would be like to be a failure. Objectively, you're still too young for the verdict to be in. There's plenty of time to turn the ship around and sail for more promising waters. But you may very well feel old, and for the very first time, mortal. It's not a great feeling.

I had just begun my formal astrology studies around this age, and fortunately I could see what I needed to do. Bored and with no chance for advancement at my well-paid but dull office job, I jumped ship three days before my thirtieth birthday to make my living as an astrologer. I celebrated my thirtieth birthday feeling pretty satisfied with the way my life was going, and never regretted my decision.

Last Chance for Success? 35–42

When people talk about the midlife crisis, they're talking about the period between the ages of about 35 and 42, when all astrological heck breaks loose. Sometime within this period, Jupiter, Saturn, Uranus, Neptune, and Pluto all make difficult aspects to their positions in your birth chart. This is a time when we come to terms with the career decisions we made at 30, with the consequences of the lives we've built for ourselves, the ideals that may or may not be panning out, and usually, some real and grim reminders that nothing lasts forever as the elder generation begins to die out.

Passing the Torch: 55–60

Ideally, this is the time in your life when you survey the landscape of your lifetime of achievement with a glad eye. You begin the process of mentoring the next generation of movers and shakers in your field. You teach, or write your memoirs. Increasingly, you feel restless in your current role, looking ahead to a rich and spontaneous retirement from public life. But this rosy scenario is dependent on your having done a lot of hard work and made a series of good decisions over the past $29^{1}/_{2}$ years since your first Saturn return. Have you achieved all you wanted to achieve? Have you collected memories *worth* preserving in a book? If not, the second Saturn return can be a hard time when you feel as though you've missed your chance for success.

As you ease into your 60s, traditionally a time for retirement, your hope lies in no longer caring about worldly achievement. Uranus's last square to its position in your birth chart, much like its first square at age 21, emphasizes individuality and freedom. Even if you haven't achieved all you might have, there's still time to shake things up—to wake up the world, and to awaken to your own originality. But it means throwing off the shackles of the security you've accumulated in the course of your career, and that can be scary.

Retrogrades

A guy walking into a bar backward would get your attention. There may be a very good reason for it, but the fact remains that it's behavior that defies expectation.

The same is true when planets are retrograde. (Apparent) retrograde motion is when a planet appears, from our earthly perspective, to be moving backwards—opposite its normal trajectory through the sky, and opposite the other planets. "Retrograde" is from the Latin *retrogradus,* or backward step. Basically, the retrograde motion of planets is an optical illusion created by the difference in speed between other planets and Earth.

 ASTRO TIP When Mercury is retrograde, we often wind up retracing our steps and redoing things repeatedly until we get them right. My astrology teacher used to say that when Mercury is retrograde, you should try as much as possible to do things you enjoy—because you'll end up doing them over and over!

Retrograde Planets

Every planet (other than the Sun and Moon) has retrograde periods. In fact, the slower-moving planets are retrograde for half of each year. Each planet's retrograde cycle symbolizes appropriate times to move forward on matters associated with the planet (when the planet is direct) and times to hold back and rethink things (retrograde):

- **Mercury** is retrograde about three times each year, for three weeks at a time. Mercury is the planet that rules, among other things, communication, technology, transportation, and learning. Its retrograde periods are times when anything and everything related to these areas of life are presumed to be vulnerable to misadventure or unpredictability. Not the best time to buy new mechanical gizmos, especially cars, computers, or phones; sign contracts or make agreements; or begin new courses of study. (See Appendix B for a table of Mercury retrograde periods through 2020.)

- **Venus** is retrograde approximately 40 to 43 days every 18 months. It's considered an unfortunate time to marry or move in with a partner, form other legal partnerships, make major purchases, hold formal social affairs (a charity ball, for instance), have cosmetic surgery, or initiate a landscaping project for your home. It can be a good time for recovering money that's owed to you, formulating a financial plan, redecorating, or reuniting with friends or loved ones from your past.

- **Mars** is retrograde approximately 58 to 81 days every two years. It's a time to reconsider the ways in which you assert and defend yourself, express anger, deal with conflict, approach your work, and handle sexuality. It's considered a difficult time to start a new job or business, enter a competition, or initiate warfare; it might not be the best time for elective surgery. It may be a good time, however, to return to a former job, type of work, or sport; investigate new skills to help you cope with anger and conflict; and catch up on your rest.

The outer planets, Jupiter through Pluto, are retrograde for half of each year. Their retrograde times are probably not enough to cause problems unless they are also making difficult aspects to planets in your birth chart while they're retrograde:

- **Jupiter's** retrograde periods are a good time to resume your education, take a long-delayed trip, reread favorite books; they're less than optimal times to gamble, open a play, or launch a career as a teacher. Businesses that begin during these periods may not prosper financially because the owner is too generous with employees or customers, expands too quickly, or bites off more than he or she can comfortably chew.

- When **Saturn** is retrograde, it's all too easy to let your personal boundaries weaken and to agree to things you know you should (and normally, would) refuse. Therefore, these aren't great times to make new commitments, but they're good times to revisit commitments you've already made and make sure they're still appropriate for you. Starting a business is not so bad, but incorporating one might not be a good idea now. Consider and reinforce the structures of your life, including problems with your home, organizational problems with your business, or discipline problems with your children.

- **Uranus's** retrograde periods are good times to ask questions, shake up routines, connect with old friends, and for an incumbent to be re-elected. Energy tends to build during these times, and rebellion can come spilling out when Uranus turns direct.

- **Neptune's** retrograde times are good for spiritual retreat and reflection, to return to spiritual places that mean a lot to you, and for psychic and intuitive work. It's easier to see things clearly when Neptune is retrograde, if we're willing to accept the reality we see instead of trying to deny it.

- **Pluto** retrograde is excellent for psychological and physical healing and cleansing. It's a time when self-control is easier to harness, and it can be an excellent time for breaking habits of addiction and addressing psychological problems such as phobias, fears, and obsessive-compulsive tendencies. Trying to control others doesn't generally work well now, and in fact will backfire; but controlling and empowering yourself is good work for Pluto's retrograde periods.

When Good Planets Turn Retrograde

When a planet is retrograde, the things associated with the planet behave unpredictably. It's as though the god for which the planet was named, who's usually looking over things to make sure they're functioning properly, has gone on coffee break and left us to our own devices. Things symbolized by the planet may be lost, or if lost before may now return. We don't see matters related to the planet very clearly.

If a planet was retrograde at the time of your birth (and since the slower-moving planets are retrograde for half of each year, it's a good bet that at least one planet was retrograde), the glyph and degree/minute of the planet will be accompanied by this symbol: R_x.

Some astrologers feel retrograde planets at your birth represent areas that require extra effort on your part to become proficient. Some feel that retrograde planets represent heightened awareness or ability. My own experience is that retrograde planets in the birth chart seem to describe areas of life in which you naturally operate differently from other people. For instance, if you were born with Mercury retrograde, you may have a different style of learning or grasping information than other people. If you were born with Jupiter retrograde, you may have a belief system that's very different from those of the people who grew up around you. I think retrograde planets also point to abilities or gifts you were born with that can't always be explained rationally. People born with Mercury retrograde, for instance, are often exceptionally perceptive and insightful, noticing things others overlook.

Making Retrogrades Work for You

Because a planet doesn't seem to function as expected while retrograde, astrologers tend to issue dire warnings about not getting your computer repaired while Mercury is retrograde and not buying a house while Venus is retrograde. There's something to these warnings, but proclamations like that always make me feel rebellious, and at the very least it's fair to ask "Why?" After all, it's not practical to spend nine Mercury retrograde weeks out of every year in communication/technology lockdown mode. In fact, what I've often found is that Mercury (mischief maker that he is) often likes to push the issue; that just before Mercury turns retrograde, the car breaks down, your computer gives you the blue screen of death, or you accidentally drop your cell phone in the aquarium. Well, what are you gonna do? If you live 20 miles from your job and public transportation isn't an option, you make your living as a website designer, or you don't have a landline—obviously, you've got to play ball with Mercury.

So what does it mean when Mercury, or indeed any planet, is retrograde? It means that you may not have all the facts you need to make an informed decision about matters related to that planet. It's the reason astrologers urge clients not to make big, not easily reversible decisions like getting married or buying a home when Venus (planet of property and marriage) is retrograde, or to perhaps rent a car instead of buying one when Mercury is retrograde, or to resist following their guru to India when Neptune is retrograde.

ASTRO TIP

Retrogrades are not, generally, the right time to begin things; rather, they're times for finishing up unresolved matters. The popular thinking is that anything that begins with "re-" is appropriate to do during a retrograde period—rethink, reissue, refinish, refresh, and, most of all, reflect.

The Shadow Period

So up until the minute the planet turns retrograde, and the minute after it turns direct, you're in the clear—right? Sorry. You also need to know about a little something called "the shadow period," which begins *before* the planet turns retrograde and extends *after* it turns direct again. These are periods when the planet is functioning in a sort of retrograde fashion even though it is, technically, moving forward.

It works like this. On April 17, 2010, Mercury turns retrograde at 13 degrees of Taurus, which for the sake of narrative interest we'll call "Disneyland." Mercury continues on its backward trajectory until May 11, 2010, when it turns direct again at 3 degrees of Taurus—let's call it "Dodger Stadium." But of course, this is not the first time in recent history that Mercury had visited Dodger Stadium; in fact, he had caught a game there on April 3, 2010, on his way to Disneyland. Now, it's well known that Mercury has a bit of a short attention span, to the extent that I rather suspect he keeps forgetting about the whole retrograde business entirely. And on April 3, when the Dodgers waved up at Mercury and told him, "See you again in a couple of weeks!", Mercury had gone on his blithe and merry way, not quite sure what to make of that comment, so distracted by it that he started losing people's mail and scrambling their phone calls and crashing their hard drives. He was still moving forward, but his mind was back at Chavez Ravine with those inscrutable, irreverent Dodgers.

So on April 17 Mercury gets to the ticket booth at Disneyland when he realizes that somewhere along the way, he's lost his wallet. He turns retrograde, to retrace his steps and find it. He's now in full-on backtracking/misplacing things/forgetting stuff mode, stumbling along until eventually, on May 11, he finds himself right back at Dodger Stadium, where the entire team snickers and veteran sportscaster Vin Sculley holds up Mercury's wallet. Mercury slaps his forehead; says, "Oh yeah. Retrograde!"; turns direct again; and starts the same tedious trip down Interstate 5 toward Disneyland, for the third time. But he's still a little rattled, plus he keeps finding lost mail along the way, discovers his lost car keys, and meets up with old friends. At last, on May 27, Mercury again reaches Disneyland, where he finally buys a ticket and gets to ride the Matterhorn bobsleds.

Working with Planetary Cycles

In Chapters 18 through 21, we'll take a look at planetary cycles moving through your birth chart. In order to get the most out of those chapters, you'll need to know how to find the current position of the planets, and how to apply that information to your birth chart. Here's how it's done:

- **Get the current planetary positions.** Chapter 2 gives various alternatives for getting your hands on your birth chart, which is essentially a record of the planetary positions on the day you were born. Use the same options to find the planetary placements for today's date, or for any other date. You can find these planetary positions in an online ephemeris, an astrological calendar, or simply by calculating a chart for today's date (in your location), using an online service or computer program.

- **Use the information with your birth chart.** Start with the position of a planet—say, Venus. As of October 20, 2010, Venus is at 10 degrees and 13 minutes of the sign Scorpio. So it's currently moving through the sign of Scorpio. Which house of your birth chart is it moving through? In your chart, find the house cusp with Scorpio on it.

In the following chart, the sixth house has 18.49 (that's 18 degrees and 49 minutes) of Scorpio on the cusp. That means anything after 18.49 Scorpio comes after this house cusp, and anything before falls in a preceding house. The previous house, the fifth, has 10.27 Libra on the cusp. Anything that falls between 10.27 Libra and 18.48 Scorpio is moving through the fifth house. And since Venus is currently at 10.13 Scorpio, the fifth house is where we'll currently find her.

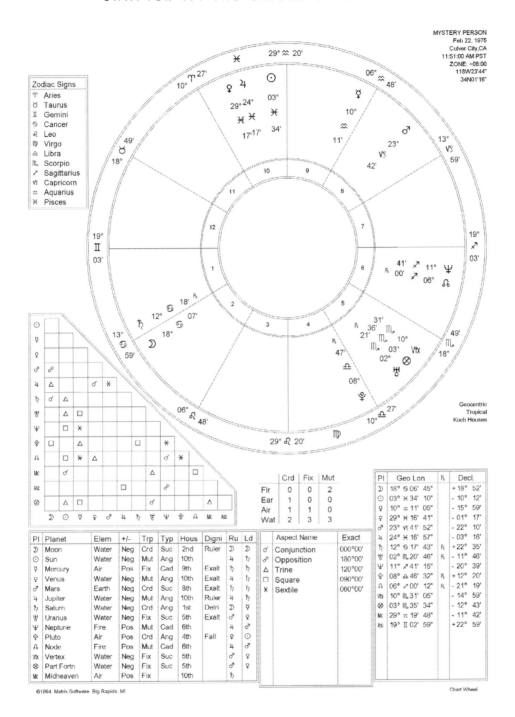

Sample birth chart.

Essential Takeaways

- Equinoxes and solstices mark the changing of the seasons and correlate to the cardinal signs and angular houses.
- Planetary cycles have varying lengths and mark the changing of your life's seasons.
- Certain ages of your life are characterized by particular planetary cycles that are common to everyone at about the same ages.
- Planets (not the Sun or Moon) periodically turn retrograde, or appear to move backwards in their orbits. These are times when the planet seems to work differently or unpredictably than its usual symbolism would suggest.
- To work with current planetary cycles, find the current planetary positions and superimpose them on your birth chart to find which house of your chart is being affected.

CHAPTER 18

Daily Planner

How the Moon helps you read the day's mood

The Moon sign by sign

Lunar aspects of the Moon

Understanding the void-of-course Moon

L ooking for a job? Signing a contract? Confronting your neighbor about his crab-grass? Understanding the Moon's current sign helps you gauge the mood of the day, present yourself to best advantage, and get what you want out of your day.

By far the speediest of our celestial neighbors, the Moon completes a lap around the zodi-ac in a mere 28 days, spending roughly $2\frac{1}{4}$ days in each sign. To find out the Moon's cur-rent sign, consult an astrological calendar or go to my website: www.bigskyastrology.com.

The Daily Mood: The Moon by Sign

Since the Moon is astrology's go-to symbol for "the public," its journey through the zodi-ac offers valuable insight into the world's mood on any given day. Each sign is associated with mythical gods and goddesses, guides, wardrobe, and activities to help you make the most of each day.

But because the Moon is a symbol of the unconscious, there's a little bit of intuition involved in reading the day's mood. For each daily Moon sign, I've offered prompts to get your intuition flowing:

- **Today's question**: Each sign has particular desires and motivations. As the Moon moves through each sign, we have a hunger to fulfill that sign's needs; asking yourself today's question (or, in the case of Gemini, making a statement) will help you do that.

- **Today's gods/goddesses:** The Moon's sign is ruled by a planet (see Part 4), and its mythology and characteristics influence the day.

- **Today's guides:** The day's guides teach you to recognize and appreciate the signs of the zodiac at work in daily life. Each sign traditionally "ruled" hundreds of people, creatures, places, and situations; a random sampling of these are presented as your guides for each Moon sign. If you encounter one of these guides today, even if it's on TV or in something you read, observe it. If one of today's guides is a housecat, keep a close eye on your tabby. Why does it do the things it does? How does it get what it needs? What can it teach you about how to approach your day?

- **Today's wardrobe:** While the Moon is in a particular sign, the public is unconsciously attracted to, and comfortable with, particular colors and other elements of style. Incorporating these into your wardrobe can both catch other people's eyes and make them feel more comfortable with you.

- **Today's assignments:** The Moon's sign lends itself to doing particular things. I've made these general enough to be applied to a variety of tasks and goals.

Today's Moon in Aries

You're driving your husband to work. You've got 25 minutes to make the 15-minute drive. The weather is clear and the traffic is light. There is no need to rush. Suddenly, from a side street, a car pulls in front of you going 10 miles an hour slower than you were driving. You sigh. You tap the steering wheel impatiently. You grumble. "What's your hurry?" asks your husband.

The Moon is in Aries today—*that's* your hurry. For Aries, the destination is not the point, and the journey is not exactly the point either. The point is how the journey is made—and it had better be made quickly.

An Aries friend once told me that in his youth, people called him "the young man in a hurry." He was 50 years old when I knew him, and he was still rushing around from place to place. The only time he ever looked unhappy was when he was standing still.

With the Moon in Aries, don't endanger yourself or others—but enjoy the feeling of being in motion. The feeling of speed. The feeling of propelling yourself through the air like an arrow, and the thrill of hitting a bull's-eye.

Daily Planner for Today's Moon in Aries

Today's mood	Impatient
Today's question	Who am I?
Today's gods/goddesses	Mars, the god of war
Today's guides	Soldiers, martial artists, metal workers, athletes, race-car drivers, percussionists, hawks, stinging insects, lifeguards, rascals, rams
Today's wardrobe	New, stylish, eye-catching
Today's assignments	Start things. Confront people. Do stuff that you've been putting off.

Today's Moon in Taurus

The lesson of Taurus is that each of us has more than we realize. Some of our blessings are easy to see: good health, a nice place to live, work we enjoy, enough money to meet our needs, friends and family to make it all worthwhile. But other blessings are subtle and fall all too often into the category of "things we take for granted."

Mellow out today. Move slowly. Listen to music, appreciate the view, and breathe in the sweet perfume of fresh air and clover. Today, there is air to breathe. There is the chance to hope that difficulties will be overcome and that good times are ahead. There is the sensation of food in the stomach, or even of hunger. There is pain. There are daytime and night, clouds in the sky, the ground beneath your feet. Against all odds, the world exists—and more unlikely still, you exist. You're alive. If you have just that, only that, you're a step ahead of the greatest, happiest, and most powerful men who ever died.

Daily Planner for Today's Moon in Taurus

Today's mood	Relaxed
Today's question	What is mine?
Today's gods/goddesses	Venus, goddess of love, desire, and sensuality

Today's guides	Bankers, gardeners, confectioners, dancers, musicians (especially singers), cherubs, children, housecats
Today's wardrobe	Conservative and well made
Today's assignments	Count your blessings. Inventory your belongings. Shop for essential, big-ticket items. Garden.

MISC.

Wearing the Moon on Your Sleeve

Each sign of the zodiac is associated with particular colors. Wear these colors on the days when the Moon is in that sign, and you will radiate ease, comfort, and simpatico. Without knowing why, others will gravitate to you as magnetically as a white cat to a black sofa. Going on a job interview or a first date today? These are the colors that will give you the edge over other candidates:

- Aries: Red
- Taurus: Green
- Gemini: Patterns
- Cancer: Silver
- Leo: Gold, orange
- Virgo: Navy, gray
- Libra: Light blue, pink
- Scorpio: Crimson
- Sagittarius: Purple
- Capricorn: Dark shades
- Aquarius: Bright blues
- Pisces: Greenish blue

Today's Moon in Gemini

You want to be delighted today. You hunger for mischief, and unexpected questions, and the twinkle of a stranger's eye. You crave words that make you think, and conversation that holds your attention—whether you say much or not, you sure feel like listening to the music of voices.

Not just human voices, either. Today, the whole world is speaking to you. The wind whispers to you through the leaves of the trees. Birds jabber about something that seems urgently important to their birdish brains. Even the half-dozen screaming bumper stickers on the car in front of you have something to say.

What does it all mean? Who cares? That's not the work of today; there will be time to contemplate meaning when the Moon enters Sagittarius. Gemini is simply in the business of collecting impressions and information, trivia, snippets of sounds and smells and colors. Experiment with some new words today … let them roll around on your tongue like tangy, delightful candy. Speak to a stranger. Take a photograph of something that made you laugh. Listen to the world today.

Daily Planner for Today's Moon in Gemini

Today's mood	Curious
Today's question	Question everything today!
Today's gods/goddesses	Mercury, messenger of the gods and all-purpose trickster
Today's guides	Smart alecks, toddlers who ask "why?" every two minutes, interviewers, writers, monkeys, birds, brothers and sisters, books and newspapers, con artists, twins, butterflies, the wind
Today's wardrobe	Whimsical and surprising
Today's assignments	Catch up on paperwork, phone calls, and visits. Write. Read. Keep the conversational ball in play.

Today's Moon in Cancer

While "house" is a word that emphasizes structure and form, "home" is the province of Cancer. The cooking smells, comfy upholstered furniture, jumbled memorabilia, pets, book bags, and discarded jackets of everyday life. The low hum of a television or radio, tuned to someone's favorite channel while dinner is prepared. The porch light turned on to meet the weary traveler, returning home after a long day of work.

Sometimes, after an especially long, hot, uncomfortable summer day, my husband and I take a twilight stroll around our neighborhood. Windows are thrown open to catch the evening breezes, and out of them spills children's voices, the drone of the evening news, the clattering of supper dishes being washed. We watch our neighbors moving around inside their homes in an intimate domestic ballet, relaxing on sofas, eating ice cream, getting the kids settled down before bedtime. I know that what I'm glimpsing through the window is not the whole story; every home holds sadness and anger, passion and joy, punctuating the quiet hum of domesticity. But there's something reassuring about glancing through a window at twilight and seeing fellow humans huddled in a womblike dwelling, engaged in the ancient ritual of creating a tribe.

What makes your house feel like home? How does it make you feel nurtured and protected? What is the "home" inside of you—and how can you share it with the world, creating an atmosphere of acceptance, nurturing, and nourishment for your friends, your neighbors, and your co-workers?

Daily Planner for Today's Moon in Cancer

Today's mood	Vulnerable, and a little sensitive
Today's question	What is home?
Today's gods/goddesses	The Moon, earth's distant and compelling sister, mysterious beacon on which we project our longings. Also, perhaps, Demeter, goddess of grain and fertility, who worked tirelessly to free her daughter Persephone from the clutches of Pluto.
Today's guides	Women, especially mothers, bakers and cooks, crabs, domestic workers, caretakers, lunatics, night birds, security officers
Today's wardrobe	Modest and conservative, even old-fashioned
Today's assignments	Nourish yourself and others with food for the mind, body, and spirit.

Today's Moon in Leo

My friend Monica says that one day when her nephew (born with the Moon in Leo) was about three years old, she offered to take him out into the backyard to "watch him" while he played. She had meant this in a figurative, supervisory sense—but her nephew took it differently. At one point, realizing Monica's attention was wandering, he halted in his tracks, put his hands on his hips, and wailed, "Look at me! *I'm playing!*"

There for you, in a nutshell, is Leo. When the Moon is in Leo it's time to play, to perform, to make the world laugh with joy, to explore the thrilling possibilities of the human experience. We can sometimes feel a bit disgusted by grown Leo types who make cheap and embarrassing bids for attention—but it's kind of sad, really, when a Leo is overlooked. There they are, playing, creating, expressing their hearts out, and no one notices. So they respond by cranking up their already incandescent personalities to an unbearable wattage, or else they slink off to the lair to nurse their wounded pride. Either way, you end up on the scary side of a dangerous animal.

The key to enjoying today's Leo lunar energy is simply to play. Celebrate your individuality. Be your own biggest fan. And remember, too, to be an appreciative audience to every person you meet; they're special, too. Pay attention to them—we don't want a lot of dangerous animals running around loose.

Daily Planner for Today's Moon in Leo

Today's mood	Fabulous!
Today's question	How can I have fun and get noticed for it?
Today's gods/goddesses	The Sun, symbol of all life-giving creative power; Helios, the Sun god and the god of sight
Today's guides	Children, performers, roosters, felines, royalty, biochemists, brokers, men in general, people in power
Today's wardrobe	Flashy and well accessorized, tiara optional
Today's assignments	Play. Create. Show off a little. Throw a party.

Today's Moon in Virgo

An applicant interviews for her dream job at a high-profile technology firm. She's bright, hard working, and talented. Unfortunately, her nails need a manicure, there's a run in her stockings, and her resumé suffers from a severe case of needs-an-editor. Thinking she needed only her sterling job record to land the job, she forgot that it's also important to pay attention to details, and to present her qualifications—and herself—as perfectly and professionally as possible.

The past couple of weeks have been a time to conceive and nurture new ideas, and it's almost time to share them with the world. So while the Moon is in Virgo, review your accomplishments. Fine-tune your work and prepare a polished sales pitch that presents your talents, skills, and creativity in the best possible light.

While the Moon is in Virgo, it's time to be a bit tough on yourself; you have to be willing to face your imperfections before you can correct them. But be sure to temper this process with humor and pragmatism; nothing—and no one—is perfect, and perfectionism run amok dampens creativity and fun.

Daily Planner for Today's Moon in Virgo

Today's mood	A little cranky, to be honest
Today's question	How can I help?
Today's gods/goddesses	Mercury/Hermes, messenger of the Gods and God of trade; Vesta, keeper of the sacred flame
Today's guides	Civil servants, maintenance personnel, editors, grain farmers, gardeners
Today's wardrobe	Tailored and deceptively, stunningly simple
Today's assignments	Analyze, soothe, untangle. Balance the books. Edit your resumé. Review contracts.

ASTRO TIP

For about two-and-a-half days each month, the Moon is in the same sign as the Sun was in at your birth. Mark these days on your calendar, because if you really need to wheedle the world into doing your bidding, these are the best times to do it. The days when the Moon is in the same sign as the Moon in your birth chart are days when you are inclined to be especially touchy. And days when the Moon is in your rising sign are days when you can hit the ground running without falling over your shoelaces.

Today's Moon in Libra

You walk into your neighborhood grocery store to pick up a few things for dinner. Gathering only the items you need, you take them to the checkout counter and realize too late that you're a dollar short. The store doesn't accept credit cards or checks for payment. What happens next?

It depends on how Libran you are. If you're a frequent customer, you might ask the storekeeper to extend credit until your next visit. You might persuade the cashier with a few carefully chosen—and possibly flirtatious—words to reduce the price on a couple of items. Or you might just return one of your items to the shelf, deciding to improvise a new dinner menu based on whatever's in your pantry and the items you can afford.

While the Moon is in Libra, the whole world is your neighborhood grocery store and you're either buying or selling. Whether the commodity is goods, services, or emotional goodwill, doing business with the world is not simply about exchanging goods; it's about exchanging words, feelings, and impressions, and about building relationships based on fairness and trust. While the Moon is in Libra, take the pulse of your relationships with others. How are you different from them, and how are you the same? How can each of you get what you want in a way that makes both of you happy?

Daily Planner for Today's Moon in Libra

Today's mood	The opposite of what anyone else around you is feeling
Today's question	What is it like to be someone else?
Today's gods/goddesses	Venus, goddess of love, justice, and fertility
Today's guides	Every other person you meet, but especially females; public relations and beauty industry workers; retail workers; diplomats; artists and musicians
Today's wardrobe	Exquisite, and hyper-feminine or -masculine (you choose)
Today's assignments	Learn about yourself through interacting with others. Play nice. Network. Negotiate.

Today's Moon in Scorpio

Every family has one: a teller of unpopular truths. There's a kid who notices the uncomfortable silence that falls over the Thanksgiving table when Uncle Ralph pours himself a third glass of cabernet, and proclaims, "Uncle Ralph is drinking so much!" Or a teenager with Morticia Adams hair and makeup who drapes herself in black and informs Mom that Dad is having an affair.

But usually there's also a caring adult in the family whose truth telling is motivated by love for you and interest in your well-being. The spouse who calls you out when you're fooling yourself, or a parent who points out that your new girlfriend doesn't seem to care for you as much as you care for her.

It hurts to hear the truth, even from someone who loves you. It's even harder to tell the truth when you risk losing the affection of the person you tell it to. But the truth must be faced in order for conditions to change, or for true intimacy to occur. Today is a day to face those truths, and to begin the process of forging deeper intimacy with the people close to you.

Daily Planner for Today's Moon in Scorpio

Today's mood	Intense, and a little testy
Today's question	What's really going on?
Today's gods/goddesses	Mars, god of war; Pluto, lord of the underworld
Today's guides	Serpents, eagles, undertakers, accountants, therapists
Today's wardrobe	Gothic bordello chic—deep décolletage, crushed velvet, heavy eye makeup
Today's assignments	Defend the helpless. Destroy your enemies. Tell it like it is. Throw away things you no longer need. Consult a counselor.

MISC.

Marriage by the Moon

The astrology of marriage is a complicated subject, and personally I can spend hours trying to nail down a really good wedding chart. But it all begins with the Moon. The best days for marriage (other things being equal!—and they often aren't) are when the Moon is in Taurus, Libra, or Cancer. Difficult days for marriage: when the Moon is in Aries, Scorpio, or Capricorn.

Today's Moon in Sagittarius

What do you eat for breakfast—eggs or cereal? Do you eat standing up, sitting down, behind the wheel of the car, or sitting at your desk? Tomorrow morning, alter your breakfast ritual. Gobble some toast and jam instead of your usual muffin. Scramble your eggs instead of poaching them. Get up 10 minutes earlier and eat your breakfast at home, sitting down, actually chewing instead of gulping.

If you're like most people, this tiny exercise will require supreme effort. Morning routines in particular—performed when you are only semiconscious and operating on autopilot—are a good gauge of your overall tolerance for change and variety. Remaining open to new possibilities is a habit of mind, a habit that can be developed through small changes (like eating something different for breakfast) as well as large ones (changing your career path).

The mood is a little more whimsical and a lot more adventuresome while the Moon is in Sagittarius. Why not try something new? This is the time to sample the new restaurant you've had your eye on, to sign up for the class you've been dying to take, or to draft a list of dream vacation spots. Your heart and mind want to go on vacation today; feed them something new, and watch them soar!

Daily Planner for Today's Moon in Sagittarius

Today's mood	Adventurous
Today's question	Why not?
Today's gods/goddesses	Jupiter, the god of thunder and pretty much the boss of all the other gods
Today's guides	Gamblers, pundits, judges, professors, jockeys, publishers, travel agents, clowns
Today's wardrobe	Sporty, something that won't rip when you bend over and will breathe when you run to catch a bus
Today's assignments	Take a chance, try something new, plan a vacation.

Today's Moon in Capricorn

My father was a Capricorn farmer who was happy spending hot, humid summer afternoons in absolute solitude, meditatively traversing his acres aboard a tractor. But even in the early 1960s small farms were struggling, so he also drove our school bus—"to support his farming habit," my mom liked to say. He did whatever he had to do to make a go of his farming while supporting his family, working long hours and odd jobs.

Capricorn has the vision to imagine the end goal of any enterprise; the leadership to enjoin others in making it a reality; and the tenacity and single-mindedness to stay on course when others would flounder. No one is more resourceful or determined than Capricorn; he simply will not give up, no matter how hopeless the situation may seem.

While the Moon is in Capricorn, envision your legacy. Examine what needs to be done to achieve your objectives. And then roll up your sleeves, hop on your tractor, and get to work.

Daily Planner for Today's Moon in Capricorn

Today's mood	Serious and determined. You know: grown-up.
Today's question	Where am I going?
Today's gods/goddesses	Saturn, god of agriculture, civilization, and social order
Today's guides	Elders, captains of industry, engineers, chiropractors, farmers, the poor, ravens, bears
Today's wardrobe	Your finest, most conservative suit. Bust out the pinstripes.
Today's assignments	Prioritize, build, discipline. Start a business. Formulate a long-term plan for your business or your life.

ASTRO ALERT The day's mood can be significantly affected by the Moon's aspects to other planets. Even if the Moon is in an upbeat, carefree sign like Sagittarius, the day's mood can be heavier and darker if the Moon is in aspect to Saturn.

Today's Moon in Aquarius

You're a six-year-old kid and it's your first day at school. Your neighborhood friends go to a different school across town, and your brothers and sisters are either too young or too old for your school. Midmorning, the recess bell rings and you wander outside with your classmates, who all chatter convivially with one another.

What happens next? Do you strike up a conversation with a friendly looking kid, join a game of dodge ball, or lurk on the sidelines, desperately wishing you were anyplace else on earth?

We're odd at heart, each and every one of us. It's both a blessing and a curse that you are not exactly like anyone else. Being unique can be something you wear like a badge of honor, part of the special something you bring to the playground, the dinner table, or the boardroom. Or it can be a stigma that leaves you feeling lonely and maladjusted, never really fitting in anywhere.

Aquarius represents the dichotomy between celebrating what is unique about you and finding a place where you belong. This is why Aquarius is the sign of friendship: friends are those like-minded souls who like you precisely *because* you're unique. Moon in Aquarius days are no time to stand on the sidelines and watch the other kids playing ball. Instead, no matter how solitary you may be by nature, this is the time of each month to make an effort to participate in society's games—and to bring all your unique gifts to bear in furthering communal interests.

Daily Planner for Today's Moon in Aquarius

Today's mood	Friendly
Today's question	Where do I belong?
Today's gods/goddesses	Saturn, god of agriculture, civilization, and of social order; Uranus, god of change
Today's guides	Eccentrics, visionaries, entrepreneurs, politicians, motivational speakers, colleagues, members of organizations
Today's wardrobe	Shiny fabric and jewelry, electric colors, anything a little weird
Today's assignments	Join a club. Gather with friends. Organize a protest. Get something pierced.

Today's Moon in Pisces

True mystics have always enjoyed hanging around with a bad crowd. This is not to say that every grungy-looking kid slouching around the corner convenience store is a mystic, or even a nice guy. It's just that if you want to learn how to truly love everybody, you should hang around with those society finds most difficult to love. You'll either turn to the bottle; end up insane, dead, or disillusioned; or become a black belt in unconditional love.

Pisces is a true mystic. Unlike his opposite sign, Virgo, Pisces has to work to develop the gift of discrimination; his nature is to get along with everyone and accept them as they are. He sees himself in everyone, but particularly identifies with the meek and powerless. And Pisces is sensitive, all right; but unlike his water sign brethren, Cancer and Scorpio, he has no crusty exoskeleton to protect him. So early on, Pisces learns the art of escape—it's his only survival technique when fisherman stalk him with nets, spears, and tasty lures.

While the Moon is in Pisces, remove your shell for a couple of days and try seeing life through another's eyes. Be humble. Practice compassion for those you feel deserve it least. And set down the burden of judgment—you'll be amazed how much more energy you have! If you find all this immersion in the human race exhausting, go ahead and escape in a nap, a day at the beach, or a favorite CD. But the best in our Pisces selves will never escape from our responsibilities to those under our care, or to whom we've made important commitments.

Daily Planner for Today's Moon in Pisces

Today's mood	It's all good, bro.
Today's question	Where is the love?
Today's gods/goddesses	Jupiter, the god of thunder and pretty much the boss of all the other gods (this explains why Pisces are not really as meek as they're made out to be); Neptune, the god of the ocean, representing Pisces's primordial connection with all other beings
Today's guides	Fish and fishermen; mystics and priests; poets, painters, and music makers; drunks and addicts; your tired, your poor, your huddled masses yearning to breathe free, the wretched refuse of your teeming shore, the homeless tempest-tossed

Today's wardrobe	Think Stevie Nicks and any male rock singer who wears a feather boa—lots of gauzy fabrics, velvet, lace, possibly feathers
Today's assignments	Just to love, and be loved in return. Oh, and maybe some meditation, a nap, a little swimming, some music, and a comforting visit or phone call to a friend in need.

Today's Lunar Aspects

Walk into a home, an office, a restaurant, almost anyplace—and you immediately sense the rhythm of the people who spend time there. Is it a steady, quiet rhythm, or a stimulating, syncopated one? Do you feel at peace there, or challenged? And have you noticed that there are some days when everything from interpersonal interactions to getting a tune-up on your car just seems to *flow* better than on other days?

In astrology, this flow of energy is symbolized by the Moon's aspects with other planets. If the Moon makes most friendly aspects to other planets in her $2^1{}_2$-day journey through a sign, things tend to go pretty smoothly. But if she makes bad aspects to other planets, the result is sort of like walking through a very beautiful house but tripping over loose rugs and hitting your shin against the corners of sharp tables. Pretty soon, you don't even notice the nice artwork on the walls, or the lovely view of the lake.

Pull out your trusty astrological planner or calendar and you'll see a list of the day's planetary aspects. If your calendar shows a day full of squares and oppositions, it's likely to be a bit of a tough day, regardless of which planets are involved.

When the Moon is in harmonious aspect to a planet, it's generally a good day to pursue matters related to that planet. If the Moon is making a difficult aspect to a planet, matters associated with that planet will require extra effort and may lead to aggravation:

- **Moon in aspect to the Sun**—Harmony (conjunction, trine, sextile) or conflict (square, opposition) between wants and needs, conscious and unconscious, actions and our responses. See Chapter 19.

- **Moon in aspect to Mercury**—Intellect and feelings are in harmony (conjunction, trine, sextile) or in conflict (square, opposition).

- **Moon in aspect to Venus**—Harmonious, affectionate, and comfortable (conjunction, trine, sextile); moodiness and domestic difficulties (square, opposition).

- **Moon in aspect to Mars**—Energy and emotional conviction (trine, sextile); aggression, impulsiveness, volatility (conjunction, square, opposition).

- **Moon in aspect to Jupiter**—Optimism and urge for adventure (conjunction, sextile, trine); poor judgment and overindulgence (square, opposition).

- **Moon in aspect to Saturn**—Benefits through hard work and discipline (sextile, trine); depression or pessimism (conjunction, square, opposition).

- **Moon in aspect to Uranus**—Readiness for change and independence, original and spontaneous (conjunction, sextile, trine); disruptions, restlessness, accidents (square, opposition).

- **Moon in aspect to Neptune**—Sympathy, intuition, imagination (conjunction, sextile, trine); impracticality and escapism (square, opposition).

- **Moon in aspect to Pluto**—Clearing the emotional air (conjunction, sextile, trine); uneasiness, jealousy, secretiveness (square, opposition).

The Void-of-Course Moon

After the Moon has finished making all of the planetary aspects, it will move into its current sign; we say that it is *void-of-course* until it moves into the next sign. (That's "without a course"—not, "void … of course!") The void-of-course period can last a few minutes or a day or more; it depends on the positions of the Sun and planets relative to the Moon.

 DEFINITION

A **void-of-course** Moon refers to the period between the Moon's last major aspect in a sign until it moves into the next sign. The void-of-course period varies in length, but there is a void-of-course Moon every couple of days.

Some astrologers regard the void-of-course Moon period as a sort of mini "day of rest." The traditional interpretation of the void-of-course Moon period is that anything you initiate under its influence is pretty much dead on arrival. So initiate nothing, say nothing, don't lift a finger, some astrologers say, as though the void-of-course Moon were the Sabbath. This seems a tad impractical for busy people with lives to lead.

I think it's more helpful to regard the void-of-course Moon as a period when things sort of ... continue. There is a momentum to the Moon's $2\,^1/_2$ day journey through a sign, a momentum that builds as the Moon grazes up against contentious or flowing aspects to other planets. And when that last aspect has sounded like a gong, we can stop in our tracks to listen to the reverberation, or we can ride along on the sound waves.

You won't be traveling through this particular area of the emotional landscape for another 28 days. So while the Moon is void-of-course, savor the reverberations of the Moon's journey here. Pause if you can, but move on to new things if you must; just understand that it's likely they'll reverberate at the same pitch as the old things.

ASTRO TIP

When the Moon is void-of-course, do take actions such as mailing your tax return, that you don't wish to lead to further actions (such as a tax audit). When the Moon is void-of-course, don't start things that you hope will continue to grow and improve, because it won't turn out that way.

Essential Takeaways

- The Moon's sign symbolizes the mood and appropriate activities of the day.
- The Moon's daily aspects to other planets describe whether the day will flow smoothly or with difficulty.
- The void-of-course Moon is a time when the Moon has completed all its aspects to other planets before changing signs.
- The void-of-course Moon is best for initiating actions that you don't wish to lead to further actions.

CHAPTER 19

Monthly Planner

The Moon's waxing phases and beginning new things

The Moon's waning phases and completing things

The Sun's cycle of energy and personal growth

Mercury's cycle of communication and learning

Venus's cycle of enjoyment, relationships, and finances

I grew up in a farm community of grizzled men in muddy coveralls and women in calico housedresses. These people took more of a "nose to the grindstone" than a "head in the clouds" approach to life, yet every household boasted a well-thumbed copy of the *Farmer's Almanac,* the popular guide to planting by the Moon. No crops were planted, no garden harvested, no animals bred, no haircuts administered to squirmy adolescents unless the phase of the moon was "right." There wasn't any discussion of "living in harmony with the cosmos"; it's simply that experience had shown these practical people that lunar cycles *worked.*

The phases of the Moon—the 28-day unfolding of the angles between Sun, Moon, and earth—are the easiest of all cycles to identify and work with. Simply look up in the sky: the Moon's appearance will tell you where you are in its cycle. During the waxing phases of the Moon (between New Moon and Full Moon), we plant; and during the waning phases (between Full Moon and New Moon), we gather. There are a few subtle variations along the way, but that's basically it.

Even if you never stick your hands in the ground and only buy your food from a market, you have things to plant—if only the intangible seeds of new ideas and intentions.

All enterprises that you hope will grow and flourish are best undertaken during a waxing Moon. Then, during the waning Moon, you can take your ideas and products to the marketplace.

Starting Things: The Waxing Moon

Between the New and Full Moon phases, the Moon is waxing. Each night its light increases until it reaches maximum illumination at the Full Moon. In fact, a good way to remember the difference between the waxing and waning moons is to think of how waxing your coffee table or your car makes it shine brighter!

New Moon

Walk outside on the evening of a New Moon, and the sky is dark; the Moon set with the Sun. Getting around requires faith in your gut instinct and the light from a sprinkling of stars. And yet as farmers and gardeners have long known, this is the best time to plant seeds. For planting is always an act of faith; seeds look as small and insignificant as stars, and you can only hope that these tiny pellets will someday look like the picture on the seed packet.

The New Moon is a time to start fresh. Where is the "soil" of your life ready to receive new seeds of inspiration? Find the degree and sign of the New Moon (see the table in Appendix B), and note which house of your birth chart they fall in. This is the house of crucial activity and insights in the month ahead. You can't know now whether the seeds you plant will come to fruition—you can only dream, plant, and have faith.

Finding the New Moon in the sky: The Moon rises and sets with the Sun, so you won't see it at all in its New phase.

Things to do at the New Moon: Initiate new ventures—a new business, job, marriage, or garden. Think about how you would like to improve yourself and your life. Make lists of things to accomplish in the month ahead.

New Moon Wishes

At the New Moon, the Sun and Moon are together in the same degree of the same sign. The house where this degree and sign falls in your birth chart represents the area of your life that is ready to receive your New Moon wishes:

- First and seventh houses: Wish for personal improvement and better relationships.

- Second and eighth houses: Wish for improved financial conditions.

- Third and ninth houses: Wish for better communication, for travel or for visitors, and for knowledge and insight.

- Fourth and tenth houses: Wish for an improved living situation or career success.

- Fifth and eleventh houses: Wish for creative inspiration, for friendships, and for fun.

- Sixth and twelfth houses: Wish for good health, peace, and enlightenment.

Waxing Crescent Moon

At the Waxing Crescent phase, the Moon begins to show a sliver of brightness—and likewise, you are beginning to "see the light." You begin to grasp both the opportunities and difficulties of achieving what you set out for yourself at the New Moon.

As the landscape becomes clearer, you may lose heart and resign yourself to the status quo. At the Waxing Crescent Moon, complacency is a sign of failure. If you've ever tried to lose weight, you know the disheartening feeling of beginning a diet with enthusiasm and determination, only to find that both are weakening within a few days. "It will take me forever to lose 20 pounds, and I might not manage to do it at all," you think. "So why don't I just enjoy myself now? Hand me that Twinkie!"

Patience and the power of your own mind are the keys to navigating the Waxing Crescent phase. As Henry Ford once said, "Whether you think you can do something or you think you can't, you're probably right."

Finding the Waxing Crescent in the sky: Look for a tiny lunar sliver in the west in the early evening, after the sun has set.

Things to do at the Waxing Crescent phase: Gather information, supplies, or other resources that you need for a project, event, or other goal.

First Quarter Moon

At the First Quarter Moon, it's time to take action. At the New Moon, you conceived a vision, and at the Waxing Crescent Moon you considered what it would take to realize that vision. Now it is time to push forward and to make a real commitment.

If you got a bit ahead of yourself at the New Moon and jumped right into something new without preparation, you might find, only a week later, that you need to alter those plans.

It's a bit like assembling furniture from a kit without looking at the instructions; it might work out fine, or somewhere along the line you might find that you're on your way to constructing a three-legged chair.

Luckily, at the First Quarter Moon, the furniture glue has not yet hardened. There's still time to make changes, and now is the time to do it. Don't be afraid to change your mind, and by all means add another leg to that chair.

Finding the First Quarter Moon in the sky: The First Quarter Moon rises in the east at noon and sets in the west at midnight. Half of the Moon's illuminated face is visible.

Things to do at the First Quarter Moon: Change your mind. Ask for what you want.

Waxing Gibbous Moon ◑

At the Waxing Gibbous phase, the Moon looks very close to full. Likewise, whatever intentions you planted at the New Moon may look fully formed and ready for harvesting. But looks can be deceiving, and *almost* is not the same as *ready*.

Anyone who has ever baked a cake knows what a Gibbous Moon is like. As you peer at that cake through the glass window in the oven door, it looks done. You test it with a skewer, which comes out almost clean … except for that one pesky spot near the center that's still a little gooey. "Maybe I should take it out now," you think. "Surely it will retain some heat and continue cooking long enough to finish that center bit, and after all I don't want to overbake it and end up with a dry cake."

I'm here to tell you that if you take that cake out of the oven now, you'll end up with a gorgeous-looking, mostly perfect cake … with a gooey center. Likewise, if you declare victory for your New Moon intentions at the Gibbous Moon, there is almost certainly something half-baked about them.

Finding the Waxing Gibbous Moon in the sky: The Waxing Gibbous Moon looks almost full; about three quarters of the Moon's illuminated face is visible. It rises in the east in the mid- to late afternoon and can be easily seen before sunset. It sets at about 3 A.M.

Things to do at the Waxing Gibbous Moon: Wait. Sometimes that is the hardest thing to do, but right now it's what's necessary. Fine-tune. Analyze.

Finishing Things: The Waning Moon

Between the Full and New Moon phases, the Moon is waning. An astrologer friend and I like to refer to this as the "whining" part of the lunar cycle; it's a time of reaping what one has sewn and reflecting on how you might need to change your approach to ensure a better outcome in the future. Ideally, it's a time of reflection and objective soul-searching—but for each of us, there comes a time when some good old-fashioned whining feels pretty satisfying!

Full Moon ◯

How did you do? Do the plants in your garden, or the projects in your life, resemble the vision you had for them at the New Moon? The light of the Full Moon reflects both the strengths of your New Moon plans and how you might correct your course to steer away from future missteps and obstacles.

The Full Moon is also a time to reflect on your relationships with other people. So review your New Moon plans—but more importantly, review the state of your heart. Are you falling into difficult patterns with the people you care about? It's not too late to change course. If you find yourself becoming too wrapped up in your own plans to be kind to the people around you, take a step back and look at things from someone else's point of view.

Finding the Full Moon in the sky: It's hard to miss! It rises in the east at sunset and sets in the west at dawn; it shines all night.

Things to do at the Full Moon: Take an honest look at where you are. Ask for, and pay attention to, feedback from customers, co-workers, family members, and friends.

Once in a Blue Moon
A Blue Moon is the second Full Moon in a calendar month, or the third Full Moon in a season (for example, from vernal equinox to summer solstice) with four Full Moons (instead of the usual three). The colloquial expression "once in a Blue Moon" refers to something that doesn't happen often. So how often do we have a Blue Moon? About once every two to three years.

Waning Gibbous Moon ◯

Why is it so delicious to get together with a group of same-sex friends to compare notes about relationships? Why are the late-night confabs over cocktails the best part of any professional conference? Why did my grandmother and her friends enjoy working together on their quilts, bending over the giant quilting frame in her living room and chatting the hours away?

Because humans are social creatures. We crave interactions with our fellow humans, and we learn from them. If something you initiated at the New Moon—a business, relationship, garden, craft project—didn't turn out the way you'd hoped, you might benefit from the advice of others who've tried the same things, perhaps with better success. And if you succeeded beyond your wildest dreams—well, it might be nice to share some of your tips with others. Astrologers call this the Disseminating Moon, and it's a good time to spread the seeds of knowledge and ideas. This is the time of the month to set up your quilting frame, pour some cocktails, and talk things over with like-minded souls.

Finding the Waning Gibbous Moon in the sky: It rises midevening and sets midmorning. As with the Waxing Gibbous Moon, the illuminated face of the Moon is about three quarters visible.

Things to do at the Waning Gibbous Moon: Discuss your progress with others. Teach, give lectures, or conduct training. Write letters and proposals.

Last Quarter Moon

At the Last Quarter Moon, it's time to take stock of your progress during this cycle. If you've veered too far off course from your New Moon goals, perhaps you can gently correct your trajectory now. It's also possible that you now have a better perspective on what those goals should have been! Begin now to think about the goals you wish to set for the next New Moon cycle, beginning about a week from now.

The Last Quarter phase is a time to develop understanding. It's time to weigh the perceptions and feedback of the Full and Gibbous Moon phases and to decide what is really true and right for you. Acknowledge that there are things you could do differently in your business, your relationships, your creative projects—but also, that there are times to stand firm in the courage of your convictions.

The Last Quarter Moon is a time of increased tension, so be gentle with yourself and with others. Misunderstandings are more likely than usual.

Finding the Last Quarter Moon in sky: Go to bed early and you'll miss it—the Last Quarter Moon rises after midnight. It doesn't set until around noon, though, so look for it in the morning sky. Half of the Moon's illuminated face can be seen—the half opposite what was visible at the First Quarter Moon.

Things to do at the Last Quarter Moon: Edit your work. Organize your workplace or home and figure out what you can let go. If you need to end a difficult relationship once and for all, now is a good time to do it.

Waning Crescent Moon

Before planting a new crop of seeds, it's necessary to let the soil rest. And as you reach the end of this month's 28-day lunar cycle, you could probably benefit from some rest yourself. So plan some downtime for this part of the monthly cycle. Don't fill your days with activity. Take some time to think about, and let go of, the things, people, and situations that no longer provide help or happiness. Let your soil rest, so you can receive the next New Moon's seeds of energy and intention.

Finding the Waning Crescent Moon in the sky: It rises a few hours before the Sun and sets a few hours after noon. Look for a tiny lunar sliver in the eastern early morning sky.

Things to do at the Waning Crescent Moon: Discard unwanted or unneeded things. Catch up on your rest. Tie up loose ends, such as billing for work already completed. Meditate. Record your dreams, as they're often numerous and rich during this phase.

The Sun: Cycles of Personal Growth

The Sun moves through the entire zodiac in about one year, spending about 30 days in each sign. The date that the Sun enters each sign can vary by a day from year to year; this is because the Sun's cycle doesn't match up exactly with our 365-day calendar year. The Sun's cycle through the houses of your birth chart shows where you are feeling most alive, and where you are ready to blossom, grow, and celebrate your own unique fabulousness.

Practically speaking, we can't live without the Sun. And in astrology, the Sun is likewise considered the animating force of the birth chart, describing your unique genius, magnetism, and sense of personal identity. As the Sun moves through the houses of your chart, it indicates where you are especially compelling and attractive and where you are most likely to attract attention and receive the recognition you deserve. If not all of that recognition is positive, it's a signal that perhaps you haven't been living up to your potential in that area of your life.

The Sun also symbolizes creative impulses and ability. You needn't write a song or paint a picture to be "creative"—creativity is simply the merging of skills with passion. A mechanic who can apply his passionate for understanding how things work to diagnosing what's wrong with a wheezing engine is every bit as creative as an actor giving an Academy

Award–winning performance. Where is your creative heart this month, and where can you best share your creative gifts with others?

Moving Through the Signs

As the Sun moves through your chart, it's important to make time for fun and recreation. It's no coincidence that Sunday, the traditional day of rest, is named after the Sun! "A change is as good as a rest," as an old expression suggests. The Sun's sign indicates the activities that will make you feel happy and alive this month, and that will give you the opportunity to grow. To make sure people listen to you, adapt your style or mode of communication to the Sun's current sign placement:

- **Sun in Aries:** Starting new things

- **Sun in Taurus:** Relaxation and enjoyment of the finer things in life

- **Sun in Gemini:** Short trips, conversation, changes in routine, reading and writing

- **Sun in Cancer:** Time spent with family, thinking about the past

- **Sun in Leo:** Vacation, recreation, creative pursuits

- **Sun in Virgo:** Cleaning, organizing, editing

- **Sun in Libra:** Collaborating, negotiating, enjoying the arts

- **Sun in Scorpio:** Introspection and spending time with intimate loved ones

- **Sun in Sagittarius:** Long trips, religious or ritual observances, celebrations

- **Sun in Capricorn:** Making resolutions for the year ahead, getting serious about your goals

- **Sun in Aquarius:** Making important changes, spending time with friends

- **Sun in Pisces:** Rest and reflection, enjoying the arts, anything that lets you escape from the everyday world

ASTRO TIP

Most likely, the houses of your chart are not all the same size. Some houses are skinny, others wide; the Sun, Moon, and planets will take much longer to move through some than others. If one is inclined to think in terms of past lives, we can safely assume the larger houses of your chart represent areas where you neglected your homework in previous incarnations and now must turn in some extra-credit assignments. (See Part 3 for details on how the birth chart is divided into houses.)

Moving Through the Houses

The Sun moving through the houses of your chart symbolizes settings and situations where you would benefit from cultural activities, entertainment, or fun getaways:

- **The Sun in your first house:** This is one of the best months all year to assert yourself. Go ahead; be a little pushy!

- **The Sun in your second house:** Celebrate life, nature, and your many blessings. Get better at relaxing and enjoying yourself.

- **The Sun in your third house:** Enjoy time with siblings and neighbors. Celebrate your creativity in writing or storytelling, and spread the word about yourself and your efforts.

- **The Sun in your fourth house:** Celebrate your roots, and the family that made you who you are. Focus on becoming the ancestor that future generations of your family will be proud to claim as their own.

- **The Sun in your fifth house:** This is one of the most creative months of the year for you. Put your whole self into your creative passions, and inspire others to explore their own creativity.

- **The Sun in your sixth house:** This is your month to shine in your workplace. You should also honestly evaluate areas for improvement, but resist the urge to become too critical of yourself or others.

- **The Sun in your seventh house:** Suddenly everyone wants to be your best friend! This is a good month to share the spotlight with others, so look for opportunities to collaborate with others on creative projects.

- **The Sun in your eighth house:** For many people, this is a low point in the year, with much self-examination, a little regret, and difficult feelings about other people that need to be resolved. Give yourself over completely to the feelings that arise, then let them go! It's the psychological equivalent of taking out the garbage.

- **The Sun in your ninth house:** This is a wonderful month for an adventure. If you've been wanting to take a big chance on something new, this is the month to do it! Also a good month to travel (especially overseas) and to share your knowledge with others.

- **The Sun in your tenth house:** If you've been needing to make a career push, do it during the month when the Sun is moving through your tenth house. Others will instinctively look up to you this month, so be sure you present yourself in a way that earns their respect.

- **The Sun in your eleventh house:** This is a great month to get your message out to a mass audience, because you will naturally shine in large groups of people.

- **The Sun in your twelfth house:** One of the lowest months of the year for physical vitality. Get lots of rest so you'll be ready to hit the ground running next month.

Mercury: Cycles of Learning

When I was growing up during the Jurassic era (before cable and DVR), late-night television was dominated by commercials for the Evelyn Wood speed-reading course. I was too young to appreciate the irony of using television to promote reading (since TV seemed destined to replace books altogether), but as an enthusiastic reader I thought speed reading sounded like the coolest thing ever. Think how many more books I could consume!

If planets could buy commercial advertising spots, Mercury would have cornered the market on behalf of Ms. Wood. Mercury moves through the zodiac in approximately 88 days, spending about three weeks in each sign (unless retrograde). Mercury is zippy—fitting for the planet of new information, variety, and (if deprived of these things) boredom. Mercury is not the kind of planet who would have stood for being in the same sign for very long; as it is, it turns pretty cranky when it's retrograde and forced to spend twice as long in a single sign!

Mercury never travels farther than 28 degrees from the Sun, so it is always in the same sign as the Sun, or the sign before or after. If the Sun is the rock star of the zodiac, Mercury is his press agent—the one who spreads the word far and wide and soothes his client with flattering words about his talent and virility. While Mercury moves around your chart, let it spread the word about your talents, knowledge, and charm.

Moving Through the Signs

To make sure people listen to you, adapt your style or mode of communication to Mercury's current sign placement:

- **Mercury in Aries:** Fast, impulsive, direct

- **Mercury in Taurus:** Slow, deliberate, unpretentious

- **Mercury in Gemini:** Quick, frequent change of topic

- **Mercury in Cancer:** Intuitive, guarded, sentimental

- **Mercury in Leo:** Dramatic, playful, creative

- **Mercury in Virgo:** Detail-oriented, critical, practical

- **Mercury in Libra:** Tactful, diplomatic

- **Mercury in Scorpio:** Silent but deadly

- **Mercury in Sagittarius:** Loud, theatrical, opinionated

- **Mercury in Capricorn:** Taciturn, authoritative

- **Mercury in Aquarius:** Quirky, rebellious, opinionated

- **Mercury in Pisces:** Gentle, humorous, artistic

 ASTRO TIP

Like an adolescent on summer vacation, Mercury tends to get into mischief when it gets bored. So give it the job of documenting your life's story. Personal journals, once all the rage, have fallen a bit out of fashion in the era of Facebook and Twitter. But while social networking is ideal for sharing updates about what you had for lunch, there is great value in recording your more private thoughts for posterity. Buy a great-looking notebook and a terrific pen and set aside a few minutes each evening to set down a few remembrances. Mercury—and your future self!—will thank you for it.

Moving Through the Houses

As Mercury flits from one house of your chart to the next, it symbolizes where you are ready for more knowledge and information. In which area of your life is it time for you to learn something new, get a new perspective, or acquire a new skill?

- **Mercury in your first house:** Talk about yourself! This is also a great month to confront people or situations that have been bothering you.

- **Mercury in your second house:** Give your finances a thorough going-over this month, and if necessary, get advice about how to handle your money and resources better.

- **Mercury in your third house:** Your best month all year for writing, reading, speaking, and taking short trips in a fast car.

- **Mercury in your fourth house:** Explore your family genealogy. Visit or call your family. Begin writing your memoir.

- **Mercury in your fifth house:** Promote your latest creative project. Take a class to learn a new creative skill, such as playing an instrument, painting, or writing a screenplay.

- **Mercury in your sixth house:** Make a list of everything in your life that needs repair. Set up a filing system or archive. Sort through those dusty boxes in the garage.

- **Mercury in your seventh house:** Pass the talking stick to your partner or closest friends. Handle communications that require diplomacy and negotiation.

- **Mercury in your eighth house:** Get some perspective on what makes you tick—talk to a therapist, psychic, or astrologer. This is also an excellent time for research and sleuthing.

- **Mercury in your ninth house:** Limit your intake of gossip, small talk, and television. This is the time to sift through all the thoughts, information, and ideas you've gathered and share them with others—through writing, teaching, or public speaking.

- **Mercury in your tenth house:** Show off your brain. Learn a new career-related skill. Take a communication-related career to the next level.

- **Mercury in your eleventh house:** Now is a good time for visits and chats with friends, and to indulge yourself in social networking. You are likely to receive unexpected flashes of inspiration.

- **Mercury in your twelfth house:** As much as possible, give your mind a vacation this month. Feed it lots of novels and reality TV, listen to music, and take naps.

Venus: Cycles of Enjoyment

Ask any astrologer what his or her clients talk about most, and the answer will almost certainly be relationships and money. In other words, if you learn nothing else about astrology besides how to understand the cycles of Venus—the astrological symbol for money and relationships—you'll probably consider your education more than sufficient.

Venus symbolizes pure enjoyment—of other people, and of all the delights earth has to offer. But although it's a symbol of finding love and money, it also describes how we bring beauty, harmony, and gifts to the lives of those around us.

In its roughly 225-day orbit around the Sun, Venus moves through each sign of the zodiac and each house of your birth chart. Venus's current sign introduces you, usually monthly (except when Venus is retrograde), to a different style of relating and enjoyment. And

Venus's cycle through the houses of your birth chart points to where romantic attraction and financial opportunities are likely to be found at any given time.

Moving Through the Signs

As Venus moves through the signs of the zodiac, there is a strong pull to handle relationships and financial matters in the style of that sign:

- **Venus in Aries:** Love at first sight; impulse spending

- **Venus in Taurus:** Sensuality; indulgence, spending on quality

- **Venus in Gemini:** Flirtation; comparison shopping

- **Venus in Cancer:** Courting; saving

- **Venus in Leo:** Whirlwind romance; lavish spending

- **Venus in Virgo:** Office romance; bargain hunting

- **Venus in Libra:** Serious relationships; spending on appearance

- **Venus in Scorpio:** Passionate intimacy; compulsive spending

- **Venus in Sagittarius:** Free love; generosity and philanthropy

- **Venus in Capricorn:** Committed relationship; investment

- **Venus in Aquarius:** Strange bedfellows; unexpected money

- **Venus in Pisces:** Unconditional love; charity

 ASTRO ALERT Venus symbolizes all that is beautiful, graceful, and delicious in life. But as we know, too much of a good thing can be hazardous to your health (and your bank account). As Venus moves through the houses of your chart, aim for a happy balance between indulgence and extravagance. Honor Venus with fresh flowers and a nice bottle of wine for dinner, but no one needs a six-course dinner at a five-star restaurant every night.

Moving Through the Houses

As Venus moves through the houses of your birth chart, it reveals opportunities to beautify your world, build better relationships with others, and find financial opportunities and insights:

- **Venus moving through your first house:** Beautify your appearance, and be cautious about moving into new relationships too quickly. Be assertive in asking for what you want, but avoid impulsive spending and borrowing or lending from friends and family.

- **Venus in your second house:** Spruce up your property and have your possessions appraised. You're drawn to relationships with people who are comfortable, reliable, and prosperous.

- **Venus in your third house:** You instinctively express yourself in a charming way this month, so it's a good time to ask for a raise or a favor. Communication, writing, and transportation are good sources of financial opportunity or insight. The way others speak or write can make them very attractive to you this month.

- **Venus moving through your fourth house:** It's a very good month to decorate your home. Real estate and domestically oriented businesses and activities are where the money is. You're most attracted to people who feel familiar, "like family."

- **Venus moving through your fifth house:** If you've ever wanted to make money from your art, this is a good month for it. It's also a splendid month for entertaining. Outgoing, generous, and confident people will be most appealing to you this month.

- **Venus moving through your sixth house:** Beautify your workplace; paint, or bring a plant or water fountain to your office. You're likely to get a raise or find a romantic interest at work. It's also a very good month to untangle your finances and get caught up on bookkeeping.

- **Venus moving through your seventh house:** Show your partners and close friends your honest affection and regard, and offer your enemies a little mercy. Your best financial opportunities this month come from networking.

- **Venus moving through your eighth house:** You may find yourself bringing brightness and grace to those in dark and difficult circumstances, and may be drawn to rela-tion-ships with moody, troubled people. Your finances may become entangled with other people's, and it's a good time for choosing investments.

- **Venus moving through your ninth house:** You're rewarded this month for being daring and innovative, and are likely to find financial opportunity through travel, foreign countries, education, or publishing. This month you might find yourself attracted to people who are from quite a different background than yourself.

- **Venus moving through your tenth house:** People in positions of authority instinctive-ly like you this month, so it's another good time to ask for a raise or promotion. (If

you're self-employed, raise your rates!) If you're looking for romance, you'll likely find it with someone who is in the same profession you are, or who is a bit younger or older than
you are.

- **Venus moving through your eleventh house:** If you've been wondering if a particular friendship might turn into something romantic, you will probably get your answer this month. Financial opportunities or insights are likely through networking, and if you were promised a raise last month, this is when you should begin to see additional income from your work.

- **Venus moving through your twelfth house:** You'll love spending time alone this month, or holed up at home with just your partner. Your best financial opportunities come through spiritual, metaphysical, artistic, or philanthropic sources such as church contacts, nonprofit groups, art and music, or metaphysical activities (tarot card readings, astrology, etc.).

Essential Takeaways

- Begin things while the Moon is in its waxing phases.
- Complete things while the Moon is in its waning phases.
- The Sun's cycle through the houses of your chart indicate where you can shine this month.
- Mercury's cycle through the houses of your chart indicate where you are curious and communicative this month.
- Venus's cycle through the houses of your chart show where you bring and attract beauty, affection, and gifts this month.

CHAPTER 20

Yearly Planner

Mars and the cycle of assertiveness

Jupiter and the cycle of exploration

Saturn and the cycle of authority

Solar and lunar eclipses

Each year, around about Thanksgiving time, I begin to mull over the prospect of writing a holiday newsletter to send to our family and friends. Yes, I'm one of "those people." On the other hand, as my friends and family will attest, I write really cool holiday newsletters. That's because I only include the highlights of the year. If the year didn't have any particular highlights (some years are like that), I make the mundane stuff superinteresting. And if I can't do that, I don't send out a newsletter.

What makes an event worthy of the holiday newsletter? First, I have to be able to remember it in late November. Someone in the household broke a leg or built a coffee roaster from scratch? Check. We took a vacation to some exotic location, or someone graduated from school? Check. Groundbreaking career achievements? You bet.

The cycles of Mars, Jupiter, and Saturn, and the tension of semi-annual solar and lunar eclipses, indicate life experiences that are generally interesting enough to fill a family holiday newsletter and not put your audience to sleep. Mars covers half the zodiac in a year, energizing fully half of the areas of your life with scrappy, feisty goodness. Jupiter covers a full sign of the zodiac, bringing the opportunity for at least one really interesting adventure. And Saturn pokes along through one half of a sign, so within any given year you're probably sizing up your ambitions in some area of your life, or else your ship is in the process of coming in, with a cargo of either rewards or disappointments. (Don't put the disappointments in the newsletter, unless you can make them funny.)

Mars: Cycles of Assertiveness

Mars is the planet of assertiveness, symbolizing where in life you tend to be an assertive and proactive hunter (or, heaven forbid, a bully), and where you're inclined to hide under the furniture like prey. Unlike Mercury and Venus, which are never farther away from the Sun than 28 and 45 degrees respectively, Mars can make every possible aspect to the Sun. So in the Mars principle, the Sun—your ego and sense of identity—encounter, for the first time, real friction and the potential of open warfare with others. A toddler discovers the word "no" around the time Mars first returns to its natal position at age $2^1/_2$, standing up for the first time to his parents, the gods of his young life. Likewise, you might find that $2^1/_2$ years into a job, a relationship, or any other kind of undertaking, you just feel *done* with it, and itchy to move on.

Mars represents your desire for newness and challenges. After $2^1/_2$ years, Mars has made a full circuit of the signs and houses from where it started. You've experienced everything at least twice—anniversaries, birthdays, annual reports, shareholder meetings—and it's time for a new challenge.

ASTRO TIP

About every two-and-a-half years, Mars returns to the same degree and sign it was in at your birth. This is your "Mars Return," and marks the beginning of a new two-and-a-half-year cycle of work, physical exertion, and challenges. It's often a time when you feel restless, bored, and ready for a fresh start.

Mars in Motion

As it moves through the zodiac, Mars indicates the nature of the challenges and conflicts that all of us face at the same time. Situations and types of people suggested by the sign through which Mars is moving tend to be energized, sexually charged, competitive, impulsive, and quick to anger under Mars's influence.

The areas of your particular life where you are energized and ready to resolve conflict are indicated by Mars's placement in the houses of your chart. About half the houses in your chart will be energized by Mars this year and the rest next year. Because not all houses are the same size, Mars may spend more time in one house than another.

Mars moving through Aries/your first house—A strong sign for Mars, so energy flows smoothly. This is a great time to begin all new projects, especially exercise routines, competitive enterprises, and jobs, especially entrepreneurial enterprises. Go after your individual goals. Don't completely forget about other people's needs and feelings, of course; but there are times in life when it's essential to focus on yourself, and this is one of those times. However, aggression is given its head. This is a time when wars begin, arguments flare up, and conflicts about territory and leadership come to a head.

Mars moving through Taurus/your second house—Taurus is not a strong sign for Mars, and energy here tends to move very slowly, with a lot of waiting and frustration. On the plus side, people make well-considered decisions. Pursue what you need to get where you want to go. Actively cultivate sources of income and stockpile provisions. However, there's a tendency to eat and spend impulsively, and conflicts may erupt over money or other resources.

Mars moving through Gemini/your third house—Energy is scattered and people are prone to restlessness and irritation. It's a great time to clear the air and really speak your mind about what's bothering you, and it's also a great time to initiate new communication businesses or routines. Speak your mind. Work with your hands. Write something. Begin learning a new language or skill. Fights among neighbors, siblings, and others in a shared community are common, and people may tend to drive aggressively or pick fights.

Mars moving through Cancer/your fourth house—A great time to do work around the house, especially renovation and in particular work that you do yourself. Spending time at home or with family can energize you now; if there are conflicts to be resolved, now is the time to tackle them. Expend physical energy at home, whether exercising, working on your home, or doing your job from home. Begin projects or businesses related to domestic or women's issues, or concerning nutrition or food. Conflicts within families or nations—the source of which are usually related to security—come to a head.

Mars moving through Leo/your fifth house—Assert yourself creatively; go after fun and attention! Conflicts at this time emerge over who should get attention and recognition, about child-rearing, and about sex. You want to have fun and you want to be noticed and admired. Give some energy to a hobby or some creative pastime that really makes you happy. Spend active time with your kids.

Mars moving through Virgo/your sixth house—A very strong time for research, analysis, problem solving, and practical solutions. Really push yourself at work right now; you've got the energy for it. You may find yourself competing at work, for a raise or for some other kind of reward; in any event, your competitive instincts are driving you at work now. You want to work alone. Handle anger well or you may become ill. Those around you are prone to nervousness and irritability; fights erupt over critical attitudes or work that isn't done well. It can also be a challenging time for health, but also a good time to change health attitudes and routines.

Mars moving through Libra/your seventh house—A good time to plot strategies and figure out ways to persuade others to give you what you want. Start a marketing or PR campaign or business. This can be a tough couple of months, because Mars requires that we assert ourselves, while Libra and the seventh house emphasize cooperation with others. You may find yourself in a series of difficult confrontations with people close to you. Moods vacillate between anger and conciliation; fights break out within primary relationships, and the underlying issue is about fairness.

ASTRO ALERT

Mars moving through the seventh house of your chart doesn't have to mean a fiery end to your most important relationships! But it's an important time for both you and your partner to be able to air your disagreements openly (and loudly, if that's your style). This will give you a better chance for a more honest relationship moving forward, one that honors each individual personality.

Mars moving through Scorpio/your eighth house—A strong sign for Mars, so energy flows well. This is the time to confront systemic, deep-rooted problems, including emotional and psychological blockages. A good time to engage in therapy. Also a good time for sleuthing and for core problem solving. Conflicts emerge about jealousy, suspicion, betrayal, lack of trust, and how to best use shared resources. You will tend to fight with your most intimate partners, but that can be pretty exciting for your sex life. It's a good time to work out investment strategies, catch up on your bookkeeping, and organize your wills and trusts.

Mars moving through Sagittarius/your ninth house—Energy is generally upbeat and abundant, and this is a great time to take a leap of faith. New experiences and adventure are the buzzwords; start a business or other project that helps people expand their minds, bodies, or spirits. It's a great time to start a higher education program, or to write a thesis, dissertation, or book. You'll enjoy spending time outdoors, and will be eager to travel. Legal conflicts and issues around religion, beliefs, and institutions (especially education) are likely to come to a critical point now. Conflicts related to religion, school, or travel.

Mars moving through Capricorn/your tenth house—One of Mars's best signs, so energy is highly focused, disciplined, and productive. Now is the time to lay foundations for the future, establish goals, and formulate business or life plans. Mars in your tenth house is one of the peaks of your Mars cycle; make the most of it by asserting yourself in your career. You may have conflicts with those in positions of authority. Conflicts emerge around who's in charge, and about rules, structure, and discipline.

Mars moving through Aquarius/your eleventh house—Energy is at a consistent level but given to sudden changes in direction. It's a good time to initiate a group or organization or something requiring a team effort. Assert yourself with your friends, or pursue a leadership role in an organization to which you belong. It's a good time for you to work with other people, even if you normally prefer to work on your own. Conflicts arise around the issue of equality, with friends and members of organizations ripe for confrontation.

Mars moving through Pisces/your twelfth house—Energy is flowing now, but does not work well if it's forced into rigid routines and particular directions. Live in the moment, and pursue musical, artistic, or spiritual goals. You'd love to sleep, rest, and give yourself over to dream states, long naps, and woolgathering. If you don't have the luxury of doing that, work hard to access your imagination and sensitivity and use them in your work. Conflicts emerge about unreliability, deception, unrealistic ideas, or faith; resist the urge to run from conflict.

 ASTRO TIP — In Chinese astrology, the 12-year cycle of animal signs originated with the orbit of Jupiter, which takes about 12 years to make an orbit around the Sun.

Jupiter: Cycles of Exploration

Jupiter symbolizes everything large, including the ways we grow in consciousness, body, and spirit. When Jupiter touches a sign, he brings a call to adventure to those parts of the human experience; when he moves through a house of your birth chart, you become like Alice in Wonderland after she ate that piece of cake and grew so large that she became trapped in the White Rabbit's house.

Astrologers don't necessarily believe that Jupiter is Santa Claus, but his movement through the chart does seem to coincide with times of opportunity, adventure, and growth. Jupiter asks, "Where have you outgrown your current life?" Where are you ready for an adventure, and a new way of looking ate things, and what kind of experiences will help you get them?

Jupiter in Motion

As Jupiter moves through the signs of the zodiac, all of us experience the potential for growth in the areas of life represented by Jupiter's current sign. If mankind at large ignores the opportunity for growth, giving in to intellectual laziness and arrogance, we lose the opportunity for this particular adventure for another 12 years.

Jupiter moving through the houses of your chart makes the impulse for growth and adventure specific to you and your life. Look back 12 years ago, when Jupiter was in the same sign and house, for clues to how to make the most of this cycle. The signs and houses share a lot of common territory, so I've combined the signs and equivalent houses in the interpretations that follow. But be sure to read both Jupiter's sign and the house of your chart that it's moving through.

Jupiter moving through Aries/your first house—It's time to upgrade your personality and outlook to something a little more inclusive and exuberant, more in line with your beliefs. Have the courage of your convictions; walk it like you talk it. This is the year you take up a new sport, do something dramatic about your appearance, go on a strenuously physical adventure, or start pursuing an educational goal.

Jupiter moving through Taurus/your second house—Put your money where your mouth is. Invest in your dreams; be generous with yourself and with others. Step out of your comfort zone. Learn more about money, appraisal, or property; don't be afraid to spend money on education.

Jupiter moving through Gemini/your third house—Think bigger. Learn a new language. Read lots of books, and try your hand at writing. Get to know your neighbors. You might not be able to get away for a long vacation to a distant land, but try to get a change of scenery on a regular basis, even if it's just going to a restaurant you haven't tried before.

Jupiter moving through Cancer/your fourth house—Expand your base of operations. This could mean moving to a new house or enlarging the one you have; it could mean adding members to your household—kids, extended family, new pets. Cook large meals, or experiment with new types of food. If you're traveling, you'll probably enjoy visiting family or returning to your hometown. You'll enjoy learning about things related to family, so you might embark on a genealogy project.

Jupiter moving through Leo/your fifth house—This year you discover that you've a lot more creative than you thought, and will probably enjoy putting yourself forward and getting attention, even if you're normally more retiring. That's cool; express yourself! Take an art class, or tour the great museums of the world (or even just the ones in your city). Be a teacher or mentor to young people, especially in the areas of sports or the arts.

Jupiter moving through Virgo/your sixth house—This year, you need a bigger job to do. Maybe it's time to change where you work, whether your employer or even your industry; maybe you just need to find a way to bring more of yourself, and your philosophy of life, to the work you're doing. Bring a little something new into your life every day.

Jupiter moving through Libra/your seventh house—This is a year when it's important to connect with people who help you see the world, and your place in it, in a bigger way. Perhaps your expectations about relationships have been too small; maybe you have been afraid to hope and reach for everything you want.

Jupiter moving through Scorpio/your eighth house—Unless you win the lottery or have a really interesting selection of people on your holiday mailing list, the big news this year will probably not end up in a newsletter. This is quieter, more private stuff, like learning to trust others and accepting their support. Like making a real intimate soul connection with someone, or learning to accept something about yourself that's always bothered you.

Jupiter moving through Sagittarius/your ninth house—You know what? You don't know as much as you think you do. The good news is, there's always more to learn, someplace new you haven't visited, and new dreams and visions to embrace. Enlarge your vision this year; look for experiences that challenge your beliefs.

Jupiter moving through Capricorn/your tenth house—This year, you'll find you're ready to be a leader, or at least to acknowledge your expertise in a particular area. You may even be ready for parenthood! Be willing to invest hope and money into a business venture, whether your own or someone else's, one you really believe in. Follow your calling, with your whole heart, and take a chance in your career that you've never before been ready to take.

Jupiter moving through Aquarius/your eleventh house—Some of the people you call your friends are no longer moving in the same direction that you are. Look for new companions in previously unexplored places. This year you envision a long-term goal that you may not reach for a while; let yourself commit to it and have faith that you'll get there eventually!

Jupiter moving through Pisces/your twelfth house—Your burdens have become much too heavy and take up far too much space in your life. This year tie a bunch of helium balloons to them, and release them into the wild. Open up space for relaxation, for rest, and for day-dreaming. Explore the fertile pastures of your imagination; write a song or a poem, or paint a mural on your bedroom wall.

Lucky Jupiter

In traditional astrology, Jupiter was called the *Greater Benefic*. It was considered the most positive and fortunate of all the planets, and its placement and influence in the birth chart a symbol of protection, luck, and happiness.

Saturn: Cycles of Authority

Saturn takes $29^1/_2$ years to complete a journey around the Sun. It spends about $2^1/_2$ years in each sign of the zodiac. As Saturn moves through the zodiac, society experiences burdens, blockages, challenges, and hardship in the matters related to each sign. If your Sun, Moon, or Ascendant are in the sign Saturn is currently moving through, these hardships take on a more personal relevance. And as Saturn takes its $29^1/_2$-year trip around the houses of your horoscope, it represents the maturity, wisdom, and self-discipline that come with confronting, working through, and achieving authority and mastery in those areas of your life.

Saturn in Motion

This year, you need to feel as though you're within a year or two of reaching an important goal related to Saturn's current sign and its house position in your chart. Saturn represents your ambitions and your willingness to invest hard work and sacrifice in achieving them. His sign and house in your chart describe the nature of your ambitions. Work hard and apply yourself, and Saturn will reward you with self-respect and the respect of others; fail to do your best, and Saturn becomes a harsh parent who lets you know he is very, very disappointed in you.

Saturn moving through Aries/your first house—If you've dreamed of living alone, working for yourself, or just learning to be comfortable eating in a restaurant by yourself, this is the year to make it happen. It won't be easy; in fact, anything that *is* easy for you this year is not moving you toward greater independence and self-respect.

Saturn moving through Taurus/your second house—If you cherish some financial goal, whether getting out of debt, achieving a certain level in your savings account, or maybe putting together a down payment for a house, this is the year to work toward that goal. Any obstacles or difficulties in reaching your goal will prove to you that you're able to take care of yourself.

Saturn moving through Gemini/your third house—If you want to be listened to, want to be a person whose words have authority and influence, want to write a book or master a new skill, this is your year. People who don't listen to you or who don't appreciate your skill are encouraging you to improve and respect your own abilities and efforts.

Saturn moving through Cancer/your fourth house—If you want to be closer to your family, to have a better home, or to feel more emotionally secure, this is the year to work on those things. Unable to rely on old foundations, this is a time to begin building a new emotional, financial, and literal home that will protect and sustain you for the next 29 years.

Saturn moving through Leo/your fifth house—Unable to connect easily with joy, fun, or creativity, you must develop a framework to let you rediscover and explore these areas of your life. Pursue something that offers joy but also requires a commitment of time and discipline—learning to play an instrument, perhaps, or having a child.

Saturn moving through Virgo/your sixth house—You may have become aware that you lack particular qualifications or technical skills that would allow you to advance in your work; now is the time to work to develop them, and it will almost certainly require sacrifice and determination on your part. Don't let yourself off the hook; you really need these qualifications or skills to succeed in the next phase of your life.

Saturn moving through Libra/your seventh house—What kind of partner do you want to have? Are you a person of integrity, discipline, and maturity? Do you *deserve* to have the kind of partner you want? If not, this is the time to make yourself a better partner. If your relationships aren't working, find where you're lacking instead of looking for faults in your partner. At the end of it all, you may or may not have the relationship you want with another person, but without a doubt you'll have a better relationship with yourself.

ASTRO TIP

Particularly important years are the ones when Saturn is moving through your first, fourth, seventh, or tenth house; when it is in the same sign it occupied at your birth; or when it is in the same sign as the Sun or Moon in your birth chart. These are years when you may meet unusually difficult obstacles, discouragement, or hard work; but they are also years that offer the greatest opportunities for maturity and achievement.

Saturn moving through Scorpio/your eighth house—One of the hardest feelings in life is the feeling that you're completely on your own, with no one to offer assistance. That's how it may feel to you now, and it may be hard for you to imagine that Saturn isn't just trying to make your life miserable. But Saturn wants you to experience the pride and satisfaction that come with being completely self-sufficient—both financially and emotionally. Address your finances realistically, especially loans and investments. And if you need emotional support, this is an excellent time to consider counseling or therapy.

Saturn moving through Sagittarius/your ninth house—You'd like to be seen as an authority when it comes to life's big questions—the meaning of life, what happens after we die, the way things work. Take your mind seriously. Finish or go back to school, read great works of literature, travel someplace that really challenges you. Real achievement for you will be proving not that you know everything, but rather that you're serious about training your mind and doing the work to become even more knowledgeable.

Saturn moving through Capricorn/your tenth house—In order to be taken seriously in your career, you need to take yourself, and your professional development, seriously. It's time to acknowledge your own authority and appreciate your achievements; if there are gaps in your ability or flaws in your character, correct them. If the world seems to be pushing you down, keep getting back up and prove that you're worth looking up to.

Saturn moving through Aquarius/your eleventh house—Someday when you're gone, what would you like to be your legacy? What would you like to see written on your tombstone, what tributes in your eulogy? Now is the time to envision and formulate a goal to create this legacy. Enlist your friends to help you; a legacy is always something that's more important than any single person.

Saturn moving through Pisces/your twelfth house—We've all made mistakes, all had bad things done to us, hurt other people, failed to live up to our potential. The question for you this year is, will you run away from these things, or can you do the work of shoring up your spiritual center? Can you take responsibility for what's gone wrong in your life up to now, forgive others and yourself? Or will you surrender to blame, victimhood, illness, and powerlessness?

Turning Points

We think of eclipses as incredibly rare and awesome events; in reality, solar eclipses happen twice each year. You may not see them where you live, but that doesn't mean they are not happening, and it doesn't mean you're not experiencing their symbolism in your life. Eclipses indicate turning points in your life; just as ancient people feared eclipses because they seemed to suspend the very laws of nature, eclipses in your life can indicate times when things seem to be turned upside down—and that can be scary.

Solar eclipses happen twice each year, when the New Moon happens within 18 degrees of one of the lunar nodes. A lunar eclipse usually occurs within two weeks of a solar eclipse. Because they're associated with the lunar nodes, eclipses have an approximate 19-year cycle through the zodiac. So if an eclipse falls at the same degree and sign of the Moon in your birth chart at age 10, another one will fall in roughly that same spot around age 29. Think back to that really big event in your life, and then flip the calendar forward nine years—what issues were demanding your utmost attention? What about 19 years later?

As they move through the houses of the horoscope, eclipses show you where the action is: where you are changing, growing, muddling through unfamiliar territory—in short, where you are currently most interesting.

Eclipse Cycles

The 18½-year cycle of solar eclipses is called the Saros Cycle. This cycle can predict when eclipses will occur in particular areas of the zodiac. Solar eclipses also belong to the Saros Series, which can take hundreds of years to complete. In her book *Predictive Astrology: The Eagle and the Lark* (see Appendix C), astrologer Bernadette Brady has done fascinating work with these cycles, interpreting eclipses according to the "birth" chart for the first eclipse in their Saros Series.

Solar Eclipses

At the solar eclipse, intuition (the Moon), wordless and irrational, overpowers your creative center and power (the Sun). The result is a bit like a short circuit of your internal wiring.

During an eclipse, the fundamental laws of the universe no longer apply. The Sun browns out, like a faulty wire that dims your kitchen light when you turn on the garbage disposal. The birds turn quiet. The world is shrouded in an apprehensive silence that you can almost hear.

In my observation, the week before and after a solar eclipse has us tiptoeing nervously through the graveyard, whistling a tune to keep the boogeyman away. Solar eclipses seem much more physically affecting than lunar ones, more unnerving, and the past themes they evoke—themes from 9 and 19 years ago—are anything but subtle. They are big events, and evoke the feeling that something big is changing in the landscape of your life.

At the solar eclipse, something is trying to get your attention—like the Moon, rising up in front of the Sun as if to say, "Just hold it a second—you're missing something!" People from the past or the present appear on the scene to behave in inexplicable ways. The person you used to be, the one you thought you'd outgrown, is trotted out in front of you as a reminder that you really haven't changed all that much; you're still the same old mess you were, back when you had the bad relationship, when you flunked out of school, when your best friend told you to get lost. Sit at the knee of the wise Moon, looming larger than usual in the sky, and know that she is reflecting the Sun in you. What is the part of your ego that is running around unchecked? What is the part of you that you're trying to disown? Let the Moon guide you, like a wise mother, toward self-acceptance and humility.

Lunar Eclipses

During a lunar eclipse, the Earth casts a shadow on the Moon, blocking it from reflecting the Sun's light. Similarly, at a lunar eclipse our ability to transmit and receive light—to channel and midwife divine inspiration—is trumped by the impulses of pure worldliness. Sometimes, it's the worldliness of physical disease or limitation that casts a long shadow; other times, the pain of earthly need and loss.

Usually, it's a pain you recognize. Eclipses have 19-year cycles, so an eclipse falls in the same sign and the same part of your chart every 19 years, and in the opposite spot every $9\frac{1}{2}$ years or so. What happens on the outside, in your outer life, is a little different each time—but the thing that's touched inside of you is exactly the same. At the lunar eclipse, an antidote to these earthly difficulties seems to lie in the celebration of earth's healing, stabilizing powers.

At the lunar eclipse, your vision is clear—or at least, you are guided by keen instinct; not the wild, emotional intuition of the Moon, but rather the quiet instincts of the earth. They are the same instincts that guide the hand of the craftsman as it chooses just the right piece of wood for his project; as it hovers for a moment over one chisel, before selecting another that's just right for the task.

At the lunar eclipse, there is something in you that longs to connect more deeply with the earth, to drink from her cool waters and lay your head upon her sweet grass. Some long-ago pain has reared up and sent you packing, returning home to mother earth for solace. As you gaze up at the half-bitten Moon, know that the earth is offering you something, some smooth block of marble, a piece of wood, a section of clay. Open your instinctive mind, and ask yourself: What is it that wants to be brought into being? And what is the right tool with which to carve it out?

Eclipses in Signs and Through the Houses

Like the lunar nodes, eclipses move clockwise through your chart, falling into opposite signs for a year and a half at a time and moving through opposite houses in your chart. The pattern goes like this:

first house/seventh house

twelfth house/sixth house

eleventh house/fifth house

tenth house/fourth house

ninth house/third house

eighth house/second house

The sizes of these house pairs, or axes, vary depending upon where you were born. For instance, people born extremely north or south of the equator will have one or two of these axes that are extremely large, while the rest of the houses of the chart are very small. Obviously, as eclipses move through your chart, they will pass more quickly through a very small pair of houses than through a very large one. On average, though, you can count on a particular set of houses in your chart being sensitized by eclipses for one to two years at a time.

Eclipses in Aries/Libra or the first/seventh houses—Eclipses falling in the first and seventh houses symbolize a time of profound changes in the balance between your individuality and your relationships with others. Romantic relationships, marriages, business partnerships—all take on heightened significance under this influence. Even when the state of your relationships is such a shambles that any change might seem welcome, you're rarely prepared for the anxiety that new relationships, even (or maybe especially) the happiest ones, inspire—anxiety that the "I" will not survive the process of becoming a "we," anxiety that the dream won't last. These are usually active times in your life, when there's a sense of being at war for the survival of your personal identity; be sure to take time out from "relating" to take care of your own needs. On the other hand, you may be getting out of a relationship and rediscovering yourself—falling in love with yourself, so to speak. If so, be careful not to become overly self-absorbed; make time to nurture the positive relationships in your life.

Eclipses in Virgo/Pisces or the sixth/twelfth houses—After the hectic activity of eclipses moving through your first house, this is a time of recuperation and healing. If you've pushed too hard with eclipses in your first house, this may be a time when you become sick or otherwise find yourself in a position of having to rely on others—or on faith. If you started or ended a relationship while eclipses were moving through your seventh house, this is the time when you must learn to live with the day-to-day consequences of that decision.

It's not uncommon to experience health problems and work upheavals during this cycle, but the real challenge lies in acknowledging your craving for solitary contemplation while simultaneously engaging in life-sustaining activities (work, household maintenance). Ideally, you will learn to immerse yourself in work as a kind of spiritual journey, instead of envisioning your spiritual journey as something that occurs in a vacuum, apart from the everyday world.

Eclipses in Leo/Aquarius or the fifth/eleventh houses—During the previous eclipse cycle, you passed through the quiet, recuperative stage of eclipses in the twelfth house. This year, it's time to get out and beat the bushes, in search of new friends and connections. With eclipses in the eleventh and fifth houses, love affairs and friendships often get a thrashing—love affairs break up, or an important but temporal relationship passes through your life for a short time. Such relationships have a feeling of "fatedness" about them, and may leave you feeling disillusioned, until you come to a better understanding of the role such relationships play in your life. Often, they serve simply to help you learn how to love better, but not necessarily to stay forever and be your life partner.

Friendships, too, go through big changes. During this cycle, it may seem that everyone deserts you at once; friends may get married or have children and have no time for you, leaving you with little audience for your self-expression. The lesson: do you give of yourself only to please an audience, or because it pleases you to express yourself?

This cycle may correspond to a change in your relationship with your parents or other mentors that allows you to transition to complete adulthood and leaves you feeling more free to express yourself completely and live your life exactly as you please. Also, since the fifth house rules children, eclipses in this house may find you considering the ultimate act of self-expression: becoming a parent.

Eclipses in Cancer/Capricorn or the fourth/tenth houses—Having gained confidence in your coping mechanisms and creative energy while eclipses moved through the eleventh and fifth houses, you face a new challenge: breaking with the past and moving with confidence toward the future. You might move to a new place, or discover your life's path; one may lead to the other. The key to discovering your direction in life (as described by the tenth house) is in first making peace with your point of origin, and especially with your family. If you are going to get anywhere in life, you must travel as lightly as possible, and that means the family baggage has got to go!

Alternately, if you've spent years pursuing your career path, this may be a time when more emphasis is placed on family. The tenth house sends you out into the world to follow your calling, and the fourth house sends you on a treasure hunt deep within yourself, examining your background and heritage. Here, you find the raw material, diamonds in the rough, that you can polish and refine into a meaningful gift to offer the world.

Eclipses in Gemini/Sagittarius or the third/ninth houses—Having made decisions about your life's purpose and making peace with the past while eclipses were in the tenth and fourth houses, it's now time to embark upon your quest. Probably, you won't feel up to the challenge; you'll doubt that you have the skills, intellect, or preparation to move forward on your journey. Schooling may become an issue, usually because you're confronted with the educational requirements of pursuing your life's work. You may return to school, or apply for a license or credential you've needed for a long time. You may develop an intense interest in a new subject, or take an existing interest to a new, journeyman level. This is also a typical cycle for leaving an unsatisfying career and starting your own business.

No matter where you are on your path, eclipses in the third and ninth houses mark a time to stretch your consciousness, expand your mental limitations, and test your faith in yourself. Eclipses in the ninth house invite you to take a chance in life, to act on faith, even though you may feel you are not up to the challenge; they also provide the impulse to develop the skills necessary to assist you on your quest.

Eclipses in Taurus/Scorpio or the second/eighth houses—Having made a daring leap of faith while eclipses were in the ninth house, you begin to wonder if the universe will support you, both emotionally and financially, in your quest. While eclipses fell in your third and ninth houses, you expanded your mind and consciousness; often, with eclipses in the second and eighth houses, you will turn to some kind of therapy or other intense, self-defining process, in an attempt to integrate your new concept of yourself.

The questions you may ask yourself during this cycle are among the most fundamental: who am I really, and is that of any intrinsic value? What's important in life? Usually you'll experience some level of psychological discomfort as you're tested in your resolve to pursue your dream, or experience loss in your life. And this cycle also tends to introduce financial discomfort, because money has a lot to do with how secure we feel about ourselves; working through financial difficulties clarifies what's really important about you, apart from your bank balance.

Essential Takeaways

- The cycles of Mars, Jupiter, and Saturn moving through your chart symbolize the development of your assertiveness, willingness to explore new things, and authority.
- Each year, Mars symbolizes where you are compelled to assert yourself and seek challenges through one half of your chart.
- Jupiter moves through one sign each year, symbolizing where you're ready for growth and exploration.
- Saturn covers a little over half of one sign in a year, and describes areas of your life where you must overcome obstacles to achieve greater maturity and authority.
- The 18-year cycle of eclipses symbolizes areas of life where you've reached a turning point.
- Solar eclipses happen twice each year and are usually accompanied, within two weeks, by a lunar eclipse.

CHAPTER 21

Long-Range Planner

Working with Uranus's cycles of awakening and rebellion

Gaining clarity during Neptune's cycles of enlightenment

Using Pluto's transformative cycles to gain insight, strength, and confidence

When you're young, you think that you and your experiences are utterly unique. No one ever thought like you, because if they did, they wouldn't be living lives of quiet desperation, working for The Man and combing their hair over their bald spot. I hope you enjoyed that part of your life. (And if you're there now—say, younger than 29—enjoy these feelings of invincibility and moral rectitude! Because generally speaking, they don't last.)

The good news is, the older you get, the more you draw comfort from knowing that, in fact, *almost everyone* has gone through most of the stuff you have. And if you learn astrology, you begin to understand that we go through an awful lot of it at roughly the same ages. This long-range planner looks at the cycles of the slow-moving planets: Uranus, Neptune, and Pluto. Their cycles form gradually and unfold over a matter of years; the processes they describe are deep and gradual, like subjects you grasp over the course of your academic career. The math you learned in second grade is vastly different than the advanced calculus you mastered in high school. But you didn't get from addition to calculus overnight—it took you 10 years.

Using the information in this cycle, you can prepare for moments of your life when rebellion is likely to flare up, and those times that you're apt to be disillusioned or to feel like life is meaningless. These can be miserable times, but they're part of being human. And by planning ahead for them, you can be an astro-ninja, using the force of these planetary transitions for your own development instead of becoming planetary roadkill.

Uranus: Cycles of Rebellion

Uranus is the planet that symbolizes rebellion against strictures, structures, and rules. It breaks the rules by having three different pronunciations of its name and by rotating on its side, like a rotisserie chicken. Uranus is weird, and he represents the uncivilized weirdo in each one of us.

Uranus takes 84 years to make a complete journey around the Sun. You read that right: 84 long, crazy years. It aspects its position in your birth chart every seven years or so, about the same time Saturn hits a rough patch in its $29^1/_2$-year cycle. (Seven-year itch, anyone?) Between Saturn pressuring us to master the rules and Uranus urging us to break them, it's no wonder we go a little crazy at ages 7, 14, 21, 28, 35, 42, and so on.

Uranus symbolizes that part of you that absolutely can't stand to be told what to do, and his cycle is designed to feed healthy rebellion. It's a good thing to be an independent person, to think for yourself and question conventional wisdom. Rebelling is a good and necessary thing; it keeps society from becoming too rigid and authoritarian. The generation that shares your Uranus sign (see Chapter 14) serves to shake up and challenge a particular set of limiting societal rules; but as Uranus moves through the houses of your horoscope, it also signifies where you are an individual change agent and iconoclast.

ASTRO TIP The ages of 21, 42, 63, and 84 are among the most pivotal years in your lifetime's Uranus cycle. These are ages when you're likely to feel rebellious and to go a little crazy, making sudden, radical changes in your life.

Working with the Cycle

How well do you answer Uranus's call for independence? Do you fear real change and lash out with inconsequential rebelliousness, or do you accept the challenge to stand up for unpopular opinions and say no to expectations and conventions that feel oppressive to you?

Track this cycle in your own life. Beginning with your birth, think about the following ages and how you were expressing your individuality and independence.

Year 0—You're born, the most shocking Uranian experience of all. Talk about independence (from the umbilical cord) and a total change of scenery! I've always thought the symbol for Uranus looks like a baby leaving the womb head first: our first great awakening.

Year 7—You may have just started school, spending the entire day away from your family. Pretty challenging, kind of scary. You have to find your way through a new set of rules and expectations, and also navigate the scary challenges of the playground, finding your place in a new group of peers.

Year 14—For many, this is a time when you move on to high school and start all over again in a new social environment. You have some freedom to choose your schedule and classes, and you get to move around to different classrooms throughout the day. Take advantage of opportunities to connect with groups, clubs, and classes that speak to your individual interests.

Year 21 (Uranus square to natal Uranus)—This is the first major challenge in your life's first Uranus cycle. For some, it's the last year of college, when you're facing the prospect of being "birthed" from the educational system in which you've spent most of your life. You're likely to be living away from your family by this age, facing an uncertain future (and in the United States, just able to drink alcohol legally). Cut loose from familiar moorings, you can feel tremendously excited and free, but also struggle to feel "normal" and connected to others.

Year 28—This corresponds with the return of Saturn to its position at your birth, and it's likely to be a time when the pressure to achieve within the limits prescribed by society is stronger than the need to be free and independent. You will likely commit to a course of action in this year; will it be one of your own choosing, or one that is designed to keep you safe, but also stagnant?

Year 35—This usually marks an itch of rebellion against the path you took at age 28. You can see 40, a milestone birthday, in the distance; if you chose the safe path at 28, now is a time you might feel you have to break free. You don't feel completely good where you are, but the alternatives seem imperfect as well. It's the dawn of the midlife crisis (see Chapter 17).

Year 42 (Uranus opposed natal position)—The next great crisis of your Uranus cycle. It's possible to look back now with fondness at your 21-year-old self, at your uncertainty but great urge to be unique and to live an exceptional life. This is an age when you can really take your life in an exciting new direction. But if you've spent your whole life living by someone else's rules and not really exerting your individuality in a meaningful way, you are likely to overcorrect, destroying personal and professional connections in your urge to gain freedom.

Year 49—Your fiftieth birthday is right around the corner, and it's tempting to tell yourself that you're too old to keep reinventing yourself. But this part of the Uranus cycle can give you a second wind, with interest in new hobbies or technologies and new social connections. Still, you're torn between trying to make one last push to reach the top of your field, or give up on all of that and just do your own thing.

Year 56—You're getting close to your second Saturn return, and your most productive working years are likely winding down. You may feel as though you want to retire right now, since you're probably fairly tired of responsibility and schedules and pushing for achievement. But really, this is the age to begin the process of disconnecting. You're probably freer now to adapt your work schedule to your needs and to leave your individual mark in your field before retiring. Embrace that, while also looking ahead to new opportunities.

 ASTRO ALERT During important years in Uranus's cycle, you can be like a giant electronic gizmo that needs to be "grounded." It's important to maintain regular routines, to cultivate healthy habits such as regular exercise and sleep, and to use some kind of meditative practice to keep yourself on an even keel during these times.

Year 63 (second Uranus square to natal Uranus)—Similar to age 21, you're preparing to leave an institutional structure that's been your world for many years. For many, you're nearing retirement from a conventional career, which means you're preparing for a radical change in lifestyle. Connecting with some worthy cause that needs your wisdom and experience will help make this transition easier, by connecting you to a new social network and helping you feel emotionally grounded.

Year 70—This can be a golden age of friendship for you, with a wide network of acquaintances and involvement in many organizations devoted to your particular interests. This is the time in your life when you can begin to embrace your eccentricities and speak your mind without fear; it may seem unlikely, but you're really at the height of your powers as a potential agent of change.

Year 77—As the physical realities of advancing age become evident, you may come to terms with the need to adapt your lifestyle to compensate. You may be dealing with the potential loss of some of your independence, and you may find you have to rely more on others than you'd like.

Year 84 (Uranus return to natal position)—Those who live to this age are, in a real sense, reborn as Uranus returns to its natal position. Even if you've spent a lifetime trying to live by the rules, you may now feel comfortable and even entitled to be a full-fledged eccentric. Your independence, mental sharpness, and irreverence endear you to others, particularly young people.

Uranus in Motion

As Uranus moves through the zodiac, it awakens society to the need for revolution in some aspect of society. As it moves through the houses of your horoscope, it awakens your need for greater freedom and change in a particular area of your own life. This is a long-term influence, with Uranus spending an average of seven years (more or less, depending on the size of the house in your chart) in each house.

Uranus moving through Aries/your first house—*Freedom to be yourself.* You have the overwhelming need to be free and unconstrained and to reinvent yourself. This cycle often begins with a change—sometimes startling—to your appearance. It's also a common cycle for moving to a new location or ending a relationship that feels too confining. Your temper might be unpredictable, and you may feel the urge to fight for causes that are important to you.

Uranus moving through Taurus/your second house—*Freedom from want.* This is a cycle when you don't want to feel tied down by possessions, financial considerations, or the need for security. You are apt to take significant financial risks, giving up security in order to work for yourself or simply to feel more independent, and may undertake a goal of financial freedom.

Uranus moving through Gemini/your third house—*Freedom of thought.* You refuse to be limited or defined by your knowledge and skill set; you may undertake studies to give you more options, but staying on track with a particular course of study is extremely challenging now. You are drawn to studies of communication and technology and bring great originality and insights to these areas.

Uranus moving through Cancer/your fourth house—*Freedom from history.* You may begin this cycle by moving to a new place, even a new country, far from your home and family. Or you may choose to stay where you are and change the existing dynamics by refusing to accept the status quo. Your mission is to dismantle your earliest conditioning and the rules you've never questioned up to now.

Uranus moving through Leo/your fifth house—*Freedom to be happy.* You won't be told how you may express yourself, how you should pursue happiness, or that you aren't that special. You know full well you're special, and that in fact everyone is unique. Anyone who tries to tell you that your hobbies are silly, your blog is self-indulgent, or your parties are boring will face an emotional lightning strike!

Uranus moving through Virgo/your sixth house—*Freedom of work.* You will often begin this cycle by changing your place of employment, sometimes more than once, because you don't want to be owned by a job. You're likely to do best working as a contractor, temporary employee, or self-employed person during this cycle. You may also dedicate yourself to a new health regimen, one that may seem unusual but suits you and allows you to pursue it at your own pace.

Uranus moving through Libra/your seventh house—*Freedom to love.* If you've been in a relationship that is unequal, stifling, or has damaged your self-esteem, you will very likely break free from it now. You are rewriting your rules and ideas about partnership, renegotiating the balance of your needs and those of a partner, and may end up in surprising and unconventional relationships.

ASTRO TIP

Uranus moving through your seventh house is a signal that you or your partner may need more individual freedom than you did before. This doesn't have to mean separate bedrooms, individual vacations, or an open relationship; it may be something as simple as negotiating evenings out with friends. Having the freedom to pursue individual interests is the key to feeling good about your relationship during this cycle.

Uranus moving through Scorpio/your eighth house—*Freedom from dependence.* You will make every effort during this cycle to free yourself from debt or other financial obligations that limit your freedom. You can't abide being supported by anyone now, and will probably commit to a program to protect yourself against depending on others in old age or if you become ill or disabled. Your relationship to sex will likely go through some changes now; you may become sexually experimental or feel somewhat asexual.

Uranus moving through Sagittarius/your ninth house—*Freedom of religion.* You'll often have a period of rebellion against the prevailing belief systems in your life and in society. Your attitudes toward religion or politics may take a sharp turn, and you will delight in taking an adversarial position in arguments about beliefs. You may wish to study or travel and find it's difficult to commit to higher education or long trips.

Uranus moving through Capricorn/your tenth house—*Freedom of direction.* Whether through your own choice or outside circumstances, the direction of your life takes a sharp, often sudden turn. Often, you are being called to a larger future than you had envisioned for yourself, but embracing that future means giving up the script you had already written in your mind. Depending on your age when this happens, you may or may not feel ready for the challenge; it is, however, ready for you.

Uranus moving through Aquarius/your eleventh house—*Freedom of assembly.* After changing direction with Uranus in the tenth house, you face the prospect of reinventing yourself within society—especially since you are probably in quite a different society than you were previously. You may lose friends and will certainly make new and important ones. Your greatest struggle during this cycle is finding a way to fit in without abandoning your individuality.

Uranus moving through Pisces/your twelfth house—*Freedom of spirit.* These may be years when you hide your "freak flag," pretending to be like everyone else so you can co-exist peacefully with others. This means you may feel most free when you're alone, and time spent in solitude can be incredibly creative and spiritually enlightening. You are extraordinarily sensitive, even psychic now, so it will be important to maintain appropriate boundaries and to protect yourself as needed, to avoid abusing food, drink, or other substances that can dull your feelings.

Neptune: Cycles of Enlightenment

Neptune's lap around the zodiac takes 165 years. It's the first of the planets for which you won't live to see its return to your natal position. It's the first planet that will never touch every house of your horoscope. You'll never completely know Neptune. And not surprisingly, it's the planetary symbol for that which is unknowable; things we believe in without any factual evidence. Dreams and imagination that help us see a future that isn't yet there. It's the quality that lets us imagine what it's like to be another person, giving us compassion and empathy. Its cycle is designed to heighten your appreciation for the unknowable hearts of others, an awe for the grand design of which you play a part you don't completely understand.

Working with the Cycle

Critical ages in this cycle are when Neptune makes aspects to its position at the time you were born.

Age 19–21 (Neptune semisquare to its natal position)—This is an age when a lack of worldly experience can lead us to have little compassion for others. We declare we'll never live like our parents, never make the same mistakes the previous generation made; the world will be better under our watch.

Age 26–28 (Neptune sextile)—After a few years in the practical world of earning a living and paying bills, you begin to see why others have compromised their ideals out of practical necessity. You may still be discontented with the world, but there are ways you can make the world better within the constraints of your everyday life, if you're willing to try.

Age 42 (Neptune square)—Part of the midlife crisis cluster of aspects (see Chapter 17), this may be a time of disillusionment and yearning, when you feel you're not being your true self. It can also be a time when you finally realize a long-cherished dream, and experience either the satisfaction of that or a feeling of being let down by reality. In any event, you begin to see that it's time for a new dream.

Age 55 (Neptune trine)—After some years of spiritual seeking, this is an age when you either find a kind of spiritual renewal, or give yourself over to the habits of escapism (TV, alcohol) or illness. Find something you can believe in.

Late 60s (Neptune quincunx)—If you haven't formulated a dream for the next part of life, you may find yourself giving in to cynicism and negativity, lacking compassion for others. It's hard to compromise your ideals of what you, other people, and the world should be like, but this is the time to embrace spiritual compromise and realism.

Age 82 (Neptune opposition)—At the Neptune opposition, we begin the process of letting go of the physical world. We find it easier to understand others, to forgive ourselves for our failings. We grow better able to love the world as it is, instead of dreaming of how we'd prefer it to be.

Sea and Sky

MISC.

The planet Neptune was named for the god of the sea because its blue gas clouds reminded early astronomers of great oceans.

Neptune in Motion

As Neptune moves through the zodiac, it awakens a societal yearning for clarity, compassion, and healing. As it moves through the houses of your horoscope, it awakens your need for peace, surrender, and spiritual awakening in a particular area of your own life. This is a long-term influence, with Neptune spending an average of 12 years (more or less, depending on the size of the house in your chart) in each house.

Neptune moving through Aries/your first house—The struggle to project a clear persona; dedicating yourself to a specific spiritual goal or compassionate cause, or to involvement in music, art, or dance. Dealing with the frailties or limitations of your physical body. An ability to blend into the woodwork.

Neptune moving through Taurus/your second house—The need to gain clarity about the physical world and take better care of your body and possessions. Working through unrealistic ideas about money, or dedicating money and resources to charitable causes. Being detached from the physical world while still being responsible.

Neptune moving through Gemini/your third house—Confronting illusions about your capabilities; are your strengths and weaknesses really what you've always assumed they were? Learning to communicate in a more compassionate way; softening your verbal approach, and engaging in imaginative writing such as poetry, songwriting, or fiction.

Neptune moving through Cancer/your fourth house—Confronting ideals about home, family, history, your nation. Are your family, your nation, your profession all that you thought they were? Forgiving your family, letting go of history, making reparations for the past.

Neptune moving through Leo/your fifth house—Are you as talented—or as untalented—as you've been led to believe? How do you really feel about children? Is time spent playing video games and gambling at casinos really enhancing your life? Creative inspiration, but also delusions of grandeur.

Neptune moving through Virgo/your sixth house—Confronting the reality that you'll never be perfect, and that maybe perfection isn't the key to happiness. The attempt to bring together mind, body, and spirit. The opportunity to make a practical contribution to a cause that's important to you.

Neptune moving through Libra/your seventh house—Examining ideals and illusions about relationship. Can you forgive partners who hurt you in the past? Are you realistic about what you expect from your current partner, or about the kind of partner you're looking for? Learning to be softer and kinder toward your partner; forming partnerships based on music, art, or spirituality.

Neptune moving through Scorpio/your eighth house—Who is really in your corner, and how much support do you really need from others in order to get by? How important is sex, and how does it fit into your notions of spirituality and love? Can you be trusted? Can you forgive those who betrayed your trust?

Neptune moving through Sagittarius/your ninth house—Confronting ideals and illusions about education (would having more make a difference?), big questions of life and death (are you a bad person, planning for your aging parent's death?)? Do your beliefs have a spiritual component or just a physical or intellectual one? Can you forgive teachers, bureaucrats, publishers, or religious figures who let you down?

Neptune moving through Capricorn/your tenth house—Examining ideals and illusions about ambition and accomplishment. Bringing a softer and more spiritual side to your work and professional reputation. Forgiving parents, teachers, bosses, the government, and other authority figures who've made you feel disillusioned.

Neptune moving through Aquarius/your eleventh house—Confronting ideals and illusions about friends, fitting in, and your future/legacy. Are your friends, community, and organizations helping you create a legacy of compassion and spiritual meaning? Can you forgive friends, organizations, politicians, the media for any ways in which they've hurt you or been untruthful?

Neptune moving through Pisces/your twelfth house—Confronting ideals and illusions about your own spiritual development; are you making a practice of examining your own motives, secrets, and suffering, or are you living in denial, drinking too much, and taking lots of naps? Are you leaving yourself open emotionally to those who are in need or in pain, or are you shutting off your compassion? Can you forgive spiritual leaders who've betrayed you, or those who've hurt you in secret, shameful ways?

Pluto: Cycles of Empowerment

Pluto, the most distant planet in our solar system, occupies the outside track in the race around the Sun; Pluto takes about 245 years to journey through the zodiac. Due to a very eccentric orbit, the time it has spent in each sign varies; since Pluto was last in Aries, it spends between 12 years (Pluto in Scorpio) and 33 years (Pluto in Taurus) in a sign.

Because it takes so long to make a journey that the Moon, say, completes in $2^1/_2$ days, we're safe in assuming that Pluto's cycles represent the kind of deep, profound, and transformative changes that take time to unfold. These deep changes involve society as well individuals, and even more so than Uranus and Neptune, Pluto moving through signs represent not just societal change or enlightenment, but movements.

Pluto represents your ability to face hard truths and your willingness to be transformed by some of life's most difficult experiences. Pluto rules power and control, and in Pluto's cycles you taste the limits of your ability to influence your own life. Sometimes—and often at ages when Pluto in the sky has reached a critical moment in its relationship with Pluto in your birth chart—life is painful, unpleasant, and unfair. Confronting mortality, powerlessness, and insignificance are the work of Pluto cycles in your life. Use them to determine whether you become bitter and caustic, or the kind of deep, mature, enlightened figure who others can come to in times of trouble.

ASTRO TIP

Pluto is known as the god of wealth. Venus is the planetary ruler of money, but Pluto is the ruler of *big* money. Pluto also rules "other people's money"—including financial collectives like banks and insurance companies, and wealthy relatives you hope will remember you in their wills.

Pluto in Motion

Unlike the other planets, Pluto's important life cycles occur at different ages depending on Pluto's sign at your birth. Most of us will never live to see Pluto travel to the halfway point of its cycle; but all Pluto sign generations experience Pluto's square (90 degrees) to its position in the birth chart. For those born with Pluto in Leo, Virgo, Libra, or Scorpio, this important cyclical passage is occurring at midlife, right in the middle of the other midlife crisis aspects (see Chapter 17). This is a pivotal moment of development in your awareness of mortality and of life stripped down to its bare essence.

There is some overlap between the Pluto generations, while Pluto was making long retrograde journeys back into the previous sign. If you were born during a year when Pluto was changing signs, you'll need to look at your birth chart to find out exactly where it was at your birth.

Critical Pluto Aspects

Critical life passages are usually represented by slow-moving planets making square or opposition aspects to their position in your birth chart. Because Pluto moves so slowly, most of us experience only one of these, the square. However, the Pluto in Cancer and Pluto in Leo generations will experience the opposition in their mid 80s, and the Pluto in Virgo generation around age 90.

When Pluto squares or opposes its position in your birth chart, loss, grief, and a heightened sense of one's mortality generally come along for the ride. Paying attention to your emotional health is important at these ages; the urge can be strong to crawl into your cave for a couple of years, but don't take hibernation to an extreme.

The age when this aspect occurs varies depending on Pluto's sign at your birth; unlike some planets, Pluto has a very erratic cycle and moves much more quickly through some signs than through others. The following table indicates the age range during which your generation experiences the Pluto square.

Pluto Cycles by Generation

Pluto's Sign at Birth	Years	Ages of Critical Point in Pluto's Cycle
Aries	1822–1852	90–93
Taurus	1851–1883	86–88
Gemini	1882–1913	74–75
Cancer	1912–1939	59–60
Leo	1938–1958	42–44
Virgo	1956–1972	39–40
Libra	1971–1984	40–41
Scorpio	1983–1995	36–37
Sagittarius	1995–2008	48
Capricorn	2008–2023	58–59
Aquarius	2023–2043	72–73
Pisces	2043–2067	86–87

Pluto moving through your first house—*Empowered personality.* The first house describes the personality and other coping mechanisms you've cultivated to help you deal with a confusing world. Now, whatever isn't working in your natural approach to the world will be painfully revealed, giving you the opportunity to respond to the world with more strength and authenticity.

Pluto moving through your second house—*Empowered security.* How have you been dishonest without yourself about the role of money, security, and belongings in your life? Perhaps you believe you can only be poor, or that you need money to be secure, or that belongings are meaningless. You're about to find out if those beliefs are really true.

Pluto moving through your third house—*Empowered message.* You notice everything, but learned early on to keep the more sensitive observations to yourself. Now it's time to tell the truth, regardless of the consequences. Keep a pure motive and avoid being honest for the purpose of being hurtful.

Pluto moving through your fourth house—*Empowered belonging.* If you had been telling yourself any half-truths about the realities of your family, parents, upbringing, early history, or genetics, now is the time they'll all be stripped away.

Pluto moving through your fifth house—*Empowered creativity.* Cut through the ego pollution. If you haven't been telling yourself the truth about your creative pursuits, your relationship with your children, and what would make your life a lot more fun, you're about to have your eyes opened.

Pluto moving through your sixth house—*Empowered service.* If you've been telling yourself that your boring job is fine, giving in to easy cynicism about the messed-up state of the world, and treating your body less like a temple than like a rest stop bathroom, you're in for a rude awakening. By the end of this transit, you should be on the path to more meaningful work, more responsible stewardship over your health, and a clearer picture of what you can do to make the world less sucky.

God of the Underworld

Pluto is the Latin name for the Greek god Hades. Hades and his brothers, Zeus (Jupiter) and Poseidon (Neptune), defeated the Titans and divvied up the spoils as follows: Zeus, god of the air; Poseidon, god of the sea; and Hades, god of the underworld.

Pluto moving through your seventh house—*Empowered partnership.* The truth about your partner, your own motivations in partnership, and the realities of the relationship itself, are revealed. What's left is the true, essential bond between you, without artifice or illusion.

Pluto moving through your eighth house—*Empowered intimacy.* How well, wisely, and honestly do you trust other people? Are you able to be truly honest about what you need from them and what you're willing and able to give? Pluto moving through this part of the chart reveals any power plays, manipulation, or deception in your most intimate and interdependent relationships.

Pluto moving through your ninth house—*Empowered beliefs.* If you've been worshipping false gods and graven images, following learned men and women with feet of clay, and pretty much thinking you had the meaning of life all figured out … well, guess what? *Nobody* has it all figured out.

Pluto moving through your tenth house—*Empowered leadership.* If your goals, ambitions, and overall life mission have been based on peer pressure, family expectations, earning potential, world domination, or basically anything other than an honest desire to provide authority and leadership for the development of mankind … this transit will not be pleasant. It's time to strip down the engine of your life, right down to the chassis, and rebuild it into something that reflects your authentic character.

Pluto moving through your eleventh house—*Empowered community.* Do you know who your friends are? It's time to find out. While Pluto moves through your eleventh house, you also get to play whistle-blower and resident burr-under-the-saddle to groups and organizations with which you're involved. Ideally, at the end of this cycle you should be connected only to those friends, groups, or causes that reflect your strongest convictions.

Pluto moving through your twelfth house—*Empowered dreams.* The twelfth house is a treasure trove of embarrassing secrets, tender fears, and sacred sorrows. Enter Pluto with his portable x-ray machine, ready to expose your soft, white underbelly to the world—or at least, to you; and even the strongest among us can be brought down by the terrors of our own psyche. By the time this transit ends, you may still have secrets, fears, and sorrows—but you'll have looked each one of them in the eye and really seen them, and they will no longer control you.

Essential Takeaways

- The slow-moving planets Uranus, Neptune, and Pluto represent major life transitions, some at predictable ages.
- Uranus's cycle symbolizes rebellion against the rules and desire for freedom. It spends about seven years in a sign of the zodiac, and roughly that long in each house of your birth chart.
- Neptune's cycle symbolizes illusions, compassion, and spiritual development. It spends about 12 years in a sign of the zodiac, and about that long in each house of your chart.
- Pluto's cycle symbolizes empowerment through the stripping away of artifice. Pluto's cycle is erratic and the time it spends in each sign and house of the chart varies.

PART 6

Bringing It All Together

L earning a language is challenging. Still, if you apply yourself, you can probably be reading *People* magazine in a second language within a year. As a language, astrology has a similar learning curve. It can take time to make the leap from understanding astrology when you read it in a book to knowing how to apply it to real world situations. Furthermore, you may decide that what you've learned in the other parts of this book are enough for you. You know how to recognize planetary placements in your chart, look them up, and get some insights about them. That's a great place to start, and for many, that's where the journey will end.

If you want to become fluent in the language, however, the final part of the book journeys into more complicated territory: using astrology to see into the future. These chapters offer a taste of how the discrete elements of astrology can be combined to reveal a portrait of a real, complex person, and how to peer into the future and make out the landscape that lies ahead.

CHAPTER 22

Speaking Astrology

Understanding the astrological alphabet

Using the correct astrological grammar

Combining key concepts: planets,signs, houses, and aspects

Approaching a chart with an open mind

A systematic approach to reading a birth chart

Sample chart analysis

Astrology has the capacity for lyricism and deep insight. But writers who created great works of art (*War and Peace,* the Old Testament, *Friends*) didn't leap from learning the alphabet one day to sitting down at a typewriter (or Dead Sea Scrolls, as the case may be) the next, ready to dazzle the world. First, they had to master a language. There were hours spent singing that wearisome alphabet song and listening to teachers drone on about grammar, punctuation, and composition, before they ever got to that neat stuff about Napoleon's invasion of Russia and the tortured romance between Ross and Rachel.

But before you can dazzle your friends with your astrological insights, you have to learn the language. I won't lie to you—there's a bit of a learning curve. This book has given you the tools, but you have to learn to wield them with skill and authority. This chapter is designed to walk you through some basic rules of astrological grammar, and to give you an example of what it might look like when you take all these disparate symbols and use them to cobble together an astrological profile of an actual person.

A Review of the Astrological Alphabet

As I discussed in Chapter 2, astrology is built on a group of basic symbols that act as short-hand for some reasonably complex concepts. The signs of the zodiac, like your ABCs, follow an established order from Aries to Pisces and are often represented by glyphs instead of their names. Each sign corresponds with a house of the horoscope and to one or more planets, which also have their own glyphs, as summarized in the following table.

Sign	Glyph	House	Planet(s)	Glyph
Aries	♈	First	Mars	♂
Taurus	♉	Second	Venus	♀
Gemini	♊	Third	Mercury	☿
Cancer	♋	Fourth	Moon	☽
Leo	♌	Fifth	Sun	☉
Virgo	♍	Sixth	Mercury	☿
Libra	♎	Seventh	Venus	♀
Scorpio	♏	Eighth	Pluto, Mars	♀ ♂
Sagittarius	♐	Ninth	Jupiter	♃
Capricorn	♑	Tenth	Saturn	♄
Aquarius	♒	Eleventh	Uranus, Saturn	♅ ♄
Pisces	♓	Twelfth	Neptune, Jupiter	♆ ♃

It's not that a sign means exactly the same things as its corresponding house or planets; it's just that there is sympathy among them, and a lot of territory in common. A doctor, a hospital room, and a white coat and stethoscope aren't the same things, but they all have something to do with health care. Likewise, the sign Taurus, the second house, and Venus all have something to do with pleasure.

This commonality becomes important to understand when you begin mixing and matching elements from different categories. Going back to our doctor example, health care providers come in different forms (doctor, nurse, dentist, veterinarian), can look or dress in a variety of ways (male, female, white coat, surgical scrubs), and might work in a variety of settings (hospital, clinic, a tent in Korea). *M*A*S*H*'s Hawkeye Pierce wearing surgical scrubs in a mobile army surgical hospital is a vastly different image from that of a nurse of the same era in a conventional hospital, wearing a crisp white hat. But they're both in the health care business.

Likewise, Venus (the concept of pleasure) can come in a variety of forms (attractive person, candy bar, lingerie, currency), look a certain way (blonde, nougaty, lacy, small bills), and be found in a variety of settings (across a crowded room, in a vending machine, Victoria's Secret, that jar in the kitchen). So a woman (Venus) who is mature and authoritative (Capricorn) and who works in communication (third house) has a certain amount in common with your boss (Saturn) who sells advertising (Libra) for a magazine (third house). They're not the same, but they have enough things in common (authority, work in communication, women's issues) that they'd probably find something to talk about at a dinner party.

Astrological Grammar

When someone who doesn't know anything about astrology wants to reference it in a "humorous" way, he might say something like, "My Moon is in Uranus." (Astrological humor almost always includes Uranus.) That's an objectionable sentence in many ways, but most importantly, it's poor astrological grammar. Here's why.

Astrological Nouns

When you learned grammar, you began with nouns. These were the words that did the heavy lifting, the people, places, and things that occupy space and perform actions, the grammatical rock stars around which the rest of the words in a sentence revolved like groupies. In astrology, planets are the nouns. Planets are described as being in signs, in houses, and in aspect to other planets or angles. In other words, a planet appears to be moving through a particular constellation (sign) and part of the sky (house), and in specific geometrical relationships (aspects) with other planets or parts of the sky. For example:

> *Venus is in Aquarius.* This means that the planet Venus is moving through the constellation Aquarius.

> *Venus is in the first house.* That is, the planet Venus is in part of the sky that the Sun occupies just before sunrise.

> *Venus is trine Saturn.* This means the planet Venus is approximately 120 degrees from the planet Saturn. The faster-moving planet is the one that makes the aspect to the slower-moving planet. (If we waited around for Neptune or Pluto to aspect something, we'd be here all day.)

Put these concepts together and you get a sentence like this:

> *Venus is in Aquarius in the first house, trine Saturn.*

Planets also rule signs; for example, Mars rules Aries. Before the discovery of Pluto, Mars was also considered the ruler of Scorpio. Most modern astrologers still consider Mars a co-ruler, or traditional ruler, of Scorpio.

To a more limited extent, signs can occasionally serve as nouns. Signs can be in houses:

> *Capricorn is in the first house.* That is, some or all 30 degrees of the sign Capricorn fall between the cusps of the first and second houses.

Signs can also be on house cusps or angles:

> *Scorpio is on the cusp of the tenth house,* or *Scorpio is on the Midheaven.*

But signs are never in planets, or in other signs. Saying something like "My Virgo is in Mars" is like saying "My yellow is in dress." It doesn't mean anything except that the person who constructed this sentence doesn't speak the language.

Astrological Adjectives

The signs of the zodiac function as astrology's adjectives, describing the nouns. For example, your girlfriend dresses eccentrically, favoring odd pairings like army boots with a tutu. In this case, your girlfriend is a Venus character (a female) who dresses in an Aquarian (eclectic, surprising) fashion.

Astrology and the Bard

William Shakespeare's plays were filled with allusions to astrology, which was very popular in Elizabethan England. From King Lear to Romeo, the characters in his plays often expressed themselves in the language of astrology—most famously, Cassius in Julius Caesar: "The fault, dear Brutus, is not in our stars, but in ourselves."

Astrological Verbs and Adverbs

Planetary movements are astrology's verbs and adverbs, showing action in the sky. The nature of that action is the adverb.

- Planets form aspects to other planets:

  Today, Mercury will aspect Pluto.

  If you want to give a little more color commentary about the aspect, you could describe the aspect:

  Today, Mercury will make a square aspect Pluto, so be on guard for sarcasm.

  Or simply: *Today, Mercury will square Pluto.*

- Planets enter signs or houses, or change direction:

  This morning, Mercury entered Sagittarius, quickly followed by my foot entering my mouth.

  Look at that—the Moon just left the seventh house and my wife walked out on me!

  Before you know it, Mercury will turn retrograde again.

  I'm living for the moment when Mercury turns direct!

Combining Key Concepts

When you start to combine planets, signs, houses, and aspects into complete sentences that make sense, it can be completely overwhelming. This is especially true because astrology is, above all, an interpretive art, so there are a number of ways you can interpret just about any astrological symbol. With practice, and with a little context about the animal, vegetable, or mineral that you're interpreting, you will eventually get better at this. For now, just get comfortable trying to do it at all. Do it by taking each element step-by-step.

Let's say you want to figure out what it means that your sweetheart was born when Jupiter was in the sign of Libra and in the sixth house. What does it mean?

1. Start with the symbolism of the planet—in this case, Jupiter. What element of your sweetie's character or psyche is under consideration? It's the inner adventurer, seeking new experiences and a broad-reaching understanding of life.

2. Consider the sign that the planet is in. This indicates the style in which he approaches the planet's bailiwick. Libra seeks balance, all things in moderation; prefers to dress beautifully and behave charmingly; dislikes gore and violence; and is preoccupied with relationships. This person prefers a balance of new experiences (Jupiter) and more familiar routines. He prefers to have company

in his adventures, and he is wary of adventures that require him to go several days without showering.

3. Consider Jupiter's house placement. Jupiter is in the sixth house, the house of health, work, daily routine, and service. He is most apt to encounter adventure in connection with his work or health, or out of a desire to be of help. He may work in the travel industry, in academia or publishing (adventures of the mind), or in a religious profession (adventures of the spirit). He may perform perfectly ordinary work (sixth house), such as chartered accountancy, in thrilling settings (Jupiter) such as Machu Pichu.

Try one yourself. What would you do with, say, Mars in Virgo in the third house?

 ASTRO TIP Chapter 16 provides a guide to interpreting aspects that is so awesomely comprehensive that it really deserves another look. So flip back and take a gander, then join us back here, won't you?

Approaching a Chart

I'll tell you a secret. I've been reading charts for almost four decades, and every time I sit down with a new one—every time without fail—it looks absolutely incomprehensible to me. The symbols swim before my eyes and refuse to hang together into anything cohesive. It's only by taking it slow and methodically, by finding an interesting thread of two and pulling at them, that I'm eventually drawn into the chart.

And I'll tell you another secret. I rarely read charts for people in person anymore, but when I did, the person who walked in the door was always completely different from what I had imagined based on his or her chart. There's an old saying: "the map is not the territory." No matter how good the map, it can't convey the reality of the landscape, and what it really feels like to be there.

Keep an open mind. Remember that symbols can be interpreted in a number of ways, so use the astrology chart as your road map. It will help you get where you need to go, but remember, a real, live person has been doing heavy construction on these roads over the course of a lifetime. There may be potholes and roadblocks that don't show up at all; some roads may have been washed away. So always approach the chart, and the person, with respect, and let them be your guide to understanding the terrain.

A Systematic Approach

There is no single right way to approach a birth chart. With time and experience, you'll have a good idea of what works for you. But when you're first getting to know the territory, it's helpful to have a systematic approach to reading the map. Here's one way:

- **Context.** First, get what you can from the birth data. When was the person born, and what is his or her current age? What are some possible concerns of someone from that generation at this current stage of life? What do you know about the city, state, region, or country of birth? There's no guarantee that place had a major impact on the person (many families move far away when a child is still very young), but it may have.

  (I can hear skeptics squealing, "That's cheating! None of that stuff has anything to do with astrology!" Maybe not, but it has everything to do with context! An astrologer will interpret the chart very differently for a man of marrying age in Nigeria than for a 13-year-old girl born and raised in Chicago. Or he or she should, anyway.)

- **Eyeball the chart.** Just look at it in a casual way, without really focusing on the details, as though you're looking at one of those 3-D posters or some cute guy sitting in the corner at Starbucks. Are some houses larger than others? Are there more planets above or below the horizon, or on the left or right side of the chart, or is the whole chart fairly well balanced? Are there clusters of planets in one or more houses? Lots of squares and oppositions in the aspect grid, or more trines and sextiles?

- **Planets on angles.** Take note of any planets that are close—say, within about 10 degrees either side—of the cusps of the first, fourth, seventh, or tenth houses. These planets are considered potent and influential; they symbolize traits and impulses you can't fail to notice, indelible qualities that are part of the person's "personal branding."

- **Aspect the chart.** Although most computer programs will generate a list of planetary aspects, I find it helpful to find the aspects myself and make a grid or list. This process, which is a bit like working a crossword puzzle, really helps me slow down and look at the relationships between the planets. Make a copy of the aspect grid in Chapter 16; start by finding aspects to the Sun, and work your way down the grid.

- **Elements, modality, and dignity.** Notice whether there is an emphasis on planets in one element (fire, earth, air, or water) or modality (cardinal, fixed, or mutable). Are there planets that are in the signs of their rulership or exaltation? Or their detriment or fall? These are important guys to look at. (Forgotten about elements and modalities? Backtrack to Chapter 3. Lost your dignities? Chapter 2 is the one you're looking for.)

- **Sun, Moon, and Ascendant.** Break down the Big Three. What is the nature of the per-son's inner hero (the Sun's sign), and in what area of life (house the Sun is in) does the hero embark on its quest? How does he or she get emotional needs met (Moon's sign and house)? What is the behavioral mask (Ascendant) the world sees?

- **The other angles.** Examine the signs on the other angles, the cusps of the fourth house (domestic and emotional needs), seventh house (approach to relationships), and tenth house (worldly calling and profession). Where is this person coming from? What's his or her calling? What kind of partner is needed to balance the personality that is on display in the first house? If you get stuck, take a look at Chapters 9 through 11.

- **Other stuff.** Interpret other chart features, including signs on house cusps, planets in houses and in signs, and planets in aspect to other planets.

Do this enough, and before you know it you'll hardly need to flip back and forth through this or any other book. You'll memorize the symbols; you'll internalize them. And when you do, all the mystifying symbols will fly together into a cohesive portrait. You'll have an intuitive feel for which factors outweigh others.

ASTRO TIP

To test whether you've spent enough time looking at the chart in depth, follow this tip from astrologer Diane Ronngren: Turn over the sheet of paper with the chart on it, and see whether you can draw it from memory. If you can't, spend a little more time peering into its inscrutable little symbols and then try again.

Sample Analysis: The Princess

As an example of how I might use those guidelines to examine a birth chart, I give you "The Princess." Born February 22, 1975, at 11:51 A.M. in Culver City, California, this young lady is now in her mid-30s. She's a member of Generation X, which came of age in the 1990s and brought us such cultural touchstones as grunge music, video games, the Internet, and $4 cappuccinos. It's a generation that has seen its share of divorced parents, stepfamilies, and ever-shifting domestic boundaries; many GenXers either put off marriage indefinitely for fear of recreating the marital disasters of the previous generation, or else work doubly hard to make their own relationships work. They also tend to have a fairly fluid approach to gender roles, and as a generation tend to take unconventional relationships and alternative lifestyles in stride. They're good at marketing (particularly the ones with Pluto in Libra), and even those who haven't paid their dues with long hours of diligent effort can go far.

Hemispheres and Houses

Here we have a well-balanced personality: a perfectly equal number of planets above and below the horizon, and on the east and west sides of the chart. She knows who she is, but she's sensitive enough to others to be collaborative and popular; she has ability to assert herself in the public eye while staying grounded.

The chart's fourth and tenth houses are a bit larger than the others; building a strong sense of family and foundation, and proving herself in a meaningful career, are where she "lives," especially with several planets (including the Sun) in the tenth house. Whatever her line of work, she will definitely be noticed.

Angular Planets

Two planets are close to the angles of the chart: the Sun, which is about 4 degrees from the Midheaven, and Neptune, a little over 7 degrees from the Descendant. We can assume she has charisma (the Sun) and an ethereal quality (Neptune), but these might also indicate she comes across as self-involved or flaky. The fact that these planets are in aspect to each other (in this case, a square aspect) indicates a dialogue between them—about how to build a strong sense of self (Sun) while remaining emotionally accessible and compassionate (Neptune)—that is one of the defining issues of her life.

ASTRO TIP

Planets that conjunct the angles of the chart symbolize defining characteristics, and their aspects (especially to each other) represent fundamental themes for personal development.

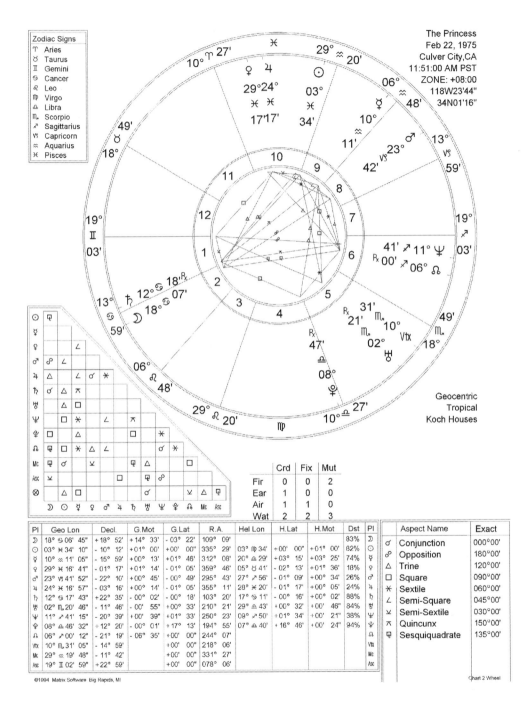

The Princess's birth chart.

CHAPTER 22: SPEAKING ASTROLOGY

Elements and Modalities: Temperament and Mode

Her Highness was born with only one planet each in a fire sign (Neptune) and earth sign (Mars); she probably had a hard time learning how to handle the practical demands of life and remain grounded (earth), and a hard time retaining her vitality and coping with attention (fire). Only three planets are in fixed signs, with the rest fairly evenly distributed between cardinal and mutable signs. She likes to initiate things, has a lot of ideas, and is good at networking with others, but probably has a hard time sticking with schedules, routines, and repetitive tasks.

Essential Dignities

The Princess was born with an enormous number of planets that are very strong by sign placement, either in the sign of their rulership or exaltation: the Moon, Mercury, Venus, Mars, Jupiter, and Uranus. Only Saturn, the planet of limits and authority, is in its detriment; she's had to work harder to develop personal boundaries and to accept leadership positions. However, the high number of planets that are strong by sign can suggest confidence, presence, and effectiveness.

The Sun: Her Inner Heroine

The Sun is in the sign of Pisces and at the top of her birth chart, near the Midheaven (career point). This is an exceptionally strong placement for the Sun and makes the case that this is a person who, above all, will stand out in a crowd and be noticed. However, Pisces is a sweet, sensitive sign and a person with the Sun here can find it exhausting to spend time in the public eye. Pursuits that allow her to indulge her imagination, connect with others emotionally, and help others awaken her inner heroine and makes her shine. If you ask Pisces Sun people what they'd like to do with their life, the answer is something like "help people" or "save the world," or perhaps something to do with dolphins.

The Sun is making several strong aspects to other planets. The square between the Sun and Neptune indicates a struggle (square) to gain a strong sense of self (Sun) despite her self-doubts and tenuous personal boundaries. Sometimes, this aspect describes the absence (Neptune) of a strong male role model (Sun); often, those with strong aspects between the Sun or Moon and Neptune use alcohol, drugs, or other substances to escape their problems. They might also lose themselves in art, music, films or TV, or dance. With the Sun trine Saturn, she might also lose herself in her work; this aspect suggests a strong work ethic, usually from a young age. With Saturn in the sign of its detriment, she may not have been good at saying no to work. And the Sun's trine aspect to Uranus in Scorpio in the fifth house gives our Princess an outrageous, even exhibitionist quality. She enjoys shocking people, and despite the ethereal qualities of Neptune and Pisces, she's a free-dom-loving rebel.

The Moon: The Inner Mom

The Moon in Cancer in a birth chart often describes someone whose mother was extremely prominent in the person's early life. Since the Moon is in the second house (security and possessions), the Princess's mom may have been preoccupied with financial security and passed these concerns on to her daughter. The Moon is conjunct Saturn, which can describe a mother who also acted as a father or was a strict disciplinarian, or who was somewhat cold or needed more mothering herself than she was able to give. Those with this planetary aspect often describe themselves as having grown up lonely or alone, and being emotionally hungry. The Moon is opposed Mars, suggesting emotional volatility and projection. And the Moon's trine to Jupiter is a person who is generally loving, emphasizes an optimistic outlook, and encourages the Princess to think big.

ASTRO ALERT   A popular misconception is that Moon in Capricorn symbolizes a person who is cold, ruthless, or selfish. I think the truth is that those born with the Moon in Capricorn or the tenth house, or in close aspect to Saturn, often felt they had to take on far too much responsibility at a young age. It's rather like being a kitten who was left on the street in a cardboard box to fend for itself: it had to figure out the world on its own and provide for itself, and that's made it tough and self-sufficient.

The Ascendant: Her Armor

Gemini was rising on the Ascendant at her birth, which gives a mischievous, chameleon-like personality, often bubbly and chatty but also extremely perceptive and a careful listener. She's interested in everything and everybody; she's probably a voracious reader and has a huge network of friends and acquaintances. Mercury, the ruler of Gemini, is in Aquarius, so she will also exhibit some of the qualities of that sign in her personality—offbeat, rebellious, and surprising. Gemini on the Ascendant is the sign of someone who makes her way in the world with words; information and connections are her currency.

The Tenth House: Career

So far, our chart interpretation has painted the portrait of a woman who is charismatic, sensitive, ambitious, emotionally hungry and volatile, who delights in shocking others and struggles with boundaries, clarity, and her own identity. Aquarius is on the Midheaven, indicating her career "style." She values freedom and originality above all other qualities in her work; Aquarius on the Midheaven is often self-employed and involved in technology, media, or professions that are considered unusual.

Uranus, the ruling planet of Aquarius, is in the fifth house, a house of creativity, self-expression, recreation, children, and performance. Along with the Sun very close to the Midheaven and in aspect to Uranus, she could be drawn to work in entertainment (especially music or film, ruled by Neptune, or television and computers, ruled by Uranus). She could also be closely aligned with humanitarian or political projects that help children. With Saturn, the career planet, in Cancer and close to the Moon, there may also be an interest in working on behalf of women's issues, homelessness, or hunger.

The Fourth House: True North

Let's look at a few other points of interest in the chart. Twenty nine degrees of Leo is on the fourth house cusp. While I haven't covered fixed stars in this book (if you're interested in learning more, see Appendix C for resources), I do keep an eye out for some of the more prominent ones. Regulus, the "Royal Star," is at 29° of Leo and is on the cusp of the Princess's fourth house. This degree on the Princess's fourth house suggests something of prominence about her pedigree. In fact, with the ruler of Leo, the Sun, conjunct the Midheaven of the chart, she might be well known (Sun conjunct the Midheaven) for her family heritage (the Sun is the ruler of Leo, the sign on the fourth house cusp).

The Descendant: Relationships

With Sagittarius on the Descendant, the partnership house, our Princess is drawn to partners who are funny, smart, and opinionated; with Neptune close to the Descendant, they might also be religious, musical, heavy drinkers, or deceptive. Since there are no planets in the seventh house, we'll look at the ruler of the sign on the Descendant, Sagittarius, for clues about her partners. Sagittarius's ruling planet, Jupiter, is strong in Pisces, the sign of its traditional rulership, in the tenth house and very close to Venus. Her ideal partner would be extremely prominent (ruler of the Descendant in the tenth house), wealthy in his own right (Venus conjunct Jupiter), and musical, spiritual, empathetic, and sensitive (Pisces).

Venus conjunct Jupiter is a classic "lucky in love" aspect; however, it's worth noting that Venus (the relationship planet) is in a wide, out of sign opposition to Pluto. Venus opposing Pluto is a sort of "beauty and the beast" aspect, and she may be drawn to partners who are brooding, cynical, controlling, or manipulative. Along with the difficult aspects to her Sun and Moon, indicating that her parents and their marriage (the Sun and Moon symbolize Dad and Mom) might not have been an example of a happy, healthy marriage, the Princess has some issues to work out before she can enjoy the full measure of the very promising symbolism of Venus and Jupiter together. To the extent she is able to face and embrace the darker side of her own nature, she'll be less likely to confront it in dark, negative partners.

How Did We Do?

Our mystery Princess is actress Drew Barrymore. Descended from the famed Barrymore acting family (called the "Royal Family of Acting"), Barrymore made her first screen appearance in a television commercial at the age of 11 months. Her breakout film role in *E.T., the Extra-Terrestrial* made her a star at the age of 6. Precocious in talent, demeanor, and habits, she began drinking and taking drugs in early adolescence, attempting suicide and landing in rehab at age 14. She got sober and began remaking her career.

Her parents split up before she was born, and she grew up having very little contact with her father. She told *People* magazine that her first memory of him was at the age of 3, when he threw her against a wall in a drunken tantrum. (The Sun can indicate the father; it's from him that she inherited her famous surname, but also the family curse: alcoholism.) Despite their estrangement, in 2003 Barrymore took over the organization and payment of her father's medical treatment until he died of cancer the following year.

Drew's mother Jaid was a struggling actress and dedicated partier who reputedly hit night-clubs with 8-year-old Drew in tow. Drew has described their relationship as "my greatest battle" (Moon conjunct Saturn, opposed Mars). At the age of 15 she petitioned a court for legal emancipation from her mother (Moon conjunct Saturn; Sun trine Uranus), and her films often explore difficult mother/daughter relationships. Promoting her film *Whip It,* Barrymore told the *Daily Mail,* "My own mom cared about Hollywood and I didn't. I wanted to act and I loved the creativity of it, but I didn't care for the lifestyle. A lot of the pain in the relationship between the mother and daughter came from my own experiences, and sections of their dialogue are verbatim conversations that took place between me and my mom. Everyone wants consistency in their family life, and that wasn't the case for me. It's why I'm so interested in telling stories about families."

In 1994, Barrymore married a bar owner (reflecting Drew's Sun square Neptune and Neptune conjunct the Descendant) named Jeremy Thomas; the marriage lasted two months. In 2001, she married comedian Tom Green, a gross-out, slapstick comic (Sagittarius on Drew's Descendant); the marriage lasted five months. She's also been in long-term relationships with rock drummer Fabrizio Moretti and comic actor Justin Long. With Uranus in the fifth house (romance), and fittingly for a member of the Uranus in Scorpio ("shocking sexuality") generation, she has described herself as bisexual and once, memorably, flashed her breasts while being interviewed by talk show host David Letterman.

Drew Barrymore has overcome a difficult childhood, substance abuse, and disappointing romantic relations to make a graceful transition from child star to full-fledged Hollywood mogul. As an actor, she remains a popular box-office draw 28 years after her first big hit, *E.T.* She recently directed her first film, and her production company is an impressive success, earning $250 million worldwide with her film remake of the '70s TV show *Charlie's Angels.* Barrymore is involved with a number of charities, notably World Food Program, which provides famine (Moon/Saturn) relief to Africa. Admired for her sunny disposition and career savvy, and for overcoming her early difficulties with grace and heart, Drew Barrymore has lived up to the promise of her Sun/Midheaven conjunction. Her personal motto might well be reflected in the tagline for her latest film: "Be your own hero."

Essential Takeaways

- Astrology is a language, and like any language it has grammar that you need to learn in order to use it effectively.
- Planets are like nouns, describing people, places, and things and occupy space and perform actions.
- Signs of the zodiac are astrology's adjectives and adverbs, describing the planets and their activities.
- When learning to interpret astrology, begin by combining the key concepts of the planet, sign, house, and aspects to other planets.
- When preparing to read a chart, remember that symbols can be interpreted in more than one way; don't make assumptions.
- Use a systematic approach to analyzing key features of the chart and follow it step by step.

CHAPTER 23

Prediction

Practical and ethical considerations for reading someone's chart

Understanding and using transits

Using progressions

I suspect prediction works best when the person you're reading for is ... predictable—that is, when the person is susceptible to societal pressures and messages and sees him- or herself as subject to the whims of fate. Even then, the birth chart is like any map: it can show us the roads that are available, but not which road we'll choose to take, or how we'll react to what we meet along the way. In short, maps—including birth charts—can tell us how to get where we're going, but not where we'll end up!

People have free will. They make choices about how to react to all the factors that influence them. That's why we hear stories of heroism and of people rising from rags to riches or overcoming terrible deprivation and hardship. Always make room in your interpretations for free will, and for the idea that a person has overcome the "lower" impulses of the symbolism in the chart.

Practical and Ethical Considerations

Be cautious about reading charts for friends and family. It's tempting to do this when you're first learning astrology; after all, who else is going to sit still and let you practice on them? The problem is that when you read a chart for someone, the power dynamic between you can subtly shift. You're the one with the answers. You've seen their eighth house, for heaven's sake! You're like the guy at the airport who gets to read the whole-body scanner and knows all about what the hot trends are in underwear.

Plus, once you get good at it, you're not going to get a moment's peace at parties, brunch, weddings, or funerals. That's when you know you've entered the Astrologer Zone and it's time to tighten up your boundaries. Professional, highly paid dentists and accountants don't spend all their time at parties gazing at errant molars and answering questions about amortization (an accounting thing, yes?). Follow their example, at least to the point of administering nitrous oxide and dropping a dime on tax evaders.

> **ASTRO ALERT**
>
> Astrology illuminates the dark corners of the psyche as well as indicates talent and potential. Before you begin reading charts for people, ask yourself how comfortable you'll be exploring touchy subjects and occasionally delivering bad news. The astrologer must use positive language and offer solutions and hope, but a reading that completely avoids tough subjects is usually not much help.

If you're interested in reading charts for total strangers for money, keep in mind that like all professions, astrology has professional organizations. In addition to hosting the usual conference schmoozefests and publishing glossy quarterly journals, astrology organizations certify astrologers and promote astrology to the public at large. Partly for this reason, they require their members to endorse a code of ethics for professional astrologers. Among other things, they usually require that their members …

- Don't claim to be infallible.

- Offer an interpretation that allows for a variety of possible meanings and outcomes.

- Don't date their clients.

- Don't perform clandestine reconnaissance missions (e.g., reading a third party's chart without that person's permission).

- Don't scare the wits out of their clients.

That last one is important: an ethical astrologer is a tactful astrologer who doesn't use predictions in a way that leaves a client paralyzed with fear. Accomplishing this isn't so hard; basically, be careful how you word the possible negative outcomes, and be sure to balance them out with possible positive outcomes. Doing this doesn't mean you're a weenie who's afraid of telling the truth; it means you're humble enough to realize you don't necessarily know everything.

Popular Tools for Prediction

There are many, many tools an astrologer might whip out of the toolbox for the purpose of prediction. Some are based on the birth chart, others aren't. Horary astrology, for instance, is based on the time someone asks a question. It's best used for important questions like "Will I get the job?", and it's helpful for simple yes or no questions. It can even help you find your lost keys. It's a specialty, though, and not all astrologers know how to do it. Then there are those (like me) who know how but just don't have the knack. So find a specialist.

Most astrologers, though, have mastered the predictive techniques discussed in the following sections.

The Current Sky: Transits

Take the positions of the planets in the sky at any given moment—say, right now. Astrologers call those "transiting planets." Observe their celestial soap opera of harmony and seething hatred, jealousy and adventure; their interactions with one another symbolize what the whole world is going through at that moment. (Remember the astrologer's motto: "As above, so below." If it's happening up there, it's happening down here.) Then, take those same planetary positions and drop them into your birth chart; that tells us how the world is treating you. What are the mighty forces (evil twin? husband back from the dead and now played by a different actor?) affecting the course of your life and urging you to react?

Transits to Transits

As they move through the sky at different speeds, the transiting planets change their positions relative to the zodiac, the earth, and to other transiting planets. Of particular interest are moments when …

- Transiting planets move into a new sign of the zodiac, particularly slower-moving planets, which change signs infrequently.

- Transiting planets change direction (see Chapter 17), turning either retrograde or direct.

- Transiting planets form exact aspects (see Chapter 16) to one another. This is particularly thrilling when slow-moving planets are involved.

Transits to Radix

The current position of the planets can also be interpreted relative to another chart. This might be your birth chart, or the chart for the birth of a company or a country or a television show. Radix is the fancy Latin word (meaning "root") for this birth chart. To look at transits to the birth chart:

1. Find the current degree and sign position of a planet in an ephemeris (see Chapter 2). For example: current position of Saturn is 10 degrees 39 minutes of Libra (October 2010).

2. Then, find where that degree and sign fall in your birth chart.

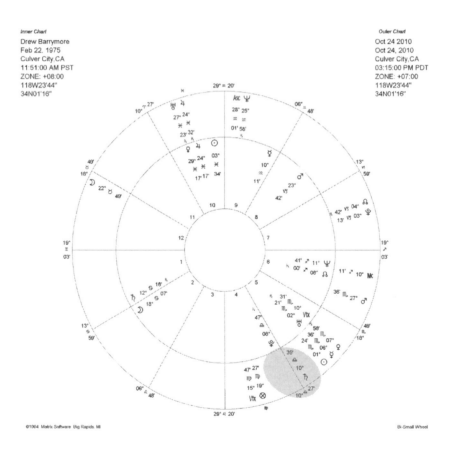

Bi-wheel with Drew Barrymore's birth chart (inside wheel) and transiting planets (outside wheel) as of October 24, 2010.

Planetary cycle—First consider the cycle of the planet so you know how long its transits will affect your chart. Saturn moves at about 3 degrees per month and takes about $2\frac{1}{2}$ years to move through a sign of the zodiac (because of retrograde periods). So Saturn is in a house of the horoscope for an average of $2\frac{1}{2}$ years, and will probably be in exact aspect to a planet for about 10 days. However, remember orbs (see Chapter 16). They apply to transiting planets as well. So if Saturn gets within 7 degrees of making an exact square to a planet in your birth chart, you're going to be experiencing its dark and sinister hand (okay, I'm exaggerating).

Also, as you learned in Chapter 17, there are certain ages when planetary cycles converge and activate major turning or crisis points. At 36, Drew Barrymore has just reached the beginning of the age range of the "midlife crisis," ages 35 to 42. In the previous chart, we see that transiting Saturn is at 10 degrees of Libra, which is making a square aspect to Saturn at 12 degrees of Cancer in her birth chart. This is one of the critical aspects of Saturn's 29-year cycle. In the next seven years we can expect to see her coming to terms with career and life decisions, ideals that may not have panned out, and some reminders that nothing lasts forever.

House position—Find the house in your chart that has the symbol for Libra on the cusp. In the previous chart, 10 degrees and 27 minutes of Libra is on the cusp of the fifth house. Since Saturn's current position at 10.35 Libra falls just after 10.27, transiting Saturn has just entered Drew's fifth house and will be there for a little over $2\frac{1}{2}$ years.

Interpretation of Saturn moving through the fifth house—The planet of maturity, responsibility, authority, and rules is now entering the house of creativity, expression, children, play, and entertainment. This is a transit that might initially be experienced as a wet blanket over the more enjoyable parts of life, as obstacles to enjoyment emerge and must be dealt with in order to move to the next level of maturity. One might deal with the question of having children, taking one's creative efforts more seriously, or the need to carve more time out of your busy schedule for pure recreation and fun. Generally, the path of your career may detour into fifth house realms, connecting with children, gaming, or entertainment.

Since Drew already has a career in entertainment and in fact owns her own production company, this might be a time when she decides to take her professional activities to a new and more challenging level, or in a direction that's explicitly aimed at children or gaming (fifth house). Also, she's at an age (36) when many women feel they need to have children if they're ever going to, so she might be dealing with the question of parenthood. This includes the possibility of a change in her relationship with her surviving parent, her mother.

Aspects to natal planets—Does 10.35 Libra form a conjunction, sextile, square, trine, or opposition aspect to any planets in the birth chart? In Drew's chart, it makes a trine aspect to Mercury, a square aspect to Saturn, a sextile to Neptune, an opposition to Pluto, and a sextile to the Moon's North Node. This tells us she is in a period when:

- She finds it relatively easy (trine) to bring discipline, maturity, and organization (Saturn) to communication and learning (Mercury).

- She is at a crisis point related to her career aspirations or sense of having reached important life milestones (transiting Saturn square natal Saturn).

- She has an opportunity (sextile) to make her dreams (Neptune) a reality (Saturn).

- Her experiences of authority figures, or of being in positions of authority herself (Saturn), are currently strongly colored (conjunction) by a need to feel in control, empowered, and acting from strength and integrity (Pluto).

- She has an opportunity (sextile) to use her position of authority or influence (Saturn) to pursue a cherished work or charitable goal (Moon's North Node in sixth house).

This is an analysis of only one transiting planet to the birth chart! As you can see, this can become quite complicated. Narrow it down more easily by focusing on the transits of slower-moving planets—say, Mars through Pluto—to the birth chart.

Progressions

Another popular technique for prediction is the use of *progressions.* Progressions don't reflect actual, physical positions of planets in the sky, as transits do. They are ways of moving your birth chart forward in time to reflect the individual's changing reality—your "progress."

The most popular form of progressions are *secondary progressions,* which are based on the idea that each day of life after your birth reflects a year of your life. So if you were born on May 3, 1983, you would look at the transits for May 4, 1983, to describe what your life is like as of your first birthday; May 10, 1983, for your seventh birthday; and so on.

A **progression** is a method of symbolically moving the birth or radix chart forward in time to reflect growth or events. **Secondary progressions**, also called "day-for-a-year" or major progressions, are a method of moving the birth chart forward in time to reflect your personal, unfolding growth. In secondary progressions, each day after your birth is thought to represent conditions in your life in the comparable year after your birth.

All planets and house cusps are progressed forward using this method, but the faster-moving planets (Sun through Mars) generally show the most activity. For this reason, it's thought that secondary progressions reflect your inner—especially emotional—development.

Secondary progressions mimic the cycle of the planets. Since the Sun takes about 30 days to move through a sign of the zodiac, in secondary progressions (in which a day equals a year) the Sun takes about 30 *years* to move through a sign of the zodiac. If you were born on the date of the vernal equinox, with the Sun in the first degree of Aries, the secondary progressed Sun would move into Taurus around the time you turn 30. If you were born with the Sun at 17 degrees of Aries, your secondary progressed Sun would enter Taurus about 13 years later (13 years = 13 degrees of motion; 13 + 17 = 30 degrees).

When working with progressions, these are the important events to look for:

- Secondary progressed planets changing sign or house
- Secondary progressed planets changing aspects to other secondary progressed planets
- Important natal aspects becoming exact by secondary progression
- Secondary progressed planets in aspect to natal planets

For example, the previous chart shows the Sun at 3° 34', or three and a half degrees, of Pisces. This tells us that when she was about $26\frac{1}{2}$ years old, in 2001, the progressed Sun moved into the sign of Aries. We can expect that, at that age, there would have been a shift in Drew's personality from the dreaminess of Pisces to a more assertive, action-oriented, even impulsive personality. On July 7, 2001, with her progressed Sun in the last degrees of Pisces, she married comedian Tom Green, a union that took fans by surprise. On July 25, 2001, her progressed Sun entered Aries, a dramatic shift and the beginning of a new 30-year cycle. Fewer than six months later, the marriage ended.

The Rule of Three

When considering whether a prediction is likely to come true, astrologers use a venerable guideline known as "The Rule of Three." If the symbolism to support the prediction appears only once, it's considered a possibility; if it appears twice, it's likely; and if it appears three times, it's a probability.

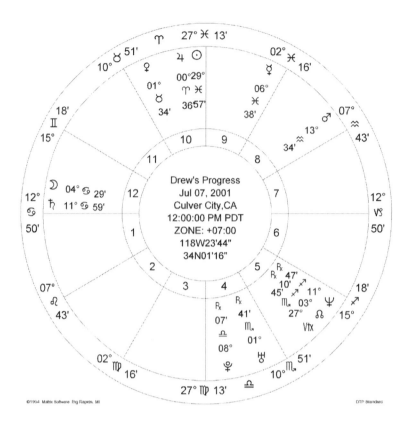

Drew Barrymore progressions to July 7, 2001.

Solar Arc Progressions/Directions

Another popular form of progressions are solar arc progressions, also called solar arc directions or degree-for-a-year progressions. These take their name from the method of calculation, in which the progressed Sun's arc—the number of degrees and minutes it's covered since birth—is added to each natal planet to derive the solar arc progressed placement. It sounds complicated, but it's actually a very easy system to use because the Sun moves about a degree each day. If a person is 26 years old, just add 26 degrees to each natal planet and you're in the ballpark.

Because they have their basis in the movement of the Sun, solar arc progressions seem to reflect outward, physical, identifiable events. I think of them as indicating *what you do* in response to the motivations of the secondary progressions or the outward pressure of transits.

Unlike with secondary progressions, aspects between solar arc progressed planets don't change over time, because they're all moving at the same rate. Slow-moving planets and (often) the Ascendant and Midheaven show more motion in solar arc progressions than in secondary progressions.

When working with solar arc progressions, pay close attention to the following:

- Solar arc progressed (SA) planets making a conjunction to an angle of the chart

- SA planets changing sign

- SA planets moving into a new house of the horoscope

- Important natal aspects becoming exact by solar arc progression

- SA planets making major aspects to natal planets

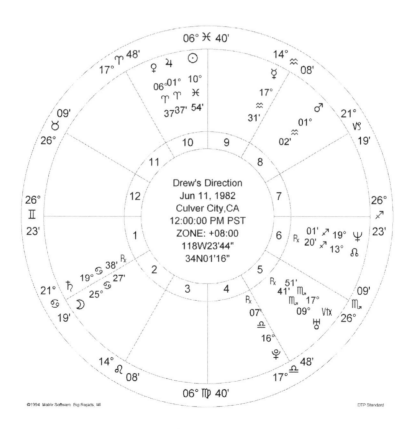

Drew Barrymore: solar arc progressions, June 11, 1982.

For example, on June 11, 1982, *E.T.: The Extraterrestrial* was released in theaters and made 7-year-old Drew Barrymore a sensation. Her solar arc directions for that day (see the previous chart) show the Sun in an almost exact square to natal Neptune (11 degrees 47 minutes of Sagittarius). The square between the Sun and Neptune, both close to angles of the chart, is one of Drew's most important natal aspects; but at the time of her birth, the Sun was still just about 8 degrees from forming the exact aspect to Neptune. We know, then, that between the ages of about 7 to 9 (1 degree of orb approaching exact, 1 degree leaving exact), the natal promise of this dramatic aspect—the Sun so close to the highest point in the chart indicating the possibility of fame, Neptune ruling movies—will in some way be realized.

Combining Natal, Progressions, and Transits

When you're just getting started, stick to two wheels at a time: the transits with the birth chart, the secondary progressions with the birth chart, and so on. But when you get used to reading these charts, you'll often combine the natal, progressions, and transits on a single page so you can easily compare all of their positions and look for common themes. Chart calculation programs usually offer a chart wheel option, often called a quadwheel, that displays all the information in a single chart.

The planetary placements of the birth chart, secondary and solar arc progressions, and transits give you a lot of data, and it can be challenging to sort through it all. Just as you did in Chapter 22 when you were learning to read a single birth chart, it's important to come up with a systematic approach to finding the most important progressed and transiting events. Here are the events I look for when I'm beginning this kind of analysis:

- Is the progressed Sun changing signs or houses or making an exact aspect?

- Where's the progressed Moon?

- Is the person in one of the critical life cycles described in Chapter 17?

- Are the slow-moving planets (Uranus, Neptune, Pluto) making a conjunction to one of the angles of the chart or an aspect to one of the inner planets?

- Traffic jams—are a whole lot of things piling up in one place?

Looking at Drew Barrymore's transits and progressions for February 18, 2001, for example, a few things jump out at me. First of all, the progressed Sun is at 29 degrees of Pisces. This tells me Drew is getting ready for a real life overhaul, as we all do when the progressed Sun changes signs; it only happens every 30 years, and it's a big deal. Since the Sun is in the tenth house of the chart and rules the fourth, I suspect a substantial shift in her living situation and public reputation. Also, this progressed Sun is conjunct Venus in the birth chart at 29 Pisces; this can point to marriage, but also to major property decisions, both of which can affect her living situation. The progressed Sun is also making a quincunx aspect to the cusp of the fourth house; she's about to have an adjustment (quincunx) in her living situation (fourth house), and it's probably going to cost some money (Venus). There is about a two-year window of opportunity for this aspect to produce results.

Progressed Venus entered Taurus about a year ago and is getting ready to exactly oppose natal Uranus; this can point to sudden relationship developments and sudden changes in property or financial status. The window of opportunity for this is about one year.

The progressed Moon—also a symbol of home—is at 29 Gemini and is currently exactly sextile the fourth house cusp. The progressed Moon getting ready to change signs gives the suggestion of changes in her living situation, and the sextile to the IC introduces the opportunity (sextile) to explore alternatives. The window of opportunity for this aspect is one month.

Transiting Mars is within 1 degree of an opposition with Jupiter, and both are square Drew's natal Sun (3 Pisces). This plays out over about a four- or five-day period.

Finally, on this date the transiting Sun is at 29 degrees of Aquarius, which is in exact opposition to her fourth house cusp. The transiting Sun moves quickly, 1 degree per day, so this is the only day this month that the transiting Sun will be in a major aspect to the fourth house cusp.

On this date, Drew Barrymore's house (Moon, fourth house ruled by the Sun) caught fire and she lost most of her possessions (Venus/Uranus). And incidentally, five months later she married her fiance, Tom Green (Sun/Venus). The marriage lasted just a few months—just long enough for the progressed Sun to move into Aries.

Some Final Thoughts

The philosopher Plato once said, "Perhaps there is a pattern set up in the heavens for one who desires to see it, and having seen it, to find one in himself." What a lyrical way to think about astrology! Indeed, in a world whose state seems to be one of perpetual chaos, I find comfort in the logic and predictability of astrology's cycles. They help me detect patterns in the world, and in myself; and when I recognize patterns, I'm in a better position to change them.

When I began my study of astrology nearly 40 years ago, books were my first teachers. I'm thrilled and gratified to have had the opportunity to take you by the arm and guide you onto your own astrological path. Happy trails, and may your astrological journey be a long and fascinating one!

Essential Takeaways

- Use good judgment in deciding whether to read charts for other people. When making predictions, balance difficult possibilities with positive ones, and don't scare the person to death.
- In astrology, transits refer to the current planetary positions. They can be interpreted relative to each other or in comparison to the planetary positions in the birth chart, where they show outer influences and situations that affect you.
- Secondary progressions posit that the planetary positions each day after your birth correspond to a year after your birth, and that these positions show your inner development and progress.
- Solar arc progressions are derived from adding the total movement of the secondary progressed Sun to each natal planet. These show your outer response to inner development and external influences.

Appendices

Glossary

air sign   One of three signs associated with the characteristics of sociability, communication, and relationship. The air signs are Gemini, Libra, and Aquarius.

angles   The cusps of the first (Ascendant), fourth (IC), seventh (Descendant), and tenth houses (MC).

angular   One of four houses associated with the cardinal signs. The angular houses are the first, fourth, seventh, and tenth. May also refer to a planet that lies close to the cusp of one of these houses.

Aquarius   Eleventh sign of the tropical zodiac, symbolized by the water bearer. Ruled by Uranus, traditionally ruled by Saturn. Associated with the eleventh house of the chart.

Arabic parts   Sensitive points in the chart that are derived from three planets, angles, or other points and which have the combined qualities of those points. The Arabic part most commonly used is the Part of Fortune.

archetypes   Idealized representations of some trait or quality in the collective unconscious.

Aries   First sign of the tropical zodiac, symbolized by the ram. Ruled by Mars and associated with the first house of the chart.

Ascendant   The cusp at the beginning of the first house, on the left side of the chart. The Ascendant is one of the angles of the chart, a powerful point symbolizing one's physical self, especially appearance. The Ascendant's sign is also called the "rising sign"

aspect   A geometric angle formed by two planets and representing harmony or conflict involving the matters ruled by those planets.

astrologer   Someone who practices astrology.

astrology   From the Greek *astrologia,* meaning "telling of the stars," astrology is essentially a language—the fine art of speaking in stars.

benefic   In traditional astrology, a planet considered especially lucky and favorable. Venus was known as the *lesser benefic* and Jupiter as the *greater benefic.*

birth chart   A diagram, usually geocentric, that shows the placement of the Sun, Moon, and planets at the time and place of birth.

Blue Moon   The second Full Moon in a calendar month, or, in a season with four Full Moons (the usually number is three), the third Full Moon in the season is the Blue Moon.

cadent   One of three houses associated with the mutable signs. The cadent houses are the third, sixth, ninth, and twelfth.

Cancer   Fourth sign of the tropical zodiac, symbolized by the crab. Ruled by the Moon and associated with the fourth house of the chart.

Capricorn   Tenth sign of the tropical zodiac, symbolized by the sea goat. Ruled by Saturn and associated with the tenth house of the chart.

cardinal   One of four zodiac signs that are associated with the qualities of leadership, initiation, action, and ambition. The cardinal signs are Aries, Cancer, Libra, and Capricorn.

centaur   From the Greek word for "hand," a mythical creature that is half-man, half-beast, often depicted as having two natures, one untamed and the other scholarly.

chart   An astrological map of the heavens at the moment of an event. Usually includes 12 houses, the Sun, the Moon, and the known planets of our solar system (including Pluto).

conjunction   A major aspect separating two objects or points by 0 degrees. It's considered a major and neutral aspect.

contraparallel   Planets the same degree of declination but on opposite sides of the equator. Similar to an opposition.

cusp   An imaginary line separating one sign or house from another.

derivative houses   A method that allows you to read a "horoscope," derived from the houses of your chart, for any person in your life. In derivative houses, a particular house of your horoscope is treated as though it were the Ascendant, and the rest of the chart is read relative to that house.

Descendant   The cusp at the beginning of the seventh house, representing the western horizon. One of the angles of the chart, it is a powerful point symbolizing relationships with equals.

dissociate   An aspect that occurs between two planets in signs that don't share the same aspect relationship. Also called an out-of-sign aspect.

earth sign   One of three signs that are associated with the characteristics of practicality, resourcefulness, and reliability. The earth signs are Taurus, Virgo, and Capricorn.

ecliptic   The apparent path of the Sun's annual journey across the sky, as it appears to move eastward relative to the fixed stars, including the constellations known as the zodiac.

ephemeris   A table showing planetary positions for a given day.

equinox   Daylight and nighttime hours of roughly the same length. The vernal equinox (March 20 or 21), when the Sun enters Aries, marks the beginning of spring. The autumnal equinox (September 22 or 23), when the Sun enters Libra, marks the beginning of autumn.

essential dignities   A system of evaluating the essential strengths of a planet based on its sign or degree. A planet is considered most strong in the signs of its rulership or *exaltation*, which are the signs whose symbolism is essentially compatible with the planet's objectives. A planet is considered least strong in the signs of its *detriment* (the sign opposite its rulership) and *fall* (the sign opposite its exaltation); these are signs whose symbolism is essentially at odds with the planet's purpose.

fire sign   One of three signs associated with the characteristics of passion, inspiration, and creativity. The fire signs are Aries, Leo, and Sagittarius.

fixed   One of four signs associated with the qualities of accumulation, stability, and resolution. The fixed signs are Taurus, Leo, Scorpio, and Aquarius.

Gemini   Third sign of the tropical zodiac, symbolized by the twins. Ruled by Mercury and associated with the third house of the chart.

hemispheres   Divisions of the horoscope using the horizon to symbolize day (above the horizon) and night (below the horizon); and the meridian to symbolize the Sun's ascent to its highest point (left of the meridian) and descent (right of the meridian) to its lowest point in
the sky.

horary   In Latin, "of the hour." The branch of astrology that attempts to answer questions based on a chart for the moment the astrologer hears and understands it.

house   One of 12 divisions of the horoscope wheel, referring to areas of the sky and symbolizing areas of the life where things take place.

IC (imum coeli)   The cusp of the fourth house, also called the nadir and one of the angles of the chart. Powerful position symbolizing one's home, heritage, and roots.

ingress chart   A chart cast for the moment of the Sun's ingress, or entry, into one of the four
cardinal signs (Aries, Cancer, Libra, or Capricorn). These charts are used by mundane astrologers to anticipate moods and events during a particular three-month period for a specific part of the world.

intercepted sign   A sign whose entire 30 degrees fall within one house of the horoscope, but which doesn't appear on the cusp of the house.

Jupiter   Planet symbolizing expansion, optimism, foreign travel, higher education. Ruler of the sign Sagittarius, traditional ruler of the sign Pisces. Associated with the ninth and twelfth houses of the chart.

Leo   Fifth sign of the tropical zodiac, symbolized by the lion. Ruled by the Sun and associated with the fifth house of the chart.

Libra   Seventh sign of the tropical zodiac, symbolized by the scales. Ruled by Venus and associated with the seventh house of the chart.

malefic   A planet traditionally thought to have a primarily bad or malicious meaning. Mars was considered the *lesser malefic* and Saturn was the *greater malefic.*

Mars   Planet symbolizing conflict, work, and sexuality. Ruler of the sign Aries, traditional ruler of the sign Scorpio. Associated with the first and eighth houses of the chart.

MC (medium coeli)   The cusp of the tenth house, also called the "zenith" and one of the angles of the chart. Represents one's career and highest aspirations.

mean node   The approximate position of the lunar node based on its motion over its entire $18^1/_2$-year cycle.

Mercury   Planet symbolizing communication, learning, intellect, siblings, travel. Ruler of the signs Gemini and Virgo. Associated with the third and sixth houses of the chart.

meridian   One of 24 imaginary lines running from the North to the South Pole at regular intervals, marking degrees of longitude from the Prime Meridian at Greenwich, England.

modalities   *See* quadruplicities.

Moon   Earth's Moon symbolizes family, mother, home, instincts, and security. In astrology, often referred to as a planet for the sake of convenience. Ruler of the sign Cancer and associated with the fourth house of the chart.

mutable   One of four signs associated with the qualities of versatility, adaptability, and intuition. The mutable signs are Gemini, Virgo, Sagittarius, and Pisces.

natal chart   *See* birth chart.

Natural Wheel   A prototypical horoscope divided into 12 houses of equal size, with Aries on the first house cusp followed by the other signs, in order, on subsequent house cusps. The natural wheel shows the correlation between particular signs and houses.

Neptune   Planet symbolizing spirituality, illness, vagueness, water. Ruler of the sign Pisces and associated with the twelfth house of the chart.

Node   The point where the orbit of a planet intersects with the ecliptic. In astrology, nearly always refers to the Moon's North or South Node.

opposition   An aspect between two bodies or points separated by an angle of 180 degrees. Considered a major and difficult aspect.

orb   The number of degrees from an exact aspect between two planets or angles within which the aspect is considered viable.

parallel   Two planets that share the same degree of declination. Similar to a conjunction.

Pisces   Twelfth sign of the tropical zodiac, symbolized by the fishes. Ruled by Neptune, traditionally ruled by Jupiter. Associated with the twelfth house of the chart.

planet   In astrology, the Sun, Moon, Mercury, Venus, Mars, Jupiter, Saturn, Uranus, Neptune, or Pluto. Planets represent particular dimensions or motivations in the psyche.

Pluto   Planetoid referred to in astrology as a planet. Symbolizes power, control, death, and transformation. Ruler of the sign Scorpio and associated with the eighth house of the chart.

progression   Method of symbolically moving the birth or radix chart forward in time to reflect growth or events. Secondary progressions equate each day after birth with the equivalent year of a person's life. Solar arc progressions (directions) add the arc of the Secondary progressed Sun to each natal position to derive the Solar Arc progressed placement.

quadruplicities   A system that divides the zodiac into three groups of four signs each. Signs of the same quadruplicity are incompatible. The quadruplicites are cardinal, fixed, and mutable.

quincunx   The aspect between two objects or points separated by an angle of 150 degrees. Considered a minor and difficult aspect.

radix   Most commonly, the birth chart; the "root" chart upon which transits, progressions, planetary return charts, and other techniques are based.

retrograde   When a planet appears to move backward in its orbit.

rising sign   *See* Ascendant.

Sagittarius   Ninth sign of the tropical zodiac, symbolized by the archer/centaur. Ruled by Jupiter and associated with the ninth house of the chart.

Saturn   Planet symbolizing maturity, boundaries, ambition, and structure. Ruler of the sign Capricorn, traditional ruler of the sign Aquarius. Associated with the tenth and eleventh houses of the chart.

Scorpio   Eighth sign of the tropical zodiac, symbolized by the scorpion or the eagle. Ruled by Pluto, traditionally ruled by Mars. Associated with the eighth house of the chart.

semisextile   The aspect between two objects or points that are separated by an angle of 30 degrees. Considered a minor and beneficial aspect.

semisquare   The aspect between two objects or points that are separated by an angle of 45 degrees. Considered a minor and difficult aspect.

sesquisquare   The aspect between two objects or points that are separated by an angle of
135 degrees. Considered a minor and difficult aspect.

sesquiquadrate   *See* sesquisquare.

sextile   The aspect between two objects or points that are separated by an angle of 60 degrees. Considered a major and beneficial aspect.

sidereal zodiac   Associates the vernal equinox with the Sun's actual position on that date, currently in the constellation of Pisces.

sign   One of 12 signs of the zodiac, based on the constellations along the ecliptic.

solstice   The longest or shortest day of the year. The summer, or aestival solstice (June 20 or 21), when the Sun enters Cancer, is the longest day of the year and marks the Sun's highest elevation in the noonday sky. The winter, or hibernal solstice (December 21 or 22), when the Sun enters Capricorn, is the shortest day of the year and marks the Sun's lowest elevation in the noonday sky.

square   An aspect between two bodies or points separated by an angle of 90 degrees. Considered a major and difficult aspect.

succedent   One of three houses associated with fixed signs. The succedent houses are the second, fifth, eighth, and eleventh.

Sun   The Sun symbolizes personal identity, creativity and self-expression, and children. In astrology it is often referred to as a planet for the sake of convenience. Ruler of the sign is Leo, and it's associated with the fifth house of the chart.

synastry   The astrological technique of comparing the planetary placements in two people's birth charts for areas of compatibility and potential friction.

Taurus   Second sign of the tropical zodiac, symbolized by the bull. Taurus is ruled by Venus and associated with the second house of the chart.

transit   Refers to a planet's current position (e.g., transiting Mercury), as well as to the planet's movement though a particular area of the chart or in aspect to a planet.

trine   An aspect between two bodies or points separated by an angle of 120 degrees. Considered a major and beneficial aspect.

triplicity   A system that divides the zodiac into four groups of three signs each, representing the natural elements of fire, earth, air, and water. Signs of the same triplicity have similar temperaments and are compatible.

tropical zodiac   Associates the vernal equinox with the first degree of the sign Aries.

true node   The exact position of the Moon's nodes for a particular day.

Uranus   Planet symbolizing nonconformity, rebellion, and unpredictable occurrences. Ruler of the sign Aquarius and associated with the eleventh house of the chart.

Venus   Planet symbolizing beauty, relationships, and material possessions. Ruler of the signs Taurus and Libra and associated with the second and seventh houses of the chart.

Virgo   Sixth sign of the tropical zodiac, symbolized by a virgin/maiden. Ruled by Mercury and associated with the sixth house of the chart.

void-of-course Moon   When the Moon has completed the last of its major aspects to other planets before leaving its current sign.

water sign   One of three signs associated with the characteristics of sensitivity, receptivity, and empathy. The water signs are Cancer, Scorpio, and Pisces.

zodiac   A band of fixed stars through which the Sun, Moon, and planets appear to move. Its constellations comprise the familiar 12 signs of the zodiac.

Helpful Planetary Tables

In the following table, find the degree and sign of the New Moon and note which house of your birth chart it falls in. This is the house of crucial activity and insights in the month ahead.

New Moon Table 2011–2020

Calculated for Greenwich Mean Time

Jan. 4, 2011	13° Capricorn 38'
Feb. 3, 2011	13° Aquarius 53'
Mar. 4, 2011	13° Pisces 55'
Apr. 3, 2011	13° Aries 29'
May 3, 2011	12° Taurus 30'
June 1, 2011	11° Gemini 01'
July 1, 2011	09° Cancer 12'
July 30, 2011	07° Leo 15'
Aug. 29, 2011	05° Virgo 27'
Sept. 27, 2011	04° Libra 00'
Oct. 26, 2011	03° Scorpio 02'
Nov. 25, 2011	02° Sagittarius 36'
Dec. 24, 2011	02° Capricorn 34'

Jan. 23, 2012	02° Aquarius 41'
Feb. 21, 2012	02° Pisces 42'
Mar. 22, 2012	02° Aries 22'
Apr. 21, 2012	01° Taurus 35'
May 20, 2012	00° Gemini 20'
June 19, 2012	28° Gemini 43'
July 19, 2012	26° Cancer 54'
Aug. 17, 2012	25° Leo 08'
Sept. 16, 2012	23° Virgo 37'
Oct. 15, 2012	22° Libra 32'
Nov. 13, 2012	21° Scorpio 56'
Dec. 13, 2012	21° Sagittarius 45'
Jan. 11, 2013	21° Capricorn 45'
Feb. 10, 2013	21° Aquarius 43'
Mar. 11, 2013	21° Pisces 24'
Apr. 10, 2013	20° Aries 40'
May 10, 2013	19° Taurus 31'
June 8, 2013	18° Gemini 00'
July 8, 2013	16° Cancer 17'
Aug. 6, 2013	14° Leo 34'
Sept. 5, 2013	13° Virgo 04'
Oct. 5, 2013	11° Libra 56'
Nov. 3, 2013	11° Scorpio 15'
Dec. 3, 2013	10° Sagittarius 59'
Jan. 1, 2014	10° Capricorn 57'
Jan. 30, 2014	10° Aquarius 55'
Mar. 1, 2014	10° Pisces 39'
Mar. 30, 2014	09° Aries 58'
Apr. 29, 2014	08° Taurus 51'
May 28, 2014	07° Gemini 21'

June 27, 2014	05° Cancer 37'
July 26, 2014	03° Leo 51'
Aug. 25, 2014	02° Virgo 18'
Sept. 24, 2014	01° Libra 07'
Oct. 23, 2014	00° Scorpio 24'
Nov. 22, 2014	00° Sagittarius 07'
Dec. 22, 2014	00° Capricorn 06'
Jan. 20, 2015	00° Aquarius 08'
Feb. 18, 2015	29° Aquarius 59'
Mar. 20, 2015	29° Pisces 27'
Apr. 18, 2015	28° Aries 25'
May 18, 2015	26° Taurus 55'
June 16, 2015	25° Gemini 07'
July 16, 2015	23° Cancer 14'
Aug. 14, 2015	21° Leo 30'
Sept. 13, 2015	20° Virgo 10'
Oct. 13, 2015	19° Libra 20'
Nov. 11, 2015	19° Scorpio 00'
Dec. 11, 2015	19° Sagittarius 02'
Jan. 10, 2016	19° Capricorn 13'
Feb. 8, 2016	19° Aquarius 15'
Mar. 9, 2016	18° Pisces 55'
Apr. 7, 2016	18° Aries 04'
May 6, 2016	16° Taurus 41'
June 5, 2016	14° Gemini 53'
July 4, 2016	12° Cancer 53'
Aug. 2, 2016	10° Leo 57'
Sept. 1, 2016	09° Virgo 21'
Oct. 1, 2016	08° Libra 15'
Oct. 30, 2016	07° Scorpio 43'

Nov. 29, 2016	07° Sagittarius 42'
Dec. 29, 2016	07° Capricorn 59'

Jan. 28, 2017	08° Aquarius 15'
Feb. 26, 2017	08° Pisces 12'
Mar. 28, 2017	07° Aries 37'
Apr. 26, 2017	06° Taurus 27'
May 25, 2017	02° Cancer 47'
June 23, 2017	02° Cancer 47'

July 23, 2017	00° Leo 44'
Aug. 21, 2017	28° Leo 52'
Sept. 20, 2017	27° Virgo 27'
Oct. 19, 2017	26° Libra 35'
Nov. 18, 2017	26° Scorpio 19'
Dec. 18, 2017	26° Sagittarius 31'

Jan. 17, 2018	26° Capricorn 54'
Feb. 15, 2018	27° Aquarius 07'
Mar. 17, 2018	26° Pisces 53'
Apr. 16, 2018	26° Aries 02'
May 15, 2018	24° Taurus 36'
June 13, 2018	22° Gemini 44'
July 13, 2018	20° Cancer 41'
Aug. 11, 2018	18° Leo 41'
Sept. 9, 2018	17° Virgo 00'
Oct. 9, 2018	15° Libra 48'
Nov. 7, 2018	15° Scorpio 11'
Dec. 7, 2018	15° Sagittarius 07'

Jan. 6, 2019	15° Capricorn 25'
Feb. 4, 2019	15° Aquarius 45'
Mar. 6, 2019	15° Pisces 47'
Apr. 5, 2019	15° Aries 17'
May 4, 2019	14° Taurus 10'
June 3, 2019	12° Gemini 33'
July 2, 2019	10° Cancer 37'
Aug. 1, 2019	08° Leo 36'
Aug. 30, 2019	06° Virgo 46'
Sept. 28, 2019	05° Libra 20'
Oct. 28, 2019	04° Scorpio 25'
Nov. 26, 2019	04° Sagittarius 03'
Dec. 26, 2019	04° Capricorn 06'

Jan. 24, 2020	04° Aquarius 21'
Feb. 23, 2020	04° Pisces 28'
Mar. 24, 2020	04° Aries 12'
Apr. 23, 2020	03° Taurus 24'
May 22, 2020	02° Gemini 04'
June 21, 2020	00° Cancer 21'
July 20, 2020	28° Cancer 26'
Aug. 19, 2020	26° Leo 35'
Sept. 17, 2020	25° Virgo 00'
Oct. 16, 2020	23° Libra 53'
Nov. 15, 2020	23° Scorpio 17'
Dec. 14, 2020	23° Sagittarius 08'

Eclipses symbolize times of instability and change. Solar eclipses occur at least twice each year and are usually accompanied within two weeks by a lunar eclipse. Use the following table to find the house where the degree of the eclipse falls in your birth chart; this indicates which part of your life is likely to be at a turning point.

Eclipses Table 2011–2020

Calculated for Greenwich Mean Time

Date of Eclipse	Type of Eclipse	Degree and Sign
Jan. 4, 2011	Solar	13° Capricorn 38'
June 1, 2011	Solar	11° Gemini 02'
June 15, 2011	Lunar	24° Sagittarius 22'
July 1, 2011	Solar	09° Cancer 11'
Nov. 25, 2011	Solar	02° Sagittarius 37'
Dec. 10, 2011	Lunar	18° Gemini 08'
May 20, 2012	Solar	00° Gemini 20'
June 4, 2012	Lunar	14° Sagittarius 08'
Nov. 13, 2012	Solar	21° Scorpio 56'
Nov. 28, 2012	Lunar	06° Gemini 40'
Apr. 25, 2013	Lunar	05° Scorpio 51'
May 10, 2013	Solar	19° Taurus 31'
May 25, 2013	Lunar	03° Sagittarius 58'
Oct. 18, 2013	Lunar	25° Aries 51'
Nov. 3, 2013	Solar	11° Scorpio 15'
Apr. 15, 2014	Lunar	25° Libra 17'
Apr. 29, 2014	Solar	08° Taurus 51'
Oct. 8, 2014	Lunar	15° Aries 07'
Oct. 23, 2014	Solar	00° Scorpio 24'
Mar. 20, 2015	Solar	29° Pisces 27'
Apr. 4, 2015	Lunar	14° Libra 21'

| Sept. 13, 2015 | Solar | 20° Virgo 10' |
| Sept. 28, 2015 | Lunar | 04° Aries 38' |

Mar. 9, 2016	Solar	18° Pisces 55'
Mar. 23, 2016	Lunar	03° Aries 10'
Aug. 18, 2016	Lunar	26° Aquarius 00'
Sept. 1, 2016	Solar	09° Virgo 21'
Sept. 16, 2016	Lunar	24° Pisces 13'

Feb. 11, 2017	Lunar	22° Leo 34'
Feb. 26, 2017	Solar	08° Pisces 11'
Aug. 7, 2017	Lunar	15° Aquarius 30'
Aug. 21, 2017	Solar	28° Leo 52'

Jan. 31, 2018	Lunar	11° Leo 39'
Feb. 15, 2018	Solar	27° Aquarius 07'
July 13, 2018	Solar	20° Cancer 41'
July 27, 2018	Lunar	4° Aquarius 45'
Aug. 11, 2018	Solar	18° Leo 41'

Date of Eclipse	Type of Eclipse	Degree and Sign
Jan. 6, 2019	Solar	15° Capricorn 25'
Jan. 21, 2019	Lunar	00° Leo 49'
July 2, 2019	Solar	10° Cancer 37'
July 16, 2019	Lunar	24° Capricorn 00'
Dec. 26, 2019	Solar	04° Capricorn 07'

Jan. 10, 2020	Lunar	19° Cancer 53'
June 21, 2020	Solar	00° Cancer 21'
July 5, 2020	Lunar	13° Capricorn 29'
Nov. 30, 2020	Lunar	08° Gemini 44'
Dec. 14, 2020	Solar	23° Sagittarius 08'

Mercury turns retrograde more often than any other planet. When Mercury is retrograde, you may observe more than the usual problems with communication, technology, transportation, and thinking clearly. The following table gives the dates when Mercury turns retrograde and when it turns direct again. The degree and sign where Mercury turns retrograde and direct indicate areas of your chart where you are most likely to experience problems in your own life.

Mercury Retrograde Table 2011–2020

Date	Degree and Sign	Retrograde or Direct
Mar. 30, 2011	24° Aries 20'	Retrograde
Apr. 23, 2011	12° Aries 53'	Direct
Aug. 3, 2011	01° Virgo 11'	Retrograde
Aug. 26, 2011	18° Leo 42'	Direct
Nov. 24, 2011	20° Sagittarius 06'	Retrograde
Dec. 14, 2011	03° Sagittarius 52'	Direct
Mar. 12, 2012	06° Aries 48'	Retrograde
Apr. 4, 2012	23° Pisces 51'	Direct
July 15, 2012	12° Leo 31'	Retrograde
Aug. 8, 2012	01° Leo 26'	Direct
Nov. 6, 2012	04° Sagittarius 16'	Retrograde
Nov. 26, 2012	18° Scorpio 11'	Direct
Feb. 23, 2013	19° Pisces 52'	Retrograde
Mar. 17, 2013	05° Pisces 38'	Direct
June 26, 2013	23° Cancer 06'	Retrograde
July 20, 2013	13° Cancer 22'	Direct
Oct. 21, 2013	18° Scorpio 23'	Retrograde
Nov. 10, 2013	02° Scorpio 30'	Direct
Feb. 6, 2014	03° Pisces 18'	Retrograde
Feb. 28, 2014	18° Aquarius 09'	Direct
June 7, 2014	03° Cancer 10'	Retrograde
July 1, 2014	24° Gemini 22'	Direct

Oct. 4, 2014	02° Scorpio 18'	Retrograde
Oct. 25, 2014	16° Libra 46'	Direct
Jan. 21, 2015	17° Aquarius 04'	Retrograde
Feb. 11, 2015	01° Aquarius 18'	Direct
May 19, 2015	13° Gemini 08'	Retrograde
June 11, 2015	04° Gemini 34'	Direct
Sep. 17, 2015	15° Libra 54'	Retrograde
Oct. 9, 2015	00° Libra 54'	Direct
Jan. 5, 2016	01° Aquarius 02'	Retrograde
Jan. 25, 2016	14° Capricorn 55'	Direct
Apr. 28, 2016	23° Taurus 35'	Retrograde
May 22, 2016	14° Taurus 20'	Direct
Aug. 30, 2016	29° Virgo 04'	Retrograde
Sep. 22, 2016	14° Virgo 50'	Direct
Dec. 19, 2016	15° Capricorn 07'	Retrograde
Jan. 8, 2017	28° Sagittarius 51'	Direct
Apr. 9, 2017	04° Taurus 50'	Retrograde
May 3, 2017	24° Aries 16'	Direct
Aug. 13, 2017	11° Virgo 37'	Retrograde
Sep. 5, 2017	28° Leo 25'	Direct
Dec. 3, 2017	29° Sagittarius 17'	Retrograde
Dec. 23, 2017	13° Sagittarius 01'	Direct
Mar. 23, 2018	16° Aries 53'	Retrograde
Apr. 15, 2018	04° Aries 46'	Direct
July 26, 2018	23° Leo 26'	Retrograde
Aug. 19, 2018	11° Leo 32'	Direct
Nov. 17, 2018	13° Sagittarius 28'	Retrograde
Dec. 6, 2018	27° Scorpio 17'	Direct

Mar. 5, 2019	29° Pisces 38'	Retrograde
Mar. 28, 2019	16° Pisces 05'	Direct
July 7, 2019	04° Leo 27'	Retrograde
Aug. 1, 2019	23° Cancer 57'	Direct
Oct. 31, 2019	27° Scorpio 37'	Retrograde
Nov. 20, 2019	11° Scorpio 36'	Direct
Feb. 17, 2020	12° Pisces 52'	Retrograde
Mar. 10, 2020	28° Aquarius 13'	Direct
June 18, 2020	14° Cancer 45'	Retrograde
July 12, 2020	05° Cancer 29'	Direct
Oct. 14, 2020	11° Scorpio 39'	Retrograde
Nov. 3, 2020	25° Libra 54'	Direct

Resources

Astrological Organizations

American Federation of Astrologers (AFA)   Formed in 1938 to promote astrological research, teaching, lecture, and practice, AFA publishes books and a monthly journal, *Today's Astrologer,* holds conventions, and offers a correspondence course and certification exams. Website: www.astrologers.com

Association For Astrological Networking (AFAN)   Incorporated in 1988, AFAN is dedicated to media accountability and public information. AFAN monitors media and responds to inaccurate or biased media coverage of astrology and astrologers. AFAN offers a legal information kit for astrologers and works to effect changes in laws that restrict the practice of astrology. AFAN sponsors International Astrology Day and works with other astrology organizations to provide funding, grants, and scholarships for astrological research and education. Along with NCGR and ISAR, AFAN co-produces the United Astrology Conference (UAC), which is held approximately every three years. Website: www.afan.org

Astrological Association of Great Britain (AA)   Founded in 1958, AA hosts astrological events and conferences. Its publications include *The Astrological Journal; Culture and Cosmos: A Journal of the History of Astrology and Cultural Astronomy; Correlation: Journal of Research into Astrology; Astrology and Medicine: The Journal That Promotes the Teaching and Study of Medical Astrology;* and *Transit, the Astrologers' Newsletter.* The AA database with astrological data on thousands of notable people and events is available to members. Website: www.astrologicalassociation.com

Federation of Australian Astrologers (FAA) A nonprofit incorporated in 1995, the FAA established a code of ethics, publishes the *FAA Journal,* encourages research, holds seminars and meetings, and offers examinations and a diploma of astrology. The FAA International Astrology Conference is hosted every two years in various cities around Australia. Website: www.faainc.org.au

International Society for Astrological Research (ISAR) Founded in 1968 and incorporated as a nonprofit organization in 1979. With vice presidents in 20 difference countries, ISAR emphasizes research techniques, hosts international conferences, publishes a journal three times each year, and offers certification. Website: www.isarastrology.com

The National Council for Geocosmic Research (NCGR) A nonprofit organization for astrological education and research that was founded in 1971, NCGR sponsors local chapters throughout the world as well as several special interest groups. NCGR publishes *Geocosmic Journal* twice each year and hosts regional conferences. Website: www.geocosmic.org

NCGR–Professional Astrologers Alliance (NCGR-PAA) A trade organization for professional astrologers founded in 2009, NCGR-PAA offers certification and mentoring opportunities for professional astrologers. Website: www.astrologersalliance.org

Organization of Professional Astrologers (OPA) The OPA is a nonprofit organization dedicated to helping professional astrologers get the information and tools they need to improve their practice. It offers retreats and a newsletter, *The Career Astrologer.* Website: www.professional-astrology.org

Books

General Reference

Bills, Rex E. *The Rulership Book: A Directory of Astrological Correspondences.* Tempe, AZ: American Federation of Astrologers, 2007. Everything in the universe can be described in by an astrological symbol, and while this book doesn't include them all, I rarely fail to find what I'm looking for in it.

Burk, Kevin B. *Astrology Math Made Easy.* San Diego, CA: Serendipity Press, 2005. Kevin Burk is an excellent astrologer, writer, and teacher, and this is also a superb guide for learning manual chart calculation.

The Michelsen-Simms Family Trust, and Rique Pottenger. *The New American Ephemeris for the 21st Century, 2000–2100 at Midnight.* Exeter, NH: Starcrafts Publishing, 2006. A nice general guide to astrology and the planets.

www.terrylamb.net   Website of Terry Lamb's Astrology, Etc., where you can also order her self-published *Beginning Astrology Math Workbook.* Terry's method is the one that ultimately made manual chart calculation not only easy for me, but a joy.

Signs

Forrest, Steven. *The Inner Sky: How to make wiser choices for a more fulfilling life.* Borrego Springs, CA: Seven Paws Press, 2007. Steven Forrest presents the planets, signs, and houses in his wise, soulful, easy-to-understand way. If I could have only one astrology book with me on a deserted island, this would be it.

Goodman, Linda. *Sun Signs.* NY: Bantam Books, 1984. When I'm dishing with my astrologer friends, nearly everyone admits that this was the book that got them interested in astrology. This introduction to the 12 signs of the zodiac is whimsical, but it's also thorough and insightful.

Houses

Herbst, Bill. *Houses of the Horoscope.* San Diego, CA: Serendipity Press, 2006. Bill Herbst's book is an indispensable primer on houses, laid out in a beautifully simple way.

Marks, Tracy. *Your Secret Self: Illuminating the Mysteries of the Twelfth House.* Lake Worth, FL: Nicolas Hays, 2010. The mysterious twelfth house, traditionally the house of sorrow, illness, insanity, and self-undoing, gets a much-needed facelift by astrologer and licensed mental health counselor Tracy Marks.

Sasportas, Howard. *The Twelve Houses: Exploring the Houses of the Horoscope.* London: LSA/Flare, 2007. In this classic, the late, beloved astrologer Howard Sasportas focuses deep psychological insights on the 12 houses.

Planets

Casey, Caroline W. *Making the Gods Work for You: The Astrological Language of the Psyche.* NY: Harmony Books, 1998. Caroline Casey has a distinctive, imaginative way with words and the ability to place everything astrological in a larger context. This book really makes the planets come to life.

Cunningham, Donna. *The Moon in Your Life: Being a Lunar Type in a Solar World.* York Beach, ME: S. Weiser, 1996.

———. *Healing Pluto Problems.* York Beach, ME: S. Weiser, 1986. Cunningham, an astrologer with a Master's in social work, brings an unflinching but reassuring approach to difficult subjects. These two are among her most popular books (and my favorites), with compassionate and sensible guidance for understanding and healing emotional issues with astrology.

Forrest, Steven. *The Book of Pluto: Turning Darkness into Wisdom with Astrology.* San Diego, CA: ACS Publications, 1994. Like Cunningham, Forrest is a friendly, positive voice, and he treats Pluto (a planet with a scary reputation) with the respect it deserves without trying to scare the wits out of anyone. This book covers both natal and transiting aspects to natal planets and is highly recommended.

Greene, Liz. *Saturn: A New Look at an Old Devil.* York Beach, ME: S. Weiser, 1976. A classic review of one of astrology's "bad guys." Interpretations of Saturn in signs, houses, aspect, and synastry (relationships).

———. *The Astrology of Fate.* York Beach, ME: S. Weiser, 1984. This is essentially a book about Pluto and Pluto issues. Greene takes a heavier approach to the topic than Cunningham or Forrest, but will especially appeal to readers who appreciate a serious, psychological approach.

Massey, Anne. *Venus: Her Cycles, Symbols & Myths.* Woodbury, MN: Llewellyn Publications, 2006. Massey explores the planet of love and beauty through its archetypal representations in myth, fairy tales, and contemporary society. The book covers Venus in aspect to other planets, as well as in houses and signs. There's also a good discussion of Venus's important retrograde cycle.

Asteroids

George, Demetra, and Douglas Bloch. *Asteroid Goddesses: The Mythology, Psychology, and Astrology of the Reemerging Feminine.* Berwick, ME: Ibis Press, 2003. This is the book that really brought the major asteroids into contemporary astrology, with an essential overview of Juno, Ceres, Vesta, and Pallas Athene grounded in classical archetypes.

www.joycemason.com   Website for astrologer Joyce Mason, an expert in Chiron. Her e-book *Chiron and Wholeness* offers an inspiring yet down-to-earth introduction to this planetoid.

www.juliedemboski.wordpress.com   Blog for astrologer Julie Demboski, where you can order her e-book *Juno in the Birth Chart.*

Lunar Nodes

Forrest, Steven. *Yesterday's Sky: Astrology and Reincarnation.* Borrego Springs, CA: Seven Paws Press, 2008. Forrest is a leading proponent of what's called Evolutionary Astrology, which presumes a belief in reincarnation. If that's not your bag, you may not warm to this one. But if you're open to these ideas, there is a lot of insight here, presented in Forrest's friendly, accessible style.

Ronngren, Diane. *Lunar Nodes: Keys to emotions and life experiences.* Reno, NV: ETC Publishing, 2005. Ronngren has been watching the lunar nodes for years and brings a lot of practical observation to this subject. Her book offers interpretations of all natal and transiting house placements and aspects to planets.

Aspects

Tompkins, Sue. *Aspects in Astrology: A Guide to Understanding Planetary Relationships in the Horoscope.* Rochester, VT: Destiny Books, 2002. Planetary aspects are notoriously hard to grasp, sometimes even for the practiced astrologer. Sue Tompkins covers every planetary combination, and this book reads like it's been written by someone who's read about a million birth charts and learned something from each one. I consult this book every time I'm preparing to give a reading.

Cycles

Gerhardt, Dana. *Moonwatching.* Self-published e-book, 2008.

Lundsted, Betty. *Planetary Cycles: That Get You from Beginning to End Without a Guide.* York Beach, ME: S. Weiser, 1993. This book sets out major planetary life cycles in a clear, easy-to-understand way.

Sullivan, Erin. *Retrograde Planets: Traversing the Inner Landscape.* York Beach, ME: Red Wheel/S. Weiser, 2006. The retrograde cycles for every planet, both in the birth chart and by transit, are thoroughly covered.

Transits and Progressions

Brady, Bernadette. *Predictive Astrology: The Eagle and the Lark.* York Beach, ME: S. Weiser, 1998. An intermediate astrology primer with practical techniques for making sense of overwhelming data to produce an astrological chart interpretation that makes sense and is helpful.

Hand, Robert. Planets in Transit: *Life Cycles for Living.* Atlen, PA: Whitford Press, 2001. Given Hand's well-deserved reputation as one of astrology's greatest living scholars, I'm always pleasantly surprised at how accessible and useful his writing is. This book gives basic but helpful interpretations for all aspects between transiting and natal planets.

Kent, April Elliott. Astrological Transits: The Beginner's Guide to Using Planetary Cycles to Plan and Predict Your Day, Week, Year (or Destiny). Beverly, MA: Fair Winds Press/Quarto, 2015. My followup to "The Essential Guide to Practical Astrology" is a user-friendly introduction to understanding and interpreting planetary cycles.

Websites

www.alabe.com   Website of Astrolabe, where you can calculate astrology charts for free or order their popular Solar Fire calculation program.

www.astro.com   Website of Astrodienst, where you can calculate a variety of astrology charts, including progressed charts, for free. Astrodienst also has a free online ephemeris and hosts a lively international discussion forum.

www.astrologysoftware.com   Website of Matrix Software. Their Win*Star Professional Version software was used to calculate the charts that appear in this book. Win*Star also sells a wide range of interpretation reports.

www.mooncircles.com   Website for Dana Gerhardt, a beloved long-time columnist for *The Mountain Astrologer* magazine. *Moonwatching,* her collection of essays about the lunar phases, first appeared as a series in that magazine.

www.quicksilverproductions.com   The website for Jim Maynard, who publishes a variety of astrology calendars each year, including the popular Pocket Astrologer. This handy pocket-sized guide gives lunar signs and void-of-course periods, and planetary aspects for every day of the year.

Index

M

About the Author

April Elliott Kent fell in love with astrology at the age of 12 and has practiced profession-ally since 1990. She is the author of Astrological Transits (Fair Winds Press 2015), The Essential Guide to Practical Astrology (Alpha/Penguin 2011, reprinted by the author in 2016), and Star Guide to Weddings (Llewellyn 2008). Her astrological writing has also appeared in The Mountain Astrologer and Dell Horoscope magazines and in Llewellyn's Moon Sign Book, Sun Sign Book, and Sabbats Almanac annuals.

A graduate of San Diego State University, April is also a member of the International Society for Astrological Research (ISAR) and the Authors Guild. She is a popular lec-turer for local astrology groups and served on the faculty of the 2012 United Astrological Conference (UAC). She currently serves as President of the San Diego Astrological Society.

Acclaimed for her warm, accessible writing style, April specializes in using real life scenar-ios to illustrate astrological principles. Her website, BigSkyAstrology.com, has welcomed visitors from around the world since 2000. She lives in a 1923 bungalow in San Diego, California, with her husband their two imperious cats.

Made in the USA
Middletown, DE
17 July 2021